AMERICAN FOREIGN ECONOMIC POLICY

Benjamin J. Cohen, EDITOR

PRINCETON UNIVERSITY

HARPER & ROW, PUBLISHERS

NEW YORK, EVANSTON, AND LONDON

For My Parents

Contents

Preface

This book is about American foreign economic policy. Its purpose is to give some insights into the major issues confronting the policymakers of the world's richest and most powerful nation in the third decade of the postwar era. It is designed for use in courses both in international economics and international politics. Foreign economic policy must take into account both economic and political considerations. The student of international economics should benefit from a systematic treatment of some of the political elements that influence the United States in the promotion of its foreign economic objectives. And the student of international politics should benefit from a systematic treatment of some of the economic elements that influence the United States in the pursuit of its national political objectives.

The design of the book is unique. It is neither just another book of readings nor just another textbook. In fact it is both, combined between the covers of one volume. Part I is an original essay on the general problems of analysis of foreign economic policy. The purpose of this essay is to provide the reader with a firm conceptual framework for examining the specific problems of United States foreign economic policy. The body of the book is divided into four additional parts; the first is concerned with the financial framework within which American policy functions, the latter three with the principal world areas of United States concern—the Industrial World, the Communist World, and the Third World of less well-developed countries. Each of these sections is introduced by an essay of my own, in which I state my personal perception of the fundamental issues of American foreign economic policy today. The remainder of each section is comprised of comments by leading economists and others on specific aspects of these issues. The book concludes with a bibliography of suggested further reading.

Much of the credit for any merit this book may have belongs, of course, to the authors who have graciously consented to the reproduction of their works. In addition, I wish to acknowledge my deep gratitude to William G. Bowen of Princeton University for his inspiration and support. I am also indebted to Robert G. Gilpin, Jr. and Anthony M. Lanyi of Princeton University, and to Wolfram F. Hanreider of the University of California at Santa Barbara, for their many helpful comments on earlier drafts of my essays. And finally, I must thank J. Edward Jones III, who, as my research assistant, was an invaluable aide during all stages of the preparation of this volume.

BENJAMIN J. COHEN

Princeton, New Jersey

Nobody has attained political maturity who does not understand that policy is politics. Economists are particularly apt to overlook these truths.
—J. A. SCHUMPETER

AMERICAN FOREIGN ECONOMIC POLICY

ESSAYS AND COMMENTS

PART I

American Foreign Economic Policy
Some General Principles of Analysis

Foreign economic policy is not an end in itself. It is part of a country's total foreign policy and to some extent serves the same goals. Yet foreign economic policy is not often discussed from this point of view; in fact, the readings in this volume are unusual in doing so. Economics deals primarily with the allocation of scarce resources and political science deals primarily with power relations. Most economists and political scientists act as if "never the twain shall meet." In their surveys and studies of international affairs, neither economists nor political scientists have devoted much serious thought to developing a systematic conceptual framework of analysis that would permit discussions of the allocation of scarce resources in support of power relations. The purpose of this essay is to start to lay the foundation of such an analytical framework. We begin in the first section with a brief, general review of some basic principles of foreign policy. The second section examines in greater detail the specific role, potentialities, and limitations of foreign economic policy and describes the proposed analytical framework. Finally, using that framework, the third section describes the major developments in the foreign economic policies of the United States since 1945 and summarizes the major themes of American foreign economic policy today.

1.

If there were one world government, there would be no need to study foreign policy—unless of course we were in communication with life on other planets. As it is, we study foreign policy because the globe is segmented into numerous nation-states, communities of men organized within a particular constitutional order pre-

1

vailing over some specific geographical terrain. These communities are, in a world of innumerable and overlapping organizations, the focal point of political power. All of them claim the right to exercise complete sovereignty over their own internal affairs. Consequently, no one of them can exercise anything even approximating complete sovereignty except within its own borders. The nation-state individually can attempt only to *influence* the external environment, using whatever instruments are at its command. All such actions intended to affect situations beyond the national jurisdiction represent together the foreign policy of the nation-state.

Ideally, foreign policy might be regarded as the reasoned product of creative leadership—concerted, purposive action arising out of a rational perception of the fundamental interests of the nation-state. Policy can mean this and often does, but often it does not, because the political processes out of which policies normally spring are not nearly so simple. To repeat, the nation-state is a community of men organized into groups of all kinds, many with extensive foreign as well as domestic interests, and every one with its provisional conception of the over-all national interest related ideologically to its own special interest. To the extent that interest is institutionalized, particular interest expresses itself with political power; and out of governmental processes of tension, conflict, and domination, the national interest and the foreign policy of the state emerge—a consensus of purposes and actions that are essentially the end products of a system of domestic power relationships.[1]

No wonder, then, that foreign policy so often seems the product of random, haphazard, or even irrational forces or events. Frequently it is an uneasy compromise formula, the result of deadlocked judgments. And frequently a country has no foreign policy

[1] A foremost exponent of this point of view is Anthony Downs, who argues that all government actions (not only foreign policy) are motivated exclusively by a desire to maximize votes; policies are merely means toward this end. It therefore follows, assuming rationality on the part of decision-makers, that general policy never represents anything more than the largest possible coalition of particular interests. See his *An Economic Theory of Democracy* (New York: Harper & Row, 1957). However, it should be noted that Downs' perspective is much too narrowly defined, for he fails to recognize that the nation-state itself may have certain general interests transcending the specific interests of domestic institutions.

at all, but, owing to indecision or the unwillingness or inability to act, simply drifts with events. Always, though, foreign policy is a function of specific lesser interests within the nation, the offspring of the interplay of powerful institutions, each trying to achieve its own particular ambitions and goals. One interesting implication of this is that the foreign policy of any single state is unlikely to serve the interests of the world community as well as it does those of the national community, for it is an inherent tendency of any collectivity of diverse interests to reconcile conflicts among their separate ambitions, as much as possible, at the expense of outsiders. After all, foreigners don't vote, but citizens do.

But foreign policy is not only a function of specific lesser interests within the nation. To insist on that view alone is to lose sight of the forest for the trees.[2] The foreign policy of a state must ultimately be legitimized by the state's national interest, and its national interest, however specifically defined, encompasses a set of general purposes that transcend the particular ambitions of domestic institutions. In managing the affairs of the nation in relation to its external environment, the government of the state acts as trustee of the separate, often disparate interests within the community, but it also acts as trustee of the interests of the community itself, the most basic of which is self-preservation—*survival.* Nothing is more important to the nation-state than the ability to defend itself against outside attack and to protect itself from outside control. National security must be the ultimate goal of all foreign policies, the irreducible core of every nation's idea of the national interest. As Nicholas Spykman has written, "the basic objective of the foreign policy of all states is the preservation of territorial integrity and political independence."[3]

Thus, even while the foreign-policy-makers of the state are expected in their regular operations to promote and protect the specific interests of domestic institutions, they are first of all responsible for the survival of the sovereign nation itself. To the extent that foreign policy is in fact the "reasoned product of creative leadership," it is designed to maximize that single objec-

[2] See Paul Seabury, *Power, Freedom and Diplomacy: The Foreign Policy of the United States of America* (New York: Random House, 1963), Ch. 4.
[3] Nicholas Spykman, *America's Strategy in World Politics* (New York: Harcourt, Brace & World, 1942), p. 17.

tive: national security. The basic problem of foreign policy is
twofold. First, it is necessary to choose a strategy of foreign policy
—that is, to identify a series of proximate goals and an action
pattern appropriate to them that will ensure the ultimate objective of national security. And second, it is necessary to make the
correct choices among the instruments of foreign policy—to allocate means to ends. These are not easy tasks, nor, as we shall see,
are they entirely discrete tasks.

The latter problem, that of allocating means to ends, is fundamentally a technical affair. The instruments available to policy-
makers must be evaluated for their potentiality, both in over-all
quantitative terms and qualitatively in terms of their suitability
for specific tasks. How effective are they, and how interchangeable
in practice? It is also necessary to evaluate the costs associated with
each instrument of policy. What are likely to be the alternative
opportunities foregone when one particular end is sought? And,
finally, it is necessary to make the actual allocation itself, hopefully to maximize policy objectives at least cost. This kind of
calculus is quite familiar to economists; it is presumably what
economics is all about, and it is certainly much of what the making
of foreign economic policy is all about. We shall return to this
problem below.

For now, let us turn our attention to the other problem of
foreign policy—the problem of translating the ultimate objective
of national security into an operational strategy of foreign policy.
This is a difficult matter, for the concept of national security is
not a precise, meaningful guide for action; it is subjective rather
than objective in content and consequently rather ambiguous.[4]
The presence of absence of external threats to the state's independence and territory can never be measured objectively. It
must always remain a matter of subjective evaluation and speculation. National security is measured by the absence of *fear* of
external threats, and fear is an idiosyncratic element in international affairs. It is well known that, for reasons only partly explained by special interest, groups within nations and even nations themselves differ widely in their reaction to one and the same
external situation. We should not be surprised, therefore, that

[4] See Arnold Wolfers, " 'National Security' as an Ambiguous Symbol," *Political Science Quarterly*, LXVII (December, 1952), pp. 481–502.

they differ in their choice of preferred foreign-policy strategy as well.

Likewise, we should not be surprised that their preferences differ when we note that the concept of national security is usually interpreted to imply not only protection of national independence and territorial integrity, but also the preservation of minimum national "core values." For the nation-state as for the individual, physical survival is not usually valued highly unless accompanied by cultural survival as well. In fact, nations have been known as collectivities to risk biological extinction through war rather than risk cultural extinction in peace. And even short of war, they tend to design and implement their foreign policies to protect not only their sovereignty and their borders, but also a certain range of previously acquired values, such as rank, prestige, material possessions, and special privileges. The problem for foreign policy is that such values are by definition subjective. Not only are nations and groups within nations likely to differ in their estimation of the range of values to be considered "basic"; even for any one nation or group that range is apt to prove elastic over time. For instance, it is a familiar phenomenon that military bases, security zones, foreign investments, or commercial concessions may be sought and acquired by a nation for the purpose of protecting basic national values, and that they then become new national values requiring protection themselves. Pushed to its logical conclusion, such extension of the range of values to include more and more marginal values does not stop short of the goal of complete world domination.

Fortunately, from the point of view of world peace, complete world domination is, at any single moment of history, an operative goal in the foreign policies of very few, if any, nation-states, although it is certainly true as well that there are always a number of governments behaving in a manner that can be described as predatory or coercive. However, most governments do not push the logic of national security quite so far and rely instead on less ambitious strategies of foreign policy. To see why, we might draw an analogy between the behavior of states in the international arena and that of competing firms in an oligopolistic market. Like the community of nations, the oligopolistic market is characterized by interdependence and uncertainty: the competitors are sufficiently few in number so that the behavior of any one has an appreciable effect on at least some of its rivals; in turn, the actions and reactions of its rivals cannot be predicted with certainty. This results in an interdependence of decision-making, compelling each firm to be noticeably preoccupied with problems of strategy. True, the oligopolist wants to make profits and consequently cannot afford to ignore such important matters as consumer tastes and factor costs. But, above all, he wants to maintain his share of the market and perhaps, if possible, to increase it —in other words, he wants to survive. This means that he must pay particular attention to long-run strategic considerations. He must scrutinize his every move for its effects on the long-term market position of his firm, for its implications concerning the firm's future freedom of action, and for the probable countermoves of the firm's rivals. Rarely is any move undertaken that is likely to threaten seriously the firm's existence.

For the individual oligopolist, a position of monopoly would obviously be preferable to the uncertainty and risk of his current status. But the goal of complete market domination is not an operative goal in the competitive strategies of many firms, for each knows that its rivals, singly or collectively, are also strongly armed with the weapons of price reductions, aggressive advertising, and product improvement. True, one does occasionally observe oligopolistic firms attempting to improve their position or to dominate a large part of the market by means of such predatory policies as price-cutting, monopolizing raw materials or distributive outlets, tying arrangements, and so on. However, most oligopolists prefer to rely on less aggressive strategies that are correspondingly less likely to provoke challenge and retaliation.[5] Some of the larger firms, for example, seem content to settle for a position of previously acquired pre-eminence, which may be considerably short of complete dominance, but which is in any event acknowledged by at least a part of the market as one of price leadership. Their strategy is to maintain their position, not augment it. Smaller firms find security in associating themselves publicly with the acknowledged price leader and conforming readily to the latter's observed market behavior. Still others, both large and

[5] See Joe S. Bain, *Industrial Organization* (New York: John Wiley, 1959), Ch. 8.

small, enter tacitly or explicitly into collusive arrangements for setting prices and dividing markets; their strategy is to ensure individual survival through mutual compromise and accommodation. And still others adopt a policy of maximum independence, eschewing any consultation or prior agreements with groups of rivals in the process of deciding on their output and prices; their strategy is to ensure survival through neutrality.

To be sure, there are many variations on these few themes, but the important point is that they represent the basic poles of conduct in an oligopolistic market. They also represent the basic strategies of conduct in international affairs: predation, preservation of existing hegemonies, association with a Great Power, compromise agreements and alliances, and neutrality. The question is: What determines the choice of basic strategy? Clearly, a multitude of variables is operative. In an oligopolistic market, the ideological inclinations and moral convictions of the corporate management are not unimportant. Nor are expectations concerning psychological and commercial developments elsewhere in the market. But perhaps most important of all is the market power that the firm can bring to bear to achieve its ends. For the individual firm, the main problem is to choose a set of proximate goals consistent with the resources at its disposal. A small firm, for instance, with little public enthusiasm for its product, no monopoly of any raw material or distributive outlets, and no special access to financial backing, is hardly in a position to elect a policy of immediate market domination. Such behavior would not be rational; much more rational would be a policy of slow accumulation of market power through price "followership" or perhaps tacit collusion. Conversely, a very large firm in a dominant market position cannot adopt a policy of maximum independence, since its actions have such an immediate effect upon and hence are so closely watched by all of its rivals. For such a firm, predation or accepting the role of price leader would be more rational choices.

Firms in the market place tend, of course, to be much more rational in their behavior than states in the international arena. It has already been emphasized that foreign policy, being very largely the product of an internal political process, often seems anything but rational. All kinds of variables enter into the determination of foreign policy, too. Even so, in its role as trustee of the interests of the national community, the government must steer the state away from destruction. National survival is its first responsibility. Therefore, even though there is a wide latitude for the introduction of irrational elements into foreign policy, that latitude is not without limits. Weak, small states cannot rationally aspire to dominate the world, and strong, large states cannot effectively isolate themselves. The proximate goals of foreign policy must fit the resources available, however tenuously. Ultimately, national power sets the limits to the nation-state's choice of a strategy of foreign policy, just as market power sets the limits to the oligopolist's choice of a strategy of competition.

The key word here is choice. In a situation of competition, interdependence, and uncertainty, the survival of any one unit is very much a function of the range of alternative strategies available to it. The oligopolistic firm with only one strategic option leads a precarious existence: if that strategy fails to result in profit, the firm will disappear. Likewise, the nation-state with only one strategic option can never truly be secure: if that strategy fails, the state will disappear or be absorbed by others or, what is more likely, be compelled to abandon certain of its national core values.[6] For both the firm and the state, the rational solution is to broaden its range of options—that is, *to maximize its power position*, since power sets the limits to the choice of strategy. This does not mean that more power must be accumulated than is available to any of one's rivals, nor does it imply that the power must be used coercively. It means only that power must be accumulated *to the extent possible* in order to maximize the range of available strategies. This is the conduct we observe of firms in an oligopolistic market. To the extent that government processes are rational, it is also the conduct we observe of states in the international arena.

What constitutes national power, and what determines the

[6] In economics, clearly, the standard of success or failure is much more visible and "objective" than it is in politics. Profits can be measured, and when they are negative the firm will be liquidated; for even while the owners of an enterprise value its survival highly, they will be willing to see it go out of business if it produces only losses. The citizens of a nation-state, however, are rarely willing to see their country "go out of business," come what may. Rather, they prefer to contract their range of core values, often quite drastically, for the sake of national survival. But since values are by definition subjective, it is a most difficult problem to know precisely when the state is producing "losses."

extent to which it can be accumulated? Essentially, power represents the ability to control or at least influence the behavior of others. This ability need not be exercised; it need only be acknowledged by others to be effective. Basically, national power derives from the entire range of the nation's resources, available or potential, and in particular from those resources that have been or could be placed at the disposal of the state's foreign-policy-makers. Foremost among these resources, of course, is the military establishment—the organizational and physical entity that wages war. But national power is more than just "forces in being"; it is a function of all of the nation's other resources as well—its industries, population, geographic location and terrain, natural resources, scientific, managerial, and diplomatic skills, and so on. In addition, it is a function of the resources available to the nation's principal rivals, for power is potent only insofar as it balances or outweighs power elsewhere. What truly matters is not so much influence in absolute terms as influence in relation to that of others. True, taking all of these resources into account necessarily implies that national power must remain an ambiguous concept; no one has yet developed satisfactory criteria for measuring its components and ranking them. Nevertheless, each state must, and in practice does, form an approximate idea of its own power and that of its main competitors. Even though the risk of miscalculation is considerable, these estimates are indispensable. They are the necessary raw material from which the choice of foreign-policy strategy is fashioned.

The extent to which national power can be accumulated is implied by the definition of that concept, ambiguous as it may be. National power can be accumulated to the extent permitted by the resources of the state. These set an upper limit. The problem of the state's foreign-policy-makers is to maximize national power subject to this constraint—that is, to make most effective use of the available resources in pursuit of the state's proximate foreign-policy goals. It is clear that these goals cannot exceed the sum of resources available. Conversely, it is clear that the available resources must be qualitatively appropriate to the chosen ends. In a real sense, therefore, national power not only sets the limits to the selection of proximate foreign-policy goals; it also provides the instruments for their achievement. This is the sense in which the two basic problems of foreign policy are interrelated: through the sum total of national resources that can be employed to influence the external environment and ensure the ultimate objective of national security. Nowhere is this interrelation more apparent than in the determination of that subset of general foreign policy labeled foreign economic policy, to which we now turn.

2.

Foreign economic policy represents the sum total of actions by the nation-state intended to affect the economic environment beyond the national jurisdiction. As such it is a hybrid, combining elements of foreign policy in general as well as of economic policy in general.

On the one hand, like *economic* policy in general, foreign economic policy is concerned with the allocation of scarce resources. Ultimately, one of its objectives is to help employ national resources in the most efficient manner possible in order to maximize the production of goods and services available for domestic absorption. The problem for the makers of the state's foreign economic policy is not necessarily to optimize the pattern of foreign trade and investment according to cosmopolitan criteria, for this might leave the nation with fewer goods and services than it could potentially attain. Rather, their problem is, in an immediate sense, to organize foreign trade and investment in whatever pattern is necessary to maximize national income. In a more fundamental sense, their rational long-term objective is to maximize national wealth—the sum total of the nation's productive possessions—since it is from these material resources that the stream of current income derives.

On the other hand, like *foreign* policy in general, foreign economic policy is also concerned with national security. Ultimately, another of its objectives is to help ensure the self-preservation of the political community. In this regard, the problem for the makers of foreign economic policy is, in an immediate sense, to provide maximum support for the chosen strategy of the state's general foreign policy. In a more fundamental sense, their rational long-term objective is to maximize the national-power position, since national power plays the same role in relation to foreign economic policy in particular as it does in relation to foreign policy in general. That is, national power both sets the limits to the selection of the proximate goals of foreign economic policy and provides the instruments for their achievement.

Even though foreign economic policy is concerned with the maximization of national power, it can actually operate on only one single element of national power—national *economic* power. What constitutes this particular element of national power? Essentially, national economic power represents the ability to control or influence the behavior of others *in economic matters*. The possibility for influence in economic matters derives from the fact that the world economy, being based on a rather elaborate international division of labor, is in fact a system of interrelationships in which to a greater or lesser extent every nation is dependent on all the others—dependent for commodities and services of various kinds, for markets and investments, for technology and skills. These dependencies are tolerated because policy-makers, presumably having learned some international economic theory, are generally aware of the tremendous benefits to be had from foreign trade and investment: the availability of goods and services that either cannot be produced at home or can be produced only at relatively high cost, the access to external sources of capital and to foreign investment opportunities, the spread of scientific knowledge. Together, these benefits enrich each nation-state and increase its material wealth. The price to be paid for these gains is dependence on others.

The dependence of one state on another gives the latter influence through its control over that for which the former depends on it. That is, if A depends on B for, say, oil, B can influence A through its ability to control—and *in extremis* to halt—the flow of oil to A. True, B may do itself harm in the process. But if in greater measure A requires oil and cannot locate alternative sources of supply, B's influence over A is effective. Likewise, even in the absence of effective control of the flow of any important commodities or services to A, B can nevertheless exercise effective influence over A if, alternatively, it either provides essential markets for A's production or supplies A with vitally needed investments or foreign aid. With respect to each of these kinds of international economic relationship, A is continuously exposed to the potential threat of a stoppage by B. Herein lies the essence of national economic power. As Albert Hirschman has pointed out, "Thus, the power to interrupt commercial or financial relations with any country, considered as an attribute of national sovereignty, is the root cause of the influence or power position which a country acquires in other countries. . . ."[7]

Ceteris paribus, the greater a state's power to interrupt commercial or financial relations, the stronger its position in international economic affairs. Conversely, the more exposed a state is to potential interruptions of commercial or financial relations—i.e., the greater its dependence on others—the weaker its position in international economic affairs.

No state, not even the United States, has unlimited economic power. On the other hand, we might note that there are some small states so weak in international economic affairs, so overwhelmingly dependent on a single large neighbor, that they essentially have no choice but to rely for their national survival on the latter's tolerance and patronage. In return for assurances of their right to exist as nominally independent political entities, they yield to the patron all effective control of their own economy. The transfer of dominion may be tacit rather than explicit, thus preserving at least the appearance of economic sovereignty, as in the cases, say, of Botswana and Malawi in southern Africa. Or it may be unambiguously confirmed in a formal economic union or other written agreement, as in the cases, say, of Bhutan and Sikkim in Asia, of Andorra, Liechtenstein, Monaco, and San Marino in Europe, and of several island-states scattered about the world's oceans. How the transfer is effected is unimportant in this context. What matters is that in all such cases, national security can be assured only by acquiescing totally in the economic hegemony of another state—in effect, by entering knowingly into the most intimate of associations with a Great (or greater) Power.

However, most states are not nearly so weak in international economic affairs. Hence, for them such intimate associations are either impossible or repugnant. In the first place, there may be no convenient patron on which to rely. The situation just out-

[7] Albert O. Hirschman, *National Power and the Structure of Foreign Trade* (Berkeley: University of California Press, 1945), p. 16.

lined requires that the discrepancy between the economic power of the two neighbors be obvious and overwhelming. Such instances are limited in number; more normally, disparities between neighbors are discernible but not decisive. Furthermore, the situation requires that there be only one logical choice of patron. In fact, many relatively small states find themselves positioned between two or more Great (or greater) Powers, between whom it would be difficult to choose without upsetting the international power balance—and perhaps the domestic power balance as well. In any event, political communities in practice prefer to determine their own destinies. Except under extreme compulsion, most are quite evidently reluctant to surrender control of the national economy to a foreign government. They want economic sovereignty as well as political recognition.

These facts are significant. Since most states neither can nor want to abdicate direction of their economic affairs, they have no alternative but to confront squarely the fact of their dependence on the international economy. If they are to enhance their national security, they must, to the extent permitted by the resources available to them, try to use their foreign economic policies to reduce that dependence—that is, to reduce the potential threat of stoppages in their commercial and financial relations. Furthermore, to counterbalance forms of dependence that cannot be avoided, they must try to increase their own influence on others. By so doing, each state individually will hope to enhance its *net* influence in the international economy by creating conditions that make interruptions of trade and financial flows of less concern to itself than to others. In short, each state will hope to enhance its national economic power.

This does not mean, though, that each state will necessarily hope to *maximize* its national economic power. In this regard, as already indicated, the rational objective of foreign economic policy is to maximize *national power in general,* of which economic power is only one single element. National power embodies political, military, geographic, and other elements as well, and while it is certainly true that all of these elements are often mutually reinforcing, it is also true that they are not always perfect substitutes. Consequently, the problem for policy-makers is to estimate costs and allocate means to ends, hopefully to achieve over-all policy goals at the least total cost. At times it may seem necessary to sacrifice one element of national power in order to exploit the more attractive possibilities of another. This is no less true of the element of economic power than of any other. Thus some less developed countries, eager to import the latest in military hardware, have in recent years been willing to sacrifice much of their economic independence by indebting themselves heavily to one or another Great Power, in the expectation that on balance this would increase their over-all national power. Likewise, in recent years the United States has willingly sacrificed a good part of its economic influence in Western Europe by promoting local programs of regional integration, in the expectation that this would enhance our joint political power in confrontation with the Soviet Union. Whether either of these specific strategies was especially wise is a matter best left for evaluation elsewhere. What we must stress here is that the objective of foreign economic policy in each case, as in many other cases that could be cited, was clearly not to maximize national economic power in particular; it was to maximize national power in general. This is the manner in which foreign economic policy provides maximum support for the chosen strategy of the state's general foreign policy.

However, foreign economic policy is also, we have said, supposed to provide maximum support for the state's general economic policy; its rational objective is to maximize national wealth, too. To what extent are these two objectives—national power and national wealth—the same? Superficially, they seem to be identical; it seems intuitively obvious that it is the rich who are powerful, the poor who are weak. And indeed often they are. But such is not always the case. Great Britain, for example, is one of the wealthiest nations on the face of the earth, yet in her dealings with the economically underdeveloped Arab states and shiekdoms of the Middle East, abysmally poor except in oil, she does not appear to operate from a position of marked strength. The Arabs' ability to control or even halt the international flow of oil gives them a considerable influence over the British. Likewise, the United States is a far richer country than France, yet the French have been able to neutralize and at times even to prevail over American strength in the prolonged negotiations on world monetary reform. Apparently France's influence stems from her recent large balance-of-payments surpluses and resulting accumulations of reserves, which have given her the ability to threaten interruptions of international financial relations.

In other words, wealth per se is not sufficient to exercise effective power in international relations: national wealth and national power are not in fact identical. Of course, it is clear that a minimum level of wealth of some sort is a prerequisite, a necessary condition, for the disposition of power. Those without any wealth of any sort have no power at all. The Arabs must be able to produce oil, the French must be able to produce balance-of-payments surpluses. But it is equally clear that the mere possession of wealth is not a guarantee of power. What matters is how that wealth fits into the over-all distribution of dependence and influence in international affairs.

These facts have important implications for the analysis of foreign economic policy. Over a broad range of policies, there can be no doubt that the two objectives of national wealth and national power are functionally equal, complementary rather than competing. Many policies that add to the nation's material possessions are also likely to add directly to its net influence in international affairs. But there is also no doubt that over a certain range of foreign economic policies, the two objectives are in direct conflict. Within this range a choice must be made, as even Adam Smith recognized, admitting that to some extent "defence . . . is of much more importance than opulence. . . ." [8]

Following Smith's advice, states often may choose to forego a certain amount of national wealth if they can thereby augment their national power. Certainly we observe much behavior of this kind in the world economy. We observe states maintaining extremely protectionist commercial policies, despite the familiar arguments stressing the gains from modified free trade. We observe states savoring balance-of-payments surpluses, despite the implied reduction of real domestic absorption relative to national income. We observe states reluctant to admit private investments or public assistance from abroad, despite the attractive charms of foreign capital and imported technology. In all these instances, current income, hence future wealth, is sacrificed for the sake of national power and security.

At the same time, we observe in many instances that states may

[8] Adam Smith, *The Wealth of Nations* (Modern Library ed.; New York: Random House, 1937), p. 431.

choose to sacrifice a certain amount of national power for the sake of current income and future wealth. Policies of this kind are not at all uncommon, either. The problem for the makers of foreign economic policy is to sacrifice as little power as possible, since power cannot be foregone without limit if national survival is to be ensured, and to sacrifice as little wealth as possible, since wealth cannot be foregone without limit if the disposition of power is to be effective. In other words, the problem is to maximize jointly two objectives. This in reality is what foreign economic policy is all about.[9]

Several years ago, Harry Johnson planted the seeds of a general analytical approach to the problem of foreign economic policy.[10] It remains for us to harvest the fruits of his efforts, for even though Johnson himself wrote specifically of only one branch of foreign economic policy—commercial policy—his analytical apparatus can be readily generalized. His article begins by noting that the traditional approach to the theory of commercial policy, like all of conventional economic analysis, is based on a clear distinction between "economic" and "noneconomic" objectives. There is, supposedly, only one valid objective of policy—the economic objective of maximizing real income, identifiable with the utility derived by individuals from their personal consumption of goods and services. Noneconomic objectives are irrelevant, since they are *ex hypothesi* irrational. This distinction keeps the analysis neat, but unfortunately it also means, as Johnson writes, that "the economist is left without a theory capable of explaining a variety of important and observable phenomena, such as the nature of tariff bargaining, the commercial policies adopted by various countries, the conditions under which countries are willing to embark on

[9] Even the mercantilists of the seventeenth and eighteenth centuries regarded wealth and power as joint objectives. According to a popular misconception, power was for the mercantilists the sole end of foreign economic policy, with wealth valued mainly as a necessary means toward that end. But in fact there is remarkably little evidence to support this interpretation of mercantilist thought and practice; most of the evidence indicates that wealth, like power, was regarded as valuable simply for its own sake. See Jacob Viner, "Power versus Plenty as Objectives of Foreign Policy in the Seventeenth and Eighteenth Centuries," *World Politics*, I (October, 1948), pp. 1–29.
[10] Harry G. Johnson, "An Economic Theory of Protectionism, Tariff Bargaining, and the Formation of Customs Unions," *Journal of Political Economy*, LXXIII (June, 1965), pp. 256–283.

customs unions, and the arguments and considerations that have weight in persuading countries to change their commercial policies."[11]

In order to make the conventional analysis more operationally useful, Johnson abandons the traditional distinction between economic and noneconomic objectives, which as he points out is ethically biased in favor of private consumption as the exclusive measure of welfare. We might also point out that it is politically unrealistic, since it totally ignores power relations. Instead of the traditional distinction, Johnson emphasizes two other distinctions. The first is between private consumption goods and public consumption goods, the latter being commodities and services that are consumed collectively and can be provided only through the government at the cost of sacrifices of private consumption. The second is between "real income" in the sense of utility enjoyed from both private and public consumption, and "real product" defined conventionally as total production of privately appropriable commodities and services. He then assumes that there exists a collective preference for industrial production, in the sense that industrial production appears as a collective consumption good yielding a flow of satisfaction to the public independent of the satisfaction individuals derive directly from the consumption of industrial products. It follows, on the assumption of rationality of government processes, that the makers of the state's foreign economic policy will protect domestic industrial production by imposing tariffs and in general carrying protection to the point where the value of the marginal collective utility derived from collective consumption of domestic industrial activity is just equal to the marginal excess private cost (product foregone) of protected industrial production. Real income will be maximized, though real product will not, since maximization of real income requires sacrificing real product in order to gratify the preference for collective consumption of industrial production. In equilibrium, the proportional marginal excess private cost of protected production measures the marginal "degree of preference" for industrial production.

To generalize Johnson's analysis, let us first substitute for his

[11] *Ibid.*, p. 257.

assumed collective preference for industrial production a preference for the collective consumption of national power (including economic power). By definition, national power can, within a certain range of foreign economic policies, be provided only through the government at the cost of sacrifices of private consumption. We have already explained, from the perspective of political science, why rational policy-makers would in fact adopt this public consumption good as an immediate objective; in addition, we need only assume that the public itself shares the government's concern for national survival. Meanwhile, let us preserve Johnson's assumption that a second objective of national policy is to maximize what Johnson labels "real product," since in fact this corresponds to what conventional economic analysis stresses as the immediate objective of rational policy-makers. And finally, let us assume that the over-all objective of foreign economic policy is to maximize "real income" in the sense of the utility enjoyed from both private consumption of real product and collective consumption of national power. From these assumptions together with the assumption of rationality of government processes, it follows that, within that range where the objectives of national power and real product are in conflict, foreign economic policies will necessarily depart from the standard production-maximization precepts of economic analysis: within that range current income will be sacrificed for the sake of national security *up to the point where the value of the marginal collective utility derived from collective consumption of national power is just equal to its marginal excess private cost.* Real income will be maximized, though real product will not. In equilibrium, the proportional marginal excess private cost of national power measures the marginal "degree of preference" for national power.

Of course, government processes are not at all as rational as this analysis implies. It cannot be emphasized too often that policy, being very largely the product of an internal political process, in fact frequently seems anything but rational. Nevertheless, since it is in their interest to maximize policy objectives at least cost, policy-makers do manifestly attempt at least a rough approximation of the sort of calculus just outlined. In formal language, they try to ensure that the marginal excess private cost of national power does not exceed the marginal degree of preference for national power. More simply, they try not to pay for net influence in the world more than they think it is worth.

This analytical approach to the problem of foreign economic policy can be very useful operationally. Its insights help to explain a variety of important and observable phenomena in this area of study. For instance, they help us to understand why, in confronting the fact of their dependence on the world economy, nations do not simply seek to avoid every form of dependence by refusing to participate at all in international economic affairs. This is the policy of autarky—total economic isolation and self-sufficiency—and it certainly does exclude the threat of interruptions of commercial and financial relations, but it does so negatively by eliminating the relations rather than the threat. This is akin to throwing the baby out with the bath water. In the view of most states, autarky represents economic security purchased at too high a price; it is just not worth foregoing all of the gains from foreign trade and investment, particularly since some of them at least should be expected to increase rather than decrease the state's net international influence.

As a matter of fact, no state in modern times has ever achieved total segregation from the world economy. Not even the Soviet Union, in the most autarkic phases of its development, ever felt that it could afford to forego all of the benefits of international economic specialization. True, for decades the Russians officially regarded foreign trade as no more than an unavoidable residual—a means for uncorking bottlenecks in the domestic planning mechanism. The price they were willing to pay for minimizing foreign influence was quite high. But it is noteworthy that in more recent years, that price has fallen dramatically. Indeed, these very same Russians have now actually renounced autarky as an official policy. Instead, they are beginning to preach the advantages of an international division of labor, albeit a "socialist" international division of labor.[12] Presumably this seemingly ideological qualification is in fact a practical one reflecting the discrepancy between the Soviet Union's preponderant economic influence within the Communist

[12] See, e.g., V. P. Sergeyev, "Economic Principles of the Foreign Trade of Socialist States," in R. F. Harrod and D. C. Hague (eds.), *International Trade Theory in a Developing World* (New York: St. Martin's, 1963), pp. 277–296.

bloc and its rather limited influence elsewhere. To that extent, the
Russians' behavior represents a rational effort to maximize their
country's national power at least cost and is wholly consistent with
the analytical approach outlined.

In summary, the over-all objective of foreign economic policy
is the joint maximization of the state's current income and its
net influence in international affairs. The practical problem of
foreign economic policy is to allocate means to ends—that is, to
make most effective use of all available national resources in pursuit of the over-all objective, the idea being ultimately to provide
maximum support for the general foreign policy of the state.
National resources here are defined as broadly as possible to include all means and instruments that can be employed in the
interest of the state to influence the external economic environment. Generally, these resources can be grouped under four principal policy headings: (1) commercial policy, (2) foreign-investment policy, (3) foreign-aid policy, and (4) balance-of-payments
policy.[13] Each of these can be discussed separately.

1. *Commercial policy.* Commercial policy represents the sum
total of actions by the state intended to affect the extent, composition, and direction of its imports and exports of goods and
services. These actions include not only the familiar direct interventions in international trade, such as tariffs, subsidies, quotas,
exchange controls, official procurement policies, state trading, and
the like, but also the many indirect interventions, ranging from
domestic revenue taxes and pricing policies to sanitary regulations,
advertising restrictions, and packaging requirements. They might
also be said to include a variety of private business practices, such
as market allocation among the domestic and foreign affiliates of
large national corporations.

International economic theory teaches that given all the Pareto
optimality conditions of the perfectly competitive market, free
trade maximizes world income. However, if the individual state
exercises any degree of monopoly-monopsony power in world

---

[13] As a fifth category, we might also list immigration policy, defined to include actions by the state affecting the outward as well as inward movement
of labor (human capital). However, we have decided to exclude discussion of
this category here on the grounds that in practice policy-makers treat it primarily as a social problem rather than as a matter of economic analysis.

markets, its own income is not maximized, and even if the state
lacks such power, its own income is likely to fall short of the
potential maximum if there are significant departures from Pareto
optimality. Consequently, some interventions in foreign trade can
be justified on conventional economic grounds as means for improving the state's terms of trade or as "second-best" corrections of
domestic "distortions."[14] Most interventions, though, cannot be
justified so easily. Most are plainly the product of special-interest
legislation, the outcome of the efforts of powerful domestic institutions to achieve their own particular ambitions and goals at the
expense of the general welfare of the national community as well
as of the outside world. As a result, most forms of trade intervention are notoriously "sticky": once enacted, they take on a
life of their own and are difficult—if not impossible—to remove.

Even so, the makers of a state's commercial policy are not
completely without room for maneuver. Most forms of trade inter-
cention can be at least manipulated in the interest of the national
community, and many can in fact be negotiated away in return
for significant concessions from others. The problem is to manipulate and negotiate to affect the extent, composition, and direction of the state's foreign trade in such a way that, subject to the
constraint of special-interest legislation that remains, the state's
net international influence is jointly maximized along with its current income. If there were no special-interest legislation at all,
any interventions lowering rather than raising income would be
justified solely as the price to be paid for maximizing this aspect
of national power.

An almost infinite variety of manipulations and negotiations of
commercial policy is possible, depending on the resources available
to the state and the proximate goals of its general foreign policy.
Assume, for instance, a small state—small in population, in geographic area, and in natural resources—trying to follow a path of
political neutrality in international affairs. Being small, it is likely
to be rather highly specialized in the relatively few lines of production in which it enjoys a comparative advantage. Consequently,
it is likely as well to be rather highly dependent on foreign trade,

[14] Harry G. Johnson, "Optimal Trade Intervention in the Presence of Domestic Distortions," in Robert E. Baldwin, *et al.*, *Trade, Growth and the Balance
of Payments* (Chicago: Rand McNally, 1965), pp. 3–34.

as measured by the proportion of exports and imports to total national production. Being neutral, however, it presumably wishes to minimize the influence on itself of the outside world in general and of any single Great Power in particular. It will therefore use its commercial policy defensively to minimize the danger to itself of stoppages in any part of its foreign trade. Its first aim will be to diversify the national production structure. This will not only reduce the state's over-all dependence on foreign trade, thereby reducing its dependence on the outside world, it will also alter the commodity composition of its foreign trade, increasing the range of exports while probably decreasing that of imports, thereby reducing the state's specific dependence on any single trade item. In addition, the state will use its commercial policy to diversify the geographic composition of its trade, in order to ensure that no single large trading partner will control too great a share of its foreign markets or sources of supply.[15]

Now, in contrast, assume a large state trying to follow a path of political predation or preservation of existing hegemonies. This state will use its commercial policy aggressively rather than defensively.[16] It will attempt to exploit the fact that, being large, it is likely already to be an important influence in world trade, even though, in relation to its own total production, its exports and imports may be rather small. Logically, its aim will be to maximize its power to threaten interruptions of the commercial relations of others, particularly of those others it wishes to dominate (or continue to dominate), at least cost to itself. Thus this state will, first of all, oppose all efforts by others to restrict or divert international trade in general, on the principle that this could diminish the power it derives from its domination of individual markets either as buyer or seller. Second, it will itself seek to divert its own trade away from states larger and richer than itself to states smaller and poorer, on the principle that this creates conditions that make the interruption of mutual trade of much graver concern to each of its trading partners than to itself. Third, it may also promote exports of highly differentiated industrial products in place of primary commodities, on the principle that importing countries can in the event of stoppage less easily switch

---

[15] Hirschman describes this last aim as "an elementary defensive principle of the smaller trading countries." Hirschman, *op. cit.*, p. 31.
[16] *Ibid.*, Ch. 2.

suppliers of the former type of good than of the latter type. And last, it may offer special price or other advantages to some of its own suppliers, on the principle that this renders more painful the diversion of a trading partner's exports to third countries.

For a final, intermediate case, assume a state that, being neither small enough to be neutral and innocuous nor large enough to be predatory or hegemonic, seeks to preserve its national security through a general foreign policy of compromise agreements and alliances. In support of this policy it is likely to direct its trade toward its friends and allies, since this would minimize the threat of potential stoppages of its trade with more hostile trading partners. It may even agree to a free-trade area or customs-union arrangement, since this would in addition maximize the group's joint power to bargain and to threaten interruptions of the trade of others. In unity there is strength. In unity there is also relatively little—if any—economic cost. In this case, the price of national security is the sacrifice of a certain degree of economic sovereignty.

These are the three principal lines of commercial policy. It seems readily apparent that in the real world virtually all states do in fact follow one or another or some combination of them. Many of the less developed countries, for example, follow the first line of policy, for the most part because of their general interest in nonalignment with any of the large power blocs, but also simply because of their political failure in almost all cases to agree on an effective approach along the third line of policy. Likewise, the first line of policy is preferred by a few of the more advanced countries, mainly those like Japan and Australia that happen to be relatively isolated at the fringes of the developed world. Most of the advanced countries, though, are more partial to the third line of policy. This is particularly true of Canada and of the small and medium-sized states of Europe on either side of the disintegrating Iron Curtain, for whom the key to survival has become compromise and alliance. The very largest countries, of course, whose principal desire is to preserve or extend existing hegemonies, favor the second line of policy, albeit modified in some proportion by the third in the interest of maintaining local alliances or strengthening bargaining power. And finally, we should not forget the very smallest countries, whose extreme application of the third line of policy has already been alluded to.

2. *Foreign-investment policy.* Foreign-investment policy repre-

sents the sum total of actions by the state intended to affect the extent, composition, and direction of private direct and portfolio investments both by residents abroad and by foreigners domestically. These actions include principally taxes and administrative regulations of various kinds, but also monetary policy to a certain extent. Their purpose is to manipulate the stock as well as the flow of private foreign investments in such a way as to jointly maximize the state's national power and current income.

There can be little doubt that with respect to the problem of maximizing current income, foreign investments benefit both capital-exporting and capital-importing countries. Otherwise, we would hardly expect to find such large flows of private capital as we do observe in the world today. For the host countries, foreign investments can bring not only short-run support of the balance-of-payments position, but also supplements to domestic savings, permitting them higher levels of gross capital formation than would otherwise be possible. For the investing countries, meanwhile, foreign investments can provide alternative outlets for domestic savings yielding higher marginal returns than investments at home, as well as eventually produce a reflow of income that can provide support to the balance of payments in the longer run. In these respects, capital-exporting and capital-importing countries share certain interests in common.

However, with respect to the problem of maximizing national power, the same is only partially true at best—and utterly false at worst. A basic motive of foreign investment is to minimize the danger of stoppages in the capital-exporting country's foreign trade by increasing the reliability of markets for exports and sources of supply for imports.[17] This ambition coincides with the security interests of the capital-importing country only if the latter is not disinclined toward close economic and political association with the capital exporter. If, contrarily, the capital importer prefers a policy of neutrality, the investments may not be welcomed at all, except possibly as a counterweight to investments from other

---

[17] Alternatively, this motive can be expressed as a desire on the part of investing enterprises to avoid uncertainty by reducing their competition; effectively, this emerges as a desire to maintain or augment oligopolistic market shares. See Stephen Hymer, "Direct Foreign Investment and International Oligopoly," June, 1965 (Yale University, Economic Growth Center: mimeo).

sources. And the investments may be actively opposed if the capital importer prefers association not with the capital exporter at all but rather with some third party. Moreover, even if the capital importer is not disinclined toward a close relationship with the capital exporter, such investments may be restricted if they threaten foreign domination of important sectors of the domestic economy.

Thus a capital-importing country will often, on security grounds, seek to constrain the flow of private investments from abroad below the level that might otherwise be dictated by purely market criteria. As a result, clear economic benefits are lost both to it and to the capital exporter. We should note, however, that there is a discrepancy in the gains foregone. Whereas the capital exporter loses only the extra profits that would have accrued from investments abroad rather than at home or in some third country, the capital importer loses the entire investment together with the increased production and improved technology that might have resulted from it. This implies that in the field of policy relating to the flow of private foreign investments, the capital-exporting country maintains one basic advantage: it has the resources; the capital importer does not. This advantage gives the capital-exporting country a considerable influence over the capital importer, since it can be used to withhold new investments, to bargain over their composition and the conditions affecting them, or even to divert them when necessary to less hostile recipients.

On the other hand, in the field of policy relating to the already existing stock of private foreign investments, the capital-importing country maintains one basic advantage: it has direct political control over the investment, the capital exporter does not. This advantage gives the capital-importing country a considerable advantage over the capital exporter, since it can be used to restrict or supervise the activities of the investment, or even to halt its operation or confiscate it when necessary. Obviously, this directly negates the basic motive of foreign investment in the first place, which was to minimize the danger of stoppages in trade. The capital exporter's rational response to such threats is to attempt, to the extent possible, to diversify the composition of foreign investments and to disperse them geographically. Where this is difficult because of the specificity of investment needs or of supply or market possibilities, the stage is set for a conflict of policies between capital exporter and capital importer, the outcome of which will depend ultimately on the price each is willing to pay for this aspect of national power.

3. *Foreign-aid policy.* Foreign-aid policy represents the sum total of actions by the state intended to affect the extent, composition, and direction of foreign public assistance given or received. Like other foreign economic policies, its purpose is to maximize jointly the state's national power and current income. Its analysis is fairly straightforward since the main economic gains all accrue to the recipient while the main political benefits all accrue to the donor. Thus the recipient will seek to maximize the benefits of foreign aid obtained at least cost in terms of dependence on other states, while the donor will seek to maximize its influence abroad at least cost in terms of foregone alternative uses of public capital. This helps to explain why, for example, recipients favor multilateral aid programs while donors favor bilateral ones, and also why donors try to concentrate their aid efforts geographically while recipients try to diversify the sources of the help they receive. And of course it certainly helps to explain why, from the point of view of the recipients, who are preoccupied with the problem of development, the donors' efforts never seem adequate.

4. *Balance-of-payments policy.* Balance-of-payments policy represents the sum total of actions by the state intended to affect the net demand or supply of foreign exchange. These actions include all of those listed under the three other categories of policy insofar as they bear upon the international payments adjustment process, as well as any other monetary, fiscal, or administrative device that influences, either directly or through its effect on private market behavior, the surplus or deficit in the balance of payments. In addition, they include all actions affecting the composition of the state's international monetary reserves.

International economic theory teaches that balance-of-payments surpluses are not inherently desirable, since they imply a reduction of real domestic absorption relative to national income. Conversely, deficits are not inherently undesirable, since they permit a nation to "live beyond its means." Nevertheless, the makers of foreign economic policy abhor deficits and prefer surpluses whenever possible. The reason is simple and relates to the inadequacies of the international payments adjustment mechanism under a regime of relatively fixed exchange rates. To begin with, it is evident that under this type of regime, persistent payments imbalances can emerge only because of conflicts within individual countries between the policies that are considered appropriate for the current state of the domestic economy and the policies that are considered appropriate for the current state of the balance of payments. If there were no such conflicts within separate countries, the payments imbalances between them would disappear. For instance, if a mutual imbalance reflected a combination of deficit and inflation in A and a combination of surplus and recession in B, there would be no internal policy conflict for either country. A would deflate, B would reflate, and balance would be restored. However, a problem arises if, as is so often the case, deficits are associated with recession (or absence of inflation) and surpluses with inflation (or absence of recession). Then there is a conflict within each country between its domestic and balance-of-payments policies—a conflict most governments prefer to resolve in favor of the former. As a result, the internal-policy conflict gets translated into an international-policy conflict. The conflict will persist for as long as the mutual imbalance of payments can be financed by the flow of gold and foreign-exchange reserves.

Now, there is virtually no limit to how long a surplus country can accumulate reserves. On the other hand, there is a distinct limit to how long a deficit country can deplete its reserves, a limit determined by the size of its reserve stock plus its access to external credit facilities. The pressures on the deficit and surplus countries are not symmetrical. Consequently, the deficit country is, more often than not, the one forced to take the initial steps to resolve the international policy conflict, usually at its own expense.[18] In this sense, the surplus country exercises an important influence over the economy and policies of the deficit country. The influence may be implicit in the former country's accumulation of the latter country's reserves, or it may be made explicit in the

[18] Actually, this statement is accurate only as a first approximation. In fact, the problem of who initiates the adjustment process and who pays the costs of adjustment is a much more complicated matter. See Benjamin J. Cohen, *Adjustment Costs and the Distribution of New Reserves*, Princeton Studies in International Finance, No. 18 (Princeton: International Finance Section, 1966).

form of conditions and "strings" attached to the extension of credit facilities or balance-of-payments support. Either way, the situation represents for the deficit country a form of dependence that it would prefer to circumvent. The easiest way for it to do so is to become a surplus country itself, capable of exercising an influence of its own. That is why the makers of foreign economic policy generally prefer surpluses to deficits, despite the evident cost in terms of real domestic absorption foregone. This cost measures the price they are willing to pay for maximizing this aspect of national power. Sometimes the price they are willing to pay is strikingly high, as in the case of France in most years since General de Gaulle first came to power.

For reserve-currency countries, the situation has another dimension. A reserve-currency country functions as a sort of banker for the world: its money is held by other states as part of their international reserves. There are several reasons why some states want to hold the money of another, but they are all based on the essential assumption of a fixed-price relationship between the reserve currency and gold, which all states still consider the ultimate international currency. Significantly, the right to alter the gold value of the reserve currency—in other words, its exchange rate—rests solely with the reserve-currency country. This right gives the reserve-currency country a considerable influence over its "depositors"—in fact, a sort of hegemony in monetary affairs—and under appropriate circumstances can largely free it from balance-of-payments constraints. For rather than risk forcing a devaluation of the reserve currency in terms of gold, the depositors are often willing to "lend" to the reserve-currency country—that is, accept balances of its currency—to the amount of any deficit the latter happens to incur; further, they are often willing to resolve the international policy conflict themselves at their own expense. In such cases, the influence afforded states by surpluses in their payments balances is neutralized by the unique advantages afforded the reserve-currency country by its control over the gold value of its own money.

However, if the reserve-currency country's deficits persist for too long, its depositors are not apt to remain quite so benign. Significantly, any single depositor has the right to convert its own reserve balance, despite the risk that by so exercising the influence afforded it by present payments surpluses or past reserve accumulations, it may be seriously jeopardizing the gold value of the balances of remaining depositors. From the point of view of the rebellious depositor, the risk may be worthwhile if it can thereby increase its net influence vis-à-vis the reserve-currency country. From the point of view of the reserve-currency country, the problem is to decide what price it is willing to pay in order to maintain its hegemonic position in world monetary affairs. That price may be counted in terms of the deviations from present domestic policies that would be required to reduce or eliminate its deficits, or in terms of the concessions—monetary or otherwise—that would be required to prevent remaining depositors from following the example of the rebel. In its current confrontation with France, a most rebellious depositor, the United States, the world's principal reserve-currency country, appears willing to pay a strikingly high price, indeed as high as General de Gaulle seems prepared to pay for his surpluses. This is not surprising, since the stakes for both are so great: in effect, predominance in Europe. Here is dramatic confirmation of the basic fact that the ultimate role of foreign economic policy is to provide maximum support for the general foreign policy of the nation-state.

3.

Since 1945 the foreign economic policy of the United States has been used openly and in a manner entirely consistent with the analysis just outlined to provide maximum support for our general foreign policy.[19] In fact, this use of foreign economic policy represents a significant departure from the pattern that prevailed up to World War II, when it was more often diplomacy that was employed to promote America's commercial and financial interests abroad; today, commerce and finance are manipulated in the interests of diplomacy. In practice, though, the change of emphasis is but one aspect of the general revolution in American foreign policy that began during the war—the shift away from

[19] For a useful survey, see H. Bradford Westerfield, *The Instruments of America's Foreign Policy* (New York: Thomas Y. Crowell Company, 1963), Part IV.

our traditional posture of insularity to a new role of active world
leadership and deliberate political involvement in every corner of
the globe.[20] Here was one revolution that was inevitable. It had
been clear to many for a generation that the United States was
the most powerful nation in the world—economically, financially,
politically, militarily. It remained only for the American government and the American people to concede that a state so large
and so influential in world affairs could not segregate itself forever
through continuing its historical policies of political isolation and
economic protectionism. Those policies ended with World War
II. Since then the United States has learned to shoulder the responsibilities as well as to exercise the prerogatives of its national
power position. In this connection it has also learned to use in
pursuit of its foreign-policy objectives all of the instruments at
its command, not the least of which are economic.

What have been the foreign-policy objectives of the United
States since World War II? Our ultimate objective has been to
ensure our national security—our independence and our way of
life—against what, once the Cold War began, was suddenly viewed
as a very serious threat from expansionist world Communism. It
does not matter whether in fact the threat was "real" or not.
What matters is that the *fear* of a threat was real. In addition, it
matters that the range of minimum national core values we then
felt worth preserving was extraordinarily broad. This helps explain
our unaccustomed willingness ever since to become involved in
"entangling" alliances, spheres of influence, and even wars in
every corner of the globe. In the Western Hemisphere we considered it in our national interest to maintain our unique hegemonic position as a predominant power without rival. In the Eastern
Hemisphere we considered it in our national interest to maintain
the balance of power against the pressure of expansion from the
Soviet Union and its allies—in other words, to "contain" Communism. Thus in one half of the world our design was to keep
Canada and the Latin American republics as closely associated
with us as ever. In the other half, it was to bolster up Western
Europe and Japan as counterweights to, respectively, the Soviet
bloc in Europe and mainland China in Asia, while at the same

[20] See, e.g., William G. Carleton, *The Revolution in American Foreign Policy*
(New York: Random House, 1963).

time competing against the attempts of Communist states to extend their influence in the nonaligned "third world" of South Asia, the Middle East, and Africa. For more than two decades these have been the principal proximate goals of American foreign policy. In pursuit of these goals, the United States has used all of the foreign-economic-policy instruments at its disposal—commercial policy, foreign-investment policy, foreign-aid policy, and balance-of-payments policy.

Geographically, American foreign economic policy divides into three primary components corresponding roughly to the three broad economic divisions of the world today: the non-Communist industrial nations of Europe, Canada, and Japan; the Communist bloc; and the less developed "third world" of Africa, Asia, and Latin America. With respect to the non-Communist industrial nations, our foreign economic policy has been plain. From the start of the Cold War, our main objective was to reconstruct the war-hurt economies of Western Europe and Japan, as well as to maintain the vigor of the undamaged Canadian economy, so that they could all be effective barriers against the presumed menace of Communist expansion. Toward this end we transferred to the former war zones huge sums of aid in the form of grants and loans, most spectacularly under the European Recovery Program (Marshall Plan), which lasted from 1947 to 1952. Toward this end, also, we stimulated an outflow of private investments from the United States, particularly to Canada but also to Europe, and we promoted through GATT a broad program of world-wide liberalization of industrial trade that frequently benefited our allies directly at our own expense. And lastly, in Europe, we encouraged various schemes of regional cooperation and integration, despite the potential threat to our own economic influence, on the ground that these would heal old wounds and substitute cohesion for fragmentation in the face of external Communist pressures. The absolute cost of these policies in terms of income foregone was in some cases quite high. Nevertheless, to the makers of policy it seemed a small enough price to pay for preserving the power balance in Europe and Asia as well as the united strength of the North American continent.

With respect to the Communist bloc, our foreign economic policy, after the start of the Cold War, was equally plain. Our main objective was the economic equivalent of political "containment": to minimize our own and our allies' trade contacts with the bloc in order to deny to the Soviet Union and its presumed satellites the major benefits of an international division of labor. East-West trade, we reasoned, was of much greater importance to the Communists than to ourselves. Hence, correct or not, it seemed possible for us to enhance our own national security at relatively little cost to ourselves in terms of income foregone. Our policy began in 1948 with the initiation of mandatory export licensing controls, and was later extended in several major pieces of legislation, including the Export Control Act of 1949, which withdrew most-favored-nation tariff treatment from all Communist states and established a list of "strategic" goods for which no United States export licenses would be issued, and the Mutual Defense Assistance Control Act of 1951 (the "Battle Act"), which tried to ensure allied cooperation with our policy by threatening to terminate economic aid to any state exporting strategic items to the Communist bloc. As a matter of actual fact, aid has never been terminated under the 1951 Act, which has always been more or less a dead letter; and under the 1949 Act a number of exceptions have been made favoring such countries as Yugoslavia and Poland as a means of encouraging tendencies toward "polycentrism" and economic liberalism within the Communist world. Even so, after two decades of Cold War, the principal emphasis of our policy remains the quasi-isolation of Communism. Indeed, vis-à-vis the Asian Communist states and Cuba, the aim is total isolation—a complete embargo on trade.

Finally, with respect to the underdeveloped Third World, our main foreign-economic-policy objective has been to cooperate in its aspirations for economic development in order to maximize our own net influence in the area and to protect our existing commercial and financial interests. Just about our only instrument of policy in this connection has been the foreign-aid program, beginning in 1949 with Point Four technical assistance and later expanding to include grants and loans by a succession of alphabetical agencies—MSA, FOA, DLF, ICA, AID, etc. Trade policy has not in fact been used much for this purpose at all, and private investors have never really received much special encouragement to seek out investment opportunities in the less developed countries. And, for that matter, the foreign-aid program itself has never been very large relative to our potential. Apparently, the United States, as a political community, has been unwilling to pay a great deal for this aspect of national power and security.

In the background of our foreign economic policy in all three of these areas has been our policy with respect to the balance of international payments. This category of policy must be discussed separately because it knows no geographic limitation; it influences and regulates our actions in every corner of the globe. The United States functions as central banker for the world: our currency of issue, the dollar, circulates widely both as the principal "vehicle" currency for international trade and investment—even the Communist states use dollars when trading outside the bloc—and as the principal reserve currency for governments and international institutions. In practice, this means that the amount of new "international" money placed in circulation year after year depends mainly on the magnitude of the annual deficits in our balance of payments. When the world's demand for new money exceeds the available supply, we, the central bank, can run deficits of almost any conceivable magnitude. In fact, this was precisely what happened during the period of the so-called dollar shortage, which lasted from the end of the war until about 1958. During these years we were effectively freed from balance-of-payments constraints to pursue whatever policies around the world we considered appropriate and to spend as freely as we thought necessary to promote objectives believed to be in the national interest. From the foreign-exchange point of view, we could afford to forego potentially profitable trade with the Communist bloc, we could afford to revive Europe and Japan with aid, investments, and trade advantages, we could afford to promote development in the Third World with substantial grants and loans, and we could afford to maintain hundreds of thousands of American military personnel abroad. In effect, despite the fact that a payments balance is by definition a mutual experience, our position as international central banker enabled us to adopt a balance-of-payments policy that was entirely unilateral: we issued the world's principal vehicle and reserve currency in amounts presumed to be consistent with our own priorities—not with those of our depositors.

Since the late 1950s, of course, that situation has changed

dramatically, for it is now manifest that the world's demand for new money no longer much exceeds the available supply. Indeed, in the view of many the dollar shortage has become a serious "dollar glut." As a result, we can no longer proceed to ignore the priorities of our depositors; we are no longer freed from balance-of-payments constraints. This has compelled us to revise our policies with respect to the balance of payments and to review our official attitude toward the role of the dollar in world monetary affairs. What payments programs are appropriate in this new situation? What are the costs and benefits of the present role of the dollar? What will be the role of the dollar in the future? And what should be our policy regarding international monetary reform? These are some of the important issues discussed in the readings in Part II below.

The readings in Parts III through V discuss other important issues of United States foreign economic policy that have arisen recently in our relations with each of the three broad economic divisions of the world. For example, with respect to the non-Communist industrial nations—often referred to as the Atlantic Community, despite the inclusion of the Japanese—a need for new policies has become clearly apparent, in large measure simply because our old policies were so markedly successful. The economies of Western Europe and Japan have been so well reconstructed that they are now both able and eager to challenge what, in the earlier postwar decades, amounted to an American economic hegemony. And Canada, too, is becoming increasingly unhappy with its role as a very junior partner in the North American economy. These problems in our economic relations with our partners in the Atlantic Community are examined by the readings in Part III of this volume.

In our economic relations with the Communist bloc, the principal problem today is, should we expand East-West trade? As already indicated, the United States has demonstrated a willingness to expand trade contacts only on a selective basis as a means for encouraging tendencies toward polycentrism and economic liberalism on the far side of the Iron Curtain. The question now is whether to expand East-West trade generally—at least as regards the Soviet Union and Eastern Europe—as a means for accelerating the broad political détente toward which events seem to be moving in that part of the world. This is the question examined by the readings in Part IV.

Finally, in our economic relations with the Third World, there are several major issues, stemming both from the growing dissatisfaction in our country with the results of the traditional foreign-assistance programs and from the growing agitation in the less developed countries for new initiatives in trade as well as aid. What is the rationale for foreign aid, and should it be provided bilaterally or multilaterally? What opportunities are there for improvements in our commercial and foreign-investment policies? And what should be our role in Latin America? These are the problems examined by the readings in Part V, the final portion of this volume.

PART II

The Financial Framework: The Issues

In July, 1944, as World War II approached its climax, representatives of the United Nations met in Bretton Woods, New Hampshire, to consider some of the financial problems that they feared would arise after the war. Their objective was to avoid a return to the monetary chaos of the 1930s—the unstable exchanges and the competitive depreciations, the exchange controls and the inconvertible currencies of that era of economic warfare. After long and arduous negotiations, they decided to return to a modified version of the gold-exchange standard of the 1920s—a regime of relatively fixed exchange rates under which most countries held their monetary reserves in the form of one or another "reserve currency" convertible into gold. (In 1944 the most important reserve currencies were the United States dollar and the British pound sterling.) To back up the revived standard the Bretton Woods Conference created the International Monetary Fund, a complex endowment of gold and national currencies designed to help deficit countries to finance temporary imbalances of payments. It was hoped that the Fund would ensure relatively stable exchanges, an early return to convertibility, and, in general, international monetary cooperation.[1]

In its more than two decades of operation, the Fund has in most respects probably exceeded the hopes of its founders. However, in the immediate postwar years, it accomplished very little. Indeed, there was very little it could accomplish, given the exigencies of the economic situation and the inelasticity of its own financial resources. The Fund was created as an international

[1] For a detailed discussion of the origins of the IMF and the evolution of the postwar international payments system, see Richard N. Cooper, *The Economics of Interdependence: Economic Policy in the Atlantic Community* (New York: McGraw-Hill, 1967), Ch. 2.

credit intermediary, and its endowment of "international liquidity" was fixed. But what the world—and particularly war-weary Europe —needed at that time was much more than a limited volume of revolving short-term credits. Rather, what was needed was an elastic supply of new international liquidity sufficient to finance the huge payments imbalances of the early postwar years and to build up national monetary reserves. In effect, what the world needed was an international bank of issue, a role the IMF was not designed to play, because the negotiators at Bretton Woods had been too preoccupied with considerations of national sovereignty to give any international institution the all-important power to create and destroy money. Nor could the role be filled by the United Kingdom, the main reserve-currency country of the 1920s; the British were then, as now, too preoccupied with their own economic difficulties.

The United States, however, the main reserve currency country of the postwar period, could and did fill the role of international bank of issue at the end of the war because the dollar was in heavy demand by other countries, both as a "vehicle" currency to finance import trade and as a reserve currency to replenish depleted reserves. Moreover, the supply of dollars was potentially quite elastic. It was a function simply of the magnitude of the deficits in the United States balance of payments. Starting in 1950, these deficits tended to be considerable, aggregating as much as $10.7 billion in the seven years through 1956. Yet no one worried. On the contrary, the world was grateful for this alleviation of the so-called dollar shortage. And the United States was pleased, too, being freed in effect from a balance-of-payments constraint on its domestic and foreign policies.

Unfortunately, this happy situation could not continue. To be sure, U.S. deficits have lasted, after a temporary surplus in 1957 owing to the Suez crisis. But the excess foreign demand for dollars has gradually eased, particularly since 1958–1960 when in just three years U.S. deficits aggregated to a sum greater than that of all of the previous decade's deficits. During those three years, the dollar liabilities of the United States continued to mount while its gold reserves continued to dwindle—that is, its net reserve position continued to deteriorate—and foreign governments became more and more concerned about the credibility of the

American government's pledge to maintain the dollar's gold convertibility at a rate of $35 an ounce. In virtually no time at all, the dollar shortage turned into what looked like a dollar glut, and pressures were soon being brought to bear on the United States to "do something about the dollar." Thus ended our freedom from all constraint of the balance of payments.

Since the late 1950s, therefore, the U.S. government has had to be increasingly preoccupied with the problem of the dollar. Initially, students of the balance-of-payments problem focused on the immediate issue of the deficits themselves. The problem, we naively supposed, was simply a matter of bringing foreign payments into line with foreign receipts. Equilibrium was the *summum bonum* of policy. But equilibrium proved to be an elusive target. Little did policy-makers realize at the time that what was really at stake was the future role of the dollar in world monetary affairs.

Academic economists were the first to point out the basic nature of the dollar's dilemma. The true pioneer was Robert Triffin, who early saw the intimate connection between our own deficits and the operation of the world's revived gold-exchange standard.[2] Under the postwar standard, he noted, the balance-of-payments equilibrating mechanism was imperfect, but the volume of transactions was increasing. The supply of international liquidity needed to finance disequilibria, therefore, had to grow continually. And since under the postwar standard the dollar was the principal component of the supply of international liquidity, this meant that the United States had to run deficits continually in its own balance of payments. However, as the deficits persisted, America's net reserve position inevitably declined, and consequently confidence in the dollar was bound to fade. In order to maintain confidence in the dollar, and so prevent destabilizing switches into gold or possibly other reserve media, our deficits had to be stopped. But if we stopped them, the supply of new liquidity would be inadequate. Either way, the system would tremble.

In effect, the international system suffered from three fundamental defects: a weak adjustment mechanism, an irregular growth of reserves, and a possibility of shifts of confidence among the

[2] Robert Triffin, *Gold and the Dollar Crisis* (New Haven: Yale University Press, 1960).

principal reserve media—mainly between gold and the dollar. Economists identified these, respectively, as the problems of adjustment, liquidity, and confidence.[3] And since under postwar arrangements the dollar was the main reserve currency—indeed, the linchpin—of the existing monetary order, it was clear that all three problems of the system were problems for the dollar as well.

It was obvious that to solve these three problems the existing monetary order had to be reformed. This meant that the reserve-currency role of the dollar had to be reformed. Here, our policy-makers came to realize, was the true extent of the problem of the dollar. Consequently, our efforts to restore external balance came to be viewed as but a single element of an evolving and necessarily much more comprehensive financial policy. In practice, balance was seen as essential, mainly insofar as it promised to reduce the influence of our creditors and so enhance our bargaining position in the long-term negotiations within the IMF and the Group of Ten concerning the future of the gold-exchange standard. The Group of Ten, which includes Belgium, Canada, France, Germany, Italy, Japan, the Netherlands, Sweden, the United Kingdom, and the United States, together with Switzerland, which is a participating but not an official member, began discussions on world monetary reform in 1964. Later, the IMF was brought into the picture, but the really important decisions are those made by the Group of Ten.

In 1967, the negotiations within the Group of Ten and IMF produced agreement on a moderate extension of the role of the International Monetary Fund through a new scheme of "special drawing rights" (SDR's). Briefly, the scheme is for an agreed amount of new SDR's to be distributed each year to IMF members in proportion to their Fund quotas. Decisions on activating the scheme and determining the size of the SDR's require a majority backing of 85 percent of IMF votes (giving the Common Market as well as the United States a veto). Countries using their SDR's are required to reconstitute only 30 percent of the

[3] See Fritz Machlup and Burton G. Malkiel (eds.), *International Monetary Arrangements: The Problem of Choice*, Report on the Deliberations of an International Study Group of 32 Economists (Princeton: International Finance Section, 1964).

total over a five-year period; the remaining 70 percent may be used as freely as owned reserves[4] Clearly, the plan is an improvement over the original Bretton Woods design. But, as indicated below, it is equally clear that it is inadequate to solve completely even one, let alone all three of the basic problems of the world monetary order; it can be regarded only as a first step toward comprehensive reform, not the last. Consequently, the Group of Ten negotiations are certain to continue for many years to come. The attention of American policy-makers, therefore, is still focused on the broad issue of world monetary reform. Equilibrium is no longer the *summum bonum* of United States policy but rather its *sine qua non*.

The first four readings below consider the question of why equilibrium has proved to be such an elusive target. Peter Kenen [1], in an acute observation, says it is because we "are engaged in a dialogue with Western Europe in which we are speaking different languages, contemplating different targets, and obsessed by different fears." Europe's surpluses are the main counterpart of our deficits, and in theory equilibrium could be restored as readily by inflation, revaluation, or relaxation of existing restrictions in Europe as by deflation, devaluation, or imposition of new restrictions by us. It all depends on who is willing to bear the costs of adjustment. James Tobin [2] argues strongly that the Europeans ought to be willing to do so to forestall the risks and costs of deflationary and restrictive policies on the part of the United States and to make good on our considerable "moral claim" on Europe, outstanding from the days when we first undertook to alleviate the postwar dollar shortage.

Unfortunately, moral claims have little impact in international politics. Tobin may be correct that "international financial policy is too important to leave to financiers," but the fact remains that policy is made by politically responsible government officials, not by moral philosophers. Policy-makers must balance costs and benefits, and against the costs stressed by Professor Tobin Europeans compare the benefits to be gained: the attenuation of inflationary pressures at home, of America's competitive strength in world markets, of our sizable investments in Europe, and of our

---

[4] For details, see International Monetary Fund, *International Financial News Survey*, XIX (September 15, 1967), supplement.

influence in world affairs. These considerations, as Kenen appreciates, weigh heavily with Europeans. And since Europeans are our most important creditors—they hold the bulk of the dollar balances which, if cashed in, could wipe out our gold reserves—they are in a position to dictate terms to us. Europe's terms are, first, that it is we, willing or not, who must bear the major portion of the costs of adjustment, and, second, that it is in the capital account rather than in the current account that the correction must be made. It is because these terms are so much in conflict with our own traditional priorities and preferences that equilibrium has eluded us.

Given Europe's terms, what can the United States do? Straightforward price and income deflation is ruled out on domestic political grounds, and in any event deflation would probably swell the outflow of capital, not diminish it, while improving our current account. Likewise, devaluation is impossible because, as Kenen explains, most other countries would also devalue in order to protect their balance of trade. With deflation and devaluation ruled out, we are relying most heavily on the so-called voluntary foreign-investment restraint program first put into operation in February, 1965. Professor Kenen claims that this program is probably "the best among second-best policies"—that is, the one most likely to restore equilibrium, within the constraints on policy, at the least cost. I do not agree with this view, for it seems that in fact the guidelines for capital exports have, repeating the words of James Angell [3], "not done much more, after the initial-impact effect, than to prevent the flood from rising at an even more rapid rate." Indeed, the evidence on this point is quite emphatic: foreign investments have remained at a very high level despite repeated stiffening of the guidelines since their inception. Professor Angell argues that drastic new control measures are called for. I do not agree with this view either, for two reasons.

In the first place, Angell's contention that the longer-run prospect for the United States balance of payments is for further sharp deterioration seems unduly pessimistic. For instance, he apparently anticipates a decline in the international competitiveness of American exports, whereas in recent years our share of the world export market has in fact held steady, not declined, and in the all-important field of research-intensive production our lead has actually grown. Again, he points an accusing finger at the rising level of American tourist expenditures abroad, neglecting to emphasize the equally rapid rise of foreign tourist expenditures in this country that has had the effect of holding the "tourist gap" virtually steady. And lastly, in appraising the balance-of-payments impact of our foreign direct investments, Angell chooses to stress the potential displacement of United States exports rather than the need for replacement imports or the return flow of income; a few subtle changes of emphasis might have altered his entire evaluation.

In the second place, Angell's contention that new control measures would be effective seems unduly optimistic. Direct controls operate by suspending the free market: excess demand is suppressed rather than eliminated. It follows that controls create a powerful incentive for businessmen to devise and attempt new methods of circumventing official authority. Surely this explains the government's need repeatedly to stiffen the guidelines for capital exports, and it suggests that further controls might meet the same fate. On the other hand, no such negative incentive for evasion would be created by an alternative measure that I have already proposed elsewhere: a Foreign Investment Reserve System under which American corporations would be offered specified and substantial tax advantages for their cooperation in rescheduling overseas capital expenditures by temporarily allocating their investment funds instead into blocked reserve accounts with the federal government.[5] The incentive created by this alternative would be a distinctly positive one—a subsidy that could be counted in dollars and cents. Consequently, the measure might be effective in persuading profit-minded businessmen to cut back on their foreign investments. Indeed, I believe that only in this way can the so-called voluntary restraint program be made *truly* voluntary in the context of the present balance-of-payments problem.

Milton Friedman [4] dissents. In his opinion, such measures as direct controls, voluntary restraints, taxes, and subsidies are merely "frantic" expedients not likely to be effective. He much

---

[5] Benjamin J. Cohen, "Voluntary Foreign Investment Curbs: A Plan that Really Works," *Challenge*, March-April, 1967, pp. 15, 16.

prefers relying on a totally free market for foreign exchange. His is the classic case for exchange-rate flexibility as the solution for any and all balance-of-payments problems—the opposite extreme from Angell's *dirigiste* approach to adjustment. It is a case that many find attractive, but Professor Friedman's presentation of it is one-sided: he emphasizes the advantages of floating exchange rates, but not the disadvantages. He emphasizes, for instance, the protection against the exchange risk of foreign trade that merchants can obtain through hedging operations in a forward market, but neglects to mention that in practice the certainty of expectations that merchants require extends quite a bit beyond the single transaction. Business decisions are not made with each separate deal calculated anew; what concerns merchants is whether it is worthwhile to carry out a succession of deals involving buying or selling abroad. Within this framework of medium-term calculations, flexible exchange rates increase the level of uncertainty over fixed rates. Consequently, a regime featuring exchange-rate flexibility is likely to contract foreign trade rather more than Friedman admits. Likewise, Friedman emphasizes that income-maximizing speculation in foreign exchange must be stabilizing. Quite true, but destabilizing speculators can also make profits on balance, even if they do not maximize them. The probability of stability in the exchanges, therefore, is rather less than he suggests.

Most important, Friedman neglects to mention the difficulties such a country as the United States would have in putting his proposal into effect. Just as devaluation is impractical for us because most other countries would follow to protect their balance of trade, so a floating rate for the dollar would be impractical if it threatened to float downward vis-à-vis other currencies. We cannot rule out the possibility of competitive depreciations by others and ultimately a return to the unstable exchanges characteristic of the 1930s. Nor can we forget the special position of the dollar in the modified version of the gold-exchange standard built up to replace the financial chaos of that earlier period. World monetary reserves today include a large "overhang" of dollar balances representing for other countries an investment in potential future consumption of foreign goods, services, and securities. These balances are held on the assumption that their value in relation to gold, the ultimate command over external resources, is fixed. A move to a floating rate for the dollar, by abrogating this fixed relationship to gold, could cause serious windfall losses for foreign governments. In effect, a floating rate would mean a unilateral renunciation of our role as an international bank of issue —a betrayal of the faith of our depositors—and while this is something that does not appear to concern Professor Friedman, who considers our reserve-currency status a nuisance anyway, it is nevertheless a foreign-policy step not to be taken lightly.

And so we are compelled to confront the basic fact, already emphasized above, that what is really at stake in our balance-of-payments policy is the future role of the dollar in international monetary affairs. Professor Friedman's solution is plausible only if we are prepared to terminate without qualification our position as the world's main reserve-currency country. If we are not, then one of the less revolutionary approaches to adjustment must be elected. Ultimately, our attitude toward the issue of balance-of-payments equilibrium must be conditional on our attitude toward the broader issue of world monetary reform. What precisely is the present role of the dollar in international monetary affairs? What are the costs and benefits of the dollar's present role? What will and should be the dollar's role in the future? These are the questions considered by the remaining eight readings in this section.

What precisely is the present role of the dollar in international monetary affairs? Messrs. Despres, Kindleberger, and Salant [5], in a "minority view," offer a unique explanation: the dollar functions as the medium of financial intermediation between European savers and European investors. Their initial premise is that liquidity preference is higher in Europe than in the United States. It then follows that "the European savers who want cash and the European borrowers who prefer to extend their liabilities into the future can both be satisfied when the United States capital market lends long and borrows short"—that is, when the United States runs a balance-of-payments deficit according to standard accounting procedures. According to Despres-Kindleberger-Salant, though, this is no deficit at all. "The United States is no more in deficit when it lends long and borrows short than is a bank when it makes a loan and enters deposits in its books." This is only a "trade in liquidity," presumably profitable to both sides and hence worth preserving. In short, Despres-Kindleberger-

Salant conclude, there is no United States balance-of-payments problem at all, only a banking problem. Consequently, world monetary reform of the kind usually suggested is unnecessary. Moreover, so long as the international difference in liquidity preference persists, attempts to adjust the balance of payments along the lines proposed by Kenen and Angell are futile and bound to fail.

The argument is elegant. However, as Robert Triffin [6] points out, "it greatly exaggerates the role of financial intermediary of the United States between liquid savings and long-term borrowings in Europe itself." In fact, a look at the statistical evidence indicates rather that the dollar has intermediated between European central banks, which accumulated dollar balances throughout most of the postwar period, and the rest of the world, where Americans spent for investment, development, and military purposes virtually without restriction. That is, by electing to hold their reserves in dollars rather than gold, the Europeans in effect chose to underwrite our foreign policies in Europe and elsewhere. This they are no longer willing to do, in part because they do not concur in all our policies, in part because, as already indicated, they have begun to fear for the gold value of their balances. Thus they want our deficits ended—and on their terms. That is why, as a policy matter, it has become imperative for us to restore equilibrium to the balance of payments. That is also why world monetary reform has become such an important issue for us. When a domestic bank makes a loan and enters deposits in its books, it need not worry about the resulting decline in its net reserve position, for in the event of a "run" by its depositors, it can always rely on the central bank, the lender of last resort. But for the United States, international bank of issue, there is no lender of last resort in the event of depositor anxiety. Consequently, as our net reserve position continues to deteriorate, we feel more and more pinched by the constraint of the balance of payments. Professor Triffin concludes that if we are determined to preserve the dollar's status as a reserve currency, either we must eventually acquiesce in an absolute European veto on our policies, or we must support the creation of some comprehensive new form of international liquidity to back up the dollar, whether through the IMF or outside it.

This raises the question of whether it is worth preserving the dollar's present role as a reserve currency or not. What are the costs and benefits of this role? Robert Aliber [7] insists that there are no important economic costs, arguing rather that the major *alleged* cost of the dollar's role, the constraint on independent domestic policies, is in fact a disadvantage that the United States would have encountered even if it were not a reserve-currency country. It is all due to the openness of the New York financial markets and the interest-sensitivity of dollar balances:

The conflict between domestic policy objectives and international policy objectives appears to arise primarily because the New York financial market enables foreign and U.S. private parties to shift funds easily from dollar assets to foreign currency assets as U.S. interest rates fall relative to those abroad, and not because of the U.S. reserve currency role; these shifts would occur even if the United States were not a reserve currency country.

On the other hand, Aliber stresses one important economic benefit of being a reserve-currency country: the greater flexibility in financing our payments deficits. He concludes that the United States obtains significant net advantages from the reserve-currency status of the dollar.

However, this conclusion is an exceedingly sanguine one. William Salant [8] points out that Aliber's line of argument is misleading in at least one important respect. It is just not true that the international constraint on United States policy arises from the sensitivity of dollar balances to interest-rate changes. On the contrary, it arises instead from the sensitivity of these balances to changes in the confidence of dollar holders regarding our ability to maintain the gold value of their assets. And this sensitivity is a function both of the size of our payments deficits and of the prospect for renewed inflation in the United States. We are constrained from following more expansionist policies than we might sometimes prefer not because of any direct impact on international yield differentials, but rather because of the possibly negative impact on the expectations of dollar holders. This is the veto stressed by Triffin, and it is for us a very real cost that can only mount as our deficits persist.

Indeed, it is a cost we are paying right now. A partial veto is already in effect. It is expressed by the terms Europe has forced us to accept in pursuit of the elusive target of equilibrium. And this in turn means that the major benefit emphasized by Aliber, the greater flexibility in financing United States deficits, is in fact no longer available to us in the same measure as it once was. That benefit is the reciprocal of the cost just described. As Salant notes, it could be exploited fully only when the demand for dollars was excessive—that is, during the period of the dollar shortage. That period has now passed, and with it has passed much of the only important economic benefit of being a reserve-currency country. Certainly we are able still to exercise greater flexibility in financing our deficits than most nonreserve-currency countries. But it is also certain that our policies have never been so constrained by our balance of payments as they are today.

Furthermore, this means that much of the political benefit of being a reserve-currency country has passed, too. William Grampp [9] describes how up to the late 1950s the dollar constituted an important instrument of political power for the United States government. Not only did our reserve-currency status oblige other governments in effect to underwrite *our* foreign policies around the globe, but it also enabled us to exploit their need for dollars as a means for influencing *their* policies as well. However, as the excess foreign demand for dollars has eased, so too has our ability to use the dollar in this way as a lever for influencing others. Indeed, today foreign governments, and particularly European governments, can use their dollar balances as a potentially even more effective lever for influencing us. Thus, it is probably true that the reserve-currency status of the dollar has by now become as much a political as an economic liability. On balance, therefore, there seems to be no compelling reason to preserve the role of the dollar in its present form.

In turn, this means that some kind of comprehensive monetary reform would be in our national interest. What kind of reform depends on the future role we envision for the dollar in world monetary affairs. The opposite poles of opinion on this issue are represented on the one hand by Milton Friedman and Jacques Rueff [10], and on the other hand by Emile Despres [11]. Superficially, Friedman and Rueff themselves seem poles apart. The former prefers freely flexible exchange rates, the latter a return to the gold standard of absolutely fixed rates. Yet the two do actually share one important element in common: the hope that the United States can be persuaded to renounce its reserve-currency role. Note, though, that whereas Friedman's principal concern is with the international constraint imposed by that role on American policy, Rueff is most concerned about the greater flexibility he believes the role affords us in financing our deficits. In this respect Friedman seems the more perceptive of the pair, although his selection was written rather earlier. Rueff makes the same mistake as Robert Aliber: he emphasizes the one important economic benefit of our reserve-currency status, apparently without realizing that it is in fact no longer available to us in the same measure as it once was. As William Salant observes, "While the United States gained flexibility in the earlier period through its role as a reserve currency center, and also as a center for private balances, the constraints imposed by that role have become increasingly tighter in the later period, and have probably become dominant."

Emile Despres does not make this mistake. He, like Friedman, recognizes that the role of the dollar in its present form is costly. However, the cost, he insists, is not due to the role of the dollar per se, but rather to the popular misunderstanding of it that has produced a "state of contained crisis." Despres, one of the authors of the Despres-Kindleberger-Salant "minority view," argues there that the United States faces only a banking problem, not a balance-of-payments problem. In [11], he adds that "This banking problem arises from an inflated demand for gold." It thus follows that the demand for gold should be curbed. And so, rather than have us renounce our reserve-currency status as would Friedman and Rueff, Despres would have us reinforce and strengthen it by a series of measures designed to replace the present gold-exchange standard with a new world dollar standard. Misunderstandings would be corrected, and the atmosphere of "nagging semi-crisis" would be dissipated. As a practical dividend, the United States would enjoy an almost unlimited flexibility in financing deficits, in effect regaining the virtual hegemony in international monetary affairs that was ours immediately after World War II.

Apart from the reservations already mentioned regarding the Despres-Kindleberger-Salant thesis, we must note here that the rest of the world is hardly likely to acquiesce without a struggle in the re-establishment of an American hegemony in international monetary affairs. Jacques Rueff's partiality to the gold standard may not be shared by many other interested parties, but his dissatisfaction with the gold-exchange standard, and especially with our remaining flexibility in financing deficits under it, most certainly is. It is all part of the broader dissatisfaction, particularly in Europe, with America's predominance and leadership in the world, and it can be counted upon to express itself in firm opposition to any reform along the lines proposed by Professor Despres. A world dollar standard cannot be considered a realistic objective of American policy. But neither, for that matter, can either the floating rates proposed by Friedman or the gold standard proposed by Rueff. For one thing, both proposals have serious economic deficiencies. More important, both would deprive the United States of the residual financial privileges that we do retain under the gold-exchange standard, and we are no more likely than the Europeans to acquiesce without a struggle in such a loss of influence. That is why the Group of Ten negotiations that culminated in the 1967 agreement on the scheme of special drawing rights tended to concentrate exclusively on rather moderate proposals for reform. Each participant could comfortably assume that the ensuing shifts in relationships of influence and dependence would at most be fairly marginal.

This point is not entirely clear from James Tobin's comparison [12] of the two alternatives to the present reserve-currency system most widely discussed before the 1967 agreement: the Collective Reserve Unit (CRU) and expansion of the IMF. When Professor Tobin was writing his article in 1965, the CRU proposal was a relatively new and relatively dramatic reform scheme being urged by the French primarily, but also by some other Europeans, as a handy means for terminating our reserve-currency status once and for all. According to the CRU scheme, all dollar balances in the monetary reserves of participating countries would gradually be replaced by collective reserve units, which were to be issued in proportion to official gold stocks and to be used in a fixed relationship with gold alone in settling payments imbalances. However, in the years since 1965 the basic concept of the CRU became considerably diluted as a result of hard bargaining in the Group of Ten negotiations, particularly by the United States. The U.S.

government initially was more partial to a relatively conservative extension of unconditional credit facilities in the IMF than to the CRU, presumably because this would be the less detrimental of the two alternatives to our international financial status. Indeed, not only would this approach maintain the dollar in its role as the world's main currency; it would also back up the dollar with a potential lender of last resort. But rather than insist on its preference, the government decided, apparently for tactical reasons, to accede to the Europeans, at the same time pressing for modifications that would be in our own interest. By early 1967 the CRU, having shed all its links to gold, was not much more than a mechanism for supplying modest but regular increments of an owned-reserve supplement to the dollar, and the United States ironically had become its most prominent advocate.

Not surprisingly, the French—and the rest of the Common Market countries—had meanwhile shifted to advocating reform within the IMF, no doubt because this alternative was now more likely than the current version of the CRU to preserve what amounted to their partial veto over our policies. Owned reserves need never be repaid; thus U.S. flexibility in financing deficits could remain as great as ever. Credits, though, must be repaid, and an additional constraint would be imposed on our policies through the balance of payments. Thus it was clear that the Europeans still were interested in curbing our privileges under the gold-exchange standard, just as we still were interested in preserving them. But it was equally clear that compromises were being made by all in the interest of achieving a reform that would yield some kind of new international money. In the summer of 1967, agreement was reached on the SDR scheme. The Europeans got the reform through the IMF that they wanted, together with a voting procedure on activating and determining the size of the plan that gives the Common Market countries a veto if they vote as a bloc. The United States, meanwhile, got a new reserve medium that, because of the provision that no more than 30 percent of drawings need be reconstituted, is virtually the same as owned money. Moreover, the effect on the dollar is likely to be minimal, because the reserve-currency status of the dollar will probably decline moderately, but not, as Tobin rightly emphasizes, its status as a vehicle currency for private international transactions, which will probably be unaffected. Thus, in the end we seem to have managed to conserve most of our residual financial privileges, and the Europeans seem to have managed to retain their partial veto on our policies. The interests of all parties have been respected.

But will this eliminate all the defects of the international financial order? Unfortunately, no. When governments negotiate, they bargain to protect the national interest, not necessarily the common interest of the community of nations. In the Group of Ten negotiations, very little attention was paid to the balance-of-payments equilibrating mechanism, so the problem of adjustment will probably remain as acute as ever. Nor does the scheme help to ameliorate the confidence problem, since it does nothing to consolidate the rather sizable overhang of existing dollar (and sterling) balances. And finally, one wonders whether the Europeans, with their strong anti-inflationary bias, would in voting to activate the plan agree to an amount of SDR's sufficiently large to deal adequately even with the liquidity problem. Thus it seems probable that the three basic problems of the gold-exchange standard—adjustment, confidence, and liquidity—will be with us for some time to come. They will continue to figure as issues in American foreign economic policy, however, only insofar as they are thought to affect our national interest—that is, only insofar as they are thought to affect our balance of payments and the international status of the dollar. The strictly limited extent to which they have figured as issues in our financial policy until now should be apparent from the preceding discussion and from the readings that follow.

1

The International Position
of the Dollar

PETER B. KENEN

What I would like to do this next half hour is simply to review the fundamental issues that underlie debates about the balance of payments—even at the risk of going over ground that is already familiar to you. I shall begin with some diagnostic comments on our balance of payments, and will move on to discuss the kinds of policies which are available to the United States. Finally, I shall try to explain why we have selected a particular set of policies, and what further choices we might make in various circumstances.

By now, we all know that the United States has a balance of payments deficit, and we all have some idea as to what this statement means. It means that the total of our spending abroad on goods, services and assets has been larger than the total of our receipts from the sale of goods and from foreign investment in the United States. There has been some discussion, this last year or so, concerning the way the deficit should be measured, and I shall say a word about that issue, but I think it fair to say that, whatever measure you use, we have run a deficit ranging between $2 and $3 billion a year for the last several years, since 1958.

We have, I believe, been measuring the deficit in a way which exaggerates its size and have, in consequence, taken an excessively pessimistic view of the payments problem. The figures which President Johnson published in his Message to Congress a few weeks ago, figures which showed a smaller deficit, particularly in 1964, provide a more accurate picture. But the deficit is alarmingly large, even on this different definition. On the measure used by the Commerce Department, the 1964 deficit was $3 billion; on the measure I would consider more accurate, it was about $1½ billion.

From Peter B. Kenen, *The International Position of the Dollar* (New York: Haas Securities Corporation, 1965), pp. 1–12. Reprinted in this form by permission.

Yet $1½ billion is excessively large especially when viewed in longer perspective—as the latest in a series of continuous deficits that have eroded our gold reserves and greatly enlarged our liabilities.

The important point to make about this payments deficit is that you cannot blame it on any single item in the balance of payments. You cannot say that the deficit is due to this flow, that one, or something else. You cannot say that it is due to foreign aid or foreign investment, to tourism or textile imports. One could as easily argue that the deficit is due to the fact that our exports are too small, that foreign tourist expenditure here is too small, or that foreign investment here is also too small. One could in short pick any item, depending on prejudice or politics, and argue that this item is too large or too small.

One should, instead, begin by asking what kind of payments pattern is sustainable, and what series of adjustments can be made. What payments can be cut, what receipts can be enlarged at least cost to our own economy and to the outside world? What are the right marginal adjustments, given our broader national goals, economic and political?

Simple arithmetic isn't always wrong, and can indeed serve as a basis for this analysis. One impressive fact about our balance of payments is that, with one brief exception in 1959, we have consistently achieved a very large surplus on current-account transactions. Our receipts from the sale of goods and services, including among services our income from investments, have been consistently larger than our payments for goods and services—for imports, foreign travel and for military purposes, and so forth. In 1964, for example, our current-account surplus was a full $7.4 billion. Our merchandise trade surplus was $6½ billion by itself —that is to say our commodity exports exceeded our commodity imports by $6½ billion. This is a small number as American economic magnitudes go. But it is one per cent of our own gross national product and, more importantly, it is close to four per cent of world trade. Let me emphasize this last point: The net U.S. balance on merchandise transactions is a pretty substantial chunk of gross world trade, so that any increase in our merchandise trade balance will also be quite large compared with total trade, and may involve substantial dislocation for other countries. I shall come back to this point again.

If our merchandise trade is in surplus and our overall current account is in surplus, why do we have a deficit? Essentially, it is because that current-account surplus is not large enough to cover a very large outflow of capital, public and private. The government capital outflow, new grants and credits less repayments, was $3.7 billion in 1964. The long-term private capital outflow was $4.1 billion, and the net outflow of short-term capital was peculiarly large for several reasons, and totaled $1.7 billion. When you add up all of these capital flows, you find that they exceeded our current-account surplus, giving us a deficit in our overall transactions with the outside world. That overall deficit is, of course, measured by the decrease of our own gold and foreign-currency reserves and the increase of our liabilities to foreign official monetary institutions.

I am not saying that the capital outflow is to blame for the deficit—that would be to violate the rules of analysis I set forth at the very beginning of my talk. All that I am saying, to organize our thinking, is that it was too large in relation to our current-account surplus, or, to put it the other way around, our current-account surplus was too small to cover the capital outflow. This description suggests, in turn, two ways of tackling the payments problem. The one would be to increase our current-account receipts; raising our exports, reducing our imports, increasing our income on foreign investment, or reducing certain other payments to foreigners. The second would be to cut back the capital outflow, making it fit into our current account earnings; this could be accomplished by cutting government aid and lending, cutting long-term private investment abroad, or cutting short-term private investment. In principle, either of these basic options is open to us.

My own preference and that of most economists is strongly to favor the first of these solutions, to increase current-account earnings. It was also the preference of the United States Government until very recently. The Government has put continual emphasis on the expansion of American exports, on the improvement of the competitive position of the United States, on the reduction of our military expenditure abroad (or the offsetting of this expenditure by foreign military expenditure here). It has taken a series of measures to enlarge the current-account surplus. I regard this as the optimum solution—the best way of going about it—for one very simple and obvious reason: By every test, the United States should be an exporter of capital to the outside world. We should be supplying capital, public and private, to other countries. We are a much wealthier nation than most others. In addition, we generate a huge volume of financial savings in this country, a phenomenon with which you are very familiar. There is no other country that can supply the quantities of capital we can supply. There is no other securities market large enough to digest a big issue of bonds, foreign or domestic. I need not dwell at length on the size of American financial markets; we are, right now, sitting at their center, and you know them very well.

But let me dramatize my point. The annual increase in the assets of American financial institutions—savings banks, savings and loan associations, insurance companies, pension funds, and others—is probably larger than the total of recorded annual savings in all of the other industrial countries combined. The savings that are channeled into our financial markets through financial institutions totalled $36 billion in 1964, comprising an enormous and continuous demand for financial assets. And I have not even mentioned the vast internal cash flow of American business, some of which, of course, finds its way abroad as direct investment, cash placements in the Eurodollar market, and so forth. All of this suggests that we are a natural capital exporter, a natural supplier of capital to the rest of the world.

Nor is it peculiar or perverse that we are investing so heavily in the other developed countries, not in the underdeveloped countries. The bulk of private capital is going to Europe and Canada; the bulk of government capital is going to the underdeveloped areas. The European countries, particularly the Common Market countries, are wealthy by comparison with the rest of the world. But the European countries, while comparatively opulent, may still be described as capital-poor countries, for a reason that may not have occurred to you. We normally think of capital formation as the acquisition of new business assets, such as plant and equipment. But one very large component of capital formation is carried out by households—residential construction and also, quite importantly, the purchase of durable consumer goods. Automobiles and major household appliances are, indeed, capital assets. The United States stocked up on these household assets in the 1940s and 1950s; we have, in fact, been building up our stock of household durables ever since the First World War. But the European household is just entering that state; personal income has just reached the levels at which households can afford to accumulate durable goods on a large scale. Remember, too, that a large part of European household capital was destroyed in the Second World War. Europe then, is investing heavily in housing and durables, making good a thirty-year backlog. In any case, Europe has a tremendous appetite for capital which we have been helping to supply, and this demand for capital, far more than wage differences, taxes and tariffs, explains the continuing flow of American capital to Europe. It also suggests that this flow of capital, if not restricted, is apt to continue for some time. I cannot agree with my good friend, Walter Salant, that the flow will end in another year or so.

The optimum solution to our payments problem would be to enlarge our current-account earnings, through additional exports, or additional income on past investments, in order to finance a continuing outflow of American capital. I might add, incidentally, that we have succeeded in enlarging our current-account surplus over the past few years. From 1960 to 1964, the current-account surplus rose from $3 billion to $7.4 billion; this was accomplished by a very impressive growth of merchandise exports and also by the rise in U.S. income on foreign investments. Income from foreign investments is now the second-largest receipt in the U.S. balance of payments, the largest, of course, being exports. This growth in income reflects a self-equilibrating process. As capital flows out steadily, accumulated assets grow, and a rising flow of income comes back to the United States, thereby financing the further outflow of capital. It is a slow process, but it works in the right direction.

As I said, the United States was at first inclined to follow the optimum path, that is, to expand our current-account earnings. In 1963, however, and with sharper emphasis in 1964 and 1965, we changed direction, deciding to crack down on the capital outflow and make it fit into the existing current-account surplus. The interest equalization tax was the first step in this direction. (Actually, there was an even earlier one, when the Treasury tried without much success to tighten the tax treatment of U.S. foreign investment. That attempt, however, should really be considered on its own merits, not as a balance-of-payments policy.) The sharper shift in policy came a few weeks ago, with President Johnson's message to Congress proposing "voluntary" limits on private foreign investment.

Why this shift in policy? Why have we turned from the attempt to expand export earnings, so as to finance investment abroad, and started instead to curtail investment? It does not imply Government hostility to foreign investment, whether long-term or short. You cannot say, in fairness and honesty, that the U.S. Government opposes private foreign investment. There are other compelling reasons for taking this new tack. Suppose we continued to rely on an expansion of the current-account surplus. How could we bring it about? We would have to make American goods more competitive in foreign markets and, for that matter, in American markets. We would have to accomplish a further movement of prices and costs in our favor. Other people's prices would have to rise faster than ours, or ours would have to fall, in order that consumers, American and foreign, would be induced to shift their purchases from foreign goods to our goods, expanding our exports and holding down our imports.

Such a shift has already occurred, but has not been sufficient. You may remember that the Brookings Report predicted a substantial improvement in the U.S. balance of payments by 1968, to be accomplished by a more rapid increase of European prices. Many of us, looking at the Brookings Report in 1963, said that you won't get that kind of increase. But the trade surplus achieved in 1964 was already as large as the one that Brookings forecast for 1968. We have had a considerable movement in prices. For that matter, the price statistics that used to frighten everybody, the export-price indexes that showed our prices rising somewhat faster than European prices, those statistics have swung around, indicating an improvement in our competitive position. But our capital outflow has outpaced the improvement in our current-account position.

There is, of course, another way of improving the competitiveness of the United States vis-à-vis other countries. A devaluation of the dollar would accomplish the same thing. It would make our goods more attractive to our own consumers and foreigners alike. But we have ruled out a devaluation, mainly because of our reserve-currency role, our position as a banker to the rest of the world. We have relied, as I have said, on the gradual advance of European prices relative to our own.

Unfortunately, Europe does not relish an improvement in our competitive position. We are engaged in a dialogue with Western Europe in which we are talking different languages, contemplating different targets, and obsessed by different fears. It is this pervasive conflict in methods of analysis, objectives, and nightmares, that explains a good deal of the recent shift in U.S. policy.

For one thing, most of the continental European countries worry less about the balance of payments than about the balance of trade. An improvement in our balance of trade, moreover, means a deterioration in their balance of trade. It may occur directly, by an increase of our exports to Europe; it may occur indirectly, by displacement of European goods in third markets. In either case, an improvement of our competitive position means a deterioration of theirs, and the trade balance is what counts for many European policy-makers, not the overall balance of payments. There are several historical reasons for this peculiar continental emphasis on the trade balance. Unlike the British and ourselves most of the continental Europeans don't think of being continuous capital exporters; instead, they tend to suppose that their capital account will balance out, over a period of years, and that their current account has also to balance out (or be in surplus). Any deterioration in their current account, such as has happened in the last few years, frightens them—and understandably so, if you study their experience. Europe, then, is anxious for us to improve our balance of payments, but doesn't want an improvement in our balance of trade.

I can give you one example, to illustrate their attitude. Some time ago, I had a long conversation with an economist at the Bank of France. This was in 1963, when two British economists, Alan Day and Nicolas Kaldor, were engaged in a public debate as to whether the pound should be devalued. My French friend told me that he was trying to figure out "by how much the French franc would have to be devalued if sterling were devalued." I hit the ceiling. "Look," I said, "you're running a huge balance of payments surplus; why the devil do you want to devalue the franc?"

He replied that 'It's not a neighborly balance of payments policy, but we cannot stand an increase of British exports, particularly of automobiles and steel; we're worried about employment in basic industries." His approach was "protectionist" or "mercantilist" (if you want to use fancy words), an approach that leads so many Europeans to concentrate on the balance of trade rather than the balance of payments.

It is indeed for this particular reason that a devaluation of the dollar is really ruled out, not so much because of our reserve-currency position, but because European countries would follow us so as to protect their balance of trade. Consider the most likely sequence. If we devalued, most other countries would have to follow us. Canada would. Britain would. Latin America would, with most of the other "peripheral" countries. In effect, there would be an appreciation of the continental European currencies relative to all the others, and that's precisely what they fear. It is, in fact, exactly what happened between 1931 and 1934, when there was, first, a devaluation of sterling, then of the dollar, leaving the European currencies greatly overvalued. At first, the continental countries resorted to trade controls to protect their own industries—as, I suspect, they would again in similar circumstances, GATT or no GATT. Then, in 1936, they themselves devalued, and when the whole cycle was finished, there was little net change in the exchange rates. The price of gold had been marked up, but there was very little change in the competitive positions of the key countries, as measured by exchange rates. Then as now, it was the European concern about balance of trade that inspired this kind of competitive devaluation.

There is another issue dividing us from Europe, pertaining to the way that "adjustment" was accomplished in the early 1960's. There has been a considerable payments adjustment in our favor, accomplished by a rise of European prices. But many Europeans describe this same process by saying that they have been obliged to "import" inflation from the United States and that the adjustment accomplished by this "imported" inflation should have been accomplished by deflation in the United States. This phrase, "imported" inflation, is a very strange phrase, because, in any very obvious sense, there has been no inflation in the United States; we have had none to export over the last few years. There has been an upward creep of our consumer price index, mainly due to the increase of service prices such as the cost of medical care. But some of this increase reflects the improvement of quality, and is hardly "exportable" in any case. If, indeed, any country has "imported" inflation during the last year or so, it has been the United States. If you analyze the recent change in wholesale prices—and the Council of Economic Advisers' *Annual Report* does it very nicely—you will discover that the one-percentage-point increase in wholesale prices during 1964 was almost entirely attributable to the prices of non-ferrous metals in world markets. The increase of our wholesale price index, then, was "imported" by way of the world-wide rise in copper prices, due to political and other developments occurring outside this country.

In what sense can one say that Europe has been "importing" inflation? The more sophisticated Europeans have an answer—and it is meaningful. Europe, they say, has run payments surpluses year after year because we have run deficits, and this has caused a continuing expansion of the European credit base. European banks have been exceedingly liquid, inundated with reserves, and this has meant that Europe's banks and other financial institutions have been open-handed suppliers of credit. They have financed business investment, residential construction and consumer spending in a fashion that has compounded inflationary pressures in the already overstrained European economy.

One might make two answers to this indictment. Firstly, one might ask why Europe has not used monetary policy to combat the expansion of credit. The answer, of course, is that higher European interest rates would simply attract additional capital from the United States, increasing bank reserves even further. In an open economy like the German or the Dutch, tight money is not always deflationary. Secondly, one might ask why Europe has not used fiscal policy to combat inflation. Then you are treated to a long, sad story. Germans will tell you that they have no fiscal policy—and that it is our fault. When you scratch your head in puzzlement, they then explain that the fundamental law of the Federal Republic of Germany, which we helped to write, spreads the vital powers to tax and spend among the state governments, rather than lodging them with the federal government. This was done deliberately, in order to prevent the central government from ever financing another war machine. Italians have a different answer; so do the Dutch and French. But all of them reduce to the assertion that Europe must rely on monetary policy much more than we do, and that monetary policy is hobbled by the balance of payments situation. In a very sophisticated sense, then, Europe has to "import" inflation from the United States. Yet the blame lies with Europe, not so much with us. In many European countries, economic doctrines and policies are not sufficiently sophisticated to cope with the technical problems posed by our deficits. They are unwilling or unable to manipulate the policy mix, as we did last year when we tightened our monetary policy and simultaneously eased our fiscal policy by tax reduction.

This brings me to a third point. The twentieth-century history of the United States has made Americans most fearful of unemployment; in consequence, we are unwilling to take deflationary measures to improve our competitive position. For similar historical reasons, Europeans fear inflation more than anything else, and are unwilling to see the correction of our payments deficit achieved by a further inflation in Europe. Each side asks the other to confront what it most fears. Europeans have been saying that we must get our balance of payments under control by deflationary measures; they have been reading back to us the lectures we used to give them in the 1940's, when we were telling them, "Get your house in order." We have been saying that we cannot accept more unemployment, and that Europe must therefore let prices rise further. Each side regards his own fears as more real and his prospects as more dangerous. Neither side fully comprehends the fears of the other.

There is, finally, one more cause of disagreement. There are those who in Europe do not want to see our payments problem solved by way of an expansion of our export surplus, but would rather see us curb our investments in Europe. This view is widely held, not just by the Gaullists who say that we are buying up the whole of Europe and taking it over, but also by more thoughtful men who fear that the power and independence of American firms in Europe will undermine European economic policies. The French—and I am not speaking only of the xenophobes—are concerned that our companies will wreck their careful efforts at economic planning. The French plan, such as it is, relies very heavily on credit control to guide and govern business investment. If a large part of French industry is American-owned and has access to credit outside of Paris, credit control may be impaired. Important investment decisions will be taken outside the ambit of French planning. One more comment, sardonic but relevant, comes to mind. "You know," a French official said to me, "we also try to operate by talking to French industry. Persuasion doesn't always work—we would admit that. But how can we in Paris even talk to a corporation whose head office is in Detroit or New York? How can we persuade corporate executives who don't even understand our language, political or literal?" Thus, many people genuinely friendly to the United States are very worried about our activities in Europe—about the size of American companies and about their independence of European policy. That is a legitimate concern.

Those who oppose American investment, regardless of their reasons, are also opposed to an increase of our exports as the way to end the U.S. deficit. They want, instead, a cutback of American investment. This is the recurrent European theme, played in unison by those who fear inflation, those who fear further American investment, and those who would like to restrict our influence in world affairs. What is more, these several views converge in another important respect. Europe demands a rapid end to the U.S. deficit.

This brings me, at last, to the General's famous press conference and his manifesto on gold and all that. Whatever its long-run doctrinal significance, France's decision to acquire gold with any further increase in its reserves, and also to convert some $300 million of dollars into gold, had an immediate tactical significance. The gold standard à la de Gaulle is not the gold standard à la Jacques Rueff. To confuse the two is an insult to Rueff and to de Gaulle. The Rueff gold standard presupposes a rigid connection between domestic and international monetary happenings. It would operate automatically to reduce the money supply in a deficit country like the United States and to expand it in a surplus country like France. The Rueff gold standard would impose deflation in the United States, but would also impose inflation in France. And if there is any single monetary system divorced or insulated from international developments, it is the French. General de Gaulle does not take the same classic view as Jacques

Rueff; he does not want to link the French economy to the French gold stock. His endorsement of the gold standard is, I think, a way to put pressure on the United States to require that we solve our balance of payments problem quickly.

The reasoning goes this way: there is no upper limit to the increase of U.S. dollar liabilities; they could assuredly climb to an unsafe level, but not to a discernible ceiling. There is, by contrast, a lower limit to the U.S. gold stock; it cannot fall below zero. If, then, the Europeans nibble at our gold stock every month instead of accumulating more dollars, they can impose intolerable pressures on U.S. policy and force us to solve our payments problem much more quickly than has been our wont. By buying gold, the French and others hope to shift the burden of adjustment onto the United States. This aspect of French policy, moreover, has attracted wide sympathy and support in Western Europe. Remember the statement, a few weeks ago, by the President of German Bundesbank, who hinted that it might be a good idea for Germany to increase the gold content of its reserves. And there are others, in private life and in central banks, who welcome the French pressure on the U.S. dollar as a way of forcing us to act and thereby of abating inflationary pressure in Europe.

How, then, do we react? If we are denied the time we would need to improve our current account some more, and are not allowed to devalue the dollar, we are compelled to reduce the capital-account outflow, to make it fit into our existing current-account surplus. If, further, the pessimists are right, and our trade figures will not be as good this year as last, the capital outflow has to be cut drastically. But how can we curb the capital outflow? Europeans tell us to raise our interest rates. This has been the standard answer, heard every week or so from one or another prominent banker and also from the Bank for International Settlements, the central bankers' club at Basle. The same thing is said on this side of the Atlantic, here in New York, where we are often told to increase our interest rates so as to make investment here more attractive or, at the very least, to make investment abroad less attractive.

Frankly, I am skeptical. International interest-rate differences have no observable impact on foreign long-term borrowing in the United States—on foreign bond issues here. There may be some sensitivity, but it is very hard to find by any sort of econometric analysis. I have worked over these figures for a long time, as some of you know, and cannot find a firm connection. There are good reasons for this. The biggest borrowers here are the Canadians; they have issued more bonds than all other countries combined. But where else can a Canadian go to borrow $100 million? He can try the Canadian market, but will only succeed in pushing up Canadian rates. If, then, we raise our rates to send him home, his attempt to borrow locally will merely re-establish the rate differential prevailing before we raised our rates, and he has again the option of New York or Canada, on familiar terms. If you examine Canadian interest rates, you will find that they run parallel to our own for precisely this reason: When the cost of borrowing rises here, Canadians go home, but push up the rates there and they come back to borrow here. It is very difficult to raise large sums in Canada—to float the big bond issues of the provincial governments; Canada's financial institutions are not as large as ours and cannot swallow large issues at one gulp. The same is true of other countries.

My point, in brief, is that a small increase in our long-term rates cannot do much to shift the locus of borrowing from New York to other centers. Let me remind you, in this connection, that most of the major capital markets abroad are still closed to foreigners, save to those who can obtain official permission to borrow. More importantly, those markets which are open, particularly the German market, charge much higher interest rates than New York.

On the short-term side, a small increase in U.S. interest rates might perhaps discourage foreign borrowing from our banks and certain other capital flows. But once again, I am skeptical, if only because the existing interest-rate differences are pretty large, especially vis-à-vis Japan, which has been the largest short-term borrower. It is not a matter of ten or twenty basis points, or even a full percentage point. In fact, many Japanese must borrow here or not at all. There is no place else for them to go. In addition, our experience with changes in short-term interest rates has been rather disappointing. One of the strategic interest rates is the so-called Eurodollar rate, and as you know, nobody takes responsibility for controlling that rate; it is free to move with other rates around the world, especially our own. Any slight increase of U.S.

interest rates is, indeed, promptly reflected in the Eurodollar rate. When, further, we did raise our discount rate in July, 1963, most other countries raised their rates, by at least as much, within the next year. One can even say, frankly and fairly, that much of the European demand for higher American interest rates is inspired by the viewpoint I have already mentioned—the conviction that Europe's rates are much too low to combat inflation. What Europeans really want is the freedom to raise their interest rates, not an increase in our rates relative to theirs. It takes two to make an interest-rate difference, and I seriously doubt that any marginal adjustment in U.S. interest rates would much reduce the net advantage of borrowing here.

It can, of course, be argued that there is another more important role for monetary policy—that an increase of U.S. interest rates would be achieved by reducing bank reserves, and a sharp fall in free reserves, a tightening of credit, would induce American banks to lend less abroad. It is even said that "credit rationing" would operate with particular force against foreigners, not against American business, so that there would be very little domestic effect and a large improvement in the balance of payments. Again, I am skeptical. I am skeptical for a number of reasons, but will mention only one. The interest rate charged on bank loans to foreigners is much above the prime rate; bank lending to foreigners is a very attractive and profitable business. I doubt, then, that you would even see a proportional reduction of lending to foreigners, and I am almost certain that you would not see a more than proportional drop in this type of lending.

To sum up, the changes in U.S. monetary policy that are within the realm of practicability would not operate sharply or rapidly enough. They would not provide the rapid reduction in capital outflows that General de Gaulle has forced us to make. This, I think, is why the President decided on the course he has charted— to ask for an immediate "voluntary" program to cut back the outflow of capital. It is, I said before, a second-best answer to the U.S. payments problem; we should be a large-scale lender to foreigners. But it may be the best among second-best policies. In the face of the French ultimatum, the demand that we put our balance of payments in order promptly or face steady loss of gold, a rapid change in policy was required.

One must surely concede that the President's program will do less to impair the efficient functioning of the world economy than a corresponding restriction of trade. We have, after all, restricted trade substantially, even if covertly. Tied aid and "buy American" procurement policies are very much like tariffs. The Defense Department, for example, is obliged to behave as though there were a tariff on certain foreign goods of 50 per cent and more, not a mere 10 or 15 per cent. Foreigners are likewise told that they must spend our aid dollars in the United States, regardless of the price differential. These restrictions, I repeat, are equivalent to tariffs, except that they operate mainly on government transactions rather than on private account. Some of the restrictions we have imposed may even distort world trade very much more than the much-abused 15 per cent important surcharge Britain has imposed. I have been slapped down for saying this, but still think I am right. The British tax is lower and more uniform in incidence than the regulations we have imposed. Should we impose more of these covert trade restrictions, or a different kind? Which would do the least damage? Speaking as an economist, but more from intuition than evidence, I contend that restrictions on capital exports of the kind we have imposed will not do as much damage in the short run as a further restriction of trade having the same effect on the balance of payments.

2

Europe and the Dollar

JAMES TOBIN

The dollar crisis will no doubt be surmounted. "The dollar" will be saved. Its parity will be successfully maintained, and the world will be spared that ultimate and unmentionable calamity whose consequences are the more dreaded for never being described. The world monetary system will stay afloat, and its captains on both sides of the Atlantic will congratulate themselves on their seamanship in weathering the storm.

But the storm is in good part their own making. And if the financial ship has weathered it, it has done so only by jettisoning much of the valuable cargo it was supposed to deliver. Currency parities have been maintained, but full employment has not been. The economic growth of half the advanced noncommunist world has been hobbled, to the detriment of world trade in general and the exports of the developing countries in particular. Currencies have become technically more convertible, but important and probably irreversible restrictions and discriminations on trade and capital movements have been introduced. Some government transactions of the highest priority for the foreign policy of the United States and the West have been curtailed. Others have been "tied" to a degree that impairs their efficiency and gives aid and comfort to the bizarre principle that practices which are disreputably illiberal when applied to private international transactions are acceptable when government money is involved.

These are the costs. Were, and are, all these hardships necessary? To what end have they been incurred?

They have been incurred in order to slow down and end the

Reprinted by permission of the publishers from *The Review of Economics and Statistics*, May, 1964, pp. 123–126, Cambridge, Mass.: Harvard University Press, Copyright, 1964, by the President and Fellows of Harvard College.

accumulations of dollar obligations in the hands of European central banks. It is fair to ask, therefore, whether these accumulations necessarily involved risks and costs serious enough for the countries concerned and for the world at large to justify the heavy costs of stopping them.

Which is easier? Which is less disruptive and less costly, now and in the long run? To stop the private or public transactions that lead one central bank to acquire another's currency? Or to compensate these transactions by official lending in the opposite direction? I do not suggest that the answer is always in favor of compensatory finance. But the issue always needs to be faced, and especially in the present case.

Several courses were open to European countries whose central banks had to purchase dollars in their exchange markets in recent years. (a) They could have built up their dollar holdings quietly and gladly, as they did before 1959. (b) By exercising their right to buy gold at the United States Treasury, they could have forced devaluation of the dollar or suspension of gold payments. (c) They could have taken various measures to correct and reverse chronic European payments surpluses. (d) By occasional withdrawals of gold and by constant complaints they could have brought tremendous pressure for "discipline" upon the United States without forcing a change in the dollar parity.

European central banks and governments chose the fourth course, with token admixtures of the third. They have made world opinion, and American opinion, believe there is no other choice. Almost everyone agrees that the pressure of the balance of payments deficit upon the United States is inescapable arithmetic rather than the deliberate policy of foreign governments. Yet for almost ten years previously, United States deficits were no problem. Clearly it is a change in human attitude and public policy, not inexorable circumstance, which has compelled us to take "corrective" actions.

It is true that the concern of financial officials about "the dollar" was only an echo—and a subdued echo at that—of the fears, hopes, anxieties, and speculations that arose in private financial circles in the late 1950s. But financial officials do not have to follow the private exchange markets; they can lead instead. By an equivocal attitude toward private suspicions of the dollar, European officials

kept pressure on the United States. Never did they firmly say that
they would not force devaluation or suspension of gold payments.
Instead, they succeeded in making the maintenance of gold-dollar
convertibility at $35 per ounce a unilateral commitment of the
United States, under three successive Administrations. Once a
banker has solemnly assured the world and his depositors that he
will never fail, he is at the mercy of those depositors capable of
making him fail.

Memories are short, and gratitude is not a consideration respected in international relations, especially when money is involved. But the United States had and has considerable moral
claim on European governments and central banks.

The present excess supply of dollars is in many respects an
unwinding of the dollar shortage of the immediate postwar period.
Capital left Europe because the continent was vulnerable to military attack, its governments were unstable, its industries were
prostrate and uncompetitive, and its currencies were inconvertible.
Capital has returned to Europe when events have overcome the
special advantages which North America seemed to have in these
respects. It is therefore relevant to recall the behavior of the
United States when the shoe was on the other foot.

During the dollar shortage the United States: gave Western
European countries (other than Greece, Turkey, and Spain) $32
billions of military and economic aid; lent them $11 billions addi-
tional (in spite of the default of European governments of debts
connected with World War I); acquiesced in substantial devaluations of European currencies, without which European exports
would still not be competitive; and acquiesced in exchange controls, capital controls, quantitative restrictions on imports, and discriminations against the United States and other non-European
countries—by no means all of which are liquidated even now.
After enabling Europe to overcome the dollar shortage, the United
States has been expected to adjust to its reversal *without* the tools
that Europe used in its turn. Rightly so, because many of these
tools were illiberal expedients—the more reason for replacing
them now with compensatory intergovernmental finance.

The United States has undertaken, at considerable cost in real
resources and foreign exchange, to defend Western Europe against
the Soviet Union. This is in theory a joint effort, but European

governments do not even yet fulfill their modest commitments to NATO. While European political leaders solicit constant reassurance that United States military power will remain visibly in Europe, their finance ministers and central bankers complain about the inflow of dollars.

The United States has not only tolerated but encouraged the development of a European customs union which attracts American capital and discriminates against American exports (especially the products of industries, notably agriculture, where North America has a clear comparative advantage).

The United States has borne a disproportionate share of the burden of assistance to uncommitted and underdeveloped nations, in which European countries have a common political and, one might hope, humanitarian interest.

The United States has provided a reserve currency. In the late forties no other international and intergovernmental money was available except gold; and the supply of gold was not keeping up with the demand. United States deficits filled the gap with dollars. It is true that this gave the United States a favored position among countries. Anyone who can print money can choose how new money will be first spent. The United States did not seek this privileged role; it arose by accidental evolution rather than conscious design. As it happens, the United States did not exploit it to live beyond our means, to make the American people more affluent. We used it rather for broad international purposes. No doubt in the long run the creation of new international money should be a privilege and responsibility more widely and symmetrically shared. But once the United States and the world are adjusted to the creation of international money via United States deficits, it is scarcely reasonable suddenly to ring a bell announcing that the world's financial experts have now decided that these deficits— past, present, and future—are pernicious.

The United States has not pushed its moral case before world public opinion. This is because many Americans believe, or prefer to believe, that balance of payments deficits, like venereal diseases, betray and punish the sins of those whom they afflict. Others regard them as simply matters of arithmetic and circumstance. Still others are afraid that making a moral argument will indicate to our all-powerful European creditors insufficient resolution to overcome the difficulties. On their side, the Europeans have neatly segregated the contexts. Their financial officials wash their hands of tariff and trade policies, agricultural protection, defense and aid appropriations, and their governments' budgets. Any European failings on these counts are facts of life to which the United States must adjust, rather than reasons for more patience or more credit.

By the narrowest of bankers' criteria—all moral claims aside—the United States is a good credit risk. Its balance sheet vis-à-vis the rest of the world, not to mention its internal productive strength, indicates the capacity to service a considerably increased external public debt. The United States has been confined to the types of credit that can be given on the books of central banks. European Parliaments cannot be asked to vote long-term loans to Uncle Sam, although the American people voted through the Congress to tax themselves to finance the Marshall Plan when Europe's credit rating was nil.

Meanwhile, European central banks are uneasy holding short-term dollar assets. They prefer gold. Why? Because they might some day force us to give them a capital gain on gold holdings when they forego this speculative possibility. But bygones are bygones; and past interest earnings are irrelevant when future capital gains beckon. On its side, the United States has had nothing to lose and much to gain in guaranteeing to maintain the value of official dollar holdings. After stubbornly resisting this suggestion on obscure grounds of principle, the United States Treasury now belatedly and selectively guarantees value in foreign currency.

The only remaining reason to refuse the United States credit is that the United States, like any other deficit country, must be "disciplined." Disciplined to do what?

To stop an orgy of inflation? The United States has the best price record of any country, except Canada, since 1958—before there was a Balance of Payments Problem. The rates of unemployment and excess capacity during the period scarcely suggest that the government has been recklessly overheating the economy with fiscal and monetary fuel.

Nevertheless, many Europeans say that when they buy dollars they are importing inflation. It is hard to take this claim seriously. First of all, if acquisitions of dollars are inflationary so are acquisitions of gold, and Europe shows no signs of saturation with gold.

Second, the classic mechanism of international transmission of inflation is certainly not operating. We have not inflated ourselves into an import surplus adding to aggregate demand in Europe. To the contrary, we have maintained a large and secularly growing export surplus. Third, although central bank purchases of foreign exchange have the same expansionary monetary effects at home as other open market purchases, it is not beyond the wit or experience of man to neutralize these effects by open market sales or other monetary actions. Fourth, United States farmers and coal producers, and Japanese light manufacturers, among others, stand ready to help European governments reduce their living costs and their payment surpluses at the same time. The truth is that Europe does not really want a solution at the expense of its balance of trade.

Perhaps we are to be disciplined to cut foreign aid. European governments do not attach the same importance as we do to aid programs, especially in the Western Hemisphere. Clearly we need a better understanding on development assistance and "burden sharing" among the advanced countries.

Should the United States be disciplined in order to cut off private exports of capital, by controls or by tight monetary policy or both? This has been a major and successful focus of European pressure. The United States authorities have responded by pushing up United States interest rates, more than a full point at the short end, and by proposing the Interest Equalization Tax. European pressure is motivated in part by nationalistic and protectionist aims—keep the rich Americans from buying up or competing with local industry. This may or may not be a worthy objective, but its worth is the same whether international payments are in balance or not.

Two other issues are involved. The first concerns capital markets and controls. Should the United States move toward poorer and more autarkic capital markets, or should the Europeans move toward more efficient and freer capital markets? Much of United States long-term capital movement to Europe does not represent a transfer of real saving. Instead it is a link in a double trans-Atlantic chain connecting the European saver and the European investor. The saver wants a liquid, safe, short-term asset. The investor needs long-term finance or equity capital and seeks it in the

United States. Unfortunately, another link in the same chain is official European holding of short-term dollar obligations. But the Europeans themselves could, through institutional reforms, do a great deal to connect their savers and investors more directly and to reduce the spread between their long and short interest rates.

The second issue is the appropriate international level of interest rates. Evidently national rates must be more closely aligned to each other as international money and capital markets improve. But surely the low-rate country should not always do the aligning. This would impart a deflationary bias to the system. In principle, easy fiscal policy could overcome this bias, but only at the expense of investment and growth. In the present situation European countries are fighting inflation by tightening their money markets rather than their budgets. They are forcing the United States to fight unemployment with a tight money-easy budget mixture. If interest rates are raised whenever a country faces either inflation or balance of payments difficulties, while expansionary fiscal policy is the only measure ever used to combat deflation, a number of swings in business activity and in payments will move the world to a mixture of policies quite unfavorable to long-run growth.

In summary, the adjustments forced on the United States to correct its payments deficit have not served the world economy well. Neither were they essential. European countries have had at their disposal several measures which are desirable in their own right, not just as correctives to the present temporary imbalance in payments. To the extent that they are unprepared to take these measures, they should willingly extend compensatory finance. International financial policy is too important to leave to financiers. There are more important accounts to balance than the records of international transactions, and more important markets to equilibrate than those in foreign exchange.

3

The Longer-Run Prospects for the
U.S. Balance of Payments

JAMES W. ANGELL

What is the outlook for the future?

I must say at once, and quite flatly, that unless some wholly unexpected event occurs, this outlook does not seem to me very encouraging. On the contrary, it is quite bleak. The overriding broad fact is that we as a nation are apparently caught on the horns of a peculiarly awkward dilemma. If we wish, we can probably achieve at least three of our major national economic and political objectives without running into serious contradictions among them. These three are the maintenance of a high rate of domestic economic growth, the maintenance and increase of our aid to less developed countries abroad, and the safeguarding of our international military and political commitments and policies. But we apparently cannot achieve all three of them, and *at the same time* achieve a fourth major and necessary objective, the maintenance of substantial equilibrium in our balance of international payments. The size of even our vast national resources seems to be too small, and the present mode of operation of our national economy too constraining on our freedom of action, to let us reach all four goals simultaneously. If this rather gloomy appraisal turns out to be anywhere near the truth, something will have to give. One or more of the four goals will have to be sacrificed, in part if not in whole, and the choice will have to be made in the not too distant future.

The grounds on which this pessimism is based lie in both the present characteristics and the probable future development of a number of the main groups of items in our balance of payments itself.

Reprinted in this form with permission from the *Political Science Quarterly*, September, 1966, Vol. LXXXI, No. 3, pp. 358–369.

First, U.S. government *military* expenditures abroad that require the purchase of foreign exchange. They seem unlikely to fall very much over the next few years, even if the Vietnam war were to stop overnight, and they may well rise. Given the kind of world we now live in, and the policies and commitments of our government, it is hard to foresee any probable major development that will decrease them substantially.

Second, U.S. government *economic* aid programs abroad. In my own view, and despite the current flood of attacks on them in Congress and elsewhere, these programs are now far too small, not too large. They should be increased to as much as one to two per cent of our Gross National Product, instead of the relatively niggardly four-tenths of one per cent asked for in the bill now before Congress. Most of this money is spent in the United States, and has a directly stimulating effect on our own economic activity. It is nevertheless also true, however, that the burden imposed on our balance of payments is appreciable, though now relatively small, and an expansion of the aid program would of course increase this burden.

Third, our merchandise exports. These exports, which clearly must carry the main burden of supplying credits for our balance of payments, have been expanding fairly rapidly. But they have not been expanding nearly rapidly enough to eliminate our payments deficits, nor are they likely to. In the last ten years, since 1956, they have grown by some fifty-two per cent—about as fast as our dollar GNP. But our merchandise imports, though smaller in total volume, grew at a more rapid *rate*, by some sixty-eight per cent. This is what has prevented our favorable merchandise trade balance from taking over an increasing share of the task of meeting our overall payments deficits. In recent years, although the trade balance has fluctuated widely, it has had an almost horizontal general trend. Moreover, the exports of the world as a whole have grown in the same period, since 1956, nearly half again as rapidly as our own exports, by seventy-five per cent. The American share of the world export market has hence declined appreciably. Finally, in the strategic field of exports of manufactured goods, where we commonly think that we have a special superiority, our share of the world total dropped from twenty-nine per cent in

1956 to only twenty-one per cent last year. Our own exports of manufactures increased by sixty-eight per cent, but the world total increased by 125 per cent, or twice as much!

In the immediate sense, these changes in our relative trade position have been due in largest part to the extraordinary industrial expansion of Continental Europe and of Japan since the Korean War. And it is also true that these latter expansions can hardly continue indefinitely at so rapid an average rate. But the situation as a whole clearly does not suggest that the international competitiveness of American exports has been increasing markedly in recent years. There is, therefore, also not much ground for hoping that any dramatic expansion of our exports will suddenly solve our balance of payments problem in the near-by future, at least not unless some drastic form of corrective action is attempted.

Fourth, our merchandise imports. Here two sets of facts are striking. First, as already pointed out, through the last decade our imports have been growing rather more rapidly than our exports. It is obvious that nothing more than a mere continuation of these rates of relative change could eventually reduce or even wipe out our present favorable merchandise trade balance. Either result clearly could be disastrous to our overall balance of payments position.

Second is a fact which in some ways is even more important. Our imports are in general quite closely and positively correlated with our dollar GNP, as is well known. Since about 1957 or 1958, however, this relation has been spectacularly close, and, if it continues into the future, can have a further and highly adverse effect upon our international payments position. Since about 1957, the average elasticity of our imports with respect to dollar GNP has been close to plus 3.3. The equation for 1957–65, using year-to-year changes and with the deltas in per cents, is:[1]

$$\Delta M = 3.26 \, (\Delta GNP - 3.56).$$

[1] This regression equation is a formalization of the ideas suggested by Walther Lederer, et al., Survey of Current Business, XLVI (1966), 17. The correlation coefficient is 0.929, and the coefficient of determination hence 0.863. The analogous equation for 1952–57 is almost the same: $\Delta M = 2.85 \, (\Delta GNP - 4.0)$.

What this means is that when the annual rate of growth of dollar GNP was less than about 3.5 per cent, imports usually fell. But when dollar GNP grew at a rate *higher* than about 3.5 per cent per year, usually imports not only rose but rose at an average rate some 3.3 times as fast as the rise in GNP! If these latter relations continue into the future, we shall obviously be in real difficulty. We are committed to trying to maintain an annual growth rate of dollar GNP which is much higher than 3.5 per cent: it is now roughly twice that. But if we succeed in this endeavor, we also virtually guarantee a large and much more than proportionate expansion of our imports, and a consequent increasingly adverse pressure on our balance of payments. We apparently will be able to have either high internal growth rates *or* balance of payments equilibrium, but not both at the same time.

Fifth, U.S. tourist expenditures abroad. They, too, are quite highly correlated with dollar GNP, showing an average elasticity in recent years of nearly plus one. They, too, will rise, and nearly in proportion, as GNP increases.

Sixth, U.S. private long-term capital exports. These exports have averaged over four billion dollars a year since 1958, as already stated, and in 1965, despite the intensive administration programs to cut them back, they totalled $4.5 billion. From at least one point of view, private capital exports constitute the biggest single leak in our balance of payments defenses.

The controversy over these capital exports has been large, loud, and heated, especially with respect to direct investments—which in 1965 totalled $3.3 billion. The business firms involved in the latter operations assert vehemently that a continued flow of new direct investment and consequent further expansion abroad is necessary, merely to maintain their competitive position in foreign markets. They also argue that the long-run benefits to the United States, in terms of the return flow of income, the indirect stimulus to subsequent U.S. exports which is produced by U.S. business operations abroad, and other gains far outweigh any initial adverse effects on the U.S. balance of payments at the time the investments themselves are made. It is also perfectly true that in every year but one since 1950, the return flow of dividends, royalties, and other income receipts from our direct investments abroad has exceeded substantially the volume of the new direct investments themselves.[2]

But there is more to it than this. First, much and perhaps the larger part of the funds used to finance our direct investments abroad has been spent initially, as a rule, for the construction of new plants built chiefly with *foreign* labor, materials, and equipment, and for the creation of new foreign production and sales organizations. Only the smaller part has usually gone initially into the purchase of U.S. goods as such.[3] Our recent direct investment has therefore not produced anything like an equal immediate demand for U.S. merchandise exports. What usually was wanted was in larger part not U.S. goods but foreign exchange. Much of this investment has, therefore, put serious adverse pressure on our current balance of international payments, and, if the recent patterns are maintained, will continue to do so—unlike, for example, the frequent British experience after the middle of the nineteenth century.[4]

Second, a substantial fraction of the income from our foreign investments is never brought home but is used to finance further expansion abroad, and hence never helps our balance of payments. This retained fraction could easily grow much larger. Third, when they first begin to operate, many of the foreign enterprises into which our direct investments flow may well continue to buy a substantial fraction of their supplies, replacement parts, and the like in the United States, thus helping our exports. Indeed, the U.S. companies involved make a good deal of this point. But with the passage of time, and as adequate foreign suppliers of the same

[2] See the study by Judd Polk, *et al.*, *U.S. Production Abroad and the Balance of Payments* (New York, 1966), p. 34. This study was based primarily on reports and questionnaire replies from a large sample of U.S. corporations with foreign interests.

[3] Polk, *ibid.*, p. 113, indicates that usually less than fifty per cent of the initial investment in plant and machinery, among the companies reporting, came from the United States. He does not say so, but presumably nearly *all* of the common materials used, labor except technicians, and the like were of foreign origin.

[4] Through "tied" loans and otherwise, a large part of British private foreign investment in the nineteenth century was accompanied by a nearly equivalent demand for British merchandise (rails, locomotives, machinery, and the like) to implement the investment itself, and hence did not put major pressure on the current British balance of payments.

things are developed, this type of demand for U.S. goods will almost certainly shrink. Why should the foreign enterprises pay freight charges from the United States and often foreign tariffs as well, when they do not have to?

Finally, and I think most important of all, the overriding consequence of our recent direct investment abroad has been not so much the increased export of U.S. *goods* as the increased export of U.S. *skills and technologies,*[5] primarily those of production but also those of organization and of selling. This is doubtless all right in itself. But the new foreign enterprises were in largest part started or expanded precisely to avoid the transport costs, protective tariffs, internal regulations, wage differentials, and the like which had previously been hampering the export of U.S. goods themselves. As the new foreign enterprises begin to turn out products more or less like contemporary U.S. products, and made largely with American technologies, they are clearly likely to have an increasingly adverse effect upon the competitive position of the analogous manufactured exports of the United States itself—both in the foreign country initially concerned, and eventually in third markets.[6]

To put it in dramatic if oversimplified terms, our direct investments abroad can end up by wrecking much of the foreign markets for our own exports of manufactured goods! This is surely an important part of the explanation of the recent decline in our share of the total world market for such manufactured exports, which was commented on above; we are beating ourselves.[7] It

[5] Polk, *op. cit.,* p. 105.

[6] This is precisely what began to happen to various classes of British exports after the turn of the last century, not so much in consequence of direct investment abroad as because of the export of British technologies, often without the knowledge or consent of the British firms concerned. But the whole problem of the primary and secondary effects of U.S. direct investment abroad on U.S. exports—including the questions listed above and a variety of others as well—is tangled, and sufficient quantitative evidence is not yet available to provide firm answers to many of these questions. Polk's study is written, on the whole, to defend rather than to attack our direct foreign investment, but it is by far the most penetrating and useful investigation of the subject that I know of. Also see the comments on Polk's study by John J. Powers Jr., in an address before the National Industrial Conference Board in New York on March 22, 1966 (mimeographed, distributed by Charles Pfizer and Company, New York).

[7] The direct investments abroad of the American oil companies are in the main a major exception to the preceding observations.

is a sobering thought, and one which does not increase one's optimism about the future contributions of our merchandise exports to the deficits in our balance of payments. We clearly face a complex problem here, and one which may not be capable of any simple solution.

Finally, the progressive deterioration of both our monetary reserves and our general international liquidity position obviously exposes us to serious short-run dangers, including the possibility of a major foreign-exchange crisis, which are *additional* to the adverse longer-run factors just analyzed.

There are also, of course, a number of favorable factors in the outlook. Of these perhaps the most important are the very fact of a continued growth of our merchandise exports, even though at too slow a rate; the increasing inflow of income from our private investments abroad, even though by no means all such income is returned to this country; the growth of foreign tourism in the United States; and the fact that, despite all our difficulties, foreigners are still holding very large and even increasing volumes of liquid dollar liabilities.

But I think—to repeat—that on balance the overall outlook is far from encouraging. Barring the wholly unforeseen, I do not look for any major crisis in the immediate future. If we keep on losing monetary reserves, however—and we have been losing them at an average rate of over one billion dollars a year since 1958—it is obvious that sooner or later a breaking point must be reached. Even at best, this will happen when our reserves have fallen to the minimum size permitted by law. And if foreigners start to cash in their liquid dollar holdings in any large volume *before* our surplus reserves are used up, as they well may, the breaking point will be reached sooner rather than later.

Clearly the time to prepare for a possible crisis is before it hits, not afterward. What can we do?

There are a number of conceivable solutions. While some of them are practicable, however, others are not. Our theoretical freedom of action is in fact limited in a number of directions.

1. We can hope for a greatly increased rate of economic growth abroad, that will stimulate the demand for our exports net of imports and thus reduce our payments deficit. Such an increase in foreign growth rates, however, does not seem very likely in the near

future. Moreover, even if it did develop, the resulting increase in our exports would expand our GNP, and this in turn would probably cause our imports to rise more than in proportion.

2. Alternatively, we can check severely or even reverse the expansion of the American economy, by fiscal and monetary measures. This would cause our imports to fall heavily. If domestic prices fell it would probably stimulate our exports, and it might thus eliminate the payments deficit. But no one can advocate this course seriously. The costs, chiefly in terms of increased unemployment, would be too severe.

3. Theoretically, we can cut U.S. military expenditures abroad, heavily or even to zero. But our wide-ranging international commitments, and indeed the whole tenor of our long-established policies, make this alternative unlikely to be a practicable one.

4. We can cut foreign economic aid still more, again even to zero. This course, however, would likewise not only reverse our long-established policies, but I believe would be completely contrary to our own long-run self-interest. Abandoning the less-developed countries would not only be morally repugnant to most of us, but would assuredly throw many of them into the greedy arms of the Communist world. Unless to meet a temporary emergency, such action would be merely stupid.

5. We can raise our protective tariffs, so far as present treaty limitations permit, and thus cut our merchandise imports. But this, too, would completely reverse the policies of trade liberalization, which we have defended and promoted for more than twenty-five years. It would also hurt our own internal growth, which is heavily dependent on imports; and in the end, by reducing the supplies of dollar exchange available to foreigners, it might cut the foreign demand for our own exports—thus helping to defeat the whole purpose of helping our balance of payments.

6. We can try to stimulate our merchandise exports directly, by means of subsidies, tax credits, and so forth. Such measures, however, would invite retaliation; and at least some of them presumably would violate the provisions of the General Agreement on Trade and Tariffs. On balance, I doubt if we can hope for much from such devices.

7. We can cut back heavily on U.S. travel abroad, or even pro-

hibit it. Such interference with individual freedom is repugnant to most of us (though various foreign countries have long enforced such restrictions); it would cut heavily into the foreign-exchange earnings of our international carriers; and unless extensive exceptions were made—and extensive exceptions would help to defeat the very purpose in view—it would have adverse effects both on U.S. business activity abroad and on U.S. education. Nevertheless, we may well be forced into something of this sort.

8. We can restrain much more severely those private capital exports which require the purchase of net additional foreign exchange, or even prohibit them entirely for a time. As pointed out earlier, such exports have been the biggest single leak in our balance of payments dike, and they deserve very serious attention. The Interest Rate Equalization Tax has had a marked effect in reducing the rate of portfolio investment abroad, but the program for voluntary controls over direct investment has not done much more, after the initial-impact effect, than to prevent the flood from rising at an even more rapid rate.

Various methods for increasing the present restraints are available, running from much heavier taxation to capital-export rationing, and even the outright prohibition of private capital exports.[8] The adoption of any such measures would produce understandably vehement protests from the business and banking interests affected. They almost certainly also would not be completely watertight. But the bulk of the desired results could be achieved if the government acted with firmness.

In the shorter run, the flow of income to the United States from *previous* foreign investment would remain undiminished, unless by deliberate action of the prospective recipients (and such withholding could be subjected to penalties). It also seems to me

---

[8] As an alternative, some students have proposed giving favorable tax treatment to investment income earned abroad that is returned to this country, to the return of capital now held abroad, and the like. Setting up and operating such a system of tax preferences, however, would encounter formidable administrative and perhaps also political difficulties; and in any event it is doubtful that the increase in the return flow of funds would be large enough to produce any great reduction in the payments deficit, unless temporarily. The present attractions of foreign direct investment are great; and as Polk's study makes clear, the current-profit motive is often not dominant.

improbable, at least in the shorter run, that restricting private capital exports further would have much effect on the demand for U.S. exports from existing United States-associated firms abroad. In the longer run, on the other hand, it is true with respect to direct investment that the foreign branches, subsidiaries, and other associates of U.S. firms *might* eventually find their competitive position abroad substantially handicapped by a lack of sufficient new dollar nourishment.[9] But recent experience suggests that this possibility may have been exaggerated. Such enterprises have already had a good deal of success in obtaining reasonably adequate supplies of funds in foreign capital markets, and at endurable costs, when they are compelled to.[10] Hence even in the longer run, the return flow of income to us and hence our balance of payments need not be seriously injured by capital-export controls. The administrative problems would obviously be substantial, and no one likes this type of interference with free markets, but the results obtainable would seem to justify the costs.

9. Finally, a good many academic economists have urged that we solve the whole balance of payments problem at one stroke by voluntarily devaluing the dollar, or even by going over to a regime of freely fluctuating exchange rates. This possible course of action has various strong theoretical appeals, and in the longer run may become unavoidable, but in the present situation of the United States I do not think it would work.

There are several difficulties. First, other countries could depreciate, too, or retaliate in other ways, thus wiping out our initial advantage. Second, even if they did not, substantial parts of the payments we now make abroad are immune to the effects of changes in the exchange rates: namely, government military expenditures and economic-aid outlays abroad, and also all other private and governmental payments that are fixed in terms of foreign currencies. Exchange depreciation would not reduce the demands for foreign exchange on these accounts by a penny, and thereby would fail in these respects to produce any corrective effect on our balance of payments. Depreciation also might actually

---

[9] See Polk, *op. cit.*, Chaps. 2 and 3, especially p. 59.
[10] Foreign borrowing by reporting U.S. corporations amounted to $967 million in 1965, and is expected to reach $1,480 million in 1966. *New York Times*, May 11, 1966.

stimulate rather than check the export of private capital. Finally, it almost certainly would be followed soon by internal price increases and other forms of domestic inflation, which would quickly wipe out much or most of the initial gains to our balance of payments in the merchandise and service accounts.[11] For the United States today, I therefore do not think that voluntary exchange depreciation offers a very attractive or indeed effective solution for the problem of our international payments deficits, as long as any other alternative is open to us.[12]

The overall conclusion to which I come is thus not very optimistic. I do not see much likelihood that, if no additional and pretty severe corrective action is taken, our international payments deficits will simply cure themselves. Indeed, both the policies and commitments of our government, and the complex relations among our GNP, merchandise exports, merchandise imports, and various service items virtually guarantee that they *cannot* cure themselves.

My further conclusion, then, is that the most desirable and least injurious major steps we can take, among those which are in practical fact open to us, are probably to enforce very substantial restrictions against U.S. travel abroad; and certainly to put much more severe brakes on those exports of private capital that require the purchase of net additional foreign exchange, especially long-term capital exports, for a substantial period. In 1965, as remarked before, long-term private capital exports alone were three times as large as the whole of our payments deficit. This is a leak we simply cannot continue to afford.

If we do thus limit private capital exports further, however, it must be in the hope, as with Mr. Micawber, that something else will eventually turn up. If only in our own long-run self-interest, we can hardly want to stop private capital exports for an indefinite period. But even imposing sharp additional limitations on private capital exports is a gamble. It may not work, in the sense that it may not wipe out our payments deficits or even reduce them to

[11] The U.S. exchange depreciation of 1933–34 was followed in the next two years by a *more* than proportional increase in wholesale prices.
[12] Exchange depreciation seems most likely to cure persistent and large balance of payments deficits when there has *already* been serious internal inflation simultaneously with over-valued exchange rates. This is hardly the situation in the United States today.

manageable size. If it does not, then I fear that the only alternative open to us will be exchange depreciation, forced on us by our eventual inability to keep on paying off our foreign short-term obligations in gold when gold is demanded of us. Yet the costs of enforced depreciation would, I believe, be very high. Let us hope that we are not thrown into it despite ourselves.

4

Using the Free Market To Resolve the Balance-of-Payments Problem

MILTON FRIEDMAN

Discussions of U.S. policy with respect to international payments tend to be dominated by our immediate balance-of-payments difficulties. I should like today to approach the question from a different, and I hope more constructive, direction. Let us begin by asking ourselves not merely how we can get out of our present difficulties but instead how we can fashion our international payments system so that it will best serve our needs for the long pull; how we can solve not merely this balance-of-payments problem but the balance-of-payments problem.

A shocking, and indeed, disgraceful feature of the present situation is the extent to which our frantic search for expedients to stave off balance-of-payments pressures has led us, on the one hand, to sacrifice major national objectives; and, on the other, to give enormous power to officials of foreign governments to affect what should be purely domestic matters.

Foreign payments amount to only some 5 percent of our total national income. Yet they have become a major factor in nearly every national policy.

I believe that a system of floating exchange rates would solve the balance-of-payments problem for the United States far more effectively than our present arrangements. Such a system would use the flexibility and efficiency of the free market to harmonize our small foreign trade sector with both the rest of our massive economy and the rest of the world; it would reduce problems of foreign payments to their proper dimensions and remove them as a major consideration in governmental policy about domestic

From Milton Friedman, "Statement," *The United States Balance of Payments*, Part III: *The International Monetary System: Functioning and Possible Reform*, Hearings before the Joint Economic Committee of the Congress (Washington, D.C.: 1963), pp. 451–459. Reprinted in this form by permission.

matters and as a major preoccupation in international political negotiations; it would foster our national objectives rather than be an obstacle to their attainment.

To indicate the basis for this conclusion, let us consider the national objective with which our payments system is most directly connected: the promotion of a healthy and balanced growth of world trade, carried on, so far as possible, by private individuals and private enterprises with minimum intervention by governments. This has been a major objective of our whole postwar international economic policy, most recently expressed in the Trade Expansion Act of 1962. Success would knit the free world more closely together, and, by fostering the international division of labor, raise standards of living throughout the world, including the United States.

Suppose that we succeed in negotiating far-reaching reciprocal reductions in tariffs and other trade barriers with the Common Market and other countries. To simplify exposition I shall hereafter refer only to tariffs, letting these stand for the whole range of barriers to trade, including even the so-called voluntary limitation of exports. Such reductions will expand trade in general but clearly will have different effects on different industries. The demand for the products of some will expand, for others contract. This is a phenomenon we are familiar with from our internal development. The capacity of our free enterprise system to adapt quickly and efficiently to such shifts, whether produced by changes in technology or tastes, has been a major source of our economic growth. The only additional element introduced by international trade is the fact that different currencies are involved, and this is where the payments mechanism comes in; its function is to keep this fact from being an additional source of disturbance.

An all-around lowering of tariffs would tend to increase both our expenditures and our receipts in foreign currencies. There is no way of knowing in advance which increase would tend to be the greater and hence no way of knowing whether the initial effect would be toward a surplus or deficit in our balance of payments. What is clear is that we cannot hope to succeed in the objective of expanding world trade unless we can readily adjust to either outcome.

Many people concerned with our payments deficits hope that

since we are operating further from full capacity than Europe, we could supply a substantial increase in exports whereas they could not. Implicitly, this assumes that European countries are prepared to see their surplus turned into a deficit, thereby contributing to the reduction of the deficits we have recently been experiencing in our balance of payments. Perhaps this would be the initial effect of tariff changes. But if the achievement of such a result is to be a sine qua non of tariff agreement, we cannot hope for any significant reduction in barriers. We could be confident that exports would expand more than imports only if the tariff changes were one sided indeed, with our trading partners making much greater reductions in tariffs than we make. Our major means of inducing other countries to reduce tariffs is to offer corresponding reductions in our tariff. More generally, there is little hope of continued and sizable liberalization of trade if liberalization is to be viewed simply as a device for correcting balance-of-payments difficulties. That way lies only backing and filling.

Suppose then that the initial effect is to increase our expenditures on imports more than our receipts from exports. How could we adjust to this outcome?

One method of adjustment is to draw on reserves or borrow from abroad to finance the excess increase in imports. The obvious objection to this method is that it is only a temporary device, and hence can be relied on only when the disturbance is temporary. But that is not the major objection. Even if we had very large reserves or could borrow large amounts from abroad, so that we could continue this expedient for many years, it is a most undesirable one. We can see why if we look at physical rather than financial magnitudes.

The physical counterpart to the financial deficit is a reduction of employment in industries competing with imports that is larger than the concurrent expansion of employment in export industries. So long as the financial deficit continues, the assumed tariff reductions create employment problems. But it is no part of the aim of tariff reductions to create unemployment at home or to promote employment abroad. The aim is a balanced expansion of trade, with exports rising along with imports and thereby providing employment opportunities to offset any reduction in employment resulting from increased imports.

Hence, simply drawing on reserves or borrowing abroad is a most unsatisfactory method of adjustment.

Another method of adjustment is to lower U.S. prices relative to foreign prices, since this would stimulate exports and discourage imports. If foreign countries are accommodating enough to engage in inflation, such a change in relative prices might require merely that the United States keep prices stable or even, that it simply keep them from rising as fast as foreign prices. But there is no necessity for foreign countries to be so accommodating, and we could hardly count on their being so accommodating. The use of this technique therefore involves a willingness to produce a decline in U.S. prices by tight monetary policy or tight fiscal policy or both. Given time, this method of adjustment would work. But in the interim, it would exact a heavy toll. It would be difficult or impossible to force down prices appreciably without producing a recession and considerable unemployment. To eliminate in the long run the unemployment resulting from the tariff changes, we should in the short run be creating cyclical unemployment. The cure might for a time be far worse than the disease.

This second method is therefore also most unsatisfactory. Yet these two methods—drawing on reserves and forcing down prices— are the only two methods available to us under our present international payment arrangements, which involve fixed exchange rates between the U.S. dollar and other currencies. Little wonder that we have so far made such disappointing progress toward the reduction of trade barriers, that our practice has differed so much from our preaching.

There is one other way and only one other way to adjust and that is by allowing (or forcing) the price of the U.S. dollar to fall in terms of other currencies. To a foreigner, U.S. goods can become cheaper in either of two ways—either because their prices in the United States fall in terms of dollars or because the foreigner has to give up fewer units of his own currency to acquire a dollar, which is to say, the price of the dollar falls. For example, suppose a particular U.S. car sells for $2,800 when a dollar costs 7 shillings, tuppence in British money (i.e., roughly £1 = $2.80). The price of the car is then £1,000 in British money. It is all the same to an Englishman—or even a Scotsman—whether the price of the car falls to $2,500 while the price of a dollar remains

7 shillings, tuppence, or, alternatively, the price of the car remains $2,800, while the price of a dollar falls to 6 shillings, 5 pence (i.e., roughly £1=$3.11). In either case, the car costs the Englishman £900 rather than £1,000, which is what matters to him. Similarly, foreign goods can become more expensive to an American in either of two ways—either because the price in terms of foreign currency rises or because he has to give up more dollars to acquire a given amount of foreign currency.

Changes in exchange rates can therefore alter the relative price of U.S. and foreign goods in precisely the same way as can changes in internal prices in the United States and in foreign countries. And they can do so without requiring anything like the same internal adjustments. If the initial effect of the tariff reductions would be to create a deficit at the former exchange rate (or enlarge an existing deficit or reduce an existing surplus) and thereby increase unemployment, this effect can be entirely avoided by a change in exchange rates which will produce a balanced expansion in imports and exports without interfering with domestic employment, domestic prices, or domestic monetary and fiscal policy. The pig can be roasted without burning down the house.

The situation is, of course, entirely symmetrical if the tariff changes should initially happen to expand our exports more than our imports. Under present circumstances, we would welcome such a result, and conceivably, if the matching deficit were experienced by countries currently running a surplus, they might permit it to occur without seeking to offset it. In that case, they and we would be using the first method of adjustment—changes in reserves or borrowing. But again, if we had started off from an even keel, this would be an undesirable method of adjustment. On our side, we should be sending out useful goods and receiving only foreign currencies in return. On the side of our partners, they would be using up reserves and tolerating the creation of unemployment.

The second method of adjusting to a surplus is to permit or force domestic prices to rise—which is of course what we did in part in the early postwar years when we were running large surpluses. Again, we should be forcing maladjustments on the whole economy to solve a problem arising from a small part of it—the 5 percent accounted for by foreign trade.

Again, these two methods are the only ones available under our present international payments arrangements, and neither is satisfactory.

The final method is to permit or force exchange rates to change —in this case, a rise in the price of the dollar in terms of foreign currencies. This solution is again specifically adapted to the specific problem of the balance of payments.

Changes in exchange rates can be produced in either of two general ways. One way is by a change in an official exchange rate; an official devaluation or appreciation from one fixed level which the Government is committed to support to another fixed level. This is the method used by Britain in its postwar devaluation and by Germany in 1961 when the mark was appreciated. This is also the main method contemplated by the IMF which permits member nations to change their exchange rates by 10 percent without approval by the Fund and by a larger amount after approval by the Fund. But this method has serious disadvantages. It makes a change in rates a matter of major moment, and hence there is a tendency to postpone any change as long as possible. Difficulties cumulate and a larger change is finally needed than would have been required if it could have been made promptly. By the time the change is made, everyone is aware that a change is pending and is certain about the direction of change. The result is to encourage flight from a currency, if it is going to be devalued, or to a currency, if it is going to be appreciated.

There is in any event little basis for determining precisely what the new rate should be. Speculative movements increase the difficulty of judging what the new rate should be, and introduce a systematic bias, making the change needed appear larger than it actually is. The result, particularly when devaluation occurs, is generally to lead officials to "play safe" by making an even larger change than the large change needed. The country is then left after the devaluation with a maladjustment precisely the opposite of that with which it started, and is thereby encouraged to follow policies it cannot sustain in the long run.

Even if all these difficulties could be avoided, this method of changing from one fixed rate to another has the disadvantage that it is necessarily discontinuous. Even if the new exchange rates are precisely correct when first established, they will not long remain correct.

A second and much better way in which changes in exchange rates can be produced is by permitting exchange rates to float, by allowing them to be determined from day to day in the market. This is the method which the United States used from 1862 to 1879, and again, in effect, from 1917 or so to about 1925, and again from 1933 to 1934. It is the method which Britain used from 1918 to 1925 and again from 1931 to 1939, and which Canada used for most of the interwar period and again from 1950 to May 1962. Under this method, exchange rates adjust themselves continuously, and market forces determine the magnitude of each change. There is no need for any official to decide by how much the rate should rise or fall. This is the method of the free market, the method that we adopt unquestioningly in a private enterprise economy for the bulk of goods and services. It is no less available for the price of one money in terms of another.

With a floating exchange rate, it is possible for Governments to intervene and try to affect the rate by buying or selling, as the British exchange equalization fund did rather successfully in the 1930's, or by combining buying and selling with public announcements of intentions, as Canada did so disastrously in early 1962. On the whole, it seems to me undesirable to have government intervene, because there is a strong tendency for government agencies to try to peg the rate rather than to stabilize it, because they have no special advantage over private speculators in stabilizing it, because they can make far bigger mistakes than private speculators risking their own money, and because there is a tendency for them to cover up their mistakes by changing the rules—as the Canadian case so strikingly illustrates—rather than by reversing course. But this is an issue on which there is much difference of opinion among economists who agree in favoring floating rates. Clearly, it is possible to have a successful floating rate along with governmental speculation.

The great objective of tearing down trade barriers, of promoting a worldwide expansion of trade, of giving citizens of all countries, and especially the underdeveloped countries, every opportunity to sell their products in open markets under equal terms and thereby every incentive to use their resources efficiently, of giving countries an alternative through free world trade to autarchy and central planning—this great objective can, I believe, be achieved best under a regime of floating rates. All countries, and not just the United States, can proceed to liberalize boldly and confidently only if they can have reasonable assurance that the resulting trade expansion will be balanced and will not interfere with major domestic objectives. Floating exchange rates, and so far as I can see, only floating exchange rates, provide this assurance. They do so because they are an automatic mechanism for protecting the domestic economy from the possibility that liberalization will produce a serious imbalance in international payments.

Despite their advantages, floating exchange rates have a bad press. Why is this so?

One reason is because a consequence of our present system that I have been citing as a serious disadvantage is often regarded as an advantage, namely, the extent to which the small foreign trade sector dominates national policy. Those who regard this as an advantage refer to it as the discipline of the gold standard. I would have much sympathy for this view if we had a real gold standard, so the discipline was imposed by impersonal forces which in turn reflected the realities of resources, tastes, and technology. But in fact we have today only a pseudo gold standard and the so-called discipline is imposed by governmental officials of other countries who are determining their own internal monetary policies and are either being forced to dance to our tune or calling the tune for us, depending primarily on accidental political developments. This is a discipline we can well do without.

A possibly more important reason why floating exchange rates have a bad press, I believe, is a mistaken interpretation of experience with floating rates, arising out of a statistical fallacy that can be seen easily in a standard example. Arizona is clearly the worst place in the United States for a person with tuberculosis to go because the death rate from tuberculosis is higher in Arizona than in any other State. The fallacy in this case is obvious. It is less obvious in connection with exchange rates. Countries that have gotten into severe financial difficulties, for whatever reason, have had ultimately to change their exchange rates or let them change. No amount of exchange control and other restrictions on trade have enabled them to peg an exchange rate that was far out of line with economic realities. In consequence, floating rates have frequently been associated with financial and economic instability.

It is easy to conclude, as many have, that floating exchange rates produce such instability.

This misreading of experience is reinforced by the general prejudice against speculation, which has led to the frequent assertion, typically on the basis of no evidence whatsoever, that speculation in exchange can be expected to be destabilizing and thereby to increase the instability in rates. Few who make this assertion even recognize that it is equivalent to asserting that speculators generally lose money.

Floating exchange rates need not be unstable exchange rates—any more than the prices of automobiles or of Government bonds, of coffee or of meals need gyrate wildly just because they are free to change from day to day. The Canadian exchange rate was free to change during more than a decade, yet it varied within narrow limits. The ultimate objective is a world in which exchange rates, while free to vary, are in fact highly stable because basic economic policies and conditions are stable. Instability of exchange rates is a symptom of instability in the underlying economic structure. Elimination of this symptom by administrative pegging of exchange rates cures none of the underlying difficulties and only makes adjustment to them more painful.

The confusion between stable exchange rates and pegged exchange rates helps to explain the frequent comment that floating exchange rates would introduce an additional element of uncertainty into foreign trade and thereby discourage its expansion. They introduce no additional element of uncertainty. If a floating rate would, for example, decline, then a pegged rate would be subject to pressure that the authorities would have to meet by internal deflation or exchange control in some form. The uncertainty about the rate would simply be replaced by uncertainty about internal prices or about the availability of exchange; and the latter uncertainties, being subject to administrative rather than market control, are likely to be the more erratic and unpredictable. Moreover, the trader can far more readily and cheaply protect himself against the danger of changes in exchange rates, through hedging operations in a forward market, than he can against the danger of changes in internal prices or exchange availability. Floating rates are therefore more favorable to private international trade than pegged rates.

Though I have discussed the problem of international payments in the context of trade liberalization, the discussion is directly applicable to the more general problem of adapting to any forces that make for balance-of-payments difficulties. Consider our present problem, of a deficit in the balance of trade plus long-term capital movements. How can we adjust to it? By one of the three methods outlined: first, drawing on reserves or borrowing; second, keeping U.S. prices from rising as rapidly as foreign prices or forcing them down; third, permitting or forcing exchange rates to alter. And, this time, by one more method: by imposing additional trade barriers or their equivalent, whether in the form of higher tariffs, or smaller import quotas, or extracting from other countries tighter "voluntary" quotas on their exports, or "tieing" foreign aid, or buying higher priced domestic goods or services to meet military needs, or imposing taxes on foreign borrowing, or imposing direct controls on investments by U.S. citizens abroad, or any one of the host of other devices for interfering with the private business of private individuals that have become so familiar to us since Hjalmar Schacht perfected the modern techniques of exchange control in 1934 to strengthen the Nazis for war and to despoil a large class of his fellow citizens.

Fortunately or unfortunately, even Congress cannot repeal the laws of arithmetic. Books must balance. We must use one of these four methods. Because we have been unwilling to select the only one that is currently fully consistent with both economic and political needs—namely, floating exchange rates—we have been driven, as if by an invisible hand, to employ all the others, and even then may not escape the need for explicit changes in exchange rates.

We affirm in loud and clear voices that we will not and must not erect trade barriers—yet is there any doubt about how far we have gone down the fourth route? After the host of measures already taken, the Secretary of the Treasury has openly stated to the Senate Finance Committee that if the so-called interest equalization tax—itself a concealed exchange control and concealed devaluation—is not passed, we shall have to resort to direct controls over foreign investment.

We affirm that we cannot drain our reserves further, yet short-term liabilities mount and our gold stock continues to decline.

We affirm that we cannot let balance-of-payments problems interfere with domestic prosperity, yet for at least some four years now we have followed a less expansive monetary policy than would have been healthy for our economy.

Even all together, these measures may only serve to postpone but not prevent open devaluation—if the experience of other countries is any guide. Whether they do, depends not on us but on others. For our best hope of escaping our present difficulties is that foreign countries will inflate.

In the meantime, we adopt one expedient after another, borrowing here, making swap arrangements there, changing the form of loans to make the figures look good. Entirely aside from the ineffectiveness of most of these measures, they are politically degrading and demeaning. We are a great and wealthy Nation. We should be directing our own course, setting an example to the world, living up to our destiny. Instead, we send our officials hat in hand to make the rounds of foreign governments and central banks; we put foreign central banks in a position to determine whether or not we can meet our obligations and thus enable them to exert great influence on our policies; we are driven to niggling negotiations with Hong Kong and with Japan and for all I know, Monaco, to get them to limit voluntarily their exports. Is this posture suitable for the leader of the free world?

It is not the least of the virtues of floating exchange rates that we would again become masters in our own house. We could decide important issues on the proper ground. The military could concentrate on military effectiveness and not on saving foreign exchange; recipients of foreign aid could concentrate on how to get the most out of what we give them and not on how to spend it all in the United States; Congress could decide how much to spend on foreign aid on the basis of what we get for our money and what else we could use it for and not how it will affect the gold stock; the monetary authorities could concentrate on domestic prices and employment, not on how to induce foreigners to hold dollar balances in this country; the Treasury and the tax committees of Congress could devote their attention to the equity of the tax system and its effects on our efficiency, rather than on how to use tax gimmicks to discourage imports, subsidize exports, and discriminate against outflows of capital.

A system of floating exchange rates would render the problem of making outflows equal inflows unto the market where it belongs and not leave it to the clumsy and heavy hand of Government. It would leave Government free to concentrate on its proper functions.

5

The Dollar and World Liquidity: A Minority View

EMILE DESPRES
CHARLES P. KINDLEBERGER
WALTER S. SALANT

The consensus in Europe and the United States on the United States balance of payments and world liquidity runs about like this:

1. Abundant liquidity has been provided since World War II less by newly mined gold than by the increase in liquid dollar assets generated by U.S. balance-of-payments deficits.

2. These deficits are no longer available as a generator of liquidity because the accumulation of dollars has gone so far that it has undermined confidence in the dollar.

3. To halt the present creeping decline in liquidity through central-bank conversions of dollars into gold, and to forestall headlong flight from the dollar, it is necessary above all else to correct the United States deficit.

4. When the deficit has been corrected, the growth of world reserves may, or probably will, become inadequate. Hence there is a need for planning new means of adding to world reserves—along the lines suggested by Triffin, Bernstein, Roosa, Stamp, Giscard, and others.[1]

Reprinted by permission from *The Economist*, February 5, 1966.

[1] For one of many good discussions of the proposals by Triffin, Bernstein, and Stamp, as well as others not mentioned above, see *Plans for Reform of the International Monetary System* by Fritz Machlup, Special Papers in International Economics No. 3, revised March, 1964 (International Finance Section, Department of Economics, Princeton University). See also *World Monetary Reform: Plans and Issues*, edited by Herbert Grubel (Stanford: Stanford University Press, 1963). For Robert V. Roosa's present views, see his *Monetary Reform for the World Economy* (for Council on Foreign Relations, New York: Harper & Row, 1965). An English translation of the suggestions by M. Valéry Giscard d'Estaing, made when he was Minister of Finance and Economic Affairs of France, may be found in various speeches published under the title *Statements Made by M. Valéry Giscard d'Estaing on International Monetary Problems*, Collection Ouvertures Economique (Paris, 1965).

So much is widely agreed. There is a difference in tactics between those who would correct the U.S. balance of payments by raising interest rates—bankers on both sides of the ocean and European central bankers—and those in the United States who would correct it, if necessary, by capital restrictions, so that tight money in the United States may be avoided while labor and other resources are still idle. There is also a difference of emphasis between the Continentals, who urge adjustment (proposition 3 above), and the Anglo-Saxons who stress the need for more liquidity (proposition 4). British voices urge more liquidity now, rather than in the future. But with these exceptions, the lines of analysis converge.

There is room, however, for a minority view which would oppose this agreement with a sharply differing analysis. In outline, it asserts the following counter propositions:

1. While the United States has provided the world with liquid dollar assets in the postwar period by capital outflow and aid exceeding its current account surplus, in most years this excess has not reflected a deficit in a sense representing disequilibrium. The outflow of U.S. capital and aid has filled not one but two needs. First, it has supplied goods and services to the rest of the world. But secondly, to the extent that its loans to foreigners are offset by foreigners putting their own money into liquid dollar assets, the U.S. has not overinvested but has supplied financial intermediary services. The "deficit" has reflected largely the second process, in which the United States has been lending, mostly at long and intermediate term, and borrowing short. This financial intermediation, in turn, performs two functions: it supplies loans and investment funds to foreign enterprises which have to pay more domestically to borrow long-term money and which cannot get the amounts they want at any price; and it supplies liquidity to foreign asset-holders, who receive less for placing their short-term deposits at home. Essentially, this is a trade in liquidity, which is profitable to both sides. Differences in their liquidity preferences (i.e., in their willingness to hold their financial assets in long-term rather than in quickly encashable forms and to have short-term rather than long-term liabilities outstanding against them) create differing margins between short-term and long-term interest rates. This in turn creates scope for trade in financial

assets, just as differing comparative costs create the scope for mutually profitable trade in goods. This trade in financial assets has been an important ingredient of economic growth outside the United States.

2. Such lack of confidence in the dollar as now exists has been generated by the attitudes of government officials, central bankers, academic economists, and journalists, and reflects their failure to understand the implications of this intermediary function. Despite some contagion from these sources, the private market retains confidence in the dollar, as increases in private holdings of liquid dollar assets show. Private speculation in gold is simply the result of the known attitudes and actions of governmental officials and central bankers.

3. With capital markets unrestricted, attempts to correct the "deficit" by ordinary macro-economic weapons are likely to fail. It may be possible to expand the current account surplus at first by deflation of United States income and prices relative to those of Europe; but gross financial capital flows will still exceed real transfer of goods and services (i.e., involve financial intermediation, lending long-term funds to Europe in exchange for short-term deposits) as long as capital formation remains high in Europe. A moderate rise of interest rates in the United States will have only a small effect on the net capital outflow. A drastic rise might cut the net outflow substantially, but only by tightening money in *Europe* enough to stop economic growth; and this would cut America's current account surplus. Correcting the United States deficit by taxes and other controls on capital, which is being attempted on both sides of the Atlantic, is likely either to fail, or to succeed by impeding international capital flows so much as to cut European investment and growth.

4. While it is desirable to supplement gold with an internationally created reserve asset, the conventional analysis leading to this remedy concentrates excessively on a country's external liquidity; it takes insufficient account of the demands of savers for internal liquidity and of borrowers in the same country for long-term funds. The international private capital market, properly understood, provides both external liquidity to a country, and the kinds of assets and liabilities that private savers and borrowers want and cannot get at home. Most plans to create an interna-

tional reserve asset, however, are addressed only to external liquidity problems which in many cases, and especially in Europe today, are the less important issue.

With agreement between the United States and Europe—but without it if necessary—it would be possible to develop a monetary system which provided the external liquidity that is needed and also recognized the role of international financial intermediation in world economic growth.

Analytical support and elaboration of this minority view is presented in numbered sections, conforming to the propositions advanced above as an alternative to the consensus.

1. The idea that the balance of payments of a country is in disequilibrium if it is in deficit on the liquidity (U.S. Department of Commerce) definition is not appropriate to a country with a large and open capital market that is performing the function of a financial intermediary. Banks and other financial intermediaries, unlike traders, are paid to give up liquidity. The United States is no more in deficit when it lends long and borrows short than is a bank when it makes a loan and enters a deposit on its books.

Financial intermediation is an important function in a monetary economy. Savers want liquid assets; borrowers investing in fixed capital expansion are happier with funded rather than quick liabilities. Insofar as the gap is not bridged, capital formation is held down. Europeans borrow from the United States, and Americans are willing to pay higher prices for European assets than European investors will, partly because capital is more readily available in the United States than in Europe, but mainly because liquidity preference in Europe is higher and because capital markets in Europe are much less well organized, more monopolistically controlled, and just plain smaller than in the United States. With unrestricted capital markets, the European savers who want cash and the borrowers who prefer to extend their liabilities into the future can both be satisfied when the United States capital market lends long and borrows short and when it accepts smaller margins between its rates for borrowing short and lending short. European borrowers of good credit standing will seek to borrow in New York (or in the Euro-dollar market, which is a mere extension of New York) when rates of interest are lower on dollar loans than on loans in European currencies, or when the amounts required are greater than their domestic capital markets can provide. But when interferences prevent foreign intermediaries from bridging the gap, and when domestic private intermediaries cannot bridge it while the public authorities will not, borrowing possibilities are cut, and investment and growth are cut with it.

The effects are not confined to Europe, or even to the advanced countries. Slower European growth means lower demand for primary products imported from the less developed countries. Preoccupation of the United States, Britain, and now Germany with their balances of payments dims the outlook for foreign aid and worsens the climate for trade liberalization. And the American capital controls are bound to reduce the access of less developed countries to private capital and bond loans in the United States—and indirectly in Europe.

2. It may be objected that no bank can keep lending if its depositors are unwilling to hold its liabilities. True. But savings can never be put to productive use if the owners of wealth are unwilling to hold financial assets and insist on what they consider a more "ultimate" means of payment. If the bank is sound, the trouble comes from the depositors' irrationality. The remedy is to have a lender of last resort to cope with the effects of their attitudes or, better, to educate them or, if neither is possible, to make the alternative asset (which, against the dollar, is gold) less attractive or less available. To prevent the bank from pursuing unsound policies—if it really tends to do so—it is not necessary to allow a run on it. The depositors can have their say in less destructive ways, e.g., through participating in the management of the bank of last resort or through agreement on the scale of the financial intermediation.

The nervousness of monetary authorities and academic economists is a consequence of the way they define a deficit and the connotations they attach to it. No bank could survive in such an analytical world. If financial authorities calculated a balance of payments for New York vis-à-vis the interior of the United States, they would find it in serious "deficit," since short-term claims of the rest of the country on New York mount each year. If they applied their present view of international finance, they would impose restrictions on New York's bank loans to the interior and on its purchases of new bond and stock issues. Similarly, the balance of payments of the U.S. financial sector consists almost entirely of above-the-line disbursements and therefore nearly equal "deficits." Between 1947 and 1964 the liquid liabilities (demand and time deposits) of member banks of the Federal Reserve System alone increased from $110 billion to $238 billion. This increase of $128 billion, or 116 percent, was not matched by an equal absolute or even proportionate increase in cash reserves. Indeed, these reserves increased only $1.6 billion, or 8 percent. Yet nobody regards this cumulated "deficit" of over $136 billion as cause for alarm.

The private market has not been alarmed about the international position of the dollar in relation to other currencies or the liquidity of the United States. Although there has been private speculation in gold against the dollar, it has been induced largely by reluctance of some central banks to accumulate dollars. The dollar is the world's standard of value; the Euro-dollar market dominates capital markets in Europe; and the foreign dollar bond market has easily outdistanced the unit-of-account bond and the European "parallel bond." As one looks at sterling and the major Continental currencies, it is hard to imagine any one of them stronger than the dollar today, five years from now, or twenty years hence. Admittedly, short-term destabilizing speculation against the dollar is possible, largely as a consequence of errors of official and speculative judgment. It can be contained, however, by gold outflows and support from other central banks, or by allowing the dollar to find its own level in world exchange markets, buttressed by the combination of high productivity and responsible fiscal and monetary policy in the United States. In the longer run, as now in the short, the dollar is strong, not weak.

3. Since the U.S. "deficit" is the result of liquidity exchanges or financial intermediation, it will persist as long as capital movement is free, European capital markets remain narrower and less competitive than that of the United States, liquidity preferences differ between the United States and Europe, and capital formation in Western Europe remains vigorous. In these circumstances, an effort to adjust the current account to the capital outflow is futile. The deficit can be best attacked by perfecting and eventually integrating European capital markets and moderating the European asset-holder's insistence on liquidity, understandable though the

latter may be after half a century of wars, inflation, and capital levies.

An attempt to halt the capital outflow by raising interest rates in the United States either would have little effect over any prolonged period or else would cripple European growth. With European capital markets joined to New York by substantial movements of short-term funds and bonds, the rate structure in the world as a whole will be set by the major financial center, in this instance New York. Interest-rate changes in the outlying centers will have an impact on capital flows to them. Higher interest rates in New York will raise rates in the world as a whole.

The effort is now being made to "correct the deficit" by restricting capital movements. Success in this effort is dubious, however, for two reasons.

In the first place, money is fungible. Costless to store and to transport, it is the easiest commodity to arbitrage in time and in space. Discriminating capital restrictions are only partly effective, as the United States is currently learning. Some funds that are prevented from going directly to Europe will reach there by way of the less-developed countries or via the favored few countries like Canada and Japan, which are accorded access to the New York financial market because they depend upon it for capital and for liquidity. These leaks in the dam will increase as time passes, and the present system of discriminatory controls will become unworkable in the long run. The United States will have to choose between abandoning the whole effort or plugging the leaks. Plugging the leaks, in turn, means that it must either get the countries in whose favor it discriminates to impose their own restrictions or withdraw the preferences it now gives them. Accordingly, the choices in the long run are between no restrictions, restrictions on all outflows, and establishment of what is in effect a dollar bloc, or a dollar-sterling bloc, within which funds move freely but which applies uniform controls against movements to all non-bloc countries.

In the second place, it is not enough to restrain the outflow of United States-owned capital. As Germany and Switzerland have found, to keep United States funds at home widens the spreads between short-term and long-term rates in Europe and also the spreads between the short-term rates at which European financial intermediaries borrow and lend, and so encourages repatriation of European capital already in the United States. For Europe, this effectively offsets restrictions on capital inflows. "Home is where they have to take you in." It would be possible for the United States to block the outflow of foreign capital—possible but contrary to tradition. If this door is left open, the $57 billion of foreign capital in the United States permit substantial net capital outflows, even without an outflow of U.S. capital. Although it would require powerful forces indeed to induce foreign holders to dispose of most of their American investments, they might dispose of enough to permit the "deficit" to continue for a long time.

4. Capital restrictions to correct the deficit, even if feasible, would still leave unanswered a fundamental question. Is it wise to destroy an efficient system of providing internal and external liquidity—the international capital market—and substitute for it one or another contrived device of limited flexibility for creating additions to international reserve assets alone? In the crisis of 1963, Italy borrowed $1.6 billion in the Euro-dollar market; under the Bernstein plan it would have had access to less than one-tenth of the incremental created liquidity of say $1 billion a year, perhaps $75 million in one year—a derisible amount. It would be the stuff of tragedy for the world's authorities laboriously to obtain agreement on a planned method of providing international reserve assets if that method, through analytical error, unwittingly destroyed an important source of liquid funds for European savers and of loans for European borrowers, and a flexible instrument for the international provision of liquidity. Moreover, agreement on a way of creating additional international reserve assets will not necessarily end the danger that foreigners, under the influence of conventional analysis, will want to convert dollars into gold whenever they see what they consider a "deficit."

But, it will be objected, the fears of the European authorities about the dollar are facts of life, and the United States must adjust to them. Several points may be made by way of comment.

In the first place, the European authorities must be learning how much international trade in financial claims means to their economies, now that it has been reduced. Europe has discovered that liquidity in the form of large international reserves bears no necessary relationship to ability to supply savers with liquid assets or industrial borrowers with long-term funds in countries where financial intermediation is inadequately performed and which are cut off from the world capital market. Financial authorities in Italy, France, and even Germany have lately been trying to moderate the high interest rates which reflect strong domestic liquidity preference and the wide margins between the rates at which their intermediaries borrow and lend, as well as (in the case of Germany) their own policies. Having scant success in getting households, banks or private intermediaries to buy long-term securities, these authorities are increasingly entering the market themselves. Investment is declining: in Germany with long-term interest rates touching eight percent for the best borrowers, in Italy despite Bank of Italy purchases of industrial securities, and in France where government bonds are issued to provide capital to a limited list of industrial investors. It is ironic that United States firms seem able to borrow in Europe more easily than European firms, as they continue investing in Europe while abiding by their Government's program of voluntary capital restraint. Given their liquid capital strength in the United States, they have no objection to borrowing short, and command a preferred status when they choose to borrow long. But their operations in Europe put pressure on European long-term rates and enhance the incentive of other European borrowers and United States lenders to evade the restrictions.

Europe's own capital markets cannot equal that of the United States in breadth, liquidity, and competitiveness in the foreseeable future. Europe must therefore choose between an open international capital market using fiscal policy to impose any needed restraints, and use of monetary restraint with an insulated capital market. The second alternative involves serious dangers. Without substantial European government lending to industry, which is unlikely, the terms on which long-term money would be available may cause industrial stagnation.

The first choice is the more constructive one, but it can work only if its implications are understood in both Europe and the United States. The United States, too, has failed to appreciate the role of New York in the world monetary system and has acquiesced in the Continental view of the U.S. payments position. It must be recognized that trading in financial assets with the United States means a United States "deficit"; United States capital provides not only goods and services, but liquid assets to Europe, which means European acquisition of dollars. Moreover, the amount of dollars that private savers in Europe will want to acquire for transactions and as a partial offset to debts in dollars, and for other purposes, will increase. This increase in privately held dollars will involve a rising trend in the United States deficit on the Department of Commerce definition, though no deficit on the Bernstein Committee definition.

But that is not all. The new liquid saving in Europe which is matched by European borrowing in the United States is not likely to be held largely in dollars, and certainly will not be held entirely so. Savers typically want liquidity in their own currencies, and so do banks. If household and commercial banks want to hold liquid assets at home rather than securities or liquid assets in dollars, the counterpart of foreign borrowing by industry must be held by the central bank of their country in dollars, or converted into gold. This implies a deficit for the United States even on the Bernstein Committee definition.

Whether householders and banks want to hold dollars or their own national currencies, the effect is the same: both alternatives now frighten the United States as well as Europe. They should not. And they would not if it were recognized that financial intermediation implies a decline in the liquidity of the intermediary as much when the intermediation is being performed in another country as when it is being performed domestically. An annual growth in Europe's dollar-holdings averaging, perhaps, $1½ to $2 billion a year or perhaps more for a long time is normal expansion for a bank the size of the United States with a fast-growing world as its body of customers. To the extent that European capital markets achieve breadth, liquidity, and competitiveness, the rates of increase in these dollar holdings consistent with given rates of world economic growth would of course be lower than when these markets have their present deficiencies. But whatever rate of growth in these dollar holdings is needed, the point is that they not only provide external liquidity to other countries, but are a necessary counterpart of the intermediation which provides liquidity to Europe's savers and financial institutions. Recognition of this fact would end central bank conversions of dollars into gold, the resulting creeping decline of official reserves, and the disruption of capital flows to which it has led.

It must be admitted that free private capital markets are sometimes destabilizing. When they are, the correct response is determined governmental counter-action to support the currency that is under pressure until the crisis has been weathered. Walter Bagehot's dictum of 1870 still stands: In a crisis, discount freely. Owned reserves cannot provide for these eventualities, as International Monetary Fund (IMF) experience amply demonstrates. Amounts agreed in advance are almost certain to be too little, and they tip the hand of the authorities to the speculators. The rule is discount freely, and tidy up afterwards, transferring outstanding liabilities to the IMF, the General Arrangements to Borrow, or even into funded government-to-government debts such as were used to wind up the European Payments Union. Owned reserves or readily available discounting privileges on the scale needed to guard against these crises of confidence would be inflationary in period of calm.

Mutual recognition of the role of dollar holdings would provide the most desirable solution, but if, nevertheless, Europe unwisely chooses to convert dollars into gold, the United States could restore a reserve-currency system, even without European cooperation in reinterpreting deficits and lifting capital restrictions. The decision would call for cool heads in the United States. The real problem is to build a strong international monetary mechanism resting on credit, with gold occupying, at most, a subordinate position. Because the dollar is in a special position as a world currency, the United States can bring about this change through its own action. Several ways in which it can do so have been proposed, including widening the margin around parity at which it buys and sells gold, reducing the price at which it buys gold, and otherwise depriving gold of its present unlimited convertibility into dollars. The United States would have to allow its gold stock to run down as low as European monetary authorities chose to take it. If they took it all, which is unlikely, the United States would have no alternative but to allow the dollar to depreciate until the capital flow came to a halt, or, much more likely, until the European countries decided to stop the depreciation by holding the dollars they were unwilling to hold before. If this outcome constituted a serious possibility, it seems evident that European countries would cease conversion of dollars into gold well short of the last few billions.

This strategy has been characterized by *The Economist* as the "new nationalism" in the United States. It can reasonably be interpreted, however, as internationalism. It would enable the United States to preserve the international capital market and thereby protect the rate of world economic growth, even without European cooperation.

While United States-European cooperation in maintaining the international capital market is the preferable route, it requires recognizing that an effective, smoothly functioning international capital market is itself an instrument of world economic growth, not a nuisance which can be disposed of and the function of which can be transferred to new or extended intergovernmental institutions, and it requires abandoning on both sides of the Atlantic the view that a U.S. deficit, whether on the Department of Commerce or the Bernstein Committee definition, is not compatible with equilibrium. Abandonment of this view, in turn, requires facing up to the fact that the economic analysis of the textbooks—derived from the writing and the world of David Hume and modified only by trimmings—is no longer adequate in a world that is increasingly moving (apart from government interferences) toward an integrated capital and money market. In these circumstances, the main requirement of international monetary reform is to preserve and improve the efficiency of the private capital market while building protection against its performing in a destabilizing fashion.

The majority view has been gaining strength since 1958, when Triffin first asserted that the dollar and the world were in trouble. Between 1958 and 1965 world output and trade virtually doubled, the United States dollar recovered from a slight overvaluation, and the gold hoarders have foregone large earnings and capital gains. Having been wrong in 1958 on the near-term position, the consensus may be more wrong today, when its diagnosis and prognosis are being followed. But this time the generally accepted analysis can lead to a brake on European growth. Its error may be expensive, not only for Europe but for the whole world.

6

The United States as a Banker
for Europe?

ROBERT TRIFFIN

This essay is a brief examination of the thesis of Messrs. Despres, Kindleberger, and Salant, according to which the American deficits of the last few years reflect essentially the mutually advantageous and equilibrating function of financial intermediary imposed upon the United States by the structural inadequacy of European capital markets.

This thesis might appear somewhat suspect to the extent that it could be interpreted as an attempt to explain the present "dollar glut" as a structural and permanent phenomenon, just as the "dollar shortage" of yesteryear was interpreted by at least one of our three authors as an equally structural and permanent phenomenon. Yet, it should not be dismissed too lightly, and I am very gratified to be able to mark my agreement with Despres, Kindleberger, and Salant on a number of vital points of their analysis:

1. American investments in Europe are in part at least the reflection as well as the cause of the accumulation of liquid assets by Europeans in the United States.

2. "Money is fungible," and present restraints on exports of American capital are likely to be largely offset by withdrawals of foreign funds from the United States rather than to succeed in eliminating the global deficit in our payments abroad.

3. The intentional accumulation of liquid assets by European owners (and by owners elsewhere) could and should facilitate sound and noninflationary growth of real long-term investments in

Reprinted in this form by permission from Robert Triffin, *The Balance of Payments and Foreign Investment Position of the United States,* Essays in International Finance, No. 55 (Princeton: International Finance Section, 1966).

Europe (and elsewhere). The role of financial intermediary assigned in each country to the banking system should not be
blocked by national borders and by the right of some hundred
"monetary sovereigns" to liquidate at any time into gold metal
the current, and even past, balance-of-payments surpluses of their
respective countries.

4. The simple creation of a new monetary reserve instrument,
à la Bernstein (or similar CRU devices), would not in any way
solve this fundamental problem.

5. A "lender of last resort" is needed to reconcile the liquidity
preferences of individual savers with the relative immobilization
of productive investments. The right to liquidate *in gold*, at any
moment, the claims of the lender is neither the only nor the best
way to prevent the borrower from following unsound policies.
"The depositors can have their say in less destructive ways, e.g.,
through participating in the management of the bank of last
resort or [should we not read "and"?] through agreement on the
scale of the financial intermediation."

These numerous points of convergence between the analysis
and suggestions of Despres, Kindleberger, and Salant, on the one
hand, and my own, on the other, allow me to be all the more
candid about our divergences.

I regret to find neither in their *Economist* article, nor in other
parallel articles by the same authors on the same subject, even a
mere shadow of the abundant statistical documentation that
would enable them to support their thesis, and particularly to
make it more precise. Europe has become again—more precisely,
sometime in 1955—a net creditor of the United States. At the end
of 1964, Western Europe's assets in the United States exceeded its
liabilities by about $5.6 billion. Our three authors are right in that
this net position is the result of an excess of net short-term claims
($12.7 billion) over net long-term indebtedness ($7.1 billion). But
more than two-thirds of the gross claims of Europe on the United
States ($10.5 billion out of a total of $15.6 billion) correspond to
official rather than private assets and are overwhelmingly made up
of monetary reserves accumulated by central banks. The International Monetary Fund estimates at about $11.6 billion the for-
eign-exchange reserves of European central banks at the end of
1964. If we deduct from this amount the sterling assets of Euro-

pean monetary authorities ($0.9 billion according to the estimates published by the Bank of England), we arrive at a figure of $10.7 billion for their short-term dollar assets, except for their modest holdings of currencies other than dollars and sterling.

One may retain as a minimal estimate of official short-term dollar assets of Europe the estimate of the *Federal Reserve Bulletin*: $9.4 billion at the end of 1964, inclusive of "Roosa bonds." The *Survey of Current Business* never fails to point out that its statistical estimates of the dollar holdings of foreign commercial banks include substantial amounts of liabilities really held by foreign official institutions through foreign commercial banks, and foreign branches of American banks.

Private short-term European holdings in the United States are probably, therefore, substantially lower than the $5.1 billion registered in official statistics and do not finance more than a very modest fraction of private American investments in Europe ($19.5 billion) and particularly of long-term investments ($17.5 billion). These are, in any case, almost exactly offset by the long-term investments of Europe itself in the United States: $17.7 billion.

The role of financial intermediary of the United States would emerge, instead, between the net balance of *direct* investments ($6.2 billion in favor of the United States) and the net balance in favor of Europe of *other* long-term investments ($6.5 billion). The main explanation of this difference in the form of investment, however, lies probably in the fact that it is far easier for American capital to take a major participation in existing firms in Europe than for European capital to penetrate or emulate in the same fashion the usually much larger firms of the United States. As far as direct investment is concerned, the initiative certainly lies far more with the American investor than with any autonomous desire of Europeans to raise long-term funds in the United States, as is assumed by our three authors.

It is in the relations between the United States and the rest of the world that there appears, to no one's surprise, an enormous surplus ($40 billion) of American private long-term investments abroad ($47 billion) over foreign private long-term investments in the United States ($7 billion). It is only since 1960 that the yearly flow of American long-term private investments to Europe begins also to exceed similar flows of European investment to the United

States: but by only $0.8 billion per year, compared with a surplus of $2.5 billion in the relations between the United States and the rest of the world.

If one adds to these exports of private long-term capital from the United States our foreign-aid programs, economic and military, the average outflow to Europe totals about $1.4 billion, compared with $6.5 billion to the rest of the world. As for short-term capital flows, exclusive of foreign aid, inflows from Europe ($1 billion per year, overwhelmingly for the account of monetary authorities) exceed outflows (mainly on private account) by $0.7 billion, while inflows and outflows with the rest of the world are practically in balance ($0.9 billion in both directions).

What remains then of my colleagues' thesis that American deficits would hardly reflect any real imbalance, but would be due essentially to the sound and mutually advantageous role of financial intermediary imposed on the United States by the Europeans' preference for liquidity and their inability to procure at home the long-term funds necessary for the development of their domestic economies? The increase of short-term European assets in the United States is not more than about a billion dollars a year, on the average. This increase is due, for the largest part at least, to dollar accumulation by the monetary authorities, accepted by them, more and more reluctantly, only in order to ward off an international monetary crisis. These short-term inflows just about offset the net long-term investments of the United States in Europe. And these investments are undertaken far more at the initiative of the American firms themselves than in answer to borrowing requests from European firms. In any case, the overwhelming bulk of American investment ($2.5 billion net) and of military and economic aid abroad ($4 billion) continues to go, as is highly desirable, to other parts of the world.

My colleagues recognize that the thirst for liquidity of the private sectors of the European economy expresses itself very largely through holdings in their respective national currencies rather than in dollars. If this were not so, the intermediation between their supply of short-term funds (to be held in dollars) and their long-term borrowings (in dollars) would balance out anyway and could not be regarded as the cause of the deficits of the United States. (This is true, of course, only if the deficit is measured *à la* Bernstein, as I have done myself for many years. The traditional measure of the deficit [*à la* Lederer] of the *Survey of Current Business* would show a deficit, even then, because of the inclusion of short-term indebtedness to private foreign sectors.) The three authors defend their thesis, however, by including in the European demand for liquid assets the balances in national currencies acquired from their central banks against transfer to the central banks of the excess dollars supplied in the private market. "If households and commercial banks [I would add "and private firms"] want to hold liquid assets at home rather than securities or liquid assets in dollars, the counterpart of foreign borrowing by industry must be held by the central bank of their country in dollars, or converted into gold. This implies a deficit for the United States even on the Bernstein Committee's definition. . . . An annual growth in Europe's dollar-holdings averaging, perhaps, $1½ to $2 billion a year or perhaps more for a long time is normal expansion for a bank the size of the United States with a fast-growing world as its body of customers."[1]

Thus it appears that, in the view of the three authors, the real problem lies in the lack of comprehension, on the part of central bankers, of the function of the United States as a financial intermediary for Europe's savers and investors. If this function were better understood, European central banks would retain the dollars which they are asked to buy; the increase of their claims on the United States, at an annual rate of $1.5 to $2 million or more, would pose no problem either to the United States or to the rest of the world.

What should we think of this thesis?

Let us note first of all that it greatly exaggerates the role of financial intermediary of the United States between liquid savings and long-term borrowings in Europe itself. It would confer, or confirm, in addition a role of the United States as intermediary

---

[1] It should be noted, however, that this extension of the intermediation thesis to the dollars accumulated by foreign monetary authorities, rather than by the private sectors alone, seems to be defended mostly by Kindleberger. One of the co-authors of the joint article in the *Economist*, Walter S. Salant, expresses, in any case, considerable doubts about it in a footnote of his paper "Capital Markets and the Balance of Payments of a Financial Center," in Fellner, Machlup, Triffin *et al.*, *Maintaining and Restoring Balance in International Payments* (Princeton: Princeton University Press, 1966).

between Europe and the rest of the world—a role far larger and politically more pregnant, as I have shown above. There is not the slightest doubt that this is a correct description of what has happened in the past. The accumulation and retention of dollar reserves by European central banks has helped the United States finance its gifts and investments in the rest of the world far more than in Europe itself, and well beyond what this country could have done if Europe had accumulated its monetary reserves entirely in gold. I have stressed for too long a time in my own writings the problem of the gold shortage—and of the irrationality of its use as an exclusive instrument for reserve accumulation—not to be in full agreement with my colleagues as to the disastrous consequences that such a policy would inevitably entail.

This does not mean, however, that the dollar should, or even could, continue to provide central banks indefinitely with the bulk of the additional liquid assets indispensable to an optimum expansion of the world economy. It could do so only if European governments and central banks were willing to abandon to the political, monetary, and banking authorities of the United States their sovereignty over the management and use of their reserves—productive or not—both in Europe and in the rest of the world. It is hard to see how they could be willing to underwrite blindly in this fashion the future deficits of the United States, irrespective of their amounts and of the multiple and variegated causes of their emergence and continuance. Let us not forget that while European governments may view favorably our foreign-aid expenditures and development financing of the Third World, some of them may also take a dimmer view, for instance, our take-over of existing industrial enterprises in Europe or of our military escalation in Viet Nam. An alternative, though equally impracticable, solution would be for the United States to confer upon its European creditors a veto right on its own policies, internal as well as external, insofar as these may influence the increase of American dollar liabilities to European central banks.

Either one of these two solutions would imply a *surrender* of national sovereignty far more drastic than the modest *merger* of sovereignties proposed in the Triffin Plan, which is limited to the creation and management of the fiduciary reserves indispensable to a sound expansion of the international economy. The time has long come to protect the creation and distribution of international monetary reserves from the hazards of gold production and speculation, Russian gold sales on Western markets, American or British deficits, waves of confidence and distrust on the part of central banks in the future stability of the dollar and the pound, and pressures which various governments may wish to apply on American or British policies.

7

The Costs and Benefits of the U.S. Role as a Reserve Currency Country

ROBERT Z. ALIBER

The constraint on expansive economic policies imposed by persistent, large U.S. payments deficits and the consequent weakening of the U.S. international reserve position, when domestic unemployment has ranged between 5 per cent and 6 per cent, has raised concern about the costs and benefits of the U.S. reserve currency role.[1] Some critics argue that the reserve currency role limits the choice of U.S. policies to eliminate or reduce the payments deficit, and thus restricts the choice of measures to achieve full employment, more so than if the United States were not a reserve currency country.

The United States is a reserve currency country because foreign official institutions hold liquid dollar assets—Treasury bills, time and demand deposits, and banker's acceptances—as part of their international reserves. At the end of 1963, holdings of liquid dollar

Reprinted by permission of the publishers from *The Quarterly Journal of Economics*, August, 1964, pp. 442–456, Cambridge, Mass.: Harvard University Press, Copyright, 1964, by the President and Fellows of Harvard College.
[1] This issue was raised in Great Britain by A. C. L. Day, *The Future of Sterling* (Oxford: Clarendon Press, 1954). Day also discussed the issue in the United States in a paper submitted to the (Reuss) Subcommittee on International Exchange and Payments of the Joint Economic Committee in *International Payments Imbalances and Need for Strengthening International Financial Arrangements* (U.S. Government Printing Office, 1961), pp. 325–30. The issue was also examined before this Subcommittee in December, 1962, by George N. Halm, "Special Problems of a Key Currency in Balance of Payments Deficit" in *Factors Affecting The United States Balance of Payments* (Joint Economic Committee, 87th Congress, 2d Session), and in the testimony of Alan R. Holmes and Theodore Geiger in the Hearings before the Subcommittee, published in *Outlook for United States Balance of Payments* (U.S. Government Printing Office, 1963), pp. 152–62. See also William A. Salant, "The Reserve Currency Role of the Dollar, Blessing or Burden to the United States," *Review of Economics and Statistics*, XLVI (May, 1964).

assets by foreign official institutions totalled $10.8 billion, exclusive of the $1.6 billion held by international institutions.[2]

Foreign official institutions hold dollars as part of their international reserves for several different reasons—when they intervene in the exchange markets to keep the price of their currencies from deviating significantly from their official parities, they buy dollars and sell dollars against their own currencies. Most foreign countries, however, hold more than the minimum amount of dollars necessary for exchange market intervention and some hold much more.

International reserves may be held in a number of different assets; the major alternatives to holding reserves in the form of dollars are holdings of gold, or liquid assets denominated in other currencies. These assets have different risks, and they offer different advantages; gold offers no income while most currency assets do. The disadvantages of gold as a reserve asset include the loss of the interest available on most other reserve assets, the negative agio between the buying and selling prices of gold, and the risk that the price of gold might be reduced in terms of some currencies.[3] The disadvantages of holding reserves denominated in currencies other than the dollar include the susceptibility of these reserves to exchange controls or devaluation and the lack of adequate opportunities for liquid investments in most other countries.

The dollar became a reserve currency for several reasons—it ap

[2] Statistical data are from *International Financial Statistics*.

[3] In current circumstances this risk may seem slight. Monetary authorities, like any prudent investor, may take the precaution of diversifying their international reserves. Forty years ago, in somewhat different circumstances, Keynes suggested that the British were unwise to hold all their international reserves in gold. "Now that most countries have abandoned the gold standard, the supply of the metal would, if the chief user of it restricted its holdings to its real needs, prove largely redundant. The United States has not been able to let gold fall to its 'natural' value, because it could not face the resulting depreciation of its standard. It has been driven, therefore, to the costly policy of burying in the vaults of Washington what the miners of the Rand have laboriously brought to the surface . . . Nor must we neglect the possibility of a partial demonetisation of gold by the United States through a closing of its mints to further receipts of gold . . . Confidence in the future stability of the value of gold depends therefore on the United States being foolish enough to go on accepting gold which it does not want, and wise enough, having accepted it, to maintain it at a fixed value . . ." John Maynard Keynes, *A Tract on Monetary Reform*, (London; Macmillan, 1923), pp. 167–69.

peared stable in value and freely convertible, less subject to exchange depreciation or exchange controls than other currencies. New York offered a broad range of financial facilities for the short-term investment of reserve funds; large purchases and sales of liquid financial assets in New York could be effected without sizable change in their prices. No other financial market, except possibly that in London, offered comparable facilities. Sterling, however, appeared subject to the risks of both depreciation and of inconvertibility to a greater extent than the dollar. For the most part the U.S. reserve currency role developed in response to ability of U.S. financial facilities to meet the needs of other countries for a satisfactory way in which to hold their international reserves. Only in the last several years has the United States taken measures specifically intended to induce foreign official institutions to hold dollar assets.[4]

Foreign private parties and commercial banks held nearly $9 billion liquid dollar assets at the end of 1963.[5] Foreign private parties hold dollars for several reasons—yield, diversification, business convenience, tax avoidance, and exchange control evasion. Since foreign commercial banks are reluctant to carry a substantial position in a foreign currency for an extended period because of the risk of an exchange loss, even within the currency support limits, they generally hold dollars at someone else's risk—these banks may be the nominees of their government, or their central bank may make it financially attractive to hold dollar assets through forward-spot swap arrangements.[6] Some foreign commercial banks hold dollars as an offset to a short position in dollars; they may have commitments to sell dollars forward or loans out-

---

[4] Recent U.S. legislation excludes the income on Treasury bills earned by privately owned foreign central banks from the U.S. income tax. The dollar time deposits of foreign official institutions have been exempted from the maximum interest rate limitations of Regulation Q of the Federal Reserve Act.
[5] Foreigners hold a sizable volume of liquid dollar assets which are not reported in the statistics of foreign holdings because they are held through U.S. nominees.
[6] The dollar holdings of foreign official institutions are understated, while those of foreign commercial banks and private parties are overstated, perhaps by as much as $1–2 billion. From time to time the German and the Italian central banks have induced their commercial banks to hold dollars through various swap arrangements. And foreign central banks have been large suppliers of dollars in the Euro-dollar market.

standing payable in dollars. In some cases their dollar holdings may be the compensating balances on loans from U.S. banks. And these foreign banks may make short-term dollar investments, because of yield and diversification considerations.

The factors which induced foreign official institutions to acquire liquid dollar assets are among the same factors which induced nonofficial foreigners to acquire liquid dollar assets.[7] These nonofficial foreigners hold dollar assets primarily because the United States plays an important role in world trade and finance, and not because the United States is a reserve currency country. If the U.S. reserve currency role were supplanted by new international reserve-providing arrangments, nonofficial foreigners probably would continue to acquire and hold dollar assets for the reasons they now do, unless such holdings were limited or proscribed.

The Benefits of the U.S. Reserve Currency Role

The benefits of the U.S. reserve currency role include greater flexibility in financing U.S. payments deficits; increased U.S. income from larger purchases of foreign goods, services, and securities; and improved efficiency of the New York financial markets, as the competition for deposits of foreign official institutions has induced U.S. banks to extend more credit to foreigners.

The major advantage of the U.S. reserve currency role has been in financing U.S. payments deficits. The willingness of foreign official institutions to acquire liquid dollar assets is a partial substitute for large U.S. gold reserves, or for international credit lines. To the extent that foreign official institutions have settled their payments surpluses with the United States by acquiring liquid dollar assets, their demand for gold from the U.S. Treasury has been correspondingly reduced.[8] Between 1950 and 1963 inclusive foreign

---

[7] The larger the holdings of one group relative to U.S. gold reserves, the smaller the demand of other groups for dollar assets. But if foreign official institutions increased their holdings of gold and reduced their holdings of liquid dollar assets, the decline in U.S. gold stock might result in a decline in the dollar assets held by nonofficial foreigners, because the U.S. international reserve position would appear less secure.

[8] The extent of this advantage depends on which countries have the payments surpluses when the United States has a payments deficit. Great Britain, for

official institutions acquired over $8 billion of liquid dollar assets, and purchased less than $8 billion of gold from the U.S. Treasury.[9] If their demand for dollar assets had been smaller, U.S. gold reserves would have declined more rapidly, and stronger measures probably would have been necessary to reduce the U.S. payments deficit more quickly.[10]

The scope of the flexibility advantage to the United States, however, may be smaller than is suggested by the amount of liquid dollar assets acquired by foreign official institutions. This is because it appears that a part of the U.S. gold stock must be held as implicit "backing" against the liquid dollar assets owned by foreign official institutions. Nevertheless until the point is reached when the implicit gold backing requirement increases on a one-for-one basis with liquid dollar assets acquired by foreign official institutions, there is a net flexibility advantage. It does not appear that this point had been reached by the end of 1963.

The reserve currency role has enabled the United States to purchase more foreign goods, services and investments, and extend more foreign aid than would otherwise have been possible; the United States earns a "seigniorage" profit from this role. Two estimates are necessary in evaluating the magnitude of this advantage. The first is the extent to which U.S. purchases of foreign goods, services and securities have been larger than they otherwise would

---

example, has a marginal gold preference of nearly 100 per cent, while the comparable ratio for the other large gold-holding countries appears to be about 65 to 95 per cent. The advantage to the U.S. reserve position is smaller the higher the marginal gold preferences of the surplus countries, or if the surplus countries have low marginal gold preferences but hold their foreign exchange reserves in sterling.

[9] In the last several years the marginal gold preference of a number of countries appeared to decline, possibly in recognition that a continued strong demand for gold would weaken the stability of current international financial arrangements.

[10] Some observers may find the flexibility advantage a mixed blessing, since it may delay attention to the need to take measures to reduce a U.S. payments deficit. The position does not deny the flexibility advantage but rather implies that U.S. authorities are poorly equipped to make good use of it. Even if the United States were not a reserve currency country, it seems unlikely, despite the payments deficits of 1950–56, that the U.S. authorities would have become concerned with the U.S. payments deficit, in the sense that it influenced their decisions about monetary policy and fiscal policy, before the latter part of 1958 or the early part of 1959.

have been because foreign official institutions have acquired $8 billion of liquid dollar assets since the end of 1949. The second is the difference between the yield on the additional foreign assets acquired by the United States, and the yield on the dollar assets acquired by foreign official institutions. These estimates admittedly are crude and were developed to suggest the magnitude of the advantage and permit a judgment on its significance.

The United States must maintain somewhat larger gold stocks as a partial offset to increased foreign official holdings of dollars. Consequently, the net increase in U.S. purchases of foreign goods, services, and securities is somewhat smaller than purchase of $8 billion of dollar assets by foreign official institutions. It is assumed that the net increase in U.S. purchases of foreign goods, services, and securities is $6 billion.

The yield on the additional U.S. purchases of foreign goods, services, and investment can be only roughly estimated; both the composition of the marginal purchases and the yields on these marginal acquisitions are unknown. It is assumed that the average yield on marginal purchases is 10 per cent. It is further assumed that the foreign official institutions earn 3 per cent a year on their liquid dollar assets. On the basis of these assumptions, the income advantage would have been about $420 million in 1963, about .8 per cent of U.S. Gross National Product. If the yield on the additional marginal acquisitions was 20 per cent, then the income advantage would have been about $1 billion. The income advantage declines as the amount of the U.S. gold stock tied up as implicit backing for the dollar assets owned by foreign official institutions increases, and as the yield on liquid dollar assets increases.

While the income advantage is sizable in absolute terms, it appears small relative to the U.S. GNP, and even to the gap between the actual GNP and GNP at 4 per cent unemployment.[11] If the costs of being a reserve currency country are sizable in terms of the reduced freedom to devalue or the additional constraint on independent domestic economic policies, it seems extremely unlikely that the income advantage would be important enough to tip the balance in favor of remaining a reserve currency country.

[11] Whether the appropriate estimate is $4 million, $1 billion, or even $2 billion is relatively immaterial; the important conclusion is that in the array of considerations, the income advantage is small.

The Costs of the U.S. Reserve Currency Role

The possible costs of the reserve currency role include the constraint on independent domestic policies, the constraint on a successful U.S. devaluation, the burden of supplying reserves to other countries, and the burden of managing private gold markets. Those costs implicit in the reserve currency role should be distinguished both from those costs which have occurred because of the way in which the U.S. authorities have managed the reserve currency role, and from the costs to other countries of the U.S. reserve currency role.

The most important alleged cost of the U.S. reserve currency role is the reduced ability to pursue an independent monetary policy, especially when the United States is in a recession. It is asserted that if the United States follows a more expansive monetary policy, the decline in U.S. interest rates and the increase in credit availability might lead to a sizable outflow of foreign-owned liquid dollar assets, and result in inconveniently large U.S. gold losses.[12]

These U.S. gold losses might reflect conversion of existing dollar assets into gold by foreign official institutions. Or they might reflect shifts from dollars into foreign currencies or into Euro-dollar deposits by foreign official institutions or by foreign private parties. Shifts of private funds from New York to foreign financial centers do not immediately result in a drain on U.S. gold stocks. The dollars first are sold to foreign monetary authorities, who then may convert part or all of the increase in their dollar holdings into gold. The drain on the U.S. gold stocks associated with an outflow of funds is not likely to be so large as the amount of funds shifted,

---

[12] The United States might be subject to substantial gold losses, not because the United States has a payments deficit, but rather because countries which hold a large proportion of their reserves in dollars have deficits, while the countries with surpluses hold a small proportion of their reserve gains in dollars. Moreover this cause of a U.S. gold loss might occur when the United States has a payments deficit, while the surplus countries hold a small proportion of their reserve gains in dollars. While this combination of adverse circumstances is always a potential problem, it does not appear to have been especially troublesome for the United States. The British experience generally, but not always, has been that when the outer sterling area had a deficit with the non-sterling area, Great Britain had a surplus with the non-sterling area.

since only relatively few foreign official institutions (although some very important ones) convert 100 per cent of their reserve gains into gold.

Two empirical issues are involved in assessing this disadvantage —the first is whether the dollar holdings of foreign official institutions are sensitive either to changes in the absolute level of U.S. interest rates, or to changes in the differentials between U.S. interest rates and interest rates in other important financial centers. The general conclusion from recent empirical investigations is that foreign official institutions do not shift funds from dollar assets into gold, or into reserve assets denominated in other currencies, in response to changes in interest rates.[13] While some foreign central banks have shifted funds into the Euro-dollar market, these shifts appear to have been smaller than the increase in their dollar holdings as a result of their payments surpluses.

The second issue in assessing this alleged disadvantage is whether the shifts of private funds in response to interest differentials, or to changes in the interest differentials, are larger because of the overhang of official holdings of liquid dollar assets. The general conclusion from the empirical investigations is that changes in interest differentials do lead to shifts of private funds between New York and foreign financial centers.[15] Some private

[13] Gemmill concluded, "The examination of the practices of foreign countries has shown no evidence that official reserves are shifted from dollar assets to gold (or vice versa) in response to short-term variations in interest rates . . ." Robert F. Gemmill, "Interest Rates and Foreign Dollar Balances," *Journal of Finance*, XVI (Sept. 1961) 375–76. Cohen concluded, "Foreign official holders do not pay attention to interest rate considerations." Benjamin J. Cohen, "A Survey of Capital Movements and Findings Regarding Their Interest Sensitivity," published in *The United States Balance of Payments*, Hearings before the Joint Economic Committee (U.S. Government Printing Office, 1963), p. 193. Kenen concluded that gold preferences of the official institutions in other countries may be increasing, but he did not tie this change to changes in interest rate differentials. Peter B. Kenen, *Reserve Asset Preferences of Central Banks and Stability of the Gold Exchange Standard* (Princeton University Press, 1963).

[14] The empirical investigations lead to conflicting inferences about the magnitude of the shifts of private funds. Gemmill concluded, "Recent experience demonstrates that the volume of foreign private funds shifted abroad could be expected to be less than $1 billion." *Op. cit.*, p. 375–76. Bell concluded that for the shifts of U.S. short-term funds, "We have been unable to uncover evidence suggesting some sensitivity to interest rates in a number of cases, involving more than half of the $600–$800 million outflow . . . which can be considered as having an adverse effect on our balance of payments

funds, however, both U.S.-owned and foreign-owned, would be shifted from New York to foreign financial centers in response to changes in interest differentials even if the United States were not a reserve currency country. To demonstrate that the reserve currency role is a burden requires evidence that the shifts of private short-term funds are larger for each change in interest differentials because foreign official institutions hold liquid dollar assets as part of their international reserves. This proposition is not easily testable empirically.

However, if these private funds are interest-sensitive, it would seem that the shifts of short-term funds are reversible in direction. If this is the case, then other countries would also be subject to outflows of short-term funds when the interest differentials change in favor of the United States. These flows—in both directions—will be larger partly because the United States is a reserve currency country, and partly because Great Britain is a reserve currency country; the relevant issue is how much larger they are solely because of the U.S. reserve currency role.

The conflict between domestic policy objectives and international policy objectives appears to arise primarily because the New York financial market enables foreign and U.S. private parties to shift funds easily from dollar assets to foreign currency assets as U.S. interest rates fall relative to those abroad, and not because of the U.S. reserve currency role; these shifts would occur even if the United States were not a reserve currency country. The U.S. reserve currency role, however, may intensify the conflict if one of two conditions prevails—either if the sizable volume of dollar assets owned by foreign official institutions leads to a larger shift of private funds from New York to foreign financial centers for any change in international interest differentials, or if the outflow of private funds induces foreign official institutions to increase their

---

position." Philip W. Bell, "Private Capital Movements and the U.S. Balance of Payments Position," in *Factors Affecting the U.S. Balance of Payments, op. cit.,* pp. 395–482. Kenen concluded that there were close relationships between interest rates and shifts of both U.S.-owned and foreign-owned capital. See Peter B. Kenen, "Short-Term Capital Movements and the U.S. Balance of Payments," published in *The United States Balance of Payments, op. cit.* Cohen concluded, "A rise in U.S. rates relative to abroad might reduce private switching out of dollar assets by as much as $600 to $700 million a year, *op. cit.,* p. 193.

marginal gold preference above 100 per cent. Otherwise the U.S. reserve currency role will partially insulate the U.S. gold reserve from an outflow of private funds, since the demand for gold from foreign official institutions, in keeping with their customary reserve management practices, may be somewhat smaller than their reserve gains.

It is alleged also that the U.S. reserve currency role prevents a successful devaluation of the dollar relative to other currencies, because other countries would counter a U.S. devaluation with proportionate devaluations of their own currencies.[15] Devaluation by small countries is less likely to lead to competitive retaliation than is devaluation by larger countries. The relevant consideration is whether the reserve currency role further reduces the probability of a successful U.S. devaluation significantly below that which results from the importance of the United States in world trade and finance. This proposition also is not easily testable empirically.

The United States is so important in world trade that devaluations by other countries to counter a U.S. devaluation would reflect an unwillingness on their part to have their international competitive position become less favorable. Even if the United States were not a reserve currency country, there would be strong pressure on other countries to devalue in proportion to a U.S. devaluation to avoid a deterioration in their international competitive position.

In the circumstances of recent years, the U.S. surplus on current account has been large, even after deduction for U.S. military expenditures abroad and after adjustment for government financed exports. The U.S. payments deficit does not mean that the dollar is overvalued, but rather that it is not sufficiently undervalued so that the United States can generate a sufficiently large current account surplus to finance the capital outflow without a payments deficit. A U.S. devaluation would attempt to increase the undervaluation of dollar goods further so that U.S. capital outflows could be financed more easily. Some foreign countries

---

[15] "The second problem concerns the restriction which the key currency country suffers . . . it may not devalue its currency," Halm, *Factors Affecting the U.S. Balance of Payments, op. cit.,* p. 549. The proposition that the United States should not devalue the dollar because of the reserve currency role should be distinguished from the proposition that the United States cannot devalue the dollar, because of this role.

may prefer the additional commodities made available from their larger import surplus because of the contribution toward more rapid growth, even if it means giving up ownership of some of their financial assets to U.S. parties. But not many foreign countries appear likely to accept this choice.

The possible additional handicap to a U.S. devaluation attributable to the reserve currency role may arise because some countries may take a capital loss on the home currency value of their dollar assets if the U.S. dollar is devalued relative to their currencies. To avoid this loss, they might counter the U.S. devaluation with a proportionate devaluation of their own.

If this is the reason why the reserve currency role limits the ability of the United States to devalue, then it can be met in two ways. The first is by use of exchange guarantees so that the home currency value of the U.S. liabilities of the countries which do not devalue will not decline; the United States could finance all or part of the cost of the guarantees from U.S. gold revaluation profits. The second way that this alleged constraint on a U.S. devaluation from an offsetting devaluation by other countries to avoid the capital loss on their reserves is to have them also revalue gold upward, but by a somewhat smaller amount than the U.S. gold revaluation. In this way the profits from their gold revaluation would offset part or all of their losses on their dollar assets arising from a depreciation of the dollar in terms of their own currencies. No doubt it would be extremely difficult to negotiate the extent of the upward revaluation of gold in the United States and in other countries. But an increase in the U.S. gold price by more than the 10 or 15 per cent recently estimated to be necessary to achieve equilibrium in U.S. international payments would be a signal to other countries that they too should revalue their gold price upward.[16]

A further contention in support of the view that the reserve currency role limits the U.S. ability to devalue is that if the United States did devalue, the international payments system would be greatly disrupted and the international monetary system would suffer an extreme liquidity shortage. Hence the consequences are

---

[16] This estimate was made by Jaroslav Vanek, "Overvaluation of the Dollar: Causes, Effects, and Remedies," in *Factors Affecting the United States Balance of Payments.*

so severe that the United States will be dissuaded from devaluing. The first contention—that a devaluation of the dollar would be disruptive—is obviously true, but this would also be true even if the United States were not a reserve currency country. The second contention—that a devaluation would lead to a reserve stringency —is based on the premise that after a U.S. devaluation, all foreign official institutions would concentrate their international reserves in gold, in the hope that they might obtain revaluation profits from a subsequent devaluation. If the U.S. revaluation increases the dollar price of gold by 10 or 15 per cent, it seems unlikely that the possibility of this amount of gold revaluation profit at some indefinite time in the future would induce many countries to change their preferences among reserve assets. If the U.S. revaluation were larger, then the increase in the value of monetary gold stocks would more than swamp the consequences for international reserves of a shift into gold by countries which now do not hold gold as part of their reserves.

The capital loss constraint to a U.S. devaluation that results from the reserve currency role appears to be a relatively less important reason for offsetting devaluations by other countries than the deterioration in their competitive position that would result from a devaluation of the dollar. If a devaluation of the dollar were undertaken to reduce the overvaluation of dollar goods rather than to enhance the extent of their undervaluation, the capital loss constraint would assume relatively more importance. This constraint still could be circumvented by the measures suggested above.

Under current international financial arrangements the supply of international reserves is limited largely to the stock of gold monetized in official holdings, official holdings of dollars and sterling, and net credit positions on the International Monetary Fund. If an individual country wishes to increase its reserves, it must run a payments surplus. If it is successful, then its reserve gains will be reflected in a decline in the reserves of the nonreserve currency countries, an increase in the liquid liabilities or a reduction in the gold holdings of the reserve currency countries, or the absorption of newly produced gold.

The supply of monetary gold is relatively fixed, and the supply does not respond to changes in official demand. If the country which wishes to increase its reserves wants to hold its reserve gains in the form of gold, then the United States may be subject to a gold loss. In this situation the United States might also be subject to gold losses even if it were not a reserve currency country. If a country which wishes to increase its reserves is willing to hold its reserve gains in the form of dollar assets, the United States can make these dollar assets available by having a payments deficit. This may weaken the U.S. reserve position in the sense that the dollar holdings of foreign official institutions increase relative to the U.S. gold stock, and the weakening of the U.S. reserve position may lead the monetary authorities in some foreign countries to reduce the proportion of dollar assets in their reserves. In this sense the more the United States incurs payments deficits to help meet the reserve needs of other countries, the more vulnerable its own reserve position becomes. And if the U.S. payments deficit continues after the reserve needs of other countries have been satisfied, then at a time when the United States would most like them to add to their holdings of dollar assets they may prove most reluctant to do so.

The dilemma of the reserve currency arrangements is that the United States may not be able to supply the reserve needs of other countries without weakening its own reserve position.[17] The United States may adopt measures to reduce its payments deficit so that the U.S. reserve position will not be weakened while other countries still wish to add to their international reserves, either in the form of gold or dollar assets. That the reserve currency arrangements may not lead to the most appropriate rate of growth of reserves for other countries may prove unfortunate, but this is not properly a burden on the United States that makes it more difficult to achieve U.S. domestic objectives.

The United States has international objectives as well as domestic objectives; and if other countries are not able to obtain the

[17] Every banking institution faces a similar dilemma in that its risk position may weaken as its outstanding liabilities increase; an international central bank would be subject to a similar dilemma. The dilemma can be lessened by devising means to reduce the risk attached to the liabilities, through insuring these liabilities or through limiting the ability of those who hold these liabilities to convert them into gold. Most proposals for international central banks or for other types of international reserve-providing arrangements include both features. Both of these features could be incorporated into the reserve currency system, if the participants are willing, so that the United States could meet the reserve needs of other countries better and with smaller risk.

reserves they need, then they may not be able to pursue expansive domestic policies and may rely on restrictive import policies. It is desirable if international financial arrangements enable these other countries to increase their reserves at a more appropriate rate, without weakening the U.S. reserve position. There are a variety of international credit arrangements which might satisfy their reserve needs better than the existing arrangements now do, although the existing arrangements might be modified to satisfy this need better. Some of these credit arrangements might meet this U.S. international objective, but at the possible cost of making it more difficult for the United States to finance its payments deficits in the future.

Another alleged disadvantage of the reserve currency role is the U.S. responsibility for the management of private gold markets, with the consequent strain on U.S. gold reserves. The London gold market is essentially a dollar market; buyers of gold must pay in dollars, while sellers of gold receive dollars. As the demand for gold increases above the new supply available to the market from current production and other sources, the dollar price of gold increases. To limit and prevent disruptive increases in the gold price may require that the authorities supply gold to the market if the increase in demand cannot be checked. No foreign country, including Great Britain (as the October, 1960, gold flurry indicated), is likely to attempt to support private gold markets on its own, unless it feels assured that it can replenish its gold stocks from the U.S. Treasury. Directly or indirectly the burden of supporting the London gold market falls on the U.S. authorities.

Even if the United States were not a reserve currency country, the burden of supplying gold to the London market would still fall on the United States as long as the United States wishes to maintain the gold parity of the dollar for private transactions. The United States gains relief from this burden only if other gold holding countries prove willing to reduce the proportion of gold in their reserves, and increase the proportion of dollars in their reserves in response to an increase in the private demand for gold.[18]

The advantage of additional flexibility in financing the U.S. pay-

[18] Under the "gold pool" arrangement for the London gold market, other countries assist the United States in supplying gold to meet the private demand, at least on a temporary basis. See *Monthly Bulletin*, Federal Reserve Bank of New York, March, 1964.

ments deficit appears to have outweighed the various costs which can be attributed to the U.S. reserve currency role. While the additional income advantage has not been insignificant by some standards, it appears extremely unlikely that it is anywhere near large enough to tip the scales if the costs should outweigh the advantage of greater flexibility.

The opposite conclusion—that the costs of the U.S. reserve currency role have outweighed the advantages—might prevail if foreign official institutions shifted funds between New York and other international financial centers in response to higher interest rates abroad, or if these institutions bought gold in response to a decline in U.S. interest rates, or if the shifts of funds by private parties were substantially greater for any interest differential because of the sizable volume of dollar assets owned by foreign official institutions, or if the likelihood of offsetting devaluations by other countries was substantially increased as a result of the capital loss on the home currency value of their dollar assets. The evidence does not support the contention that foreign official institutions have shifted significant amounts of their reserves from dollar assets into other assets in response to changes in interest rates. Large shifts of interest-sensitive private funds, both U.S.-owned and foreign-owned, would have occurred even if the United States were not a reserve currency country. While the proposition that the shifts of private funds are larger because of the reserve currency role is not testable, it seems likely to be significant only when suspicions develop about the maintenance of the gold or exchange parities of the dollar. The contention that the reserve currency role would have made it more difficult for the U.S. authorities to devalue the dollar successfully also is not testable, although the capital-loss justification for a retaliatory devaluation by other countries appears much less important for recent years than a justification based on the resulting deterioration in their international competitive position from the further undervaluation of dollar goods.

The major constraint on the choice of domestic policy attributed to the reserve currency role, the sensitivity of short-term funds to changes in interest differentials, is a disadvantage that the United States would have encountered even if it had not been a reserve currency country. The causes of this disadvantage—the depth and breadth of U.S. financial markets, and the importance of the United States in international trade and finance—are factors which led to the development of the United States as a reserve currency country, and which appear likely to prevail even if the United States ceases to be a reserve currency country. If U.S. monetary policy had been more expansive in recent years, the U.S. payments deficit would have been larger, partly because of increased imports, and partly because of increased outflow of short-term funds.[19] Indeed the reserve currency role may have ameliorated this disadvantage, since U.S. gold losses have tended to be smaller than the outflow of short-term funds.

In recent years, nevertheless, the choice of domestic U.S. economic policies has been constrained by their consequences for the U.S. balance-of-payments position and the U.S. reserve position. The flexibility advantage of the U.S. reserve currency role has eased the conflict, but it has not eliminated the conflict. Alternative international credit arrangements, however, also might have resulted in large flows of credit from foreign countries to the United States, perhaps even in larger amounts than the credit extended the United States under the reserve currency role if they had been in existence, but they were not in existence.

That the United States has obtained net advantages from the reserve currency role in the past does not mean that the benefits will continue to exceed the costs in the future. Nor does it mean that the advantages to the United States might not have been larger under alternative arrangements for meeting international reserves needs. But there may be a significant gap between the optimal and the attainable international credit arrangements, and the combination of benefits and costs under the latter may prove less advantageous to the United States than under a strengthened reserve currency role.

[19] Those who contend that the cost of the reserve currency role have exceeded the benefits are obliged to answer the questions of how the U.S. payments deficit would have been financed or how it would have been reduced if the United States were not a reserve currency country.

8

The Reserve Currency Role of the Dollar: Blessing or Burden to the United States? [1]

WILLIAM A. SALANT

Since Professor Triffin launched his plan five years ago, the international liquidity problem has been the subject of vigorous discussion. The debate will probably reach a climax this year aná next when the IMF and the Group of Ten complete their studies of the subject.

Some proposals for international monetary reform would retain the role of the dollar as the principal reserve currency, perhaps strengthening it by further building up what Under Secretary Roosa has called its "perimeter defenses." Others envisage that the dollar would share that role with other currencies, as in the Posthuma and Lutz plans, or with a new international unit which would represent a claim against the International Monetary Fund, as in the proposals advanced by Chancellor of the Exchequer Maudling in 1962 and by E.M. Bernstein in 1963. Finally, Triffin's original plan would transfer the reserve currency function outright from national currencies to an international unit.[2]

Reprinted in this form by permission of the publishers from The Review of Economics and Statistics, May, 1964, pp. 165–172, Cambridge, Mass.: Harvard University Press, Copyright, 1964, by the President and Fellows of Harvard College.

[1] This paper owes a special debt to Robert Z. Aliber's article entitled "The Costs and Benefits of the U.S. Role as a Reserve Currency Country," published in the Quarterly Journal of Economics, because it was largely stimulated by reaction to Aliber's article.

[2] R. V. Roosa, "The Beginning of a New Policy," remarks addressed to a meeting of the American Bankers Association in Rome, May 17, 1962, reprinted in Subcommittee on International Exchange and Payments of the Joint Economic Committee, Factors Affecting the United States Balance of Payments, 1962, p. 327; S. Posthuma, "The International Monetary System," Banca Nazionale del Lavoro Quarterly Review, Sept., 1963; F. Lutz, The Problem of International Liquidity and the Multiple-Currency Standard, Princeton Essays in International Finance, No. 41, Mar., 1963; R. Maudling

Most of the discussion has centered around the relative merits of the different plans in providing adequate, effective, and stable arrangements for supplying international reserves and settling international balances—and rightly so, since this is clearly the crucial issue. A subsidiary question, which has recently received some attention in the United States and has been discussed for some time in the United Kingdom, is whether a country gains or loses by having its currency used as an international reserve by other countries. This question is closely related to the central issue, and is also of particular interest to the reserve currency countries. It is the subject of the present paper. Space limitations make it necessary to confine the discussion to one aspect of the question.[3]

The Gain in Flexibility

The principal advantage that the United States is said to gain from the use of the dollar as a reserve currency is greater "flexibility." "Flexibility" in this context arises from the fact that deficits can be financed in part through increases in the dollar reserves held by foreign monetary authorities. To the extent that they are financed in this way, a given deficit will be associated with a smaller loss of gold than would otherwise be the case, or, to stand the same point on its head, with a given gold reserve, the United States can afford to run a larger cumulative deficit than would otherwise be possible.[4]

in International Monetary Fund, *Summary Proceedings of the Seventeenth Annual Meeting of the Board of Governors*, Sept., 1962, pp. 63–68; E. M. Bernstein, "A Practical Program for International Monetary Reserves," *Quarterly Review and Investment Survey*, 4th Quarter, 1963; R. Triffin, *Gold and the Dollar Crisis* (New Haven: Yale University Press, 1960).

[3] This issue was discussed briefly in the Brookings report on the balance-of-payments, of which the writer is a co-author. See Walter S. Salant, *et al.*, *The United States Balance of Payments in 1968* (Brookings Institution, 1963), 257. The present note can be regarded as an elaboration of that discussion. In it, however, the writer speaks only for himself and not for the other authors of the Brookings report.

[4] The gain in flexibility has been cited by Roosa and Alan Holmes of the Federal Reserve Bank of New York in their statements to the Reuss Subcommittee of the Joint Economic Committee (see *Outlook for United States Balance of Payments*, Hearings before the Subcommittee on International

This flexibility entails two advantages. First, it means that the United States has more time and scope to deal with a payments deficit, and thus has increased freedom to resort to slower acting but more constructive remedies rather than harsh and restrictive ones. By the same token, it can take greater risks in adopting economic policies that might have adverse effects on the balance-of-payments.

The second advantage is that the inflow of foreign reserve balances places additional resources at the disposal of the United States, which, if not invested in larger gold reserves, can be used to finance additional net purchases of goods and services, additional foreign lending, or additional foreign aid. This advantage is distinctly secondary, and we shall not consider it further.

The Cost in the Form of Constraints on Policy

As long as foreign monetary authorities hold large reserves in the form of dollars without any commitment to keep them in that form, withdrawal or reduction of these balances is always possible.

Exchange and Payments of the Joint Economic Committee (Dec. 12, 13, and 14, 1962), pp. 119, 154), by Aliber in the article cited above, and by others. Aliber points out, however, that the gain is reduced to the extent that the United States feels obliged to hold higher gold reserves because of its short-term liabilities to foreigners. Alternatively, one might say that it is reduced to the extent that the United States is sensitive to changes in its net liquidity position, as measured by the payments deficit as defined by the Department of Commerce, rather than simply to gold losses.

Jacques Rueff considers the freedom afforded to a reserve-currency country to run larger deficits over a longer period as a serious danger rather than an advantage, both to it and to the world. According to Rueff, it allowed the United States to live for a time in a fool's paradise in which it could ignore the deficit, oblivious of the fact that the day of reckoning, though postponed, would be all the harsher when it came. See J. Rueff, "The West Is Risking a Credit Collapse," *Fortune*, July, 1961, p. 126.

Looking at the matter from the other side of the street, French Finance Minister Giscard regards the lack of reciprocity in access to credit as a defect of the reserve-currency system. While reserve-currency countries can easily obtain credit when they are in deficit, they, ". . . might not accumulate so readily the currencies of their new debtor . . ." if the payments situation should be reversed. See the statement by V. G. D'Estaing in International Monetary Fund, *Summary Proceedings of the Eighteenth Annual Meeting of the Board of Governors*, Sept. 30–Oct. 4, 1963, p. 61.

The principal cost imposed on the United States by its position as a reserve center arises from this possibility. Unless accompanied by a surplus in the United States balance-of-payments, a reduction in foreign balances will drain gold from the United States. A large enough drain would free, or at least threaten, either the suspension of gold payments or an increase in the selling price of gold, that is, a devaluation of the dollar against gold in one form or another.

Because of the role of the dollar as a reserve currency, devaluation would have particularly serious consequences. It is argued by some that, quite apart from any moral obligation to foreign holders of dollars, devaluation must be ruled out entirely because it would disrupt the world payments system and lead to worldwide deflation. Thus, it is said the United States is denied a possible remedy for payments deficits that is open to all nonreserve-currency countries, while at the same time it is exposed to special risks. Others, while not ruling out devaluation categorically, would agree that the position of the United States as a reserve center and as an international money and capital market, as well as the leading trading country, make it a step that could be considered only as a very last resort.

Thus, it is argued, the United States must follow policies which will induce foreign monetary authorities to retain their dollar reserves and, if the United States is in payments deficit, increase them if possible. Such policies, however, may be undesirable on other grounds. In particular, if aggregate demand is deficient, policies designed to expand activity may be inhibited because they entail some danger of inflation and payments deficits, or may be thought by foreign holders of dollar balances to do so.[5]

[5] For a statement of the position that devaluation is out of the question for the United States, see G. Halm, "Special Problems of a Key Currency Country in Balance of Payments Deficit," in *Factors Affecting the United States Balance of Payments*, cited above, p. 546–547. Halm argues further that a reserve-currency country is inhibited in following policies aimed at high levels of employment and rates of growth not because such policies are necessarily inflationary, but rather because they ". . . may easily expose [a country] to inflationary pressures, . . . and . . . lead to balance-of-payments difficulties." The usual escape from such difficulties, devaluation, is not open to a reserve-currency country. (See pp. 549–550). In other words, a reserve-currency country cannot sail as close to the wind as others because the consequences of miscalculation are potentially too serious. The policy constraint is also

The contention that the reserve currency role of the dollar imposes a constraint on the United States appears to clash head on with the claim that it provides the United States with flexibility by giving it more time to deal with deficits and thus greater latitude in its policy options. It would appear that, if one argument is right, the other must be wrong.

In fact, either can be valid depending on the time and circumstances. Borrowing allows a person, or a country, to spend in excess of its receipts (from sources other than the proceeds of loan). The obligation to repay debt, an unwelcome if sometimes inescapable product of past borrowing, may force expenditure (apart from debt repayment) below receipts. If a country performs international banking functions and its debt takes the form of deposits payable on demand, its customers' decisions whether to increase or decrease their deposits may determine whether it borrows or repays short-term debt.[6] These decisions depend largely on the depositors' views as to the attractiveness of the reserve currency as compared with alternative reserve assets.

Until about 1958, the position of the dollar was thought to be impregnable. Payments deficits were moderate and thought to be temporary, the dollar was still the only major convertible currency apart from the Swiss franc, foreign balances were small, though growing, and the United States gold stock remained close to its peak level. Consequently, foreign holders did not hesitate to increase their dollar balances.

Payments deficits aggregated just over $10 billion in the period 1950–1956. Almost half of this amount was financed by a build-up of official dollar holdings, about one-quarter by an increase in private balances, and one-quarter by gold sales. Its position as an international banker enabled the United States to borrow ". . . in

---

emphasized by Theodore Geiger's statement before the Reuss Subcommittee in the 1962 Hearings on the *Outlook for United States Balance of Payments* cited above, p. 165, and by Harry Johnson in his statement to the same Subcommittee in *International Payments Imbalances and Need for Strengthening International Finance Arrangements*, Hearings, May 16, June 19–21, 1961, p. 204.

[6] This compressed statement is designed to establish that the decisions of foreign depositors determine whether an international bankers' liabilities rise or fall. It should not obscure the fact that throughout the period when its banking debts were rising, the United States continued to run a surplus on current account, although the balance of all payments was in deficit.

almost an imperceptible fashion, without the necessity of arranging and negotiating loans as other borrowers must do."[7] In this period, the reserve currency role provided flexibility without imposing constraint.

Since 1958, United States deficits have run at a higher level, the major European currencies have been made convertible, foreign dollar balances have risen greatly, and the United States gold stock has fallen by one-third. The withdrawal of foreign balances, including official reserve holdings, has, at least intermittently, been a subject of real concern.

The published figures do not, in fact, reveal any net withdrawal of official balances except for very brief periods. The published figures, however, do not tell the full story. It is generally believed that some of the largest official holders of dollars have continued to add to their balances not because they wanted more dollars, but because they felt that the stability of the world payments system, and therefore the security of their own previous accumulations, required them to do so. Furthermore, the United States Government has held down the deficit by arranging for advance repayments on debts owed by European governments and advance payments on military sales to Germany and perhaps other countries. In addition, it has borrowed from a number of European governments and central banks in their own currencies. All of these devices reduced the need for settlement by gold sales or increases in dollar reserve holdings.

Of a cumulative deficit of $18 billion in 1958–1963, $7 billion, or 40%, was financed by gold sales. Foreign official balances increased by about $5 billion, private balances by the same amount, and dollar holdings of international institutions, primarily the IMF, by about $1 billion.[8]

While the United States gained flexibility in the earlier period

[7] See Roosa's statement to Joint Economic Committee in *Outlook for United States Balance of Payments*, cited above, p. 119. Figures are based on Brookings report, cited above, Table I-2, p. 10.

[8] Based on 1958 to 1962 figures from the Brookings report cited previously, Table I-2, and preliminary 1963 figures from various sources, partly estimated. Increase in U.S. subscription to the IMF is excluded from all figures. The increase in official dollar holdings is somewhat understated because it does not include official holdings of Euro-dollars, which are believed to have increased substantially.

through its role as a reserve currency center, and also as a center for private balances, the constraints imposed by that role have become increasingly tighter in the later period, and have probably become dominant.

International Constraints and Domestic Policy

A number of arguments can be made against the proposition that the pressure to retain foreign reserve balances has inhibited the adoption of policies best suited to promote full employment and growth. We shall summarize and evaluate them briefly, while trying not to become too involved in the complex problem of the relation between internal and external policy objectives.

First, it can be argued that international considerations have imposed no undue constraints on the pursuit of domestic objectives, and that the policies followed have been appropriate to those objectives.[9] This is not the place to discuss the merits of domestic policies. I shall merely state my own view that domestic objectives have often called for more active policies of expansion than those actually followed from 1958 to 1963.

Second, it can be argued that, while domestic expansion has not been pursued with sufficient vigor, the reason lies not in international constraints but in other causes. It can be argued persuasively, for example, that because of a cultural lag, both the responsible policy-makers and the public were still unduly concerned about inflation long after the real problem was inadequate demand. While this may have been true up to a certain point, it ceased to be true in recent years.

Critics who feel that central bankers have a chronic deflationary bias would argue that, in the absence of international pressures, the Federal Reserve authorities would have found other reasons

[9] It has also been argued that the monetary authorities have created an inflationary excess of liquidity in the United States. According to this argument, which is associated particularly with John Exter, this excess liquidity has spilled over into an excess of external spending over receipts, and is thus responsible for the payments deficit. In the absence of this external outlet, it would have manifested itself in the form of inflationary price rises in the United States. See especially Exter, *The Gold Losses* (First National City Bank, 1962).

for keeping the monetary screws too tight, or for tightening them too soon in the cycle.

As regards fiscal policy, Gardner Ackley has maintained that expansionist measures have been delayed, not by international constraints, but rather by the prevalence of irrational inhibitions against budget deficits.[10] I have no disposition to quarrel with this interpretation of recent fiscal policy. Nevertheless, it does not dispose of the fact that, in the absence of international constraints, monetary policy might have been used more actively to promote expansion, leaving less of the burden to fiscal policy.

Third, it is often argued that while international considerations have constrained the standard methods of applying the conve .- tional instruments of economic policy to domestic objectives, policy makers have refined both the tools and their application so as to evade these constraints. (This argument is a special form of the first one, noted above, that policy has in fact been appropriate to domestic objectives.) The argument applies primarily to the "twist" in monetary policy and to the use of the appropriate mix of fiscal and monetary policies, and secondarily to special measures designed to influence the international flow of capital, such as intervention in the foreign exchange market, higher rates on time deposits, and the proposed interest equalization tax on income derived from foreign securities.

As to the "twist," it is all to the good that the Federal Reserve authorities have discarded their self-imposed limitation to "bills only," and now feel free to extend open market operations to the entire maturity range of government securities. Nevertheless, the "twist" cannot be effective beyond certain limits. Communication between the sectors of the capital markets limits the differential between long- and short-term yields. Furthermore, while international capital movements are no doubt more sensitive to short-term than to long-term rates, the latter also have an impact, as is indicated by the fact that the Treasury felt it necessary to request the interest equalization tax.

Inhibitions on the use of fiscal policy, already referred to, are all too evident, notably in causing the long delay in passage of

[10] G. Ackley, "The Economic Policies of the Kennedy Administration," address before Midwest Economics Association, April 26, 1963, processed, pp. 16–20.

the tax reduction bill, which was introduced in the beginning of 1963 and might well have been submitted half a year earlier if the climate of opinion had been considered more receptive. Fiscal policy is not yet a sufficiently flexible instrument in this country to be relied on as the principal short-term regulator of aggregate demand. Thus it is not often possible to obtain the mix between fiscal and monetary policy which could best reconcile domestic and international objectives.

Moreover, there are domestic objectives other than the level of aggregate demand which should be allowed to affect the mix. Tight money and a loose budget produce a different composition of demand than easy money and a tight budget. A policy of encouraging investment in the interest of growth through low interest rates, as advocated by some, conflicts directly with the international objective of attracting capital through relatively high interest rates accompanied by more expansionist fiscal policy.[11] Furthermore, at the cost of conceding too much to popular mythology, I would also maintain that there is an optimal rate of expansion of public debt which should also play a role, albeit a subordinate one, in determining the fiscal-monetary mix.

The possibilities of gaining greater freedom of action by innovations in technique have not necessarily been exhausted. Among the devices that have been proposed toward toward this end, the one that is most relevant to the reserve currency role of the dollar is the guarantee of the gold or foreign exchange value of official dollar balances against devaluation.

Last, some would concede that international considerations have constrained domestic economic policy, but would deny that the reserve currency role of the dollar bears a major responsibility for this constraint. Instead, they would place the onus mainly on the balance-of-payments deficit, the position of the United States as a private money and capital market, and the freedom of Americans to export their capital.

It is said, for example, that the international constraint arises in

---

[11] P. A. Samuelson, "Fiscal and Financial Policies for Growth" in American Bankers Association, A *Symposium on Economic Growth*, Feb. 27, 1963, pp. 97–99, and J. Tobin, "Economic Progress and the International Monetary System," in *Domestic and International Financial Policies of the United States*, Proceedings of the Academy of Political Science, May, 1963, p. 85.

great part from the possibility of short-term capital outflows in response to interest rate incentives. Since the evidence indicates that official dollar holdings are not sensitive to interest rates, their presence does not create a problem, although private balances, which are interest sensitive, may do so.[12]

This argument, it seems to me, is based on a misconception of the nature of the problem. The problem is not that official balances might be shifted to other money markets because of a change in yield differentials, or converted into gold because an absolute decline in interest rates makes the added safety of gold more attractive than the reduced yield obtainable on dollar assets. It is rather that the confidence of official holders of dollar balances in the ability of the United States to maintain the relation between the dollar and gold and other currencies may diminish. Such a loss of confidence might be associated either with adverse developments directly affecting the balance of payments, or with official holders' estimates of the possibility of inflation in the United States. Expansionist economic policies increase the possibility of inflation, or at any rate are commonly thought to do so. It is for this reason, rather than because of any direct effect on yields of easier monetary policies, that domestic expansion may be constrained by the fear of withdrawal of foreign reserve balances. In short, any danger would arise because changed expectations as to the possibility of inflation would shift the schedule of foreign asset holding preferences, not because changed yields would give rise to marginal changes in holdings of dollar assets associated with shifts along unchanged preference schedules.

It is impossible to assess the relative importance of the reserve currency role of the dollar as compared with other external factors in limiting the freedom of policy makers to pursue domestic economic objectives. The size of foreign dollar reserves, and the availability of gold as an alternative form in which to hold reserves, suggest that the contingency of a reduction in the reserves can never be far from the minds of responsible officials in the United States. On the other hand, large depositors in a bank are inhibited from reducing their balances by the knowledge that their actions may set off a run by other depositors, thus endangering the safety

[12] This argument is advanced by Aliber in the article cited above.

of their own remaining balances and, in the case of the dollar, causing a breakdown of the entire international monetary mechanism.

This inhibition has given rise to considerable self-restraint on the part of official holders of dollar balances, and is in part responsible for the consultation, cooperation, and mutual support that have developed in recent years. These in turn have further reduced the likelihood of withdrawals. At the same time, they have brought the domestic economic policies of the United States under formal review (in the Economic Policy Committee of OECD), a fact which has both advantages and disadvantages from the point of view of securing greater freedom of action. It is questionable how long the spirit of interdependence and cooperation would continue if important foreign monetary authorities became convinced that the United States was following unsound policies, but the United States now has a forum in which it can explain and justify its policies.

It would be hard to arrive at a consensus on the question whether constraints associated with the reserve currency function have hampered the pursuit of other policy objectives. Differences of opinion on this question arise partly from disagreement as to the goals of policy and the means of pursuing them, partly from differences as to the interpretation of the course of events; it is especially true of contemporary history that every man is, to a large extent, his own historian.

My own views can be summed up as follows: Policies of economic expansion have been pursued with insufficient vigor and boldness. While other factors have hampered the adoption of more active policies, inhibitions associated with concern about the balance-of-payments deficit and the international position of the dollar have played a significant part, especially with respect to monetary policy. Use of refined techniques and selective controls has somewhat softened the conflict between the internal and the external objectives of policy, but has fallen far short of resolving it. The reserve currency function of the dollar is responsible for a significant part of the constraint due to international factors.

9

International Politics and Dollar Policy

WILLIAM D. GRAMPP

The purpose of dollar policy is, I suggest, mainly political: to use the dollar as an emblem of United States power and also as an instrument of power itself by creating a financial network that enables the U.S. to influence the decisions of other governments. My view is different from that of most economists. They analyze the effects of the policy on the economic, not the political, position of the U.S. and the effects on the world's monetary system rather than on the distribution of political power among nations. Their analysis implies the purpose of dollar policy is economic, or ought to be. But if the purpose is actually political, their analysis is beside the point. Some economists do say the U.S. is using the dollar to secure prestige, but then briskly dismiss the point as irrational or of no consequence. Their analysis does not so much miss the point as refuse to consider it.

One of the noticeable features of the debate over the dollar is the fact that more has been said by economists than by anyone else (than by bankers or political analysts, for example), and yet what they have said seems to have had little effect on the making of policy. If policy does change, and there are some faint signs that it may, the reason probably will be political and will not be the massive criticism that economists have directed at the government.

To say the purpose of policy is political does not mean that what the government is doing may, after all, be more sensible than it seems. To believe the government is acting properly (which I do not believe it is), we first must believe the dollar is capable of being used politically, and that it should be so used. Whether or

Reprinted by permission from *Challenge*, The Magazine of Economic Affairs, a publication of Challenge Communications, Inc., February, 1965, pp. 20–23.

not it should be is a difficult question to modern economists. Their forebears of the classical school, one may recall, were not troubled by the question at all. They always put national power before national wealth, or said they did. But fortunately for ourselves, the question may not have to be answered. It may be set aside if we believe the circumstances are no longer present that make the political use of the dollar feasible. There are two of them, and in fact they do not appear to be present. One is that the American economy must dominate the world in the sense that no other currency can rival the dollar as an international reserve, and the other is that the U.S. be the dominant political power so that its decisions will prevail over those of its allies.

These two conditions were present, and with great force, between the end of World War II and the start of the Korean war. The United States had a monopoly of nuclear weapons for most of that time, and for all of it the military power of the U.S. was supreme. There were, to be sure, many political differences between the U.S. and the non-Communist countries, but in the end it was the American view that prevailed in major questions. The policy of containing communism was established by the U.S.; it was followed by the system of regional alliances, notably NATO; the action in Korea was begun unilaterally by the U.S. and promptly supported by the U.N. Security Council. In the world economy, only the U.S. could produce the goods its allies desperately needed and only dollars could buy them. This was the period of the dollar shortage. The dollar at that time was obviously a symbol of American power, but it was something much more. It was the money of the world, at least the non-Communist part, and was used as a reserve for national currencies.

The reserve dollars were obtained by special arrangements with the U.S., like loans and grants, that added to the dollar stock of foreign countries or enabled them to conserve what they had. The dollars were not obtained, as they were later, by selling goods and securities to the U.S. in such an amount that the sellers obtained a trade surplus. The United States was then the surplus country— selling more on balance than it was buying and lending, and giving its customers the difference. The U.S. controlled the world use of the dollar by regulating its loans and grants. At this time there was the possibility of trade relations being established between the Communist and non-Communist blocs. Had this occurred, the recovery of Western Europe probably would have been delayed, and the political power of the dollar could have been maintained for a longer time. Hence the Russians, as by an invisible hand, brought U.S. supremacy to an end before it otherwise would have occurred. Their economic position, however, was not thereby improved; it, too, is slipping in the world. What happened may have yielded some *Schadenfreude*, but that is about all.

During the Korean war, the U.S. imported unusually large amounts of raw materials and as a result reduced the surplus in the current account of its balance of payments. The change lessened the dollar shortage and reduced the dependence of Europe on the United States (but did not eliminate it). At about the same time the production of Europe had reached its prewar amount. The recovery came sooner than was expected, and the reason seems to have been the high productivity of labor. Europe discovered that the destruction of capital, although extensive, did not have nearly the calamitous effect that was supposed, and this was because the population was a much more valuable economic resource than had been recognized. Another indication of the growing power of Europe was the formation of the economic communities in the late Fifties. The effect of both the Free Trade Area and the Common Market was to increase aggregate demand in the member countries, to bring into use substantial amounts of unemployed or underemployed resources, and to give some of the countries a surplus position in the international payments system. One should add that the nonmember countries also improved their economic position, and so did some of the non-European countries.

As they became surplus countries, the U.S. became a deficit country. The total amount which it spent on foreign goods and to buy foreign securities became larger than the amount it received from the sale of American goods and securities. In technical language, the sum of debits in the current and capital accounts of the balance of payments was greater than the sum of credits; the difference is the deficit. This development changed the world position of the dollar. It no longer was or is scarce, but is in surplus. The position of other currencies also changed. Those of the surplus countries became stronger, and some have become, in a limited way, rivals of the dollar as a reserve currency. They have not, I hasten to add, replaced it, nor are they likely to in the near future. But their greater strength is a loss of power for the dollar. It still has power as a symbol of the United States and as an instrument for influencing other governments. But the power is less because the economic need for the dollar is less. It still is needed as a reserve for national currencies and it is needed to make certain kinds of international payments. But it no longer is needed in order to make payments for what is bought from the U.S. The world has all the dollars it needs for that purpose because it is selling large quantities of securities to the U.S. each year and obtaining a quite sufficient supply of dollars for them. Not every country is doing this, but the world in its entirety is.

While the economies of other countries were recovering, then growing, and finally flourishing, there were some important political changes. The economic recovery of the countries of Western Europe was accompanied by greater political stability. The formation of the Common Market was accompanied by an increase in the international power of the member countries. They now constitute an international force over which the United States no longer can always prevail. One may note in passing that an increase in political power was the major purpose of the Treaty of Rome by which the Common Market was formed, and that the economic collaboration was only a means to that end and no more. The growing political power of Western Europe is the most visible change of its kind in the world, but not the only one. The Latin American states are more consequential in world affairs now than they were in the early Fifties. So are the Arab states, so too are the nations of Africa and Asia which did not even exist in the immediate postwar period. These changes have obviously reduced the influence of the U.S., not of course to the point of putting it in an inferior position (as one would suppose from some writings and speeches), but simply to a position in which it no longer can always make its views prevail over those of other countries. The Soviet Union has experienced the same change in the Communist world.

The world today is much different from the world in which the dollar became the principal reserve currency. Hence, the ability of the U.S. to keep the dollar in that position is no longer as great as it was. More than this, the United States is securing less and less advantage from keeping the dollar in that position. Finally, the need of other countries for the dollar is becoming less and their ability to displace it is becoming greater.

To the countries using it as a reserve, the dollar never has been altogether satisfactory. On the economic side, it has substantial drawbacks. The supply of it ought to increase as they need more dollars, which they do need as their foreign trade increases. What has happened instead is that the supply of dollars increases as the U.S. incurs a deficit in the capital account, which means that other countries get more dollars if Americans want to buy more foreign securities or if the United States government makes dollars available. Another drawback is the lack of complete confidence in the dollar. A foreign holder of them will want to get rid of his dollars if *he* believes *other* holders believe the value of the dollar will decline or its usefulness in some other way will be reduced. Or the holder may want to get rid of his dollars because he himself has lost faith in it. Distrusting the dollar is by no means unwarranted. It is in a weak position and one that is, moreover, perversely unstable. The world can trust the dollar as long as the U.S. has sufficient international reserves of its own to convert or support it, like gold, foreign currencies, the ability to borrow them, etc. As the dollars held outside the United States increase, the reserves against them usually decrease. The decrease weakens the dollar and makes it less acceptable. The perversity lies in the fact that what makes the dollar less acceptable to the world is the very need the world has for it. As the need increases and the quantity of dollars held abroad increases, the proportion of U.S. reserves to dollars outstanding then declines. The dollar is thereby weakened. If dollar holdings were prevented from rising, the reserve position would be improved and the dollar would be strengthened. But that would deprive the world of the money it needs. Nevertheless when it gets that money, the acceptability is threatened, etc.

The United States Treasury is of the opposite view. Robert Roosa, [former] Undersecretary of the Treasury for Monetary Affairs, has said the dollar is weak because foreign holdings are too large and foreign banks are trading off the excess for gold. His view seems to be like that of a bank which believes it could prevent a run on its reserves by limiting its checking accounts to just the amount its depositors need for transactions and liquidity. Just how the bank would adjust every deposit, I do not know. Just how the Treasury would limit the dollar holdings of foreigners to just that amount which would preclude conversion into gold, I do not know either. There are of course only a few large dollar holders and there is a well-bred chumminess among the financial great of the world. Perhaps Roosa believes these factors make such control possible. He perhaps may be mistaken.

On the political side, there are other objections to the dollar. Just because it is a symbol of U.S. power, it also is a symbol of the inferiority of other nations, or at least of the fact that they are not consequential enough for any of *their* currencies to be a reserve currency. The resentment of the dollar has now become apparent even among the friends of the United States. *The Economist*, usually so tactful, could not resist saying, when it proposed the devaluation of the pound, that one result would be "to knock the dollar from its perch."

There is a greater political disadvantage in holding dollars. It is more immanent than actual, but no less real for being that way. The U.S. has a certain influence over the governments of countries that are large dollar holders. The influence comes from the fact that the countries are dependent on the dollar. They are, moreover, dependent on the continued willingness of the United States to convert their dollars into gold or other currencies at par. The countries could be discomfited, to say the least, if the U.S. prevented them from acquiring the additional dollars they need as a reserve, and something worse would happen to them if the U.S. made their dollars inconvertible. The governments of these countries must be aware of the position in which dollar holdings put them and do not have to be told how the U.S. could, if it would, coerce them. They are aware of their position because some have themselves used inconvertibility as a weapon. Such a use is extreme and is an act of economic warfare. Would the United States ever do such a thing? "Never!" a colleague has declared to me. Actually it not only would do such a thing, but it has a number of times. The most recent was against Cuba, whose assets in the U.S. were frozen, i.e., declared to be unusable by their owner. "But Cuba— Cuba is a hostile nation," is the reply. Of course it is, and so would

France or Germany be if they threatened what the U.S. government regarded as its essential interests.

Admittedly, the major dollar holders are in a much stronger financial position than Cuba is. They are surplus countries—receiving more payments from the rest of the world than they must make to it—and the loss of their dollars would not immediately reduce their ability to import. However, the loss would deprive them of a major part of their reserves. The effect would be psychological but still disturbing, as if, for example, a perfectly solvent and profitable business firm was deprived of liquid assets. The longer run effect could be economic and would be if the countries moved into a deficit position.

The United States government has acknowledged in an oblique way that the dollar has political power. The indications have come from President Johnson, from the Treasury, the Federal Reserve System, and from the monetary authorities of the Eisenhower Administration. Federal Reserve Board Chairman William McChesney Martin has said that any major departures from dollar policy "would have undermined our position of economic and political leadership of the free world." Mr. Roosa said that the use of the dollar as the major reserve currency gives it "a role which naturally accompanies our leading economic and political position."

These statements do not prove my view that dollar policy has a twofold political purpose (as an emblem and instrument of power). They are only consistent with it. They become more convincing when they are added to other actions that also are consistent with the view. The U.S. has employed measures that support the political value of the dollar. They are too numerous and detailed to describe. All of them are meant to support what Roosa has called the convertible gold-dollar system, which is a system that will make the dollar usable by other countries as their reserve currency. The U.S. also has refrained from employing any measures that would lessen the political value of the dollar, such as those that would weaken the convertible gold-dollar system. The U.S. has, for example, refused to consider devaluation (which is not a permanent guarantee against it) because that, again according to Roosa, would leave the world without a major currency "generally acceptable as a supplement to gold." The United States, moreover, has acted in a way that is inconsistent with the purposes that economists usually impute to dollar policy. The purposes are: to conserve the U.S. gold supply, to maintain convertibility at the present price of gold, to correct the U.S. balance of payments position, and/or to provide the world with a reserve currency for the sake of the world and not the United States. If the U.S. is trying to do any of these things, it certainly is acting in a foolish and inefficient way (which indeed is just what some economists say it is doing). It often has acted in that way in economic matters, but it very probably is not now. There is too much consistency in dollar policy, and there are too many able economists making it.

Nevertheless the policy is, I believe, mistaken. It no longer can achieve the political purposes it clearly seems to have. Whether or not the dollar should be used in this way is a question that may be ignored. The conditions no longer are present that make such a use feasible. I do not mean that the dollar already has been knocked from its perch and that it no longer adds to U.S. prestige and influence. It still adds to both. But it does not contribute nearly as much as in the past, and at times fails so completely that it is a political embarrassment.

Consider some of the measures of dollar policy and how they detract, rather than add, to the prestige and influence of the United States. In order to keep the dollar in its reserve position, the U.S. tries to regulate the supply and demand of dollars in such a way that each year the world will add to its dollar holdings just the amount it needs for reserve and payments purposes and no more than that amount. If more were added, some dollars would be converted to gold, and the decline in the U.S. gold stock would threaten the dollars that were not converted. If fewer were added, the world would not have adequate reserves and either would curtail its trade or turn to some other form of international currency, neither of which is to the interest of the U.S. To achieve this nicely calculated less and more, the U.S. uses all sorts of devices. Some of them jeopardize the political position of the U.S. in the world. The President, for example, invited the Japanese to invest in the United States, and the invitation later appeared in periodicals abroad. The U.S. has entered the international tourist trade and at the same time has limited the spending by Americans abroad. Are these measures trivial? Perhaps. But out of such trivia the national image is pieced together, or the effigy. There are, of course, other pieces in it: the space program, foreign aid, the national income and wealth, and the inventory of nuclear weapons. Yet by how much are they discounted when the world observes the cheeseparing and huckstering that are a part of dollar policy ... when for example a Frenchman in Chicago comes away from the Museum of Science and Industry where he has seen a manned satellite and returns to his hotel where he is asked in halting French if he would not like to part with a few more francs?

There are other measures that cannot be called trivial in any sense. There is nothing trivial in the United States government selling bonds abroad and making them payable in foreign currency. The Treasury and Federal Reserve System have borrowed foreign currency on a stand-by basis and use it when it is needed to absorb an excess supply of dollars. These "swap" arrangements have to be made with foreign central banks, treasuries or governments, and however they are concealed in euphemistic language, they represent borrowing by the United States for the purpose of managing borrowing that was done earlier. A debtor who must borrow to manage an earlier debt is not a figure who stands high in the esteem of the international financial community. The community, by the way, is an important part of dollar policy and hums with the comings and goings of U.S. representatives. They must be almost *en famille* in Basle. Some may reflect in private on how the ways of the world have changed when the U.S. government must solicit the "cooperation" of the bankers of one of the smallest countries in the world. They may recall the closing lines of "The Hollow Men."

There are some faint signals that the U.S. government believes the sovereignty of the dollar is about over and is itself preparing to alter dollar policy in a fundamental way. The signals are taken for a clear report in some circles abroad but probably are not meant that way. What they seem to indicate is a willingness of the United States to consider, in a way it has not been willing to consider before, some substitute for present dollar policy. Mr. Roosa, in the statement quoted above, called upon the industrial countries of the world to share some of the "responsibilities" that the dollar alone now bears. President Kennedy, in his message to Congress proposing an interest-equalization tax, said "we shall be discussing possible improvements in the payments mechanism with our friends abroad, and our minds will be open to their initiatives."

If the United States were to stop using the dollar for political purposes, the change would be quite consistent with other changes it has made in its foreign policy or seems about to make (the test-ban treaty, the deference shown to France and West Germany, the acknowledgement of a lesser role in the U.N., trade with Soviet countries, the closing of missile bases in Italy and Turkey, the willingness to consider disarmament closely, and above and beyond all of these, the possibility of a U.S.–Soviet détente). The changes can be taken as a tacit admission that the world today is not constructed as it was in the postwar period. It is a world of several economic and political powers instead of just two: it resembles oligopoly more than duopoly. The changes could continue, and in the future there could be many, not several, powers, making the structure more like monopolistic competition than anything else. The structure is probably the most inefficient imaginable. It also is the most harmless. No single firm (or government) can count for much. For that very reason it cannot do much harm.

10

The Gold Standard

I read in *The Economist* last weekend an article whose title made a great impression on me: "My Lords, Bankers and Politicians, Pray Silence for Sterling." My first reaction was to send a cable to say that I had better refrain from speaking on International Monetary Problems—since this must inevitably to some degree involve speaking about sterling. But on reflection I concluded that I was neither Lord nor Banker nor Politician. May I say, however, that if I touch very discreetly upon the problem of sterling it will never be to discuss the actual position of the British currency. What I have in mind is only the situation of the West as a whole. When in 1961 I published the article on the dangers of the gold exchange standard I called it "A Danger to the West." I didn't say a danger to France, a danger to the United States, a danger to Britain: I said a danger to the West, because I consider that what is in question is the stability and prosperity of the West altogether; my concern with sterling—or with the dollar—arises simply from this wider view. In any case, as you will see, I offer no advice whatever to the British Government. They have not asked me for any—and we have a proverb in France which says that "advice pleases those who give it"; so it is not advice that I will offer, it is only facts.

Speaking after Professor Triffin and Mr. Maudling makes my task easy because we all start from the same point. We all agree that the present system is at an end and has to be replaced. Perhaps I could devote a few minutes to explaining why. It has been explained by the two previous speakers but perhaps not in exactly

Chapter from Francis Cassell (ed.), *International Monetary Problems* (London: Federal Trust for Education and Research, 1965), pp. 35–41. Reprinted by permission.

the same way. Under a full gold standard a central bank can issue money against gold or claims in national currency (notably Treasury bills and commercial bills). Under the gold-exchange standard a central bank can issue money against gold, claims in national currency and also against foreign exchange payable in gold—which in the 1920s meant sterling and dollar and which since the last war has meant essentially dollar. What is the result of this system? It is that when a key-currency country (let us say the United States) has a deficit in its balance of payments, it pays in its own currency—i.e., dollars, in Paris, in Bonn, in Tokyo, or in Rome. But dollars are of no use in Paris, Bonn, Tokyo or Rome. They can be interest-bearing only in the United States: so the very same day that they are received, they are lent by cable on the New York money market. Thus the money flows back instantly to its place of origin and the debtor country does not lose what the creditor country gains. That is the main feature of the present regime that has led me to say that it is the most absurd system of payment imaginable. You have only to appreciate it to imagine what would be the case if you found a shopkeeper who would agree whenever you purchase something to return immediately to you as a loan the money paid to him. Your own "balance of payments" would always be in deficit! That explains the deficit of the United States.

But the receiving country when it lends the money to the United States gets a claim on the United States and these claims are the famous dollar balances that represent the counterpart of the U.S. deficit and increase every year as long as the deficit in the balance of payments persists. This creates a system in which the debtor country, since it does not feel the effect of the deficit, can remain indefinitely in deficit. Some countries, however, do not keep the dollar balances, they ask for some gold; so you have a situation (as in the last five or six years) in which the United States has lost every year about $1 billion of gold and the total of dollar balances has increased every year by about $2 billion. To say the least, if such a system continues for long it must lead to a very dangerous situation.

Of course, my friends in Washington say: "We agree that the gold standard would have tended to correct the deficit, since there would then have been an effective transfer of purchasing power and we would have lost what the creditor country gained. But what is not done in our system by the automatic reaction of the gold standard can be done by day-to-day credit policy." And that is true. You can very well imagine that the Federal Reserve, seeing a deficit of $3 billion a year tries to contract the credit structure to the same or to a greater amount, and therefore tries to create the reaction that would have been the result of the workings of the gold standard. But there is a very great difference between the two methods. In the case of the gold standard, the effect on the market is produced by day-to-day settlements and, therefore, in small installments that nobody feels. In the other case, it is produced by a massive decision that everybody can see and comment on. It has a massive action—and, let me tell you, it is extremely difficult, especially in a country which has a Parliament. In fact, it has not been done; and I think I am right in saying it will never be done. You know that the basic doctrine in the United States is cheap money and whatever the deficit in the balance of payments, the authorities have not been able until now to create a restriction of credit. Therefore the deterioration of the credit system of the United States continues, the dollar balances increase while the gold assets diminish and the very least that can be said is that it creates a very dangerous situation because somewhere, some day, there will be an event in the financial markets—I don't know where, in Japan, in Italy, or anywhere—and people will try to get back what they have invested in New York. This is the exact mechanism of the catastrophic collapse of 1931, so we must be very careful.

So much for the dollar balances. But the sterling balances are also the result of a certain kind of gold exchange standard, which is characteristic of the sterling area. They are also dangerous; but the situation is somewhat different because the bulk of the sterling balances are in the hands of countries that are united to London by economic and political links—and it is easier to have a gentlemen's agreement than a common policy. Nevertheless in the last year or so there has been some trouble with the sterling balances and London has reacted in a very courageous way—quite different from the way that the United States has reacted—with a very strong, and it seems effective, credit policy and a discount rate of 7 per cent. This restrictive credit policy, however, is a great ob-

stacle to the maintenance of London's position as an international
financial center.

If we want to return to a policy which is not hampered by the
existence of these foreign balances—in other words which is not
limited in its possibility of expansion by the need of a restrictive
policy to maintain the foreign balances, we must get rid of the
gold-exchange standard. We must avoid the formation of new
balances and we must get rid of the existing balances. Well, as I
told you, I consider that in fact the deficit in the U.S. balance of
payments will disappear only when we return to a system of payment that is a real one—in the sense that the debtor country loses
what the creditor gains. You can imagine various kinds of standard: you can imagine a platinum standard; some people are speaking of a merchandise standard. I think that the only practical
proposition is at the moment—I don't say forever—the gold
standard. We have always seen that a restoration of a real system
of payment restored in a short period the balance of payments
itself. There is no foolproof system in the human field. If you have
internal inflation the balance of payments will run into deficit
and you will lose gold; after a certain time the gold standard itself
will collapse. But if you have no internal inflation the gold standard seems to me the necessary condition for restoration of balance
in international payments.

Suppose that we say tomorrow that all the major countries agree
with the proposal of General de Gaulle that in future all international payments balances should be settled in gold. Please note
that that is the only thing that he has said. He has not discussed
the ways and means of doing that. He simply proposed that the
world should return to payment in gold. Well, suppose that this
was agreed. Do you really believe that countries will continue to
keep dollar balances when they would be required to pay their
debts in gold? Certainly not: being asked to pay in gold, they will
demand gold for these dollar balances. What would be the situation? The United States has now just under $15 billion of gold.
The dollar claims in the hands of overseas central banks amount
to rather more than $14 billion. Suppose that the reimbursement
of these claims is required in gold. The United States will be left
with such a small amount of gold that it is absolutely unthinkable.
So ways and means have to be found which would enable the

United States to repay these dollar balances without losing virtually all the gold it has.

It is suggested that this might be done by giving to an international authority the right to create an international currency not payable in gold. I fully agree that this is absolutely logical. But I am not much in favor of giving to an international authority the power to create an inconvertible international currency. I think it would open dangerously the door to creeping inflation. In any case, I really don't believe that it is in the realm of possibility that governments will agree to transfer so much power to an international body. In other words, despite the fact that it is very logical I don't think that the plan will be adopted, in the near future. I may be wrong, but I don't believe it will. What else then, if the dollar balances are to be repaid?

We could remark that the price of gold was fixed in 1934 by President Roosevelt at $35 an ounce and that since that time all prices have at least doubled in the United States. Suppose for one moment that we would do what President Roosevelt did in 1934 when he raised the price of gold from $20 to $35 an ounce, restoring the price of gold to its normal place in the hierarchy of prices; this would approximately involve doubling the dollar price of gold. If we do that, the nominal value of the U.S. gold stock will be raised from $15 billion to $30 billion. The claims of the overseas central banks, however, are in dollars: they have no gold clause and you know that no court in the world would admit that a claim without a gold clause could be presumed as having a gold clause. These claims could thus be repaid in full and the United States would be left with approximately $16 billion of gold ($30 billion minus $14 billion)—which is rather more than it has now. So the base of America's credit structure would not be diminished at all, and no one can speak on this point of a danger of deflation. If this operation were carried out soon, while America's gold stock is still very substantial, there would be no deflationary impact on the U.S. credit base. With respect to the creditor countries, they would lose their dollar balances but would receive an exactly equivalent amount of gold. Thus there would be no risk of any deflationary consequences on their own money supplies.

Many people, however, argue that the more likely danger is that a revaluation of gold would be inflationary. This is because

most countries have no currency balances to repay to foreigners—
and therefore, no opportunity to offset the rise in the nominal
value of their gold stocks. These countries—say Germany, Belgium,
Canada, Spain, France, Italy, Japan, Netherlands, Sweden and
Switzerland (there are others having gold but I have no figures
here)—hold gold stocks totalling about $18 billion at the present
price of gold. If the price were doubled, the value of these stocks
would rise to $36 billion. It is true that it might be dangerously
inflationary for them to enlarge their structure of credit correspondingly. And it is for this reason that I should like to turn now
to discuss the problem of sterling balances, since the repayment
of these could provide a way of neutralizing some of the impact
of a revaluation of gold.

I have never before given my full thoughts on this question
of the sterling balances because I wished so far as possible to be
discreet. Let me say at once that these are personal thoughts
(despite the fact that one of our well-known authors said that
personal thoughts are so called because you ought to keep them
to yourself): I must state emphatically that they have not been
communicated to the French Government, they are not an offer
from the French Government, they are purely my own. If we
accept the first proposition, that an increase in the price of gold
will be the most likely solution (before or after a crisis), we must
face the problem of the surplus monetary reserves that this will
create for some countries. I would suggest—tentatively—that part
of these surplus reserves might be used as a loan to Great Britain
to repay the sterling balances—provided that Britain wanted to
repay them, which is not sure. Such a loan would probably absorb
rather less than half of the surplus. The remainder, I think, ought
to be absorbed in the amortization of the government debt to the
central bank—which would be merely an accounting operation
that would neutralize any inflationary impact on the domestic
money supply. Thus I think it would be very easy to avoid any
danger of inflation from a revaluation of gold and hence that it
is possible to restore the full mechanism of the gold standard without any fear of trouble for the future.

People are sometimes afraid that the gold standard is not flexible
enough and is indeed an obstacle to full employment and growth.
Let me insist on this point, it is entirely wrong to say that the gold

standard does not maintain the superstructure of credit which exists in all of our countries. On the contrary, it would make un-necessary the restrictive credit policy which is typical of the present situation in Britain. It would make it possible to re-establish London as a full financial center; moreover, it would certainly realize a great dishoarding of gold. We have seen after all financial reforms a reduction in long-term interest rates, a great increase in the possibility of investment and I am quite sure that it would generate a long wave of very powerful expansion and development in the world.

What are the objections? Those I have seen come chiefly in the United States. They said it would be a devaluation of the dollar; but this is not so because if the price of gold was changed simul-taneously in all convertible currencies there would be no change in the parity of the dollar with other currencies. They say it would be a breach of contract. I say it would not: there is no gold clause covering the dollar or sterling balances. They said it would be un-just. I am very sensitive to this argument; let us see what it means. Maintaining the price of gold at the present level means that the people who are producing steel or wheat now get for one ton of their product twice as much gold as they would have got in 1934. Is it really justice to give such a windfall profit to people who are producing useful goods—twice as much gold as they would have got when gold was at its normal price? Is it not an invitation to purchase gold, a temptation to transform useful resources into hoarding of gold?

I think that the situation is very similar to what we have seen in the field of housing. In our countries we have maintained during a long period rents at an artificially low level: in consequence the supply of housing has been persistently smaller than the demand, and because the construction of new houses was discouraged the State had to intervene and put public money in. The situation in respect to gold is exactly the same. We are short of gold because the price is maintained at an artificially low level. Let me tell you a story about that. Two weeks ago I was in the United States. I saw a very important Senator there. He told me he was very angry about my country. He told me: "Oh, I see very well what you have in mind, you want to take all our gold at the present price and when we have no more gold then you will double the price and make a great profit against us." I told him: "My dear Senator it's exactly the reverse that I am proposing. I am proposing that you increase the price of gold now, when you still have some gold, and give us only half of the gold that we are now entitled to get at the present price." "Then," he said "if so I am with you." Well it is very interesting to see the amount of misunderstanding that is connected with this question of gold.

Then last week a very important friend of mine in the United States said to me: "But, after all, for us it is a matter of honor. Three Presidents of the United States have successively said that we shall not change the price of gold." I said: "That may be so. I wouldn't propose as an excuse that every Government on the eve of devaluation has always said that they would not devalue the national currency. But if it is a matter of honor the first condition for a debtor is to maintain himself in a position to repay his debt. . . ."

Well that shows how I see the problem. The future is not known. Personally I believe that a measure of this kind is very necessary. If it were adopted, as it ought to be, it would entail an international convention that would contain the following stipulations:

1. Central banks would undertake not to increase their dollar and sterling holdings in future.

2. The price of gold would be simultaneously increased in all countries with convertible currencies by an amount to be agreed by them.

3. The rise in the value of the gold stocks of the U.S.A. and U.K. as a result of the increase in the gold price would be used for the immediate repayment of existing dollar and sterling balances.

4. An appropriate proportion of the increased nominal value of the gold stocks of the countries having no currency balances to repay would be lent to the U.K. for a period of at least 20 years.

5. The remainder would be used, where the local situation makes this appropriate, for the amortization of government borrowings from the central banks.

Such an agreement would free the world from the threat of economic crisis which now hangs over it. The West would be able once more to continue, in security and for a long period, its triumphant march towards well-being, security and progress.

I am sure that in the end a solution of this kind will be adopted. I don't think that there is any real solution outside the change of the price of gold. We have seen in the 1930s that the U.S. tried everything and finally in 1934 they increased the price of gold from $20 to $35 an ounce and that was the beginning of the recovery from the Great Depression. The only question is to know when it will be done: whether it will be done before the crisis or after it. I consider that if we do nothing we shall have a continuation of the increase in the dollar balances (though not the sterling balances) and that some day the United States will be unable to pay its obligations abroad. This is not just a theoretical possibility. I know very well what it means. In 1958 when I had to look at the French finances, we had no foreign exchange at all and we were informed that we could not get any more credit anywhere. So we had no choice: when you have no foreign exchange you can do nothing else but establish an embargo on gold, quotas on all imports, restrictions on travel abroad and various other measures that are extremely bad for the welfare of the people, for the development of production—and also for international relations. If we now do nothing, I am personally convinced that that is what will happen someday.

The problem seems to me to know whether there is enough realism and courage to do what is necessary and co-operatively before we are forced to do it. The main question is to know whether a plan of the kind I have outlined today will be adopted before the crisis or after the crisis. I strongly hope that it will be adopted before—and that we shall spare the world the suffering of a new Great Depression.

11

A Proposal for Establishing a World Dollar Standard

EMILE DESPRES

A proposal for strengthening the international monetary system which was originally circulated in the spring of 1965 is outlined below. Its adoption—and, perhaps, merely its serious consideration—would bring to an end the state of nagging semi-crisis in the international economy which has persisted since 1959, and it would reverse the present growth of mercantilist restrictionism.

The central postulate underlying this proposal is that the dollar is not only "as good as gold" but is, fundamentally, much better than gold. In the present day world, gold derives its desirability as a monetary asset from the fact of its unlimited convertibility into dollars at a fixed price. The dollar is not merely a national currency; it is, indeed, the predominant international currency. It is widely used for commercial settlements not only in trade with the United States but in trade between foreign countries. It is the principal unit of account in international lending and borrowing, both long-term and short-term, even when both borrower and lender are foreign entities. Free world central banks and monetary authorities, other than those of the sterling area and the French community, settle their deficits and surpluses, in the first instance, by taking in or paying out dollar balances.

Except by special arrangements, gold is no longer used directly in settlements between foreign countries. Although foreign countries may elect to exchange dollars for gold or gold for dollars, the dollar is the medium of payment and gold simply a potential source of, or use for dollars. The United States is the only country

Reprinted and title changed by permission from "Statement," *New Approach to United States International Economic Policy,* Hearings Before the Subcommittee on International Exchange and Payments of the Joint Economic Committee of the Congress (Washington, D.C.: 1966), pp. 39–42.

which stands ready to buy gold on demand or sell gold to foreign central banks and monetary authorities. Although other countries have defined the legal parity of their monetary units in terms of gold, all IMF members except the United States have taken advantage of the option provided under the Articles of Agreement of the International Monetary Fund to set the upper and lower support limits in terms of dollars. Since so large a part of the free world's international obligations—commercial and financial—is denominated in dollars, it is, in the last analysis, dollars and not gold which are desired for international settlements. The evolution of credit money over the past four or five centuries has proceeded to a point where gold has become a dollar substitute, rather than the dollar a gold substitute.

Whatever may have been the case in the past, the desire for gold as a monetary asset is today contrived and artificial. It rests upon the confident assumption that the United States government will always stand ready to supply dollars in exchange for gold without limit and at a price not less favorable to gold holders than $35 an ounce. Certainly the anxiety which the U.S. government has shown in the face of gold losses has done nothing to weaken the confidence with which this assumption is held. Nevertheless, the United States, although completely committed to defending the dollar, has no comparable commitment to the defense of gold.

A second postulate is that the United States, as the world's financial center, faces a banking problem and not a balance-of-payments problem. This banking problem arises from an inflated demand for gold, itself a result of the present United States gold policy. The present state of contained crisis of the international monetary system can be corrected only by bringing about a genuine change in prevailing asset preferences—reducing the desire for gold and increasing the desire for dollars. Such a shift in asset preferences can be brought about by United States action and not by international negotiation to create some supplementary reserve asset. Within the context of prevailing asset preferences, any international agreement would be too limited in scope and too rigid in its operation to permit the needed re-establishment and development of an unrestricted, integrated, international capital market based upon the United States. By distributing liquidity on a symmetrical formula which does not take account of the special banking problems of the financial center, it would give reserves to countries that do not need them without appreciably easing the positions of those who do.

The present inflated demand for gold rests upon persistent belief in the possibility of dollar devaluation and the confident expectation that, in any event, gold can always be converted into dollars without limit at no less than $35 an ounce. A change in asset preferences can be effected only by changing these expectations. Only in this way will the actual demand for dollar assets be brought into line with the underlying character of the dollar's international role.

Despite repeated official statements of the U.S.'s determination to defend the dollar and the steps which have been taken for this defense, belief in the possibility of dollar devaluation underlies the bulk of the private speculative demand for gold and probably exerts some influence upon the decisions of central banks and monetary authorities with respect to the composition of their reserves. So long as we stand ready to convert gold into dollars without any limit at $35 per ounce, the holding of gold becomes a safe potential source of dollars, risking little more than the interest foregone. The desirability of gold as a monetary reserve asset depends upon the fact that the conversion of gold into dollars is universally taken for granted. If convertibility of gold into dollars were convincingly limited, gold not eligible for purchase by the United States would lose its usefulness as an international monetary asset. International settlements between foreign countries are largely carried out in dollars, not in gold, and it is scarcely conceivable that foreign central banks and monetary authorities would agree to use in settlements among each other an asset not freely exchangeable for dollars.

The kinds of steps which, in my judgment, the United States should take to alter prevailing asset preferences are given below:

1. The present 25% gold reserve requirement against Federal Reserve notes should be repealed and it should be made more explicitly clear than at present that all the monetary gold which the United States holds would be used if necessary in defense of the dollar. Gold should be treated not as a last line of defense to be conserved and husbanded but as a readily available reserve to be employed alongside swap credits and forward exchange opera-

tions and IMF drawings and other newly developed financial devices. Although we have reiterated our determination not to devalue, continuation of the existing reserve requirements against Federal Reserve notes together with U.S. zealousness to avoid gold losses whenever possible has created a widespread impression that in the face of persistent gold losses, the U.S. would resort to devaluation long before its $13 billion of monetary gold has been exhausted.

It is widely accepted that if a devaluation of the dollar should occur, this would be accompanied or immediately followed by a general devaluation of other currencies. Consequently, devaluation of the dollar would do nothing to improve the competitive position of the U.S. in world markets, even if such an improvement were desired for balance-of-payments reasons. The chief effect of a devaluation of the dollar would be the change in the U.S. liquidity position through a writing up of the dollar value of monetary holdings. If a 50% devaluation were undertaken with a $13 billion monetary gold stock, the new value of the stock would be $26 billion. This is the only advantage, if it be deemed an advantage, to be gained from dollar devaluation. (Since devaluation would greatly weaken the rest of the world's willingness to hold dollars and dollar claims, even this advantage would be illusory.) It should be noted that devaluation would be utterly pointless even in terms of the liquidity position of the U.S. if it were deferred until our gold holdings were exhausted, since with a monetary gold stock of zero, there would be nothing to write up. A general devaluation of currencies at a time when U.S. gold reserves were exhausted would only increase the dollar fetching power of foreign gold holdings and of newly mined South African and Russian gold. Although exhaustion of the U.S. monetary gold stock would doubtless necessitate a suspension of gold payments, it would not necessitate devaluation, which is a very different thing, and would, in fact, render devaluation pointless, except as a means of providing massive windfalls to foreign monetary authorities and gold speculators and mining interests. It is well understood, of course, that the U.S., without gold of its own, would not find it attractive to supply such a windfall to others. Belief in the possibility of dollar devaluation rests squarely, therefore, on the assumption that there is some floor to United States gold reserves not far below present levels and that if this floor is reached, the United States would feel "forced" to devalue. This belief would be greatly weakened if convincing evidence were provided that there is no such floor. Elimination of Federal Reserve requirements against Federal Reserve notes, together with greater use of gold along with swap credits and other financing devices for day to day international payments purposes would go far to destroy belief in the possibility of devaluation.

2. In addition, the United States should announce a new policy with respect to the purchase of gold. While continuing to stand ready to sell gold without limit at the statutory price of $35 an ounce, the U.S. should impose strict limitation upon the amount of gold which it stands ready to buy at this price and should substitute firm credit lines for the monetary gold rendered redundant by quota limitations on U.S. purchases. This proposal involves no change in the price at which we would stand ready to buy gold. However, it would end the unlimited convertibility of gold into dollars, and it would substitute credit for the monetary gold made redundant by the quota limitations.

Special limitations regarding gold purchases would be made for underdeveloped countries, dollar reserve countries and Great Britain. In the case of all other countries, the United States should declare its readiness to enter into a series of bilateral and reciprocal gold purchase plus credit agreements along the following lines:

i. The U.S. would stand ready to make net purchases of gold at $35 an ounce in an amount not exceeding ⅓ of the monetary gold held by the other party to the agreement at the time of announcement of the new U.S. gold buying policy. The other party would agree to sell gold to us only when necessary for balance-of-payments reasons. (The remaining ⅔ of the other country's gold reserves, together with such gold, if any, as might be subsequently acquired, would be ineligible for purchase by the U.S.)

ii. Reciprocally, the other country would stand ready to buy up to this amount of gold from the U.S. when necessary for balance-of-payments reasons.

iii. Firm reciprocal credit lines (swaps) permitting drawing without specified maturity and covered by an exchange value guarantee would be established in amounts equal to twice the reciprocal commitments with respect to gold purchase. It would be mutually agreed that drawings under these credits would go hand in hand with gold sales in the ratio of two units of credit utilization to one of gold sales. Under such an agreement, a country wishing to obtain, say, $150 million for international payments purposes would sell $50 million of gold to the U.S. and draw $100 million under its credit line. Thus, access to dollars through gold and credit combined would remain unimpaired, credit replacing the gold rendered unusable by U.S. purchase limitations.

In the case of countries holding the major portion of their reserves in the form of dollars (e.g., Japan, Canada) and of all underdeveloped countries, it seems appropriate to make eligible for purchase by the United States at $35 an ounce all gold reserves held by the monetary authorities of these countries on the date of announcement of the new gold policy. Swap credits would then be unnecessary. Any gold subsequently acquired by these countries would be ineligible for purchase by the United States.

Great Britain's position as a financial and reserve currency center justifies special arrangements. The U.S. should propose a reciprocal gold plus credit agreement similar in form to the reciprocal agreements outlined above, but making British gold eligible for purchase by the United States in an amount equal to the full British central gold reserve on the date of announcement of the new gold purchase policy. Britain would, in turn, stand ready to purchase an equal amount of gold from the U.S. and gold transactions would be meshed with drawings under swap credits in the ratio of 1 to 2.

Measures would also have to be taken with respect to the IMF in order (1) to assure that gold ineligible for direct sale to the United States did not reach us indirectly through the IMF as intermediary, (2) to assure the convertibility into dollars of existing IMF gold holdings, and (3) to prevent the IMF from becoming a dumping ground for gold ineligible for sale to us. These are matters of technical detail which raise no insuperable difficulties.

The steps outlined above surely would result in a marked shift in asset preferences from gold to dollars and would remove the elements of weakness which impair the effective operation of the existing system by preventing the United States from performing its appropriate banking function. A dollar reserve system would be established free of the critical weaknesses of the existing system.

The proposal outlined above should not be considered a rigid blueprint. It is undoubtedly susceptible of modifications and improvements. More important, its adoption or even its serious consideration in U.S. official quarters would require a radical change in prevailing official doctrine regarding the dollar's relationship to gold and the applicability to a world financial center of traditional notions of balance-of-payments equilibrium. So long as present doctrines are adhered to and so long as solutions are sought by attempting to negotiate multilateral agreements for supplementary reserve assets which do not give recognition to the inherent asymmetry between the position of a financial center and that of its clients, there is little reason to expect much improvement in the condition of contained crisis which has prevailed during the sixties. Thus, a radical change in the prevailing doctrine is needed. With such a change, the task of devising appropriate measures to end the crisis and provide an international monetary environment favorable to growth and development, and to commercial and financial liberalization, would be a simple task. It could be accomplished either by steps of the type outlined above or by other measures having equivalent effect.

The result would be the establishment, in effect, of a world dollar standard under which loan finance, short and long term, would be available to borrowers with credit standing at the market rates (with aid to underdevoloped countries at concessional terms). United States monetary policy, and the resulting level of interest rates, would have to be determined in full consultation with foreign governments and appropriate international agencies in order to provide financing terms consistent with world economic growth and stability. Purely domestic stabilization policy would then rely largely upon fiscal instruments, unless the requirements of both domestic and international stabilization coincided in pointing to a need for greater monetary expansion or restraint.

12

The Future of the Dollar
as International Money

JAMES TOBIN

As General de Gaulle has characteristically reminded us in a
recent press conference, the United States dollar occupies a unique
position among national currencies. It is used as money throughout the world, not just in the country of issue. Will the dollar
continue to perform this special international role, lately called
into question by events as well as by the General? Does the United
States have a national interest in the perpetuation of this external
use of its currency? In what alternative ways could the international functions of the dollar be performed?

Foreign users of dollars are both *private* (banks, businesses,
and individuals) and *official* (central banks, governments, and
international institutions). For reasons that I shall develop, I
believe there are good prospects for continuation and even expansion of private uses of dollars. However, I think the dollar is likely
to lose sooner or later its position as a "reserve currency" for
central banks and governments. I shall explain why I feel we
should not be dismayed by this development, and I shall discuss
some suggestions for replacing the dollar in the international
monetary system.

Today foreign holdings of dollars amount to $24 billion of which
private holdings represent $11 billion and official holdings $13
billion. I exclude international institutions, which hold another
$5 billion. I refer to foreign holdings of *dollars*, but of course I
do not mean dollars in the literal sense of coin and currency. Very
little takes that form. Rather I am speaking of obligations to

Delivered as Carl Snyder Memorial Lecture at the University of California,
Santa Barbara, March, 1965. Reprinted by permission from James Tobin,
National Economic Policy (New Haven: Yale University Press, 1966), Ch.
17. Copyright © 1966 by Yale University.

foreigners payable on demand or within a year by U.S. banks or the U.S. Treasury. Increases in these liquid short-term liabilities to foreigners are what we count, together with outflows of gold, as deficits in our balance of payments.

Foreign Private Dollar Holdings

Why do private banks, businesses, and individuals abroad hold dollars rather than their own national currencies? Sometimes, of course, they are speculating that their own currency may depreciate in value. Normally, however, these dollar holdings are working balances, maintained in preparation for making future dollar payments. They are analogous to the working bank balances of American households or corporations. The dollar is the unit of account, and medium of exchange, not only for the $40 billion of annual payments by foreigners to U.S. residents but for many other transactions in which neither party is a U.S. resident.

The dollar plays this role for several reasons. One is simply the size of the country and of its transactions with the rest of the world. Another is historical. After the Second World War, the dollar and the Swiss franc were the only currencies convertible on demand into any other national currency. Other currencies were subject to all kinds of exchange controls and to considerable risks of devaluation. The dollar's value was assured, less by U.S. possession of almost all the world's monetary gold in the free world than by the seemingly inexhaustible appetite of foreign countries for U.S. products. In these circumstances it was natural for exporters and importers, lenders and borrowers, to make their contracts in dollars.

A third reason is the high state of organization and efficiency of U.S. financial institutions and financial markets. The holder of a working balance naturally seeks to earn some interest return on his funds. Likewise, he wishes to be able to put funds in or take them out at any time conveniently, inexpensively, and quickly. The only places that really offer such facilities, through banks and a short-term money market, are New York and London. The checkered career of sterling since 1931 has confined its use as international money pretty much to the "sterling area," composed mainly of Commonwealth and ex-Commonwealth countries.

The Euro-Dollar Market

During recent years, it is true, strong competition with New York has developed in London and elsewhere in Europe. The new institutions and markets pay the dollar the sincerest kind of flattery. For they deal in "Euro-dollars," i.e., short-term liabilities to pay dollars, undertaken by foreigners rather than by American residents. When the debtor is a reputable London bank, his promise to pay dollars is virtually as good as "real" dollars in New York.

Euro-dollars are substitutes for real dollars just as bank deposits are substitutes for the coin and currency that they are obligations to pay. Thus the development of Euro-dollars has reduced world demand for dollars—not, of course, one-for-one. Banks and other dealers who have undertaken Euro-dollar obligations presumably keep some genuine New York dollars as reserves. Otherwise they might have to scramble to raise the dollars needed to meet their dollar-dominated obligations when they come due.

Of course they make loans expressed in dollars too. But, as in any banking operation, the loans are less liquid and more risky, as well as higher yielding, than the deposits. This difference is responsible both for the profit in the operation and for the need for fractional reserves. I don't know what the reserve fraction is in the Euro-dollar market, but it is probably quite low. Even if it were as high as one fifth, every Euro-dollar substituted for a real dollar in international working balances would mean a net reduction of 80 cents in the demand for dollars.

The major attraction of Euro-dollars has been that they pay a higher interest rate than deposits in New York or U.S. Treasury bills. At the same time, Euro-dollar market banks are able to make loans at rates competitive with U.S. lenders. The profit opportunity which has called for the Euro-dollar market is the gap between deposit interest rates and loan interest rates in the United States. This gap was in part due to the legal ceiling imposed in the U.S. on the rates commercial banks may pay on time deposits. Although the Federal Reserve has raised this ceiling in several steps over the past three years, it still handicaps the U.S. in the international competition for funds. The ceiling should be abandoned altogether.

So far as foreign demand for dollars is concerned, the obvious reduction due to substitution of Euro-dollars is offset only to the extent that fractional dollar reserves are held against Euro-dollars, which are substituted for holdings of other national currencies. The offset cannot be large, although I do not know of any successful attempts to pierce the mysteries of the Euro-dollar market and measure the effects.

The economy of dollars accomplished by the Euro-dollar market is by its nature a once-for-all phenomenon. The dollar may already have survived the main blow it is going to suffer from this source. Once the initial profit opportunity is exploited—and Euro-dollar rate margins are very narrow now—the market will grow at roughly the same pace as the world economy, and so will its need for genuine dollar reserves.

Besides the competition of Euro-dollars, adverse speculation has reduced private demand for dollars in recent years. In spite of these two disadvantages, private dollar holdings abroad have been rising by about $1 billion a year. This seems to me impressive testimony of the strength of the world economy's normal demands for dollars for working balances. In satisfying these demands, we can probably run a balance-of-payments deficit, according to the Commerce Department of the term, of $1.5 billion a year without putting the dollar under pressure in the foreign exchange market.

Official Dollar Holdings

I turn now to the official use of dollars. Some official holdings are working balances, similar to the private holdings I have just been discussing. The central banks of other countries are committed, under the Articles of Agreement of the International Monetary Fund, to maintain the values of their currencies in the foreign exchange markets within 1 per cent of the declared official parities. They do this by buying or selling dollars for their own currencies. They have working balances of dollars both as a result of and in anticipation of their interventions in the exchange markets.

But the current dollar holdings of foreign central banks and governments greatly exceed their needs for working balances. The dollar has been used as a "reserve currency," and the bulk of official holdings abroad represent reserves that nations hold against adverse development which threaten their exchange rates or their ability to pay for needed imports.

Gold is the most important reserve asset. But, especially after the Second World War, many nations began to use dollars in place of gold or in combination with gold. Dollars could earn interest; they were directly usable in the foreign exchange markets; they were convertible into gold at the U.S. Treasury; they commanded American goods and services. Until the late 'fifties, therefore, the U.S. could count on foreign central banks to hold gladly any dollars that came their way.

This buildup of dollar reserves, moreover, served an important international purpose. Without them, Europe and the rest of the world could have built up their own reserves only by depleting the U.S. gold stock. This would have forced the U.S. to take, early in the postwar period, deflationary and restrictive measures. New gold production is not able to keep pace with the demand for reserves in a growing world economy.

The reserve-currency system grew like Topsy; it was never deliberately and consciously created. But its internal logic is that foreign countries will accept unlimited quantities of dollars in payment for their goods and their properties. As General de Gaulle and his unofficial monetary adviser, M. Jacques Rueff, have so eloquently pointed out, the principle of the reserve-currency system is indefensible. It is as if an individual citizen of the United States had the power to print dollar bills for his own use. We have long since centralized and nationalized the power to create national currency. For similar reasons General de Gaulle is unassailable when he asks that international money "not bear the mark of any individual country."

Of course the reserve-currency system has not been operating according to its internal logic in recent years. On the contrary, the United States has been faced ever since 1960, at the latest, with the distinct possibility that General de Gaulle and others will ask us to convert into gold not only the dollars currently accruing to them but also those which they happily accepted in the halcyon days of the reserve-currency system. This has made our supposedly privileged position much less comfortable, to say the least, than it would be if dollars really continued to be the unquestioned equivalent of gold.

I do not think it is simply nationalistic bias that leads me to assert that the U.S. did not abuse the privileged position of owning a printing press for international money. We did not flood European countries with worthless paper, forcing them into inflation while we carted home the products of their toil and thrift. On the whole, we used our international monetary privilege to finance the responsibilities we had assumed in the common defense of the West and in assistance to the underdeveloped world.

It is true that American investors have been acquiring large and presumably profitable industrial and commercial interests in Europe. As a nation, we have financed these acquisitions by pouring dollars into Europe central banks. It would be hard to judge whether this is an abuse of the reserve-currency system, or whether it is a result of the formation of a customs union that at the same time attracts American capital and excludes American exports. But in any event a European country with nationalistic objections to the U.S. capital invasion can handle the problem by direct measures. Were the international monetary system otherwise satisfactory, the fact that it has facilitated this movement of capital would not be a reason for changing it. Indeed facilitation of capital movements is one of the principal *raisons d'être* of the system of fixed exchange rates.

But it is really beside the point to argue whether or not the U.S. has abused, or is abusing, its reserve-currency status. General de Gaulle's monetary restlessness is of a piece with his general restlessness, shared in some measure by other European governments. Europe will no longer accept without question and participation U.S. international leadership, no matter how benevolent. We will undoubtedly have to construct more symmetrical arrangements for making international decisions and sharing international responsibilities in the fields of defense and foreign aid, as well as more symmetrical international monetary arrangements.

Some countries, particularly those in the Western Hemisphere, may continue to find it in their interest to hold the bulk of their reserves in dollars because of their close trading ties with the United States. Similar arrangements exist within the sterling area, and within the franc zone, which includes most of France's former dependencies in Africa.

In particular, the United States and Canada may find it in their mutual interest to move toward a monetary union. We would give Canada a large line of credit; in return Canada would agree to hold all its reserves, above a minimal gold stock, in U.S. dollars. This would formalize what is already true, i.e., that a consolidated North American balance of payments is of much greater relevance to the strength of the two dollars than their separate accounts. Capital outflows across our northern border should not really be a cause for concern about the U.S. dollar, as they are in present statistical practice. Such outflows tend to be offset sooner or later by Canadian imports from the U.S. or by increased holdings of dollars by the Bank of Canada.

Outside a "dollar area," however, I believe that we in the United States must face squarely the inevitable prospect that other countries will cease to hold dollars as official reserves above minimal working balances. They will insist on a more symmetrical or neutral international money. Recent French conversions of dollars into gold are a dramatic indication. Perhaps the handwriting on the wall can be read even more clearly from the unobtrusive way in which Germany, which has no political reason to embarrass the U.S., has been steadily reducing the dollar content of its reserves. And even when conversions are not made, the threat hangs over our heads like the sword of Damocles and forces us to take all kinds of measures that conflict with U.S. foreign and domestic policy.

Alternatives to the Reserve-Currency System

What could take the place of the dollar in official reserves? And how could the transition to a new kind of international money be arranged? One proposal, of course, is to adopt a pure gold standard. Nations would hold only gold metal as international reserves. Balance-of-payments deficits resulting in claims by one central bank upon another would be settled in gold. Presumably central banks and governments might extend each other credit. But deficit countries would have no automatic or presumptive rights to such credit. This is the system favored by Jacques Rueff, among others.

Any abrupt institution of the gold standard would involve massive conversion of dollars into gold. U.S. gross reserves would decline drastically, and total world reserves would contract by an equivalent amount. To avoid this shock, most advocates of the gold-standard solution favor an increase in the price of gold in terms of all currencies. By marking up the value of its gold stock by 66⅔ per cent, the U.S. would be able to pay off $10 billion of its short-term debts in gold and still have, as now, $15 billion in gold reserves. Other countries' reserves would be increased by two thirds of their current gold stocks. Most gold-standard advocates would regard this expansion of world reserves as inflationary. They would prefer an increase in gold price of the order of 33⅓ per cent, which would be just sufficient to enable reserve currency holdings outside the currency "areas" to be replaced by gold without changing the total of world reserves. In this case the U.S. would have only $10 billion in gold left after the two operations: revaluation of our stock to $20 billion and conversion of $10 billion of outstanding dollars. Our loss of $5 billion in reserves would be balanced by increases in the reserves of other countries.

All major governments have repeatedly opposed this solution and expressed their determination to avoid it. The main national beneficiaries would be South Africa and the Soviet Union, the principal gold producers. The main private beneficiaries would be the gold speculators and hoarders who have already caused so much trouble. A rise in the gold price now would encourage similar speculation and hoarding some time in the future. It would put more world resources into an essentially wasteful activity, and even so there would be little prospect that gold production would augment reserves at a sufficiently rapid or regular rate to meet the needs of an expanding world economy. Surely in this day and age man can contrive a better solution than to reinforce the ancient irrational myth of gold.

The French government has promoted discussion of one alternative scheme, the Collective Reserve Unit or CRU, and I suspect this, rather than a literal metallic gold standard, was in the back of General de Gaulle's mind. In its essence the proposal would increase the value of gold in official monetary gold stocks, but not the value of unmined or privately hoarded gold. CRUs, which may be regarded as paper gold, would be issued to participating nations roughly in proportion to their gold stocks. They would be issued by an agent—the French propose the Bank of International Settlements in Basel—with whom the participating countries would deposit equivalent amounts of their own currency. Thus a CRU would represent, say, 50 cents in U.S. dollars, 10 cents in French francs, 12 cents in German marks, and so on. Deficits would be settled in gold-cum-CRUs in fixed proportions corresponding to their shares in aggregate reserves.

CRUs would replace dollars in monetary reserves. Assuming that the initial issue was designed to change the form but not the total of reserves, it would be about one third of the aggregate monetary gold stock and have the same effect on U.S. and foreign reserve positions as a 33⅓ per cent increase in the price of gold.

The CRU proposal has two great merits. It would be a truly international fiduciary money, based on a portfolio of national currencies rather than any single national money. It is vastly superior to gold, because no resources need be wasted in producing it; and its supply can be deliberately controlled rather than left to accidents of mining economics and technology and the whims of private hoarders and the Soviet Union. Nevertheless, the proposal has decisive disadvantages for the world, and particularly for the United States.

First, the French wish to confine the participating group of nations to a big boys' club—ten or twelve leading monetary powers. These countries would print more money for themselves, and from this new mine of paper gold the rest of the world would benefit only indirectly. There already exists a worldwide monetary organization, the International Monetary Fund. The French proposal would diminish its importance by entrusting the most important monetary function to a select group, outside or only nominally inside the Fund.

Second, replacement of existing dollar holdings with CRUs, of which the dollar component is only fractional, inflicts on the

United States a considerable loss of total reserves. As I argued above, the U.S. need have no apologies for the past. Its deficits were incurred for good international purposes and were essential to the international monetary system. We should insist that any new system consolidate the past without penalizing the United States. The first installment of CRUS should be backed 100 per cent by the dollars they replace in foreign reserves.

Third, the proposal has a restrictive and deflationary spirit and bias. This is not intrinsic to the proposal but reflects the French view that the current total of world reserves will be adequate for some time to come. They wish the new system to function like the gold standard described above; countries would have very little access to credit to relieve the necessity of settling deficits with metallic or paper gold.

In principle, the participating countries could regulate the supply of world reserves by agreeing to issue themselves, from time to time, new CRUS in the agreed national proportions. But since this would require a unanimous vote, doubts would probably be resolved by doing nothing.

The major alternative is to replace dollars with credits against the International Monetary Fund. The Fund already is a pool of national currencies from which members can draw. Some of their drawing rights are automatic; these should be, and increasingly are, regarded by member countries as international reserves on virtually the same plane as gold and reserve currencies.

These automatic rights arise in two ways. First, 25 per cent of members' quotas are subscribed in gold, the remainder in their own currencies. The gold "tranche" is automatically available. The total of gold tranche rights is now about $3.5 billion, and it will rise to about $4.5 billion under the 25 per cent increase in Fund quotas that has just been negotiated. Gold tranche drawing rights do not augment world reserves, since they only replace the gold paid into the Fund by member governments.

Second, a fiduciary creation of automatic drawing rights occurs as a by-product of Fund lending operations. For example, in the past when the Fund lent dollars to other members, typically underdeveloped countries, the United States obtained new automatic drawing rights—so-called pre- or super-gold-tranche rights —in equal amount. To the extent that the borrowing countries were using not solely the gold tranche of their quotas but the non-automatic credit tranches, the new automatic rights created for the U.S. were not offset by any reduction in the automatic rights of other members. In recent years the U.S. was able to use more than $1 billion of rights previously accumulated in this way to finance its balance-of-payments deficits. At present, the net automatic rights of Fund members thus created amount to about half a billion dollars.

There are several ways in which the IMF could create more reserves than it has in the past. One is to make another 25 per cent of quotas, the first "credit tranche," as automatic as the gold tranche. This would increase world reserves by more than $4 billion initially. It would also mean that future increases in quotas would add to world reserves *more* than they subtract in gold subscriptions.

A second device, which also has considerable appeal to me, is for the Fund to engage in investment operations. The Fund would purchase national currencies with pre-gold-tranche drawing rights. Members would share in these purchases in fixed proportions, probably governed by their relative quotas in the Fund. Fixing the proportion has the advantage of avoiding highly arbitrary political decisions each time an operation is undertaken. It makes these reserve-creating investments essentially neutral monetary operations, like the open-market operations of national central banks. They would be clearly distinct from extensions of credit to help individual countries, which are analogous to the discounting functions of national central banks.

There may be objections to Fund investments in the obligations of members with inconvertible currencies, which are not usable in Fund drawings. To meet these objections while still giving the underdeveloped world a share in the benefit of Fund reserve creation, an appropriate proportion of Fund investments could be reserved for purchase of the obligations of the International Bank or its affiliates.

Finally, it is essentially to avoid total inaction whenever there is disagreement. Therefore, it should be provided that, unless the Fund board specifically votes to do otherwise, Fund investments in any year should be sufficient to make total automatic drawing rights grow by an agreed percentage. The chosen figure should be designed to make total world reserves, including gold as well as IMF credits, expand along with world trade and production.

Simultaneously, the usefulness of automatic drawing rights on the Fund could be increased by making them directly transferable between members. At present they can be shifted from one member to another only with the intervention of the somewhat cumbersome currency-drawing procedures of the IMF.

As just outlined, the proposal does not solve the transitional problem of consolidating existing dollar balances. This too could be done by the Fund, through an initial purchase of dollars from the countries now holding them. Or, it could be done separately, outside the IMF, by funding our current short-term dollar debts into long-term debts payable in the other country's currency. The attractiveness of this funding could be enhanced by providing that the lending country could cash them early, with the United States, another country, or the Fund, in case it encountered balance-of-payments difficulties of its own.

The proposal for Fund investment in a package of national currencies and World Bank bonds has obvious kinship with the CRU idea. But it avoids the disadvantages of the CRU. It is located in an established worldwide organization, and all countries share in its benefits. It does not replace existing dollar balances in a manner unfair and injurious to the U.S.; this consolidation must be separately managed. The IMF investment proposal is flexible and it does not have a deflationary or restrictive bias.

The creation of international money, for circulation among central banks, is entirely feasible. The institutional setting for this development already exists in the International Monetary Fund. The way is there; what is needed is the will. Progress is blocked, on the one hand, by French distrust of money creation in the IMF and, on the other hand, by U.S. insistence on the sanctity of the dollar's status as a reserve currency. In my view, the U.S. should now be willing to accept an orderly consolidation of dollar balances in return for new arrangements to provide reserves through the IMF.

The United States no longer has blank check privileges, and official holders of dollars are restless and unhappy. Nevertheless the U.S. government continues to insist that we will consider no reform of international monetary arrangements that threatens the

reserve-currency position of the dollar. This insistence has contributed to the current impasse in international discussion of monetary reform. But it has not, of course, prevented the dollar's
reserve-currency status from eroding anyway.

The reluctance of U.S. financial circles to accept a solution that
recognizes the decline in the reserve-currency status of the dollar
seems to be based on a misunderstanding. It is feared that such
a solution will also displace the dollar from its role as the principal
medium of exchange in private international transactions. This
would lose New York and the country some financial business and
income, and the nation would no longer enjoy the ability to finance
payments deficits from the yearly increment of private foreign
demand for dollar working balances.

But no one is proposing to create an international money for
private circulation. There the dollar will remain unchallenged,
save for the imitative competition of the Euro-dollar. The sources
of its advantages, which I tried to explain above, are in no way dependent on the dollar's continued use as an official reserve currency. Indeed, any international monetary reform that removes
the danger of a run from dollars into gold can only strengthen the
world's private demand for dollars. More important, it can free
U.S. policy from our current obsessive concern with gold.

PART III

The Industrial World: The Issues

From the point of view of American foreign economic policy, the "Industrial World" consists of—besides ourselves—Canada, the non-Communist nations of Europe, and Japan. The categorization is not an accurate one because it includes some states that can hardly be called manufacturing giants, e.g., Greece, Portugal, Spain, and Turkey, and excludes some that are by no means primitive, most notably the Soviet Union, Australia, Israel, and South Africa. Still, it is a handy way of distinguishing our policies toward the relatively rich Free World from those affecting either the Communist World or the Third World of less developed countries.

In our economic relations with Western Europe, the major themes of United States policy have been European unity and Atlantic partnership. Since the beginning of the Cold War, we have stressed European unity for two reasons: as a means for burying the nationalistic animosities that had already caused two world wars in this century, and as a means for strengthening the area as a barrier to Communist expansion. Unity was to be achieved through financial and commercial collaboration and eventually through an integration of Europe's economies. Thus as early as 1947, when Marshall Plan aid was first offered to the nations of Europe, our generosity was made conditional upon local efforts to cooperate in economic matters and to coordinate activity on a regional scale. The Europeans responded gladly by joining together in what became known as the Organization of European Economic Cooperation (OEEC). Soon a program of intra-European trade liberalization was begun, a payments union was formed, and by 1958 it was even possible to restore a degree of convertibility to all of Europe's currencies.

The year 1958 also witnessed the birth of the European Economic Community (EEC), a broad economic union conceived by France, Germany, Italy, and the three Benelux countries after the success of their earlier coal and steel union (ECSC, 1950). In a sense the Community represented a victory for American policy, which had actively promoted a total integration of Europe's economies. But it could hardly be called a total victory, for not all of Europe's economies were included. Great Britain had objected to the formation of a common market, preferring instead a much more diluted variety of economic collaboration. When the six EEC countries refused to compromise their objectives, a stalemate ensued, and subsequently Britain sponsored the formation of the European Free Trade Area (EFTA). As a result, Europe split into two rival blocs: an "Inner Six" and an "Outer Seven." At the end of the 1950s, the unity of all of Western Europe remained an unfulfilled objective.[1]

The same is true of the objective of Atlantic partnership. In general, the aim of U.S. policy-makers was to foster the closest possible political relations between ourselves and Europe, presumably to guarantee that they would never tip the scale against us in the postwar balance of power. Economically, the partnership between America and Europe was to be cemented by a global liberalization of industrial trade—the trade that is of prime interest to the countries on both sides of the Atlantic. Unfortunately, the legislative branch of the U.S. government did not make the job easy for the executive branch. For instance, in 1948 the Executive midwifed an International Trade Organization (ITO), only to discover it had been a stillbirth: Congress refused to ratify the Havana Charter. The Executive then retreated to a transitional arrangement set up a year earlier, the General Agreement on Tariffs and Trade (GATT), hoping that it could thereby continue to exploit its existing authority to negotiate reciprocal tariff reductions. That authority, however, was delegated by Congress and had to be renewed periodically. At each renewal it was narrowed so much that by the end of the 1950s, after several rounds of GATT-sponsored tariff negotiations, there were very few trade

[1] For a history of Europe's uncertain progress toward unity, see Michael Curtis, *Western European Integration* (New York: Harper & Row, 1965).

concessions left that the United States could offer in the interest of freer commercial relations across the Atlantic.[2]

John F. Kennedy came to the Presidency determined to reinvigorate U.S. efforts to promote European unity and Atlantic partnership. This was his "Grand Design" in foreign policy. In 1962 he persuaded Congress to pass the Trade Expansion Act, granting him for five years sweeping new powers to negotiate reciprocal tariff reductions. To further liberalize Atlantic trade, he was authorized to reduce all tariffs by as much as 50 percent. In addition, in all commodity categories for which the United States and the EEC together accounted for 80 percent or more of world exports, he was authorized to move the entire distance to free trade. This latter provision was designed to further promote the movement toward general European integration that had been revived that year by Great Britain's decision to seek membership in the Common Market. Everyone understood that without the British the free-trade provision would be meaningless. But with the British and with the rest of EFTA as either members or associates, it could be of great importance.

Thus with one stroke it seemed we might accomplish our Grand Design after all. Unfortunately, we failed to reckon with Charles de Gaulle, who had a grand design of his own. As Randall Hinshaw notes [13], de Gaulle's conception of European unity—a conception that has since come to be shared by many Europeans—was of a Europe free of all traces of American power. Consequently, the French president almost immediately vetoed the British application for Common Market membership, labeling Britain in effect a "Trojan horse" for the United States. This action, for all practical purposes, killed the free-trade provision of the Trade Expansion Act and left us with only the 50 percent provision as a basis for a new round of tariff negotiations in GATT. Dubbed the "Kennedy Round," it got under way in 1963, but here too de Gaulle proved to be a firm opponent of American policy. Although the EEC negotiated as a single unit, it was dominated by France, and in the hard bargaining of the next four years the French re-

---

[2] On our commercial policy in the postwar period, see Paul H. Douglas, *America in the Market Place: Trade, Tariffs, and the Balance of Payments* (New York: Holt, Rinehart and Winston, 1966), Chs. 7–8.

sisted all concessions that might perpetuate or extend America's influence in Europe. For the most part, they were successful. When the Kennedy Round finally ended in 1967, the results fell far short of its namesake's original vision. True, the Kennedy Round reduced more tariffs by more than any other round of GATT negotiations in the postwar period. Indeed, thousands of individual tariffs were cut by the full 50 percent provided for in the original Trade Expansion Act. However, many other duties were cut by considerably less, and some of the most important tariffs of various countries were not cut at all. As William Diebold [15] makes perfectly clear, the commercial restrictions that remain with us—not only the tariffs but even more important the nontariff barriers—are by no means negligible. Atlantic trade is still very far from being free.

The frustrations engendered by the experience of the Kennedy Round are vividly apparent in the selections by Randall Hinshaw [13] and David Steinberg [14]. Although both economists wrote well before the conclusion of the negotiations, both anticipated the Round's relatively limited accomplishments, and so their comments remain quite relevant in current discussions of United States commercial policy. What should our post-Kennedy Round policy be? Both Hinshaw and Steinberg answer that freer trade is in our national interest, and I agree. Not only is it in our economic interest as a consuming nation and as a highly effective competitor in world markets, it is also in our political interest as the world's most important trading state. Relatively speaking, foreign trade is not so important in this country as it is elsewhere; in other words, we are less dependent on trade than most other countries. At the same time we buy and sell more, in absolute terms, than any other country on the face of the earth: we have more influence in trade matters than anyone else. Consequently, we can on balance probably enhance our own economic power position by promoting a further liberalization of world trade. The question is, what kind of liberalization?

Steinberg advocates a complete liberalization of all trade by all of the industrialized nations—in effect, absolutely free trade within the Industrial World. This is the classic GATT objective and of course eminently worthwhile in principle. However, the experience of GATT illustrates how very difficult it is to achieve in actual practice: free trade is just not a politically realistic objective for American policy. Protectionist sentiment remains potent in almost every country in the world, as do nationalistic sentiments that oppose any extension of America's foreign economic influence. Feeling on this issue has become particularly strong within the European Economic Community, which is trying to maximize its own economic power position by preserving its common external tariff and agricultural policy. Feeling is strongest of all in Gaulist France. In the Kennedy Round it found expression in the firmness and inflexibility of the Common Market's bargaining position, a position not likely to be relaxed much in the future. In my opinion, we simply cannot hope to persuade the Six to join us in a commitment to absolutely free trade.

On the other hand, it might be possible to persuade some of the industrialized nations to join us in such a commitment. Hinshaw favors by-passing the Community and concentrating instead on building a free-trade area to include the EFTA countries together with any others that might wish to participate. As a group, the EFTA countries are less self-contained than the Six. In general, therefore, they share an interest with the United States in freer world trade. Indeed, in the Kennedy Round some of them were prepared to liberalize trade even more than we were, and most would probably welcome any new free-trade initiatives by this country. Thus a basis does appear to exist for what Hinshaw calls "a creative response by the non-EEC countries."

However, it is a most uncertain basis and not at all the creative response it might seem. As Steinberg warns, "it overlooks the fact that participation of the EEC countries . . . is essential to the success of any trade negotiation and indispensable to our overall foreign policy mission." The fundamental reality for the EFTA countries is that they trade considerably more with the Six than with us. If free trade for the whole Industrial World is ruled out, then they would benefit much more from participation in the Common Market than from membership in an Atlantic free-trade area excluding the EEC. Consequently, it should not have surprised anyone when in 1967, as the Kennedy Round drew to its rather disappointing conclusion, Britain and most of her EFTA partners once again queued up in Brussels to apply for either full Community membership or associate status. It was the logical thing for them to do.

The logical—and creative—thing for us to do is to support this latest development. European unity is still a valid objective of American policy, even though circumstances have changed somewhat since the days of the Marshall Plan. They have not, after all, changed *that* much. It is still no more in our interest now than it was twenty years ago to harden the economic and political divisions within Western Europe, which is precisely what we would do if we tried to form an Atlantic free-trade area excluding the EEC. On the contrary, it is in our interest to bow to what is inevitable anyway and broaden the European Community. Europeans today are in large numbers opposed to any extension of America's economic power position at their expense; in fact, they want our predominance in their economies to end. They are not necessarily opposed to the old principle of an Atlantic partnership, but if there is to be any kind of partnership, it must, they insist, be on the basis of parity between America and a strong and, if possible, integrated Europe, not on the basis of our postwar economic hegemony over European affairs. In other words, it must be on the basis of the freest possible trade within Western Europe, not on the basis of completely free trade across the Atlantic. In short, if we wish to retain any political influence in Europe at all, they say, we must be prepared to tolerate a further decline in our net economic influence. This is the reality with which our commercial policy in Europe must deal. In practical terms, it means that we can hope for no more than a rather limited or gradual liberalization of Atlantic trade, such as the liberalization that resulted from the Kennedy Round.

This is also the reality with which our foreign-investment policy in Europe must deal. As C. F. Karsten [16], a European, observes; "The days are now past when committees from Western European countries queued up at the doors of huge American corporations to invite them to establish factories in their cities or districts, and when governments one after another—secretly or not—offered attractive fiscal advantages." Today's Europeans are becoming increasingly hostile to what is now labeled an "invasion" by those very same American corporations. Many are resentful of what they view as the overwhelming competitive strength of inflowing United States investments, said to be derived from the greater size of our firms as well as from our lead in research and development and our superior access to financial resources. American strength, it is feared, will be used to "take over" European businesses, to dominate whole sectors of European industries, eventually to evade the control of European planning—in short, to perpetuate America's predominance in Europe's economies. This, to repeat, Europeans oppose, and many are ready to back up their opposition with discriminatory and restrictive measures if necessary.

Karsten admits, of course, that the fears of his fellow Europeans regarding American investments have tended to become exaggerated, even hysterical. Nonetheless, he argues—and I would agree —"the current situation cannot go on in an unrestricted form." In view of Europe's sensitivity to any extension of America's economic power position, some form of additional restraint on the high level of our investments seems inevitable. From the public-relations point of view, if would appear to be in our interest to accept the inevitable and do the restraining ourselves.[3] It simply does us no good at all to exacerbate the Europeans' apprehensions by continuing to invest in their industries at our present rate. As in trade policy, if we wish to retain any political influence at all in Europe, we must be prepared to tolerate a further decline in our economic influence.

If Europeans fear American influence in their economic affairs, Canadians dread it, and not without cause. As both Jacob Viner [17] and Harry Johnson [18] indicate, the economy of Canada is exceptionally dependent on that of the United States. Professor Viner stresses the trade connection and the disparity in economic size between the two countries. The economies, he notes, are complementary: broadly speaking, Canada has the raw materials, the United States the manufacturing capacity. The result is that in absolute terms the volume of trade between them is considerable. Not in relative terms, however; in this respect, the trade picture

[3] For a suggestion of how to accomplish this, see the essay on pp. 36–52, "The Financial Framework: The Issues," and B. J. Cohen, "Voluntary Foreign Investment Curbs: A Plan that Really Works," *Challenge*, March–April, 1967, pp. 15–16.

is strikingly different, mainly because the American economy is so much larger than the Canadian. As Viner emphasizes, "because of the disparity in size, the Canadian economy, while important to the United States as export market and source of supply, is not nearly as important to the United States as the latter is to Canada." About three-fifths of Canada's export trade and more than two-thirds of her import trade are with the United States, whereas for this country the corresponding ratios vis-à-vis Canada are only each about one-fifth. Thus it should be no surprise to find that Canadians are extremely sensitive to developments in our commercial policies, which, they complain, do not take sufficient account of Canadian vital interests. Nor should it be a surprise to find, as Viner does, that because we are rather less sensitive to Canadian developments these complaints are often justified.

Professor Johnson stresses the investment connection and the disparity in financial strength between the two countries. Historically, Canada's economic growth has been powered by foreign investments, and since World War II these investments have been almost entirely American. Much of the capital from the United States has been invested in manufacturing facilities, particularly in the automobile and rubber industries, which are now almost completely American-owned. In all, some 45 percent of Canada's manufacturing production is controlled by United States investors, as well as some 60 percent of her petroleum and natural-gas output, half of her mining and smelting, and 10 percent of her utilities. For Europeans, the threat of an American corporate "takeover" remains primarily a fear; for Canadians, it has become a reality.

Indeed, the underlying reality is that the Canadian economy has already been informally integrated into that of the United States, not only by the extensive penetration of American capital but also by the large volume and complementary nature of intratrade. Harry Johnson suggests that an appropriate objective of policy would be "some form of reciprocal free trade"—in effect, formal economic integration. And certainly, from a strictly economic point of view, this would seem to be a rational solution, for it makes little economic sense to preserve the mutual barriers that remain. Likewise, from the American point of view, this would seem to be a logical objective, since it would consolidate our predominant position north of the border: Canada would be incorporated as the very junior partner of the United States. But for just that reason many Canadians can be expected to be hostile to any such idea. Nationalist sentiment, as both Viner and Johnson note, is strong in Canada, and as in Europe it tends to find expression in opposing any extension of America's commercial or financial influence. Indeed, as Johnson describes, many Canadians are willing to sacrifice a considerable amount of current income and future growth for the sake of reducing our hegemony over their economic affairs. For that reason, a formal economic union would not be a realistic policy objective for the United States.

On the other hand, it would not be realistic for the Canadians to aim at suppressing American economic influence by as much as the Europeans apparently hope to do. Canada's population is too small for her to go it alone, and her unique geographic situation reduces her chance of finding other more equal partners. The American predominance in the Canadian economy is bound to continue, but this is not likely to discourage Canadians from seeking to exploit every opportunity to moderate our influence marginally or to shape it to their advantage. The outlook, therefore, is for continued tension between us, sometimes breaking into the open, sometimes remaining beneath the surface. For the makers of America's foreign economic policy, the problem is to preserve our position in Canada and whenever possible to extend it, as in the 1965 agreement for mutual free trade in automobiles and parts, without sparking off a new round of Canadian anti-Americanism. That will be a delicate task, to say the least.

In our economic relations with Japan, the major theme of United States policy throughout the postwar period has been reconstruction. In 1945, Japan was a prostrate nation, and at first our impulse was to keep it that way. However, as soon as the Cold War began, our policy shifted. Very soon our objective became, in the words of Warren Hunsberger [19], "an economically strong and politically stable Japan." Since the late 1940s, this has been the operational goal of our economic policy in the Far East. To help achieve it, we primed the Japanese economy with the expenditures of our military forces, provided economic assistance and private capital, granted easy access to our huge domestic market and to our latest technology, sponsored Japan's membership in the GATT and other international bodies, and even used our ability to influence third countries in Japan's behalf. In turn, the Japanese exploited with great effectiveness the advantages and opportunities offered them, and as a result Japan today is one of the healthiest and most vigorous industrial powers on the face of the earth. Hunsberger is quite correct when he writes that "Americans can take a great deal of satisfaction in the tremendous economic successes Japan has achieved in the postwar period. The United States has contributed much to these successes."

Hunsberger is also correct when he writes that the United States now faces "some new questions of policy," for just as Japan is no longer so weak and dependent as she was a decade or two ago, so the United States is no longer as influential in international economic affairs as before. Consequently, we can no longer afford to be quite as generous with our commercial and balance-of-payments policies as we once were. On the other hand, though, if we are not generous enough, we may force Japan into actions that would conflict with other of our foreign economic policies. The Japanese desperately need external markets, and if we threaten to withdraw some part of our own on account of foreign-exchange difficulties or domestic protectionist sentiment, they may have no choice but to expand trade with the Asian Communist states instead, states against whom we are still trying to impose a trade embargo. In this respect the United States is caught on the horns of a rather difficult policy dilemma that Hunsberger discusses with considerable perception and insight.

13

European Integration and American Trade Policy

RANDALL HINSHAW

Whatever its effect on the American economy, the European Economic Community has already had a major impact on the foreign economic policy of the United States in the passage of the justly acclaimed Trade Expansion Act of 1962. Unfortunately, the premises on which that Act came into being have, to say the least, been called into question as a result of the statements and actions of President de Gaulle in early 1963, and a re-examination of the direction and focus of American policy, particularly in matters of trade, is therefore in order.

The Logic of American Policy

It should first be emphasized that American policy toward European integration has been at least as much influenced by political as by economic considerations. Consequently, any policy conclusions on European integration which rest solely on economic grounds are open to the valid charge of missing the point. For, despite the threat to its international economic position, the United States since the early days of the Marshall Plan has, under a bipartisan policy, strongly supported the cause of European integration, at first in the interest of European recovery and, later, in the interest of European political unity and economic strength. The hope was that these objectives, if realized, would make Western Europe an effective partner in promoting a promising future for the free world.

Reprinted in this form by permission from Randall Hinshaw, *The European Community and American Trade* (New York: Frederick A. Praeger, 1964), pp. 162–178.

From the outset, moreover, the United States has consciously accepted the commercially discriminatory implications of European integration. In the early postwar years the United States acquiesced in a strictly intra-European attack on trade barriers, because the dollar shortage appeared to rule out a global attack. The disappearance of the dollar shortage removed this basis for a regional approach in Western Europe, but the emergence of the European Economic Community introduced a new set of considerations in which political judgments were dominant—on both sides of the Atlantic. From a European viewpoint the importance of political considerations can be seen even in what at first sight might seem a strictly economic exercise: the steps taken by the Community to form a customs union. In the thinking of the Community's founders, political objectives were of major significance both in the internal removal of tariffs and in the establishment of a common external tariff. Internally, tariffs and other obstacles to the free movement of goods, labor, and capital were to be removed not only to increase economic efficiency, but also to bind or "cement" the member countries more firmly together politically; externally, the formation of a common tariff wall—whatever its economic rationale—likewise was to serve a political function as a symbol of the geographical limits of this unity.

In terms of geographical scope, unfortunately, the Community could hardly be regarded as an ideal instrument of European integration since it embraced only the "Little Europe" of the Six. Nevertheless, the United States—again on political grounds—vigorously supported the Six as the nucleus of what it hoped would eventually be a much broader grouping that would include most or all of Western Europe, and that might ultimately become an Atlantic or even a Free World Community. On this ground the American government, despite the possibility of adverse economic consequences, strongly encouraged Great Britain in its effort to become a full member of the Community. And it hoped that British membership would shortly be followed by similar arrangements for other EFTA countries, thus ending the unfortunate division of Western Europe into two large rival regional blocs.

With this pattern of evolution in mind, Congress in 1962 courageously passed the Trade Expansion Act under which bold reciprocal tariff cuts, apart from safeguarding American access to the Common Market, would perform the same "cementing" function for the Atlantic Partnership that reciprocal tariff reductions within the Six were performing for the European Economic Community. In addition to the general authorization to cut duties in half, authority to move all the way to free trade was granted for certain product categories, one of which could have been of great importance if Britain had been permitted to join the Community.

American Policy and De Gaulle

Unluckily, this creative response to the "Common Market challenge" almost immediately received a grave blow at the hand of President de Gaulle, who made it clear in January 1963 that his objection to British membership was based on grounds that were diametrically opposed to the American conception of the Community's role in the free world. These grounds were primarily political rather than economic. In his celebrated press conference the French President indicated that he opposed British membership because of his fear that it would open the door to a "colossal Atlantic community" which not only would include, but would be dominated by, the United States. Against this conception of the Community's future development, de Gaulle, from his earliest writing on European unification, had made it abundantly clear that he regarded the role of a united Europe to be that of a "third force"—dominated by France, independent of "Anglo-American" ties, and prepared to pursue policies detached from those of the two giant nations through which postwar conflict has been polarized.[1]

---

[1] Referring to the period 1944–46 and to opinions which date back to 1940, de Gaulle has written: "I intended to guarantee France primacy in western Europe by preventing the rise of a new Reich that might again threaten its safety; to cooperate with East and West and, if need be, contract the necessary alliances on one side or the other without ever accepting any kind of dependency; . . . to persuade the states along the Rhine, the Alps, and the Pyrenees to form a political, economic, and strategic bloc; to establish this organization as one of the three world powers and, should it become necessary, as the arbiter between the Soviet and Anglo-American camps. Since 1940, my every word and act had been dedicated to establishing these possibilities; now that France was on her feet again, I tried to realize them." Charles de Gaulle, *War Memoirs: Salvation, 1944–1946* (London: Weidenfeld and Nicolson, 1960), pp. 178–179.

Though the future is clouded, two matters seem clear. First, after a period of considerable uncertainty in 1963, the European Economic Community appears to be here to stay; and, second, it is dominated for the time being by a leader who has a conception of its role very different from that held either by its founding fathers (including, notably, that other great Frenchman, Jean Monnet) or by the many Americans who have placed so much hope in its future. More specifically, the Community is led by a man who has no interest in lowering trade barriers as a means of "cementing" an Atlantic Partnership and who appears to be equally unimpressed by any other reasons for significantly reducing the Community's level of external protection.

This does not necessarily mean, of course, that the French President will be permanently able to alter the direction of the Community's development. Conceivably, after an interruption in the timetable, the Community will resume the pattern of evolution contemplated by its major architects. In the meantime, however, the major attack on Atlantic trade barriers envisaged in the Trade Expansion Act may be virtually paralyzed unless certain questions are squarely faced.

The Basic Question

The central question which must first be answered is whether a bold move toward free trade remains a compelling American objective in spite of the abrupt calling into question of the political assumptions underlying the Trade Expansion Act. Here the author can only state, then attempt to support, his own strong conviction that, entirely apart from political considerations involving the future course of European integration, a drastic move toward American free trade has long been overdue.

The reason can be compactly stated. The first, though least important, consideration is that the economic case for American protectionism, such as it is, has long since disappeared. The case was first made—and made with great skill—by Alexander Hamilton in his celebrated *Report on Manufactures* of 1791. This carefully argued report is well worth a thorough reading, if only because it reveals how different the conditions of eighteenth century America were from those of today.

Hamilton's views strikingly foreshadow the preoccupations of many a developing country of the 1960s. His basic concern was that, in the absence of protection, the United States might be doomed to remain an agricultural country, precariously—and perhaps permanently—dependent on Europe for its supplies of manufactured goods. Like many leaders in developing countries today, Hamilton was impressed with the instability of agricultural export earnings, which he attributed not only to "natural causes" but also to foreign "artificial impediments"—a phrase which recalls that the problems of farmers have a long history.

Hamilton is an early champion of what most economists would regard as by far the most important and respectable economic argument for protection, namely, the "infant-industry" argument. Briefly, the argument is that protection may be temporarily justified in cases where a country, with the help of such protection, may be able to establish industries which are potentially efficient and fully competitive but which are unlikely to get started without initial assistance in the form of tariffs or subsidies. Within its assumptions, the infant-industry argument provides a straightforward case for protection, but only for temporary protection. As Hamilton observed, the retention of protection "on manufactures long established must almost always be of questionable policy, because a presumption would arise in every such case that there were natural and inherent impediments to success." Protection, that is to say, is justified on infant-industry grounds only in those cases where production is eventually in a position to be profitable on a free-trade basis, and is to be discontinued when no longer necessary.

The Hamiltonian case, then, applies pre-eminently to developing countries, such as the United States in its earlier years and the less developed countries of today. It provides no support whatever for American protectionism in the 1960s, and those who invoke Hamilton in support of the existing American tariff clearly have no understanding of his logic. But this is essentially a negative argument, which one can accept without proceeding to the difficult political judgment that the United States should undertake a vigorous move toward free trade. For the author, the latter judgment is derived mainly from two additional considerations.

In the first place, in spite of years of whittling away at the American tariff, the United States clearly remains among the high-tariff countries. In view of the American position of leadership in the free world, this situation can only be described as an anomaly without any valid excuse. The situation is deplorable particularly because it is abundantly clear that protectionism on the part of the United States and other high-income countries is bound to cause increasing frustration within the free world as the low-income countries gradually become more competitive in manufacturing. If this problem is taken seriously, as it must be if the United States is not, in President Kennedy's phrase, to "disdain the future," it is difficult to escape the conclusion that the "cementing" function of tariff reduction is at least as important in relation to the low-income countries as it is in relation to our Atlantic partners.

In the second place, if the United States attaches a high priority to its own economic strength and economic growth—a priority dictated by considerations both of security and of economic welfare—it can ill afford the luxury of protecting high-cost production. In this connection it is necessary to separate the basic economic argument from those which are essentially peripheral. In enlisting support for the Trade Expansion Act the Administration made its economic case largely in terms of the favorable effect of reciprocal tariff cuts on the American balance of payments and on the number of American "jobs." Official statistical studies reached the conclusion that the mutual lowering of trade barriers would increase American exports more than it would increase American imports, thus reducing or removing the pressure on the balance of payments. At the same time the increased exports, it was concluded, would create more jobs for American workers than the increased imports would replace, thus yielding a net increase in employment. While these conclusions may have been correct and, moreover, may have been important in achieving support for the new legislation, they had little bearing on the basic economic case for tariff removal, which is concerned with the more fundamental consideration of economic efficiency.

At the risk of offending those who have successfully weathered a respectable course in elementary economics, it may be briefly stated that the primary economic argument for freer trade—an argument which applies unequivocally to all developed countries —is that the reduction or removal of trade barriers would increase economic efficiency by promoting a transfer of economic resources from less efficient to more efficient employment. The case is most easily understood, and in fact is strongest, where the move toward free trade is jointly undertaken by a substantial number of countries. In these circumstances labor and capital would move from high-cost industries, previously sheltered by tariffs from foreign competition, to more efficient employment in the export industries now enjoying increased orders from abroad. The result of such a transfer of resources would be an average increase in output per worker and thus, at a given level of employment, an increase in production.

How much efficiency would increase would depend on the initial degree of protection, on the degree to which protection was reduced and, last though not least, on the number of countries participating in the move toward free trade. Since the American tariff is high, a vigorous move toward free trade would doubtless yield major benefits in increased economic efficiency, particularly if the move, as contemplated in the Trade Expansion Act, is jointly undertaken with other countries. For while it can be shown that the United States could gain economically from unilateral tariff reduction, it would stand to gain much more from a multilateral effort embracing Western Europe and other high-income areas. The reason for this is that a multilateral attack on tariffs would make possible a higher degree of international specialization and thus, for each participating country, a more productive use of economic resources. Moreover, because of the increased demand from abroad, each country could remove tariffs with less fear of a net reduction in employment.

The latter point is important because, as experience has amply demonstrated, unemployment and freedom of trade are implacable enemies. It was mass unemployment which brought free trade in Britain to an end three decades ago—the clamor for protection, in the last analysis, being a clamor for jobs. Thus, while only confusion can result from arguing that tariff reduction tends to increase employment—an argument that could not possibly apply to every country undertaking a joint move toward free trade—it is likewise folly to overlook the necessity of insuring that any move toward free trade be combined with adequate safeguards to maintain the level of employment.

But this is not just a matter of tariffs. What is clearly needed are policies to assure a labor market that is adequate to absorb all workers released from less efficient activity, whether their former jobs were in high-cost production sheltered by tariffs or in production that has become high-cost because of advances in technology. The problem, in other words, is to maintain an economy which is continuously able to take full advantage of the increased efficiency made possible both through greater freedom of trade and through never-ceasing innovation. But this is a problem which, with present knowledge, can be effectively dealt with provided sufficient attention is given to two needs: first, the need for adequate facilities to retrain workers released from less efficient employment and, second, the need for maintaining a high level of demand.

The Question of Method

So much for the central question of whether a vigorous move toward free trade remains a compelling American objective. Subject to the foregoing qualifications, this question has been answered emphatically in the affirmative.

But how may the objective best be achieved? If a major breakthrough in American policy is to be achieved and sustained, this second question merits as much consideration as the first, for the answer is far from obvious. The immediate task, of course, is to make as much progress as possible under the Trade Expansion Act and, in particular, to bring the "Kennedy round" of tariff negotiations to a successful conclusion. At the same time two points should be emphasized. The first is that, in view of recent developments within the European Economic Community, it will be difficult even with the most skillful negotiating to achieve anything approaching the steep across-the-board reductions in Atlantic tariffs contemplated in the Trade Expansion Act. The second point is that, whether the negotiations are disappointing or notably successful, the results will fall far short of what is needed if the conclusions of this chapter are accepted. To achieve significant further progress, however, it will be necessary not only to expand American authority to reduce tariffs—an objective which could be achieved by amending the Trade Expansion Act—but also to consider whether existing ground rules provide an adequate basis for a major new attack on trade barriers. In particular, it will be important to re-examine two basic premises of American commercial policy: the premise that trade concessions should be reciprocal and the premise that trade concessions should be nondiscriminatory.

These two principles have long been cornerstones of American policy. Both were embedded in the Reciprocal Trade Agreements program; both, with strong American support, were incorporated into the General Agreement on Tariffs and Trade; and both underlie the Trade Expansion Act of 1962. Any attack on these policies must therefore be regarded as bearing the burden of proof. Nevertheless, in a world in which, under existing procedures, one industrial country can be in a position to block an effective multilateral program of tariff reduction, the question must at least be raised whether reciprocity and equal treatment should be retained as working principles.

With respect to reciprocity, it is difficult to escape the conclusion that the American position is basically right. As we have seen, the case for a multilateral attack on trade barriers is much stronger, both on political and on economic grounds, than is the case for a unilateral attack. The same arguments which strongly support a bold American move toward free trade apply with equal force to other high-income countries; and further, the economic benefits for the United States—or for any other individual country—would be much greater from a multilateral than from a unilateral effort. Thus, the position that tariff concessions should be reciprocal is entirely reasonable. Reciprocity, indeed, is a *sine qua non* of any multilateral program of tariff reduction, and there is everything to be said for making the most of American influence and bargaining power to assure that American action toward freer trade is widely matched by corresponding action abroad.

In this connection, however, there is a serious difficulty. A really bold program of multilateral tariff reduction is likely to founder in midstream if the entirely proper emphasis on reciprocity is accompanied by a similar insistence on equal treatment. Where tariff reduction is carried on at a leisurely pace, as it was under the Reciprocal Trade Agreements program, the conflict between reciprocity and equal treatment may not be particularly obvious. By careful bargaining between "principal suppliers" on a commodity-by-commodity basis, the concessions extended to outsiders under the most-favored-nation clause can be kept to a minimum, and no serious friction is likely to arise, particularly where the tariff cuts themselves are modest. The situation is profoundly different, however, where a major multilateral move toward free trade is contemplated. In these circumstances it may be exceedingly difficult to persuade countries to make sweeping tariff reductions if they are required to extend concessions not only to countries which are prepared effectively to reciprocate but also to those which are not. Such reluctance, however regrettable, is entirely understandable, and must be fully taken into account if major new multilateral advances toward free trade are to be achieved.

It is here that there may be an important lesson to be learned from the Six and the Seven. Members of the European Economic Community and the European Free Trade Association have been removing internal trade barriers on a basis of strict reciprocity, the reciprocity taking the form of successive across-the-board tariff cuts under rules which apply uniformly to the members within each group. Two matters are particularly worthy of note. First, the criteria for reciprocity are simple and completely unambiguous. Reciprocity in this context means simply that tariffs are jointly reduced by a given percentage—usually ten per cent—on given dates. Second, the step-by-step concessions are extended only to countries which are jointly engaged in the same program. While this type of behavior is generally regarded as a deviation (though an authorized deviation) from most-favored-nation treatment, it can be looked at, alternatively, as a form of conditional most-favored-nation treatment—the condition of course being that such treatment (ultimately free trade) is extended only to those who reciprocate.

As has often been pointed out, the Trade Expansion Act has taken one leaf from the Rome Treaty (and from the Stockholm Convention) in the form of provision for across-the-board tariff cuts on a reciprocal basis. It has not, however, taken the other leaf of limiting tariff concessions to countries which are prepared fully to reciprocate in a multilateral program. The Act specifically provides that concessions negotiated with other countries are to be generalized on a most-favored-nation basis—a requirement which in any case is imposed on the United States and other contracting parties by the General Agreement on Tariffs and Trade.

The question now to be considered is whether, in the interest of a vigorous multilateral program to tariff reduction, there is a strong case for modifying the traditional American policy of equal treatment. It will be argued that, subject to certain important qualifications, there is such a case. The first qualification is that there is no case whatever for dispensing completely with the most-favored-nation clause or for adopting a conditional form of the clause in which the conditions—for example, "reci-procity"—are vaguely defined. Either course would be a recipe for chaos, an invitation to endless retaliation, and a long step backward in international commercial relations.

Alternatives to Equal Treatment

But these are not the only possibilities. As the Six and the Seven have shown, it is possible to establish completely unambiguous standards of multilateral reciprocity which effectively rule out what could otherwise be a source of endless bickering and back-tracking. For example, the General Agreement on Tariffs and Trade might be modified in such a way as to permit a group of countries to establish, perhaps in a series of steps, a common tariff ceiling—say ten per cent *ad valorem*—which would apply only to countries prepared to accept this ceiling.[2] Thus, if the group were to include the United States and Canada, American imports from Canada would be subject to duties which could not exceed 10 per cent, while American imports from nonparticipat-ing countries would not be bound by this restriction. In effect, members of the group would have a two-tariff system: a pref-

---

[2] Instead of a tariff ceiling, the criterion might be a tariff average. A tariff average, however, would be a much less satisfactory standard for two reasons. In the first place, even a very low tariff average—for example, 5 per cent— is consistent with a high degree of protection for particular industries. In the second place, an average which inevitably is derived from hundreds of in-dividual duties provides much more scope than a ceiling for evasion and dispute.

erential tariff, bound by an agreed ceiling, which would apply to participants; and a nonpreferential tariff, not bound by the ceiling, which would apply to nonparticipants. Such an arrangement would involve not an abandonment, but a modification, of the most-favored-nation clause. Most-favored-nation treatment would be extended, that is to say, to the possibly large number of countries prepared to accept the tariff ceiling.[3]

Of various intermediate possibilities, this one appeals to the author, both because it is highly flexible and because, unlike most other departures from equal treatment, it is not a prescription for utter confusion. But there is another approach which, in the author's view, would be still better if the necessary agreement could be obtained. It is an approach, moreover, which would involve no change in the General Agreement on Tariffs and Trade. If the United States were to join other interested countries in a program to form a customs union or free-trade area, no GATT regulations would be violated, provided the free-trade arrangement conformed to GATT standards—i.e., provided internal tariffs were completely removed on "substantially all" internal trade within a "reasonable" length of time.

From an American standpoint, as has been pointed out, the primary objection to participation in regional free-trade arrangements is their exclusiveness. A strictly Atlantic arrangement, for example, would undoubtedly be regarded by the low-income countries as a rich man's club. It is possible, however, to conceive of regional arrangements so broad in their geographic coverage that this essentially political objection would virtually disappear.

This is a possibility which, in the author's opinion, should not be lightly brushed aside. Indeed, it deserves the most careful consideration. If, for example, the "Kennedy Round" of tariff negotiations should reveal that the European Economic Community, because of its present domination by President de Gaulle, is willing to make little more than token reductions in its external trade barriers, a creative response by the non-EEC countries might be the creation of a much larger regional arrangement of an

---

[3] Alternatively and preferably, most-favored-nation treatment could be extended not only to participants, which presumably would be high-income countries, but also to the low-income countries, which could be excused, on infant-industry grounds, from observing the tariff ceiling.

"outward-looking" character. It might include as full members the United States, the present EFTA countries, Canada, Australia, New Zealand, and Japan and, as associate members, the countries of Latin America, non-Communist Asia, and non-EEC Africa. As in the European Economic Community, associate members (after a transition period) could be granted free access to the markets of full members, while being permitted, with appropriate safeguards, to retain protection for infant industries. Alternatively, in the interest of solidarity, all participating countries could be given the rank of "full" members, with certain privileges granted to countries where the per capita income was below an agreed level. Such privileges might include access to financial assistance as well as the right to protect infant industries.

The purpose of such an arrangement would be to achieve as large a free-trade region as possible—including at an early stage, hopefully, the European Economic Community. Although the Community might not be prepared to participate, at least in the beginning, a central objective would be the inclusion of the Community, by one means or another, in the broader grouping. In the meantime the high-income members of the proposed arrangement, after a transition period, would retain tariffs only against nonmembers which, for the time being, would include the Common Market countries. But the sole purpose of imposing tariffs against the Community would be to retain a measure of bargaining power in the hope of negotiating an early marriage between the two groups.

An American Opportunity

Actually, the two approaches just described differ only in degree and, in their intermediate stages, would be virtually indistinguishable. Of the two, the second is clearly the more ambitious in calling for a broad multilateral move toward mutual free trade.

Anything approaching free trade of course goes well beyond the aims of the Trade Expansion Act and, at first glance, would seem an impossible counsel of perfection. Yet it should be remembered that one great country actually pursued such a policy for several decades, and abandoned it only under conditions of *force majeure.* Like certain other legacies of the nineteenth century, free trade in Britain was a victim of the Great Depression, which provided the stern lesson that the economic gains from freedom of trade are little appreciated under conditions of mass unemployment.

But in this sphere we have learned much. The causes of large-scale unemployment—so deep a mystery three decades age—are now widely understood, and our former inability to deal with this evil can no longer be used as a weighty argument for protection. If we take full advantage of our present economic knowledge, substantially free trade is surely the right goal for American policy, both in the interest of American economic strength and in the interest of free world solidarity. Such a goal should not be pursued frenetically, but approached gradually—and, to the maximum extent, reciprocally—with firm confidence that this is the creative trade policy for as long as anyone can foresee.

14

New Forces and Old Impulses in a Changing World Economy

DAVID J. STEINBERG

The GATT negotiations in Geneva will reveal (a) the extent to which the EEC and EFTA—the pace-setters among the world's regional communities—grasp the implications and the responsibility of what they have created, and (b) the determination of the United States, the world's largest and strongest free-market economy, to fulfill the mission of its "Kennedy Round" initiative. The EFTA countries as a whole seem ready to make these negotiations the success envisaged by those who planned the Geneva meeting. The EEC as a whole seems less interested, its delaying tactics tarnishing its announced support for the GATT conference. The United States has in turn made or has at times seemed ready to make so many protectionist moves that it unwittingly may have weakened the reliability of its declarations in support of freer trade, and lessened the interest of other industrialized areas in exerting themselves to ensure the impressive success of these negotiations.

The negotiations will test more than the readiness of the Atlantic powers to make substantial progress down the road of trade liberalization in partnership with one another and with other industrially advanced countries. They will test the durability of the General Agreement on Tariffs and Trade as the guardian of fair play and forward-looking principles in international commerce. They will test the very credibility of the policy declarations of the Atlantic nations as seen from the under-developed parts of the world. The industrialized members of GATT are a minority of its membership, but it is they who hold the decisive power that will determine the General Agreement's success or failure in coping

Reprinted in this form by permission from *Atlantic Community Quarterly*, Spring, 1965, pp. 81–92.

with the two major problems of today's trading world—economic regionalism and the trade needs of the less-developed areas.

The developing countries seek dependable, freer access to the developed markets of the world, in manufactured goods as well as primary commodities. They are not confident of the ability of the industrialized countries to prevent deep economic recessions; nor do they place much confidence in assurances that the "Kennedy Round" will go far toward opening new markets for their goods. Reports of the readiness of the industrial powers to settle for much less than a 50 per cent across-the-board negotiation feed these doubts. So do the various attempts the United States has made— with some success, as in the case of cotton textiles—to negotiate international restrictions on trade in manufactured goods without any prior, economically sound, objective finding as to whether or to what extent such restrictions were necessary.

Such frustrations could also induce regional blocs of less-developed nations to explore closer trade ties with Communist countries. The chances of this happening may be greater than opinion on either side of the Iron Curtain has yet acknowledged. The regional unit may be better equipped than its individual members to negotiate trade deals with countries on the other side of the "great divide," especially where member countries may on their own be afraid to enter into such arrangements.

Regional nationalism in Latin America and other developing areas unaligned with the European Common Market could well grow in response to the competitive handicap they encounter in the preferential privileges the Common Market accords its associates from the southern hemisphere, mainly France's present and former African colonies. Under-developed countries fending for themselves as individual nation-states, particularly those heavily dependent on exports to the EEC, may be expected to react in a similar manner. The concern of giants like the United States and the United Kingdom over the effect of the EEC on their trade provides some insight into the anxiety of developing countries much more dependent on the EEC market than are the U.S. or the U.K. If EEC trade barriers affecting developing countries outside the Community are not reduced substantially, the growing strength and unity of the strong through regional integration would end up aggravating the weakness of the weak, widening the development gap between the world's rich and poor.

The United States has announced its intention to seek special concessions from the EEC to help developing countries not associated with the Community expand their exports of tropical products. However, the export problems of the developing countries are not all in tropical products. Manufactured goods have risen noticeably in the export expectations of the less-developed parts of the world, arousing growing concern among producers of competing products in the industrialized countries. (Japanese exports encounter a similar problem.) Even where the United States is ready to include such goods in the GATT negotiations, the EEC may not be so agreeable. The United States will have a difficult enough time getting concessions from the EEC on matters of more direct importance to the U.S. economy; additional concessions of special importance to the developing countries may be lost in the shuffle.

Small countries outside the EEC are likely to have considerable difficulty in negotiating special trading arrangements with the Community. GATT rules require that such import concessions be applied to all suppliers; otherwise the Community will be resorting to discriminatory practices. But if they were applied to all, they would most likely evoke strong opposition from EEC producers of the affected products—especially in the absence of reciprocal concessions from markets offering substantial export potential. The smaller outside countries whose needs sparked such special agreements in the first place are in most cases not the main suppliers of the particular products and hence not the main sources of foreign competition. Nor are they major export markets or able to offer significant import concessions that might substantially enhance their market potential for European exports.

As countries outside the EEC run into trade obstacles there, and are not able to work out an association or a special trade arrangement with the Community, they will exert greater export pressures on alternative markets, particularly the United States. With problems of their own, these alternative markets may respond with new import restrictions. Nationalist reactions are not impossible in the United States itself as it feels the effects of these pressures. The U.S. propensity to restrict trade is already cause for concern among proponents of trade expansion at home and abroad.

There seems no meaningful alternative to a far-ranging negotiation involving all of the Free World's major trading areas and committing them to substantial concessions to the entire world trade community. The current GATT conference is the time and the place.

Options in the Kennedy Round

If so much hinges on the outcome of the "Kennedy Round," what should we do if it founders and seems certain to fail—and how should success or failure be measured?

It is clear that the original objectives of the Trade Expansion Act, reflected in the negotiating authority which the Administration obtained from Congress, will not be realized.

Some say that since any trade liberalization is progress, "Let's take whatever we can get," and go after more in the next round of negotiations (whenever that might be). Supplementing this line of reasoning is the contention that economic growth in the Common Market will lead to increased imports even if the cuts made in the Community's regional external tariff are much less than what we had envisaged.

These points, supported by existing trade data on U.S. and other exports to the EEC, miss the main issue in the current negotiations—the need to minimize the growing trade discrimination (its full impact has not yet been felt) created by the two emerging free trade blocs of Western Europe. This is a necessity for West European unity, to protect the substantial export interests of the outside world in both these areas, and to prevent the retreat of the outside world into economic nationalism, national or regional.

If we delay in pushing hard for the most we can hope to accomplish under existing legislation and are ready to settle for whatever we can get, we shall be (1) hurting our own trade expansion prospects, (2) letting down the rest of the world, which had been led to believe that so much would be accomplished by the new U.S. initiative in trade policy, (3) lowering sights of our closest trade policy allies and giving them excuses for yielding to their own strong protectionist pressures, and (4) setting off a series of counter-moves around the world, with harmful economic and political overtones. A world that throbs with rising expectations cannot be expected to wait patiently—or even impatiently—for later laborious rounds of trade negotiations to make up for what the "Kennedy Round" failed to accomplish. It will react, defensively and divisively.

If the 50 per cent standard and significant cuts in non-tariff barriers, both industrial and agricultural, cannot be achieved because of what world opinion regards as the unreasonable protectionism of a major industrial trading area (the Common Market is the most likely candidate for such a role), what should we be prepared to do—assuming as we should that no negotiations at all would signal the collapse of our objectives and those of European unity, and that much less than the 50 per cent standard, even if averting disaster, would still be injurious?

If the major difficulty is a conflict between the policy ambitions of France and those of nations (including some in the EEC) seeking a design more grand than French grandeur, it might be suggested that we wait until 1966 when France loses her veto leverage in the Common Market. This, however, would be a naive policy choice. The world will not stand still waiting for that moment. France may not be prepared to be out-voted on issues of substantial national interest. In other words, the veto power may be only the formal expression of a power that exists without it. If the EEC majority gave first priority to preservation of the Community, it would yield to French threats of pulling out or finding some way to hamstring the Community. On the other hand, if the EEC majority without France was determined to join the United States, EFTA and others in a successful negotiation despite French threats to withdraw, this would mean the collapse of the Common Market.

It has been suggested that, if serious difficulties are encountered with the EEC, the United States should seek trade agreements with other major trading areas, invite the EEC to take part, and deny equal tariff treatment to the Community if it should continue to be "unreasonable." Follow-through would have to be intended and clearly credible if the idea is to be practical both in policy terms and as a basis for business decisions.

How credible, in terms of enlightened U.S. self-interest as the world may be expected to interpret it, is a proposal that would intensify the division of Western Europe and violate the basic tenet of the General Agreement on Tariffs and Trade—all for the sake of extricating some trade agreement, however limited but more than the EEC seems ready to support?

At what juncture of the negotiations would we propose such an option? Refusal of the EEC to agree to any negotiating package up to and including the 50 per cent standard does not offer sufficient justification for such a drastic move. Moreover, the trade policies of a major member of the world's trading community would not be affected by such negotiations. Nor is there any assurance that the threat of exclusion would induce that member to play the game as the others want it played. Nor do the huge policy price and the undependability of such a drastic move as a basis for business decisions suggest that the EFTA countries, Canada, and other possible participants could be expected to join in such an arrangement (based on the present limitations of the "Kennedy Round") for the sake of preferential tariff treatment in the U.S. market in competition with the EEC.

Another proposal would have the United States negotiate a free trade area with the EFTA countries, Canada and any other areas that wanted to participate. Denying equal tariff treatment to those areas that did not participate would not violate the GATT charter.

The "free trade area" proposal involves many policy problems, both domestic and international. It is beyond the scope of the President's existing authority, and a major change would be necessary in the Trade Expansion Act to permit the United States to take part in such a plan. On the assumption that a decision on some option would have to be made before the Act expires in mid-1967, the President could make a tentative commitment before then and later seek Congressional authority to implement it (either in the legislation to take the place of the Trade Expansion Act or even earlier in an amendment). However, the proposal has many tactical and strategic shortcomings internationally.

As a reaction to EEC protectionism it shares a basic weakness with the earlier idea of a "Kennedy Round" without the Common Market: it overlooks the fact that participation of the EEC countries, because of the region's importance to the rest of Europe, to the United States and to the rest of the trading world, is essential to the success of any trade negotiation, and indispensable to our overall foreign policy mission.

If the United States joined a free trade area and went to free trade only with other members of such a group, we would be overlooking this country's special role as a world power and the international repercussions of such a U.S. alignment. Any such step to form a new free trade area would set off defensive, nationalist reactions in the rest of the world.

If the developing countries were given a "free ride"—i.e., if the trade liberalization in the free trade area were extended to their goods without requiring equal reciprocity because of their weak position—this would be an additional and highly significant step toward total free trade on the part of the industrialized countries. That being the case, it would be better to call a spade a spade, eschew proposals that both confuse the issue and invite suspicion, and work for a programmed free trade commitment that would catch the imagination of the world and raise the sights and prospects of the "Kennedy Round." *Nothing less than this could adequately justify the denial of concessions to industrial powers that refused to participate. This turns out to be the option—the démarche—to which policy imperatives and the logic of events seem to lead.* Envisaging a form of free trade area, it would not violate GATT, except for the special treatment to be accorded to developing countries. Provision for such exceptions could be negotiated.

U.S. readiness to take the lead in charting complete free trade by the industrialized countries within, say, ten years—making a 50 per cent standard in the "Kennedy Round" the first step, and denying concessions to advanced economies that refused to take part—stands a better chance of achieving the level of negotiations to which the strongest supporters of the "Kennedy Round" have aspired. (All the details of the ten-year free-trade charter need not be worked out in the modified "Kennedy Round." However, a commitment would have to be made by the signatory countries and regional instrumentalities regarding the target date(s) and the broad outlines of the charter.) A clearly enunciated free trade objective would be more likely to stimulate the EFTA countries and Canada—the areas whose participation would be indispensable —to participate in a modified "Kennedy Round" than would a negotiating alternative limited by the 50 per cent standard. Because of its drama as well as the prospects of a free market in the participating industrial countries, it would be more likely to stimulate the more outward-looking members of the EEC.

Free trade is logically the ideal to which the whole process of trade liberalization is moving. The need to make a major move toward that goal, even more rapid than a general 50 per cent cut, was clearly recognized (even if more visionary than practical) when the Trade Expansion Act was designed and enacted, and it has not disappeared just because U.K. membership in the EEC was rejected by General de Gaulle. Charting a free trade timetable in the "Kennedy Round" would only move the objective forward to meet urgent needs. It has become an imperative of the time in which we live and toward which we are dynamically moving.

Free Trade Commitment

In procedural terms, the industrially advanced countries would strive for the 50 per cent standard in the current negotiations but *as part of a more advanced policy framework*. This would consist of a commitment (a) by the industrial members of the General Agreement to eliminate all barriers to international trade not later than 1975 (with rigorously limited provisions for postponement), and (b) by the other members to liberalize their trade controls as quickly as circumstances permit and according to certain standards of progress. Special provision would be made for each rung on the international ladder of economic development, with a fast-moving timetable for the most advanced economies and an individually slower pace for each of the others. The charter would provide for special interim negotiations on issues found to be obstructing the scheduled progress of the free trade plan, and on others where negotiated solutions might accelerate it. Accountability to the GATT membership for delays in carrying out such commitments would be required, with provisions for penalties if waivers could not be negotiated.

A free trade commitment by all the major industrial countries would probably dissolve the issue of tariff disparities from which much of the delay in the current negotiations has stemmed. An accelerated move to zero by all the Contracting Parties would solve that problem.

The point may be made that, if elimination of the external tariff walls around the EEC and EFTA communities is so important to the outside world, a ten-year schedule of free trade—meaning nearly ten years from 1966, about the time each of these blocs will have eliminated their internal trade restrictions—is too slow. The answer is that such a commitment, together with the achievement of free trade within these areas and assuming impressive economic progress, will in fact stimulate periodic acceleration of the scheduled elimination of trade barriers. Having set the course to internal free trade, both EEC and EFTA soon stepped up the pace, and target dates were accelerated by three years. A similar experience would be likely for the broader agreement.

Fulfillment of a free trade agreement, and of subsidiary commitments that also exceed the authority of the Trade Expansion Act, rests on authorization by Congress. The next scheduled reassessment of U.S. policy in this field is the enactment of legislation in 1967 when the Trade Expansion Act expires. Executive commitments contingent on future enabling legislation are within the President's inherent authority. He would probably consult with Congressional leaders before proceeding with such a course. If he makes such commitments, he should undertake to keep Congress closely informed on (a) the steps taken and programmed under the charter by the United States and the other signatories, (b) the effects of trade liberalization on U.S. trade and the U.S. economy, and (c) the adjustment problems encountered by U.S. producers, workers, and communities, and the steps taken and programmed by the Government and other domestic interests to facilitate the necessary adjustments.

Is it realistic to depend on getting enabling legislation? If the President could not fulfill such an international commitment made on behalf of the United States, the damage to American prestige and influence would be substantial. However, the damage would also be substantial if Congress did not continue its lower-key series of trade agreement authorizations that began in 1934. That is when the long, laborious move to free trade in fact began. If the next regular step due in 1967 can be depended upon, the more decisive step is not beyond reason—*provided the Administration can secure nationwide understanding and support for such a policy. The effort will patently demand much more than the proponents of a liberal trade policy have ever mounted in the past. And it would require the earliest possible attention to a national program—sparked by the Federal Government, but calling for appropriate steps by state and local governments—to stimulate and facilitate adjustment to change from whatever quarter. This initiative in domestic economic policy is not only a vital dimension of a policy of external free trade. It is also likely to be indispensable to broad public acceptance of such a trade policy.*

If the EEC resisted participation in the free-trade charter because of the opposition of one or two members, the plan's strong appeal to the more receptive members could lead to (a) reversal of the Community's position, or (b) dissolution of the Community as presently constituted. The outward-looking members—most likely regrouped into a new bloc—would then be free to associate themselves with the new charter. The others would most likely follow, after carefully weighing the merits of the alternative courses. The possibility that the EEC countries might under all circumstances refuse to participate in the charter, and thus prefer to encounter the many disadvantages of such a course including trade discrimination in the markets of countries which did subscribe to the charter, is an extreme contingency hopefully ruled out by the logic of contemporary dynamics in world affairs. Otherwise, the Free World is close to falling apart at the seams.

The trade policy maneuver would require meticulous calculation, careful timing, and politically astute execution to enhance its acceptability and ensure against the very division which the maneuver is designed to prevent. Various subsidiary steps may have to be considered to help ensure its success. One may be an effort by the United States, Canada, EFTA countries, and Japan to expand trade with Eastern Europe (within realistic political limitations and justifiable for other reasons), showing the EEC that the considerable potential of the East European market was not a special preserve it could capitalize on, without much competition, to offset trade losses elsewhere.

Another step may be agreement by the participating less-developed countries, as part of their participation in the free trade charter, to deny equal tariff treatment to industrial areas that refused to participate. Another imperative is continued assertion of U.S. determination to use the ultimate in military weapons to defend Western Europe. Such reassurances are necessary because the U.S. world mission, already suspect in many places around the world, would come under new attack from considerable numbers of people in the EEC.

If the "Kennedy Round" is concluded successfully without such an extraordinary fillip, the United States must still be prepared to proceed with early plans for complete free trade by the Free World's industrial areas. In fact the announcement of such intentions may help dissolve many of the roadblocks now impeding or threatening to impede the negotiations. It may, for example, induce Germany to be much more liberal in its agricultural policy, thus facilitating agreement within the EEC and a more liberal EEC approach to the "Kennedy Round." It may also induce certain countries (Canada, for example) to participate more fully in the "Kennedy Round" than may be their present inclinations. Canada feels that 50 per cent cuts would do little for its exports (mainly crude or semi-manufactured commodities facing low tariffs abroad) and hurt Canada's import-competing industrial plants since it would not adequately open up foreign markets for finished goods.

If we are not ready to make the free trade proposal, we may find that a successful "Kennedy Round" has fired the idea in Western Europe. EEC and EFTA are methodically and rapidly approaching free trade within their respective areas. The diagram of forces at work in that part of the world would show two closely related sets of regional centripetal forces impelled toward each other by the momentum of their respective internal free trade dynamics, by the lowering of the barriers between them, and by the vision of West European unity.

A closer link between the Commonwealth and the Community would come within reach. If the momentum is maintained, perhaps accelerated through an enlarged and more effective OECD with its instrumentalities of policy coordination and its targets of economic growth, a definitive timetable for total free trade on the part of the more advanced countries would be a not-too-difficult next step. Before this is done, a European free trade area, with the EEC functioning as a member and with special arrangements to accommodate the Commonwealth and the Sterling Area, might be an interim move. The trade liberalization generated by such an extended free trade community would tend to dampen the regional nationalism detected from time to time in the smaller, more compact EEC.

A free trade proposal embracing all of the industrialized Free World would be the next step. The United States might find itself ready for it. If we have adequately prepared for such an overture, we should be ready to take the initiative in proposing it, and at an earlier date to serve more immediate policy needs. When the Trade Expansion Act expires and something must be drafted to take its place, new legislative authority permitting something close to free trade should be the next step in any event.

Free trade as a policy option may not at the moment seem politically practical. It will have to be made so in the interest of credibility for our whole national purpose in the kind of world which today's dynamics seem to be shaping. It can be made so if the nation's ability to make the necessary adjustments, and if the gains to be won if those adjustments are made, are set forth convincingly by the President and those to whom he delegates responsibility in this field of public policy. The international negotiations will be extremely difficult. They will have to include commitments regarding fair labor standards, provisions on dumping (with up-to-date definitions and criteria), and prohibitions against domestic policies that might vitiate the trade agreement. Agricultural protectionism, a drag on liberal trade policies everywhere, may make the task seem impossible. But success is not beyond reason if a determined effort is made to achieve it, and *if the day-to-day policies followed by those who take the lead prove its sincerity.*

The resources and resourcefulness of government and of the free enterprise system, if properly marshalled to cope with the domestic consequences of this new international policy imperative, will find ways to cushion the impact, in fact to maximize the contribution of all sectors of the economy to the new economic strength which the new policy can generate. With respect to agriculture, for example, the phasing out of import controls should be coupled with various programs of farm adjustment. Provisions could be made for direct payments to sustain minimum incomes of needy farmers who satisfied government standards regarding agricultural adaptation (including individual efforts to obtain alternative employment). Obviously, a vigorous program of economic development in the manufacturing and service industries—in every state of the Union—is an essential concomitant of a successful agricultural adjustment effort, aside from its impressive merits on other grounds. It should be a long-overdue commitment to full employment, now made necessary by a commitment to free trade. New meaning would be given to President Kennedy's vision of a "new frontier" at home and a "grand design" abroad, each the inextricably connected counterpart of the other in a new American initiative.

The United States—not only the national government, but state and local governments as well—should set its sights now on a free-trade commitment, adjust its economic policies to that target, and thus prepare itself for the free-trade strategy suggested by the policy momentum of the past three decades and possibly accelerated by the exigencies of the current Geneva negotiations. If the policy is pursued in the proper fashion, seeking maximum support at home and abroad, opportunities for trade expansion and economic growth are likely to outweigh pressures for trade restriction. Forces for unity are likely to overcome the persistent forces of division which often bring the society of free nations uncomfortably close to disarray, and which today stand ready to capitalize on the disillusionment which a disappointing "Kennedy Round" would generate.

Impressive success in the "Kennedy Round" would be a major step toward the objective of this new U.S. initiative. And the readiness of the United States to take such initiative could well ensure the impressive success of the "Kennedy Round." Failure to achieve that standard of success might turn out to be a drop backward beyond the point of no return which we thought we had passed.

15

New Horizons in Foreign Trade

WILLIAM DIEBOLD, JR.

Unless there is new legislation, the President will, at midnight on June 30, 1967, lose his power to cut American tariffs in trade bargains with other countries. The situation is familiar enough. Eleven times already the country has faced the question of renewing the grant of power first made in the Trade Agreements Act of 1934. Each time, Congress has prolonged the power, sometimes enlarging and sometimes reducing it. Mixing long-run policy and short-run tactics to get the best possible terms for the renewal of trade legislation is an old art in Washington. But this renewal is different.

It is different because if the Kennedy Round—the tariff negotiations that have been going on in Geneva for the last few years —comes out as it seems likely to, we shall be on the threshold of a period in which trade negotiations among industrialized countries will take on new forms and a greatly enlarged scope. Sooner or later, though not necessarily in 1967, the President will have to be given new kinds of powers to engage in trade negotiations: an extension of the existing ones to cut tariffs will no longer suffice. (And if the Kennedy Round does not live up to reasonable expectations, the issues involved in a 1967 renewal will look different again, but for other reasons.)

Though trade negotiations may not be quite as unpredictable as dice or cards, it is surprising how much agreement there is among those who have looked into the matter as to what may come out of the Kennedy Round. The main impact will be on trade in manufactured goods among the advanced industrial areas—North America, Western Europe and Japan. Some important products will not be touched, but for many others duties will be cut in half (the largest possible reduction under American law, with a few exceptions). For still other goods there will be some kind of in-between cut, especially if one country has very high tariffs and another very low ones. Averaging tariffs is a questionable practice, but some brave souls find it reasonable to say that the total effect will be a reduction of tariffs amounting to perhaps 25 percent or, with luck, as much as 35. Something may also be done about non-tariff barriers, but for the most part this will be unfinished business, opening questions for the future. Agricultural exports are important for the United States, but it is hard to see how anything more can be expected than tariff concessions on a few products, some temporary understandings about the course of trade over the next few years in some major products and the beginning of a serious effort to negotiate in quite new ways so as to mitigate the costly clash of national farm policies in the future.

All this sounds prosaic enough. Where are the new horizons? Only as we look at the problems that will have to be dealt with after the Kennedy Round does the new prospect unfold.

The tariffs that remain after the Kennedy Round will not be negligible, and any new legislation aimed at them will have to start by renewing at least the President's existing powers. But would another 50 percent reduction be worth the trouble of going through the mill of another massive multilateral tariff negotiation? Simpler ways can be found, provided, of course, governments are willing to make further cuts. For example, tariff rates might be reduced a certain percent each year. Or levels could be set to which all countries would reduce their duties on certain products, thus producing a degree of "harmonization" which many people feel desirable. Rules can be devised to allow enough flexibility to permit each country to move a little more slowly on its hard cases if it moves a little more rapidly on others, or to permit a country with low duties to reduce them more slowly than those with higher rates. Formulas are neither magical nor scientific, but one can see that a general rule of this sort would simplify trade negotiations and probably enhance their effect.

Tariffs on trade among the industrial countries have been reduced much more than is generally realized. Many are far lower than at any time since the depression or, in some cases, since the end of the last century. The United States has quite a few rates that are one-quarter of what they were in 1934 and many that are almost as low. Within the Common Market and the European Free Trade Area, tariffs will soon disappear. If the Kennedy Round cuts duties by another quarter or a third, much of the world's trade in manufactured goods will move at tariff rates of less than 10 percent *ad valorem*, or not much more. Inevitably one asks, "If that much can be accomplished in twenty years without great disturbance, why not more?" Can the remainder not be removed in, say, another ten—gently, year by year?

This picture may, however, be illusory. The last quarter of a tariff may be what really protects, so that it would prove harder to remove than the first three quarters. A 10 percent tax can be very important in a highly competitive market; also, it may be equivalent to several times that much if what is being protected is only the cost of manufacturing, when raw materials are imported at low or no duties. (But then past cuts may also have been greater than they seemed.) An opposite view of things after the Kennedy Round would be that if tariffs are low enough they make so little difference to trade that they may not be worth the effort of removing. The evidence on all these points is limited and conflicting; generalizations are unwise. The fact of the matter is almost certainly that some low tariffs have a significant effect while others do not, and that negotiations will reveal more than analysis will about which further steps will be relatively easy and which very hard.

We can be sure in advance that governments will not be willing to apply simplified procedures for the reduction of tariffs to all their trade. Some of the hard cases might be attacked instead by a new way of negotiating that is taking shape during the Kennedy Round. Called the sector or industry-by-industry approach, it largely grew out of the fact that there was a danger of no significant tariff reductions being made in several major industries because one country or another wanted to hold out key products from the across-the-board cut of 50 percent. Consequently others were unwilling to make their best offers. So long as the approach was product by product, reluctance in the most timorous country blocked all action, often to the disadvantage of other parts of the same industry. In chemicals and steel, for instance, several major countries have both an export interest and a protected sector. By looking at each of these industries as a whole, the negotiators opened the possibility of working out balanced bargains covering tariffs and non-tariff barriers as well. Too little is publicly known as yet to make a confident appraisal of this technique. It suggests questions about relations between governments and businesses and among producers in various countries that will have to be looked at warily. Still it is noteworthy that Eric Wyndham White, the Director General of the General Agreement on Tariffs and Trade, has suggested that this approach could provide a way of moving toward free trade in a number of industries, particularly those with large enterprises and fairly advanced technologies.

If that technique works in the hard cases, and deep cuts are made in other across-the-board duty rates, then the Kennedy Round will have opened the prospect of the elimination of tariffs on trade in manufactured goods among industrial countries. Free trade, so long an impossible ideal for some and a worrisome spectre for others, will become, for the first time in nearly a century, something that can be seriously contemplated as a reasonable objective of policy. But the Kennedy Round has also made clear—if there was ever any doubt—that the removal of tariffs does not by itself produce free trade.

One of the advantages of the industry-by-industry approach has been to clarify the significance of non-tariff barriers in each industry and to help link their removal or modification to tariff changes. But no matter what technique is used, non-tariff barriers will have a prominent place in future trade negotiations. So far as quotas and exchange controls are concerned, the question is largely one of enforcing existing rules. But large numbers of other barriers fall outside any agreed international code and present difficult problems. Their variety is great. Some devices enhance the effect of tariffs—for example, by using artificial prices to calculate duties and assigning goods arbitrarily to customs classifications with higher duties. There are suspected abuses of legitimate practices, as in the application of anti-dumping duties. "Buy American" laws are only the best-known example of the very widespread practice of discriminating against foreign goods in governmental purchasing. Some European countries have taxes that fall disproportionately on large (and therefore largely American) automobiles. Sanitary rules, marking and labelling requirements, copyright and trademark laws, and many other regulations may also have the effect of restricting trade. So do some private business practices. Sometimes restriction is a by-product of activities that have other major purposes, but many practices are undoubtedly subterfuges. How damaging each is, and to whom, are matters still in dispute.

These barriers are too numerous and too diverse to be dealt with in a simple, comprehensive way. Some would require detailed agreements; some might yield to a more general code; others will undoubtedly have to be dealt with case by case, or under some kind of complaints procedure. Concern with non-tariff barriers is not entirely new, but the Kennedy Round has moved them to a new position of prominence and set them firmly on the agenda of future trade negotiations. As tariffs become less restrictive, non-tariff barriers become more important; and they affect the pace of tariff reduction as well. For example, European countries may link their reductions of duties on chemicals to the modification of the "American selling price" rule which has the effect of raising United States duties on some of their products. Other non-tariff barriers are likely to be treated in the same way in the future. What Percy Bidwell christened "the invisible tariff" is becoming more visible.

This prospect that the Kennedy Round has opened leads to another one. To start talking about non-tariff barriers is to open a subject that has no logical end. All manner of government activities undertaken for all sorts of reasons may have the effect of restricting trade, or at least of putting foreigners at a disadvantage compared to domestic producers. What is a trade barrier? When will it be brought into international negotiations? These are questions of new scope for the future. For example, border taxes related to domestic turnover taxes and the like have traditionally been regarded as not affecting foreign trade. Now that idea is being called in question, but the implication of change reaches deep into national tax structures and raises questions about exchange rates as well. And as tariffs fall, national laws and policies about prices, wages and business practices take on a new international importance. The foreigner's concern with depreciation allowances, shipping laws, government-financed research and the more recondite forms of subsidy grows. Only far in the future can one imagine international negotiations covering quite so wide a range of subjects, but much sooner there will be questions about these practices and others that influence trade negotiations.

Agriculture, for so long the bad boy of international trade liberalization, is already posing similar questions. For decades large segments of agricultural trade have not only been exempted from the general process of lowering trade barriers but have been subjected to new restrictions. More than simple protectionism and the political strength of farmers went into this process. Many of the restrictions were the logical consequence of domestic farm programs like those in the United States which kept domestic prices above world levels and often sought to limit output as well. In the Kennedy Round the United States and other producers outside the E.E.C. found themselves faced with a complicated new agricultural policy applied to the whole Common Market. Close and ingenious attention had been given to working out its implications for imports with a degree of logical rigor that promised to create something very much like a self-sealing mechanism. For some important products the outside world seemed likely to be put in the position of being able to supply the Six only when their own production fell short. The effect was enhanced by an increase in production and productivity coming not only from the prices offered under the new policy but even more from a technological revolution in agriculture comparable to that which put the United States back into its historical position as a low-cost exporter.

There is no way out of this impasse if negotiations are confined to trade barriers alone. So long as countries adhere to policies of this sort, there is little hope of liberalizing agricultural trade except by agreements that affect the policies themselves, not just the tariffs, quotas and variable levies that support them. If there is to be progress at all, governments have to be willing to talk, negotiate and give undertakings about such things as price-support levels, subsidies, production control and the financing of surpluses, as well as about the regulation of imports. This awkward fact is widely recognized, but whether governments will be willing to act on these premises, will be able to reach agreement and will then be able to overcome the obvious domestic political obstacles to putting agreement into effect are questions which give some inkling of the difficulties of future trade negotiations. The most the Kennedy Round can do is to start the process—and it could fail in the effort.

Agriculture as a mid-sixties exemplar of future international trade negotiations is about as unlikely a picture as one could imagine. The reasons are peculiar to agriculture. The agreements that might be made are not at all like those to be sought in negotiations about manufactured goods. The position in agriculture has been reached through the impossibility of dealing with trade barriers in the conventional way, while in industry it results from success in removing them to the point where other barriers stand revealed. And yet the two have something in common: both indicate that the trade policy of the future, if it is to make progress at all, will entail international discussion, negotiation and perhaps agreement on a whole range of things normally regarded as domestic.

That conclusion is not quite as shocking as it may seem at first sight. Defense and its economic impact have been of mutual concern of the United States and its allies for a long time. We made the domestic economies of Europe and Japan our business from the end of the war on. It is not just our difficulties with the balance of payments that have given other countries reason to be concerned about American recessions, inflation, interest rates, wage policies and general economic health. From concern has come international discussion, sometimes negotiations and, in varying degrees, undertakings. National autonomy has not given way to international obligations but it has not been left immune either. So it is not surprising if trade, the biggest international economic nexus of all, should lead in the same direction.

At the same time that what was thought to be domestic is becoming of greater international concern, the international economy is developing in ways that raise questions about what is any longer national. Europeans and Canadians ask themselves whether American ownership of segments of their industries and American involvement in their financial systems are denationalizing their economies. In underdeveloped countries some people who long ago thought they knew the answer to that question are now beginning to wonder if the expansion of the economy that is theirs to control does not depend in part on a willingness to accept more foreign enterprise. Oil-producing countries that are financially weaker than some of the companies that operate within their boundaries are finding ways to balance the seesaw while the international companies try to become good citizens of a dozen countries at once. Americans too have some questions. In 1964, manufacturing companies in Western Europe of which Americans owned at least 25 percent, and which they usually controlled, had sales equalling $16.5 billion, over twice the amount of U.S. exports to Western Europe that year. The figures are not strictly comparable and they are obviously very different in their economic meaning, yet they raise questions. Can one fully understand the American trade interest in Europe by looking at exports alone? What is the relation of American investments to European trade barriers? More fundamentally still, what is the American economy? Clearly it is not just a geographical entity surrounded by a tariff and an invisible monetary line. Our foreign trade is not just something that crosses the customs frontier or involves the exchange of dollars for other currencies. But how to define the economy is not clear, and so there must be doubt about how to define the national economic interest as well. With the United States government and most foreign governments declaring, in common but for different reasons, their interest in American investment abroad, it takes no vivid imagination to see how the area of international discussion will broaden.

. . . .

No trade legislation in the coming year can deal with all these issues. Some are not ready for action, others not yet well enough understood for us to know just what to do. Whatever is done in 1967, whether modest or ambitious, cannot be the solvent for trade-policy problems for the indefinite future, but whatever is done, particularly if it is ambitious, ought to take account of the new prospects that have been opened by the Kennedy Round.

Whether to ask for little or to ask for much is one of the classic problems of the renewal of trade-agreements legislation. A cogent case can be made for the view that with so many new problems arising the best course would be an extension of the existing act for a year or two. That would permit the President to tie up the loose ends the Kennedy Round is bound to leave, while preparing at home and abroad for the kind of approach that will be needed to deal with the problems of the future. The contrary view is also cogent: equip the President to take broad initiatives immediately, in order to build on the momentum of the Kennedy Round and guard against erosion or stagnation here or abroad. This view has its attraction. President Kennedy took the plunge when treading water would have been understandable, and he got the greatest advance in trade legislation since 1934. But he had some advantages that are now absent: the chance to break with a stagnant trade policy; the widespread feeling that the United States had to meet the challenge of the Common Market; and the wish to find a concrete expression of "partnership." No political equivalent of that situation exists now. The idea of an Atlantic free-trade area, which attracts some people, not only lacks charisma but has a negative political charge in the present state of transatlantic relations. It might also create more trade-policy problems than it would solve.

Still, the possibilities warrant something more than temporizing and some positive action would be a better earnest of American intentions than putting the decision off.[1] It should not be too difficult to draw up sensible proposals for broadening the President's power to cut or remove tariffs; to start on the problems of non-tariff barriers; to act on some of the issues of concern to the less developed countries; and to negotiate effectively with the Communist countries. How much can be done depends on a number of circumstances that are not now predictable—not least on what sort of agreement the negotiators bring home from Geneva and especially its agricultural provisions. And if instead of the satisfactory outcome of the Kennedy Round assumed earlier in this article there should be a very disappointing result with only dribs and drabs of unimportant trade concessions, still another situation would exist. Then the case for delay would be strong, to give time to consider whether the failure of the most

---

[1] The Council on Foreign Relations will shortly publish a succinct analysis of future needs and specific proposals for the extension of the President's powers by John Evans, an experienced negotiator who for years headed the American delegation to GATT. I have gained much from talking with Mr. Evans and from reading his manuscript.

elaborate effort yet made to reduce trade barriers might not mean that we needed new ideas about how to approach the subject. That kind of outcome would also raise very serious doubts about what the American people are willing—or ought to be willing—to do in trade policy.

There is another possibility, one hopes an unlikely one. That is that the Kennedy Round will become a political sacrifice, killed or made barren by some effort to strike at the United States, the *demandeur* who has been more interested than others in its success. If that happened, we would have many decisions to make, and trade policy would quite properly have to be looked at primarily in terms of what use it might be as an instrument of foreign policy. Choices that would be considerably less than second best from the point of view of trade—such as trying to form some kind of trading group omitting the Common Market—would have to be seriously considered. But the prospects of a broad liberalization of world trade are more likely to be set back than advanced by that course.

The less dramatic course suggested earlier does not imply a divorce of American trade policy from foreign policy. Quite the contrary, it assumes that long-run American interests are on the whole well served by persistence in the long and slow process of trade liberalization. There are moments when some foreign-policy aim can hasten the process by galvanizing the country to action it would not otherwise take. There are also risks of setting back the process in the effort to make trade policy respond too closely to relatively short-run political circumstances. Certainly the United States can afford economic sacrifices for foreign-policy ends; it makes them every day. But it is also easy to exaggerate the value of trade policy as a political weapon.

Perhaps trade relations among the industrial countries of the free world—though not East-West or North-South trade—have reached the point at which they should ordinarily be looked at as workaday matters rather than as a form of diplomacy. Certainly the prospects sketched in the earlier part of this article are not those of a preacher's promised land to be attained by those who will be moved to action by a vision. They emerge naturally out of what the advanced industrial countries will have done over the past twenty years and more. That experience has not proved that tariffs and other trade barriers are of no importance or that their removal is the key to prosperity or peace—just that they can be removed without great disturbance and with real benefit.

To look ahead to where we can go after the Kennedy Round is not the same as showing how to get there or laying down a time schedule. The balance of payments of leading countries, and perhaps especially the United States, will offer obstacles; so will difficulties of adjustment and resistance to it. Elections, diplomacy and particular circumstances in one country or another will be at work all the time, more often to slow the process than to speed it. Protectionism is not dead and sometimes takes on new forms. The creation of regional trading arrangements liberalizes segments of trade but at the same time introduces new distortions. And the external tariff of such a group may become not just a trade barrier but also a form of political cement, as we have seen in the Common Market. Broadening the range of trade negotiations to include national policies and practices not ordinarily thought of as trade barriers will itself generate new kinds of resistance and stimulate political fright.

The next stages of trade negotiation will be more complicated than those in the past. Maybe they will be harder. There is nothing inevitable about progress toward freer trade; it depends on what governments are willing to do. Trade barriers do not fall, they are removed. That governments ought to persist in their useful if sometimes pedestrian efforts is clear enough. That conclusion was valid in 1945 when the vision of a postwar liberal trading world was new and hopes of moving rapidly toward it were high. It was valid ten years later when the obstacles to free trade seemed great and the will to pursue it was flagging, and again in 1962 when the United States made its bid to link Europe's internal trade liberalization with the world. What is new in 1967 is not the validity of the case for further liberalization but the prospect that its result will be a new concept of trade relations between nations.

16

Should Europe Restrict U.S. Investments?

C. F. KARSTEN

One does not have to be a "stranger in paradise," as the popular American song lyric puts it, to notice in recent months in Europe a growing concern with regard to the steep increase in the amount of direct investments by U.S. business in Europe.

The days are now past when committees from Western European countries queued up at the doors of huge American corporations to invite them to establish factories in their cities or districts, and when governments one after another—secretly or not—offered attractive fiscal advantages.

Anti-Investment Chorus

Most of those special inducements have been cancelled. Ever louder are the voices of those who demand that measures be taken to stop this alarming flood of U.S. investments. Suddenly we hear again the notorious word *Uberfremdung*—foreign control—so well known from the 1930s; one newspaper after another takes up the theme, without verifying the facts, without even trying to find out the facts. Why this sudden change?

I think that the problem is much more complex than it seems at first sight. And as some of the causes are of a psychological nature, they will explain the intensity of the outbursts. For example:

There is the reaction of those European industrialists who are confronted with intense competition from their American col-

From *Harvard Business Review*, September-October, 1965, pp. 53–61. Reprinted in this form by permission.

leagues or competitors. This competition sometimes gives them—
by its intensity and effectiveness—a feeling of helplessness. Consequently, they join the chorus of "no"-sayers.

There are, on the other side, those Americans who by their
action, which is not always suitable in the European field, stand
on so many toes at once that it must lead to protests.

But there are, of course, economic reasons, as well:

There is the problem of overemployment in most of the European countries, so that the desire for creation of new employment
opportunities has completely disappeared. Now the existing industries fear a loss of labor if a new industry is established in their
district. And less labor means less production and less profit.

Last but not least, one hears the argument that we have paid
for these U.S. investments ourselves. The basis for this argument
is found in the continuous deficits of the U.S. balance of payments
which correspond more or less with the export of capital. It is
suggested that this capital export has only to be stopped in order
to solve the balance of payments problem. And as we have not
demanded gold for our dollar balances, Europe has in effect
financed our American investments.

But even if some of the arguments mentioned above may have
a true ring to them, it does not necessarily mean that something
has to be done. This has to be studied more carefully. Before we
go into it, however, I want to make one observation.

Is it really fair of us Europeans, now that the necessity for such
investments is less pressing, to protest so loudly when 10 years ago
(or even more recently) we invited the Americans to come? Are
our economies not in much better shape because U.S. businessmen
accepted those invitations? Would Europe have experienced the
same degree of wealth it now enjoys without this postwar influx
of know-how and capital? And even if we do recognize this fact,
is it fair to forget that our very shaky economies 15 years ago got
the shot in the arm they needed so much from Marshall Plan aid?

Agreed this is a question of sentiment; and if there are real
dangers in the present investment situation, we should act, since
our American friends too can only benefit from a healthy Europe.
But where most of the advocates of restrictive measures are basing
their attitude on national consciousness, it seems right to me to

point out an important aspect. A proper feeling of gratitude tells me we should be very careful before acting.

Other Statistical Data

More pertinent for our problem than the dollar amounts is the relative importance of these figures compared with the local investment totals. The available statistics, however, are not very illuminating. There are several statistical sources which give U.S. book values and turnover and export volumes, but there is no certainty that these figures correspond with the comparable European statistics.

Interesting, however, is the written reply which the European Parliament gave on the question raised by René Pleven, French politician and member of the European Parliament Assembly, on March 15, 1963, regarding U.S. investment in the six European Economic Community countries. The reply stated that the gross direct investment in the Common Market on an annual basis is not more than 2% of the total private investment (excluding housing) in this community, and its relative position is not increasing. In the same answer figures were given for the individual EEC member countries. From these figures it appears that the highest proportion is in West Germany—3.1% (according to Fritz Berg, President of the Association of Industrialists, the percentage is between 3% and 4%). The percentage is lowest in France—1.4%.

All figures are such that the word "alarming" is totally misplaced. However, one should not forget that the percentages for individual types of trade may be quite different. Of the total of $584 million which was invested in 1964 in buildings and equipment, $214 million (36%) went into the transportation equipment industry, mainly the automobile industry; $104 million (18%) into the machine industry; and $83 million (14%) into the chemical industry. Before finishing with quoting figures, let me offer still one more. The total sales of U.S.-owned industrial output in West Germany in 1963 were $3,090 million or 3.2% of gross national product.

U.S. Overseas Growth

What are some of the reasons why in the last 10 years American industrialists decided to an ever-growing extent to invest abroad?

In the first place, of course, there is the purely economic reason: looking for new markets which promise good chances. In particular Europe, after it had recovered from the worst effects of the war, and Canada looked the most attractive, since the potentialities of those markets were rather great. It must also be acknowledged that the Americans may have realized more quickly than the Europeans themselves the possibility of the growing unity of the Common Market.

Perhaps it was that U.S. businessmen may have been more easily impressed by slogans. Or, more likely, they did not have any great mental reservations about the possibilities of the Common Market. Market increase, however, can also take place by simple export. But during the first half of the 1950's, Europe was still chronically short of dollars, and therefore its import possibilities were limited. On the other hand, the potential of the future market, coupled with relatively low labor costs at that time in Europe, justified the establishment of U.S. production units. This was made the more attractive, as has been said before, by offers of fiscal advantages and other inducements.

At the same time, a situation had been created in the United States which induced the leaders of American industry to invest overseas. The ever more narrow interpretation of the antitrust laws, making pure bigness even more suspect, discouraged big industry, which already had an important share of the domestic market, from using its surplus funds for investments in additional domestic ventures. Since investments abroad are not likely to fall under the jurisdiction of the U.S. antitrust laws, the dangers were practically nonexistent there. Gradually, reasoning of a psychological nature came into being; U.S. investments abroad became a fashion, and a factory overseas became a status symbol.

But, apart from the status factor, one has to recognize that since pure size is so important in the United States to be competitive, some industries had to follow their leading competitor overseas in order to keep up with their rival's growth. "Follow the leader" was therefore another important reason why the U.S. industrialist decided to invest abroad. In the areas of service industries and advisory agencies it became necessary to follow the client overseas in order not to lose him at home. In the oil industry, for example, engineering bureaus were established wherever refineries were built. Similarly, advertising agencies were set up overseas to serve American clients abroad; and, last but not least, American banks followed to serve these firms abroad, which, in turn, gave them an introduction to the parent companies and a lead over their competitors domestically.

A final reason for investing abroad is found in the general tendency toward decentralization as production units become too big to manage efficiently. Once the decision is made to decentralize, it is obvious that future production units are going to be established near their potential markets.

All the arguments given above clearly pointed in favor of making U.S. investments abroad a decade ago. That Canada was the U.S. businessman's first choice is understandable. The fact of Canada being a neighboring country and the sharing of a common language, together with high—at one time even too high—expectations of the exploitation possibilities of the various minerals in Canada, led to a sudden stream of U.S. investments in that country in the early 1950s.

Shortly afterwards, particularly as the first scare of Communist action in Europe had somewhat subsided and the first signs of a coming unity in Europe had begun to show, that continent came into the picture. The possibilities on that continent were so much more attractive than in other, mostly underdeveloped, nations— all the more so as the chances of a rather high return on the investments were obvious and the political risk was very much diminished.

Four Investment Forms

What, then, were the various forms of organization in which those investment opportunities might be realized? There were four possible approaches open to the U.S. businessman. He could, for example:

Establish a direct branch operation.

Set up a wholly owned subsidiary in the form of a new local company.

Enter into a joint venture in which the American company would own only part of the shares of a local company, with the other shares being in the hands of the local business associates.

Institute a take-over in which the American company would buy all or a majority of the shares of an existing local company.

The first two forms of organization are, in the light of our discussion, the simplest. My impression is that the form of a *direct branch* of the parent company is used only in a few cases. Probably there are fiscal and organizational, or perhaps even legal, difficulties which prevent the widespread use of this form.

Both the *joint-venture* and the *take-over* approaches lead, from time to time, to difficulties, and most of the critical remarks which have been made are about these methods. *The Economist*, in its January 23, 1965, issue, reported that the French government has been considering restrictive measures against these two types, while leaving the organizational forms of direct branches and wholly owned subsidiaries—for the time being—free.

It may surprise some people that the *joint venture* is suspect. At first sight it looks like the most ideal form, for it combines American production know-how with the market experience of the local partners. Of course, in every partnership, as in all marriages, there is the possibility of an *incompatibilité d'humeur*. But I think that there are more lasting marriages than divorces; and in the case of the joint venture, the interest of both partners seems to be parallel.

While it is true that I know of some very successful joint-venture cases, unfortunately there seems to be one serious objection in practice—namely, the inequality of the partners. As a general rule, the *bigger* American companies go into such ventures overseas, while often it is the *medium-sized* or *smaller* companies in Europe that participate. This inequality manifests itself after some years. If the joint venture is not a success, which usually also means a difference of opinion between the partners, then continuation of the arrangement is quite often difficult, since the European partner usually lacks the funds to finance his share of the losses. The reverse is also true if the joint venture is a big success and a big expansion move is foreseen. The local share has to be diminished then for practical reasons. Thus the joint venture is, in my opinion, only suitable in very special cases between partners of roughly equal size.

The main objection to the *take-over* is not so much economical as psychological. Often it is simply the feeling that the local firm has been sold too cheaply. It is even questionable whether this is really true. An article in *The Economist* of January 23, 1965, stated that in West Germany the Americans pay 20 times earnings, while the Germans themselves in similar cases are not prepared to pay more than 12 times earnings.

No doubt there can be found cases where the local company was bought very cheaply. But, on the other side, who will tell us what is cheap or expensive, and what is the objective value of goodwill? I have seen auditors of world repute who could not agree among themselves. Of course, in many cases it is valuable for Americans to execute a take-over of an existing company instead of starting from scratch. Particularly at a time when labor is scarce, it is of interest to have immediately an organization and a staff.

The European owner of a smaller business organization may not always be completely equal in the negotiations, the more so if we see on the American side of the negotiations usually a full team of lawyers and other acquisition experts. But is it justified to reproach the Americans because they are good negotiators? If the European businessman needs help, he can get it from his local lawyer or banker.

In my opinion, therefore, there is no valid reason to discriminate among the four forms of investment. It is true, however, that in the case of a take-over the export exponent is, per definition, nil. Consequently, the argument that "we have financed it ourselves" has a truer ring than in the other cases. I will refer to this again later. In the case of taking measures against one or another form of establishment, such action should not be dictated by sentiment but only by effectiveness.

One hears many critical remarks with respect to the management of U.S.-owned companies. The argument often runs that the managers are not top level, or even near top level.[1] I do not

[1] See Edward A. McCreary, "Those American Managers Don't Impress Europe," *Fortune*, December, 1964, p. 138.

intend to go too deeply into this aspect for several reasons. First, we have here not a question of principle, but a question of organization. If mistakes are made by sending the wrong people to Europe, no doubt U.S. top management will soon find this out and send other people. Secondly, the critics are usually the same people who see such a great danger in this American penetration. They should be rather happy that these mistakes are made.

But a more important reason for not going too deeply into this is that I am not at all convinced that the complaint about management is justified. Of course, it is difficult to prove it one way or another, but, after all, what is important is whether the average manager of those U.S.-owned companies is better or worse than his colleague in local enterprises.

What we do see is that in many cases the management of the European subsidiaries has very little freedom of action, since the locus of decision-making is very centralized in the parent company. Insofar as this is a question of internal organization, it does not concern us, although, in my opinion, too much interference with management overseas does not increase its efficiency.

More important, however, is the question whether centralization means that the European subsidiary is seen as nothing more than a factory at a distance. Where this is the case, it means that the subsidiary is run on principles which do not necessarily agree with the interest of the country of residence.

Perceived Dangers

What are the real objections—so far not mentioned—against a further numerical increase of U.S. direct investments in Europe?

The main argument cited is the difference in relative size between the European companies and their competitors in the United States. The argument is that due to the difference in size, the Europeans fight a losing battle because they are smaller. Actual free market competition is only possible between competitors of roughly the same size. Without any doubt, this points to a real potential danger. In most of the publications, however, where this argument is discussed, it is only pursued to the extent that some figures are quoted (i.e., turnover of General Motors is 11 times that of Volkswagen). One has to realize, though, that nearly every comparison is misleading, since it is very difficult to find the right yardsticks. Even the two automobile companies mentioned above are not quite comparable.

Also, nobody so far (at least I have not seen such a study) has compared the size of the U.S. companies which operate subsidiaries in Europe. It may have been that in the beginning the U.S. giants usually went overseas, but that is no longer true.

Those U.S. giants which operate in Europe are also as a rule very successful, and a comparison of them with the big companies in Europe shows that the European companies are usually much smaller.[2] Remarkably enough, this argument is one which the Americans, when confronted with it, resent most. It is more or less felt as an insult. The U.S. contention is that the U.S. companies do not abuse their European competition by undercutting prices (dumping) or other sharp practices. On the other hand, American businessmen reproach European industrialists for controlling the market through cartels or other agreements.

A further U.S. argument is that the size of the parent company is of no consequence for the competitive position in Europe; only the size of the overseas subsidiary is of importance.

In my opinion, all these arguments are open to criticism. It is not the potential employed locally that is important, but the whole power—the name and the research facilities of the parent company —which counts. Particularly, research is one of the big cost factors nowadays in industry. Here the U.S. giant has an advantage because the costs are spread over greater production runs.

While there was a kind of balance between Europe and the United States in 1930, as both spent some $60 million on research, the situation is now quite different. During the fiscal year 1964–1965, the Americans spent about $20 billion on research. Moreover, although 200 firms alone spent 70% of this money, the same firms received 96% of the U.S. government subsidies. Europe spent $7 billion[3] in the same period.

[2] See "The 500 Largest U.S. Industrial Corporations" (The Fortune Directory), *Fortune*, July, 1964, p. 179; and "The 200 Largest Foreign Industrial Companies," *Fortune*, August, 1964, p. 151.
[3] These figures are quoted from the French report, *Recherche Scientifique et Indépendence*, of the Délégation Générale à la Recherche Scientifique et Technique, September, 1964.

The more this situation deteriorates, the more European industry will be outdistanced in its modern technology. Really big industry has, of course, a considerable advantage over smaller companies, for it can spend more on research with less risk to itself.

Apart, however, from research, modern technology—with its tendencies to bigger and more costly production units and bigger turnover volumes—works in favor of the large U.S.-owned companies.

Significant for the lead which the American companies have had with their market penetration in Europe was the ease with which they found local credit, usually at a cheap price. Even when they refused an outright guarantee for their subsidiaries (and in most cases this was refused, which does not mean, of course, that they were not prepared to pay up if something happened), they got loans for factories which still had to prove that they could be profitable. These loans were usually larger than the capital amounts most European industries would have been able to get.

These factors are, in the long run, decisive in the marketplace and tip the balance in favor of the big companies, even if they are very scrupulous competitors.

The main objection from the U.S. side that the Europeans, through their cartels and other agreements, control the marketplace may carry some truth in some branches of industry. On the other hand, every agreement can be broken or dodged, but the big corporation remains a unity. Moreover, we Europeans are very busy in the Common Market to forbid some of these cartel agreements, thereby dropping one of our best defensive aids.

The potential of these "powerfuls" is, however, not the only danger of the penetration in our European economy. Also important is that the policy of some major industrial companies is not directed in Europe, but in the United States. There is no guarantee that the interest of our economy runs parallel with that of the U.S. owners.

For instance, the U.S. parent company decides which factory is to serve which export market. Also the political question is important (trading with the enemy act). One hears often, "We are not allowed to act this way by 'Washington.'" Look at the case of U.S. banks refusing to subscribe to the rules of the European banking community.

Actions such as these make the American viewpoint morally weak. I believe that the U.S. industrialists are completely within their rights if they oppose discrimination against them (although they discriminate many times themselves in the United States), but then they must obey both the local laws and unwritten rules. The laws are, of course, strictly obeyed, but the unwritten rules are often not for them.

Here we have the question of difference in mentality. There is a great difference in social philosophy between Europe and the United States. Even if one states these differences, this does not mean that one can claim a moral superiority for the one or the other; but, nevertheless, the differences lead to controversies. These controversies may not be important from a purely business point of view, but along with other psychological objections they color the atmosphere and give the impression that all the U.S.-owned factories have an aggressive mentality. One of the leaders of a great American bank once said: "We will teach these European banks what competition is." The question is whether the European entrepreneur (nonbanker) has a need for this type of competition. America's system of free competition has advantages, but it also has consequences which most of us in Europe do not like.

More and more the question is heard, usually in rhetorical form: Is it not true that we Europeans have paid for these investments ourselves? The people putting the question point out the continuous deficits of the U.S. balance of payments in the last few years—deficits through which the European countries, in particular, have amassed big dollar assets. As these dollar assets, by U.S. government request, were not exchanged into gold, the Americans have, according to this argument, made European investments they could not have otherwise made if their balance of payments had been in balance.

In order to avoid any misunderstanding on this point, I want to state first that this argument looks only at the macroeconomic aspect. This seems to be self-evident, but already I have met many American managers who were irritated by this argument, since they had paid for their own investments.

Stating the problem is easier than answering it. One would simplify the problem if one would draw the conclusion that the argument is right because the deficits are more or less equal to the absolute increase in the value of American direct investment abroad. Available statistics are absolutely insufficient to give a well-founded answer, as they only show the *net* figures on U.S. capital inflow and outflow.

However, the net U.S. capital outflow was not on the level of the increase in direct American investments abroad; in 1962 it was $1,654,000 and in 1963 it was $1,888,000, while the corresponding figures for net European cash flow were $548,000 and $573,000. The rest of the investments were paid for through self-financing and locally acquired loans.

Moreover, the export exponent of these U.S. overseas investments is unknown; at least I have not been able to find out anything about it. It is known, for example, in the case of military aid and aid to developing nations that the exponent is very high. Nevertheless, a big decrease in the dollar amount of this aid would not mean an equal decrease in the deficit on the balance of payments. To what extent this factor is of importance in the case of direct investments is difficult to judge, but it is evident that some exports—for assembling as well as exporting of equipment —must take place.

What is known is the extent to which the U.S. companies have invested through self-financing (retained profit and depreciation) and how far they have taken up money locally (long-term government loans, short-term bank loans, suppliers' credit), although not over a sustained period. In 1963 about 31% of the money invested in all assets was taken up locally.

Since more precise figures are unavailable, my remarks must remain of a general nature. It seems without doubt that Europe, by its willingness to accept short-time dollar claims, has made it possible for the Americans to invest on a long-term basis.

This brings us to the economic and financial arguments in the area of monetary policy. It cannot be denied that the U.S. policy of stimulating business by keeping interest rates low, especially on the capital market, has contributed to a very great extent to the continuation of the balance of payments deficit. It has to be admitted that while this policy has been principally aimed at the achievement of a high level of employment, production, and growth domestically, its consequences externally have been largely belittled.

I have the feeling that the U.S. authorities gradually have come to realize that a change in monetary policy would be desirable. However, the difficulty is to convince the average American who has no or at best few foreign interests. After all, the balance of payments question appeals much less to the imagination of U.S. citizens than to Europeans who are used to living in much more internationally open economies.

Countries which finance the deficits of the U.S. balance of payments have, as a consequence, a continuous increase in the amount of their money in circulation. The U.S. government creates through these deficits not only international liquidity, which is not necessary for the financing of normal international trade, but simultaneously also extra national currency in the countries which have a positive balance of payments. Since we have reached the point where several of the Western European countries are already in a position of overemployment, this additional buying power stimulates these economies in an undesired way.

Through our willingness to accept the ensuing inflation, we have acquired know-how and employment for our labor force. Whether this price has been too high is still difficult to judge now. After all, it is always difficult to know what would have happened if all this U.S. investment overseas had not occurred. But what we can say is that 10 years ago, and even after that, we were willing to pay the price; only gradually and very recently this preparedness has disappeared.

Authorities such as Hermann Abs, German banker and President of the German-American Economic Association, and Jonkheer Emile van Lennep, Netherlands Treasury official, who is Chairman of the Monetary Committee of the EEC, have said that it is now up to the U.S. authorities to put their house in order by really trying to change the balance of payments position. And one of the steps on that way has to be the curtailing of U.S. direct investment abroad. This would be a very effective step.

While Abs thinks that the initiative has to be fully American, van Lennep presses for measures on both sides of the ocean. In my opinion, Abs is right in the view that it would be wiser if the Americans would take the full initiative. After all, that gives them an opportunity later, if the situation changes fundamentally, to reverse the measures.

The U.S. direct investments in Europe have indeed been increased strongly, and the available figures point at a tendency toward a further acceleration of the increase. However, seen in the light of the overall total private investments in Europe, the amount of U.S. investment is relatively so small that this does not yet warrant restrictive measures. It has to be admitted, however, that in some branches of industry the penetration has gone considerably further, but also in those same cases the situation is not such that one can speak of an emergency.

Notwithstanding this, one cannot deny that a certain alertness is justified, as there are some underlying factors which in the long run may exert a competitive influence in favor of the American subsidiaries (In this respect it should be taken into account that in order to be competitive in the marketplace, it is definitely not necessary to have anywhere near 50% of the market turnover.) These underlying factors are the differences in actual research expenses on both sides of the ocean and in the relative size between the companies in America and Europe.

If, however, one is of the opinion that the current situation cannot go on in an unrestricted form, then it should be recognized that discriminatory measures against U.S. investments should be avoided. They should be avoided if only for the reason that such actions might seriously endanger the Atlantic relationship which, after all, is the basis for the continuation of a free Western world.

I would prefer that corrective measures originate on the U.S. side, since the current danger lies more in the balance of payments argument than in the other objections.

By urging a voluntary restraint on foreign bank loans and on the expenditure of dollars earned abroad by U.S. industry, President Johnson has made clear that he seriously intends to change this situation. Although I welcome the voluntary nature of this plan, I doubt whether it will be really effective in the long run. My doubts are, in the first place, because of the fact that the measures are more directed at the effects of the deficit on the balance of payments than at the real causes of such a deficit. Secondly, it is always difficult for a voluntary plan to keep up its momentum for a sustained period.

Apart from these objections, I am very much disappointed by that part of the plan which advocates "Buy American" even if the American goods or services are more expensive. Such policies, if effective, could easily lead to similar countermoves on the other side.

From the European viewpoint, measures will have their greatest effect if they are positively directed. This means greater efforts on the research side, and a realization that the current merger movement should extend itself over the frontiers.

As long as top management in the United States does not recognize the special situation in the overseas subsidiary, no corrective measures will be successful. It is therefore most important that we encourage a better understanding in the United States of the practical realities—namely, that European countries have traditions as well as laws, and that sometimes it is better accepted to break the laws than the traditions. I hope this article may help somewhat to bring about the better understanding.

17

Canada and Her Giant Neighbor

JACOB VINER

In this lecture I will deal with the economic relations of Canada and the United States with special reference to the significance for Canada of the disparity in economic size between the two countries. A few figures will suffice to indicate how close is the integration of the Canadian economy with that of the United States. About 60 percent of Canadian total commodity exports go to the United States and about 75 percent of total Canadian commodity imports come from the United States. In 1956 Canada's net import of capital, mainly from the United States, amounted to about one-third of her total annual net capital formation and her gross import of capital amounted to about 40 percent of her total annual net capital formation.

These are all exceptionally high ratios for economic relations of one country to another. They cannot be matched, taken together, I feel certain, for any other two countries in the free world. These high rates cannot be accounted for solely by the relative size of the two countries, or even by relative size plus proximity. An additional factor operative to tie the Canadian into the American economy is the complementary character of the two economies; Canada has surpluses of raw materials of which the United States has deficiencies; standard American capital goods are well adapted to Canadian production techniques; the consumption standards and tastes of the two countries are almost identical, so that American consumers' goods find a ready market in the United States. But relative size has a great deal to do with it.

Also largely, though not solely, because of the disparity in size,

From Chapter 2 of Jacob Viner, *Canada and Her Giant Neighbor*. Reprinted in this form by permission. Alan B. Plaunt Memorial Lectures, Carleton University, Ottawa, Canada, 1958.

the Canadian economy, while important to the United States as export market and source of supply, is not nearly as important to the United States as the latter is to Canada. Out of this disparity in importance there arise for Canada some problems, some fertile sources for justified, for doubtful, and for gratuitous misgivings, and some great economic blessings.

I have concocted a list of criticisms made in recent months by Canadians of American official commercial policy. It is perhaps a grossly incomplete list, since my search has been far from exhaustive. I nevertheless have some confidence in its adequacy, since I have been unable to think up possible additions to it of real consequence. The list of criticisms by Canadians of American commercial policy that I have found is as follows:

1. American import duties and quota-limitations on Canadian agricultural products, minerals, forest products, and fisheries products are excessive.

2. Given the levels of these duties, it is unfair, or unkind, or both, of the United States to impose still higher rates of duty on processed than on unprocessed or less-processed products.

3. American commercial policy is unreasonably unstable.

4. The United States buys too little from third countries, which lessens their capacity to buy Canadian exports.

5. The American agricultural policy, and especially its price-support and export-subsidy policy for wheat, is unfairly and seriously injurious to Canada.

6. American customs procedure is unreasonably und unnecessarily burdensome, inequitable, and restrictive of trade.

7. The United States buys less from Canada than it sells to Canada.

8. The United States is not giving strong enough leadership to the promotion of a more liberal trading pattern in the western world.

In my discussion of friction-points in Canadian-American commercial relations, I will follow a one-sided procedure. I will confine myself almost wholly to the Canadian complaints about American behaviour which I have just listed. Except perhaps for a few occasional lapses, I will ignore the *a priori* probability that there is also some basis for American complaints about Canadian tariff behaviour. My main reason for doing so is that I am much better acquainted with the defects of American commercial policy than with either the merits or the defects of Canadian commercial policy. I do know that American students of Canadian commercial policy are less ready than I am to assume that Canada conducts its own commercial policy primarily with the interest either of demonstrating to the United States how neighbourly a good neighbour can be if it tries hard enough, or of making manifest to the world at large the dedication of Canada to the free-trade species of the universal brotherhood of man. I will on the whole disregard this, however, in partial acceptance of what I presume is the Canadian belief that the disparity in economic size of the two economies justifies at least a moderate disparity in the commercial policies of the two countries. In the standard account of the famous debate between the kettle and the stove on the colour question, the outcome was a draw. I would neither be much surprised, nor very disapproving, if I were to discover that it was part of the Canadian cultural pattern for parents to teach their children a special Canadian version in which the kettle emerges from the debate triumphant by resort to the clinching argument that after all it was a small kettle while the stove was a very, very large stove.

I have neither the disposition, nor the slightest sense of obligation, to defend American commercial policy. As a near-free-trader from the point of view both of my interpretation of the United States' national economic interest and of my interpretation of what are the international obligations of the United States both in terms of international equity and in terms of higher foreign policy in a critical stage of world history, I accept substantially, as having substantial validity, all but one of the criticisms of American policy that I have enumerated, and I do not reject even that one outright. You will therefore not hear a defence from me of American commercial policy, except in a very qualified sense of the word defence. I will defend present American commercial policy as compared to what it has been in the past, and, I regret to say, threatens somewhat to become again in the future. I will offer also some comments in explanation of American commercial policy, but these will not be intended as defence except perhaps as my explanation points to the conclusion that no phase of

American commercial policy is the result of American malice directed against Canada or against the outside world.

To take up first, the American duties and quotas, past, actual, and prospective, on imports from Canada of lead, zinc, cattle, petroleum, rye, and so forth. The United States is well into a recession at the moment [1958]. Signs of recession came early in the field of the non-ferrous metals, of petroleum production, and of agriculture, before it became at all evident that the recession was to be widespread and possibly severe. Much of the American non-ferrous metal mining industry is in genuine distress. The American oil industry has to operate under severe official restrictions of its domestic output. It is normal practice for governments which import substantial fractions of their consumption of particular commodities to come to the assistance at such times of their depressed domestic industries by imposing additional restrictions on imports. This is not to me the right way to deal with the problem. I am sure that it can hurt Canada more than it can help the depressed American industries and that it will not help the American economy as a whole sufficiently to warrant the injury to Canada. I assume that the American action is within the letter and the spirit of American treaty obligations, but I do not think that the United States should be content so to conduct its international relations as to make adherence to treaty obligations the only obligation of real weight. I believe, in particular, that one of the worst offences to international comity is to resort as a remedy for internal distress to measures which export that distress in aggravated degree.

When the United States levies higher import duties on imports of processed articles than on imports of the raw materials they contain, as, except through Congressional inadvertence, it always does, it of course is thereby endeavouring to assure that the processing of raw materials produced abroad for the American market shall be carried out in the United States and not elsewhere. I regard this as uneconomic and unneighbourly policy. But criticism of it comes, I think, with better grace, or without as much need for explanation, from a near-free-trader like myself than from, say, a Canadian who approves of his own country's tariff, of which the duties on imported processing, as measured by the ratio to processing margin of the excess of total duty over duty, if any, on raw materials, are often much heavier than most of the American ones.

There has long been a mild tendency in Canada to seek to countervail the effect of the American import duties on processing by restricting in one way or another the export from Canada of unprocessed materials. Export restrictions seem to me in principle to be on a parity with import restrictions, no worse, and no better. If used successfully as bargaining instruments, to obtain the removal or moderation of another country's import restrictions, a positive case can be made for them. If applied only to offset the effect of another country's import restrictions on the location of processing, they can also be defended even from a free-trade point of view. As applied to the Canadian situation, however, they face some special difficulties and hazards.

First, the producers in Canada of these raw materials, whether they be Canadians or non-Canadians, have presumably been encouraged to invest their skills, if they are employees, and their capital, if they are entrepreneurs, in the development of the facilities in question; export restrictions would operate to depress the prices at the point of production of these commodities; export restrictions would therefore be injurious to them and would be in violation of what had been their reasonable expectations. Second, such action could result in the loss of export markets for the product in either processed or unprocessed form, so that the remedy would be incomparably more damaging to Canada than the disease it was intended to cure. Third, any such action would create a new barrier to rapid development of the natural resources of Canada, whether by Canadians or non-Canadians.

It is reasonable for the commercial partners of the United States to complain against instability in American commercial policy, since this can be a costly and disturbing burden to them. With the exception of a small number of commodities, however, the actual range of instability in an upward or more restrictive direction in American import barriers has been since 1934 not only less than ever before in the United States, but less than has been normal in recent years in most countries of the free world. The American record has been less good with respect to *potential* instability, to apparent risk of impending increases of restrictions, although even here the record to date is not really a bad one, as such things go. It is true, however, that the adverse impact of such instability, actual and potential, as has prevailed, has been mainly on a few countries, notably Canada and Switzerland, but this has been fortuitous and not by design.

The complaint, that because of its restrictions on imports the United States buys less from third countries than it otherwise would and thus impairs their capacity to buy Canadian products, is merely another form of the general complaint that American trade barriers are too high. I agree. Unlike the case in some other countries, the effective American tariff is much lower than it seems, but it is not nearly as much lower than it was in the days before 1934 as official American propaganda for external consumption claims. The effective American system of import barriers is a heavily restrictive one on my standards, but not so on the prevailing standards of probably at least 80 percent of the free world. I learnt long ago not to expect the rest of the world to stay with me in the age of Cobden and Bright.

The complaint that by its price-support programme the United States has unduly encouraged the production of agricultural staples and by its direct and indirect export subsidies has disturbed world markets and created for other exporting countries serious and in some cases probably unmanageable burdens, I accept as fully valid. American agricultural policy is in my belief unjustifiable even in terms of American national economic interest. From a broader and more international point of view, it is inexcusable and irresponsible.

I feel reasonably confident that a referendum of the American people would condemn the agricultural price-support policy, though probably in milder terms than I have used. That the American Administration is unhappy about it is no secret, especially now that it is proposing to Congress revision of the programme, and especially authorization of support price minima of only 60 percent of parity which if accepted and enthusiastically administered would within a few years eliminate the worst sting of the programme for other countries exporting the commodities involved.

As contributing further to explanation, though not to defence, I draw your attention to the sharp distinction between "Administration" and "Legislature" in the American system of government,

to the great power of the legislature as compared to the Administration, and to the limited resources available to the Administration to influence or coerce a Congress which has views differing
from its own. I would add to this that the political parties as such
are also, as compared to many and probably most other countries
in the free world, relatively powerless in dealing with individual
Congressmen and Senators, and that through resort to log-rolling
and other cooperative devices individual American legislators can
and freely do magnify their inherent power to resist coercion by
party leaders or party organization, by the Administration, by
national public opinion, and by world opinion. Add to this that
the farmers, as the result of historical and geographical accident
and of deliberate contrivance, are grossly over-represented in both
the House of Representatives and the Senate, and that American
legislators do not systematically govern their behaviour by what
national referenda show, or could be expected to show, as to the
state of national public opinion on particular issues. It seems, in
consequence, to be the prevailing judgment that there is not the
slightest chance of the Administration's proposals as they now
stand being accepted this year, an election year, and that if the
Administration seriously presses its proposals it will manifest a
degree of courage in a good cause which is magnificent but not
politic. But I advise you, as I fear I often in all justice have to
remember for myself, not to sell the American Congress too short.
As in the case of American education, it also can rise to supreme
peaks. One should exercise restraint in charging with disregard
of international obligations a legislative body which has since
1945 voted, even if reluctantly at times, over $58 billions in eco-
nomic foreign aid.

For Canada, the major concern is wheat. The whole wheat situation in the world at large is a manifestation of a loss of faith in
the recent past in the adequacy of free-market processes as regu-
lators of production and of patterns of sale, with consequent substitution of government agencies, of price-fixing, of official
gambling on the trends of world prices and of production. Wheat
is much more important for Canada than for the United States
and for this reason, as well as because the United States is a richer
country, the United States can afford to give its wheat away on a
more lavish scale than can Canada. Aside from this, the two coun-

tries seem to me to be, as far as wheat is concerned, very much in the same leaky boat, uncertain as to where they came from and why, and where they are now, and where they are going. It was less American misdeeds, and more Canadian official misjudgment as to the future trend of wheat prices, which was the major cause for the present huge surplus of unsold and unsaleable Canadian wheat. Both countries are in trouble, because they have meddled overmuch with free-market prices, and because they have failed to solve for democracy the problem of how to cope with organized producer-groups who have mistaken views of what is good for themselves in the long run, who have the conviction that what is good for themselves is good for the country, and who have irresistible, or at least unresisted, political power. I do not ask you not to condemn harshly the American Administration or Congress for failure to solve the agricultural surplus problem. All that I would suggest is that in drawing upon your available resources of reproof and blame for this purpose you keep enough in reserve to take care of urgent domestic needs.

There is one line of solution of the American surplus-stock problem which would not injure, or would keep within moderate limits, the injury to wheat-exporting countries like Canada and Australia, which would bring gratitude to the United States rather than blame from the rest of the world, which the United States can afford, and which may conceivably be politically possible, and that is for the United States to lower moderately its support prices, and to give away the bulk of its surplus stocks of wheat to very poor countries where undernourishment is chronic but, because of poverty, imports of food of any kind are normally small, the wheat to be used for current consumption and as reserves against famine, but with strict avoidance of re-export. In the absence of such a programme, I see no substantial relief in sight for Canada's wheat-surplus problem except such as may come from a succession of bad harvests in the United States or in Europe.

The complaint that American customs administration is unnecessarily burdensome and inequitable is justified, and in fact is made most strongly by American importers. There have been significant administrative and legislative improvements in recent years, however, and more are in prospect.

The complaint recurs in Canada that the United States sells to

Canada more than it buys from Canada. In 1956, for example, Canada's import surplus in its commodity trade with the United States exceeded one and three-quarter billion dollars, and exceeded the over-all Canadian import-surplus. I am not sure that the complaint does not rest on the notion that import surpluses are bad per se. The Canadian import surplus, as of recent years, is of course primarily the natural and inevitable consequence of the Canadian import of capital. Unless the latter is bad, the former is not bad. That the import surplus is concentrated in the trade with the United States may be valid ground for complaint in so far as this is the consequence of American barriers on imports from Canada, and in so far as these barriers can reasonably be held to be unreasonable by persons or countries themselves protectionists and who regard their own trade barriers as part of the providential order of nature. Except, however, on the assumption, which I am not prepared to concede, that in past tariff-bargaining between Canada and the United States the Canadian negotiators were tricked or bullied into reducing Canadian import duties to lower rates than were in the circumstances in Canada's best interest, the fact that Canadian importers choose, at equal or higher rates of duty, to buy American products rather than those of third countries, seems to me a legitimate ground for moderate pride to American manufacturers but not a legitimate ground for Canadian complaint against either the American Government or the American people.

The last in my list of Canadian grievances against American commercial policy is the alleged failure in recent years of the United States to give adequately strong and effective leadership to the movement toward a more liberal pattern of international trade in the free world, and especially the failure of Congress so far to approve American participation in G.A.T.T. on a firm statutory basis. This criticism also I accept as valid. Once more, therefore, my comments will be in the nature of explanation, rather than of defence.

The American movement towards more liberal commercial policy which started in 1933 was at no time the response to an upsurge of American popular sentiment. It was the product primarily of dedicated, some would say fanatical, leadership on the part of a small group of high officials in the Department of State, and especially of Cordell Hull.

Since then there has been a change in party control of the Administration in Washington. The Republican Party is traditionally enamoured of exports and hostile to imports, and inherently suspicious on principle of international economic cooperation. Even Democratic Congressmen, moreover, would naturally give more whole-hearted support to a liberal economic foreign policy when it was the policy of a Democratic Administration than when it is, as at present, the policy of a Republican Administration. Added to this is the fact that the South, the traditional stronghold both of Democratic Party allegiance and of liberal commercial policy, in consequence of its industrialization and the changed status of its agriculture, has ceased to be a reliable supporter of programmes of trade liberalization.

President Eisenhower is personally a firm believer in liberal commercial policy, both on economic and on higher foreign policy grounds. In the nature of things, however, the demand on his time and attention is always heavy, and at the critical moments trade policy has in the past tended to slide downwards on his list of priorities. The burden of getting the required legislation through Congress has fallen therefore in larger part than was expedient on his Cabinet and Administrative staff. In the light of the professed economic foreign policy of the Administration, the high officials with major responsibility for carrying American official policy into practice are an odd lot, indeed. The present Secretary of State, when he was a Senator, voted against renewal of the Trade Agreement Act, the only statutory barrier to a relapse to the tariff levels of the Hoover age. The Secretary of Commerce, before he came to Washington, was a high officer of the Boston Home-Market Club, an organization which has for generations been an outstanding practitioner of cultural lag, with its interest in uplift confined strictly to tariff rates. The Tariff Commission has been packed with unreconstructed protectionists. The official in charge until very recently of the administration of economic foreign aid was notoriously and openly hostile to economic foreign aid. Such are the men who have to persuade Congress that it should act vigorously and promptly in support of G.A.T.T. and of further lowering of trade barriers. The only comforting idea that has come my way with reference to this seemingly desperate conjuncture is that if responsible officials with such a past press upon Congress the necessity to move in the direction of freer trade, Congress will be persuaded that the urgency on grounds of higher foreign policy of such movement must indeed be great.

An additional factor which has operated unfavourably for the success of the Administration's economic foreign policy is the downgrading of the status of the egghead in the processes of Washington policy-formulation. This began under the Truman Administration and has progressed much further under the Eisenhower Administration. In consequence, the former role of the trained economist has been in large part taken over by the businessman and the lawyer. It is only the recognition that I cannot expect any audience to credit me with full and unalloyed objectivity in this matter which restrains me from revealing how unfortunate a development I think this has on the whole been, above all in the field of economic foreign policy. I do not claim, however, that even in this field there operates a law such that the trained economist necessarily makes a superior civil servant in the American pattern as compared, say, to the successful businessmen. The record of Will Clayton, one of Cordell Hull's aides, for one, provides clear evidence to the contrary.

Despite these unfavourable factors, I would not advise Canadians to be more than moderately gloomy about the prospects for American commercial policy in the near future, and about the consequences for Canada. American commercial policy is not nearly as important as the level of American economic activity in determining the volume in which and the prices at which the United States makes its Canadian purchases. It is clear that 1958 will not be a good year. But since the coming of the statistical age, there has been only one period longer than fifteen months in which the American economy ceased to expand, the one exception being the aberration of 1929 to 1932. The National Archives Building in Washington has carved on its front the inscription "The Past Is Prologue." A Washington taxi driver makes it his practice to interpret it to sightseeing visitors as meaning: "Mister, you ain't seen nuthin' yet." That is also my opinion as to the future of the American economy, and as to the long-run prospects which the American market offers to Canadian exports, even if American import barriers remain very much as they are, and even if they should undergo a moderate rise.

Canadians express concern about the extent to which Canada's national prosperity is dependent on exports to the United States. In the past two decades the American market has been for Canada, on the whole and on realistic standards, a fairly dependable one. It has been a market profitable to Canada beyond all previous expectations and beyond all comparison with what has been available to Canada elsewhere or to other countries anywhere. If Canadians nevertheless are not happy with it, they would be even less happy without it. A young lady, upon being told that it was St. Paul's opinion that those who married did well, and those who remained unmarried did better, replied that she had no ambition to do better than well. Canada's power of choice is even more restricted than was hers. Canada has no visible alternatives, even inferior ones. The movement in Europe for a Common Market and a Free Trade Area; the movement in Latin America for regional preferential arrangements; the large proportion of the world's population which is Communist; these facts seem to point decisively against any major decline in the early future in the relative proportions in which Canada's exports must seek an American market. It will also not be soon, although I feel sure there will be a time, when Canada will be able to have declining exports and increasing prosperity simultaneously.

None of this is intended to discourage Canada from pressing, and from pressing hard, for ameliorations in the American trade-restriction pattern. It seems easily predictable, however, that such pressure is more likely to bring concrete results if it is not permitted to rest too openly on a conviction that in commercial negotiations with the United States the reciprocity should be all on one side. I would advise, moreover, that any Canadian bill of complaints should concentrate on the more important and more substantial grievances and that argument be confined to what can be argued with reason and with force in the general setting of Canadian-American relations and of American political and other obligations to third countries.

18

The Ottawa-Washington Troubles

HARRY G. JOHNSON

The nationalistic policies of the new Liberal government of Canada have surprised and perplexed many Americans as well as Canadians. The preceding Conservative government, led by John G. Diefenbaker, had secured election by appealing to Canadian nationalist and anti-American sentiment, and in many ways had made itself a thorn in the flesh of American foreign policy. Diefenbaker's refusal to honor his government's agreement to accept U.S. nuclear warheads for Bomarc missiles sited in Canada precipitated the election a year ago in which Lester Pearson's Liberals won a plurality.

With the election of a well-known international and Nobel Peace Prize winner, it was thought that Canada had at last returned to its customary path of sane and sober government. But that belief has been rudely and rapidly dispelled. The new government has adopted economic policies more extremely nationalistic than those of its predecessor—notably increased tax discrimination against foreign (mostly American) investment, and subsidization of exports of automotive products aimed at Canadian subsidiaries of big American firms. A succession of incidents, such as the proposal of the interest equalization tax, criticism by the U.S. labor movement of the Canadian action in placing the corrupt Seafarers' International Union under trusteeship, and U.S. criticism of various aspects of Canadian wheat-selling operations, have again aroused Canadian nationalist feelings.

The expectation that the election of Pearson would inaugurate a new and more cooperative phase of Canadian-American relations was, of course, politically very naive. For one thing, the major

Reprinted by permission from *Challenge*, The Magazine of Economic Affairs, a publication of Challenge Communications, Inc., June, 1964, pp. 25–27.

Canadian political parties, like the American, are loose coalitions of divergent interest groups, and even a strong leader—which Pearson is not—must survive by catering to the objectives of these groups. For another, to secure and retain power a party must appeal to the dominant sentiments of public opinion, presenting itself as the party best equipped to serve the national interests as the public sees those interests. And finally, in the British system of government on which the Canadian is modeled, the permanent Civil Service has a more powerful influence on policy than is true in the United States—and the Canadian Civil Service has in recent years become powerfully nationalist, where formerly it was internationalist.

For these reasons it has been natural enough for the new Liberal government to follow and reinforce the nationalistic policies of its predecessor, and to defend these policies on the same arguments of "sovereignty" and "national independence." But to understand the strength of economic nationalism in Canada, and the precise forms in which the policies of Canadian economic nationalism express themselves, some insight into the broad sweep of Canadian history and the postwar economic development of Canada is required.

Central to an understanding of Canadian political history is the fact, appreciated by very few Americans, that Canada represents the losing side in the War for Independence. The economic heart of Canada, southern Ontario, was settled by Tory refugees; and for most of the century after the revolution, Canadians lived in fear of annexation by the United States.

Canadian nationalism from the first meant anti-Americanism; and Canadian policy reflected the desire to build in the northern half of the continent an independent nation rivaling the United States in economic accomplishment and political importance. This objective was implemented by the "National Policy" of Canada's first Prime Minister, Sir John A. Macdonald—a policy of heavy tariff protection for manufacturing, transcontinental railway building to unite the widely separated regions of the country, and encouragement of immigration, especially of people of British stock.

The National Policy, which has remained the basic framework of Canadian economic policy, emphasized the export of Canadian resource products to Britain and other European countries, and used the tariff to promote industrialization, thereby serving the two major goals of economic development and political independence of the United States. Up until the First World War, and particularly during the wheat boom immediately preceding it, the policy worked reasonably well. But since then the political and economic realities facing Canada have changed sharply. Politically, the usefulness of the British connection has waned as the power of the United States has waxed, and Britain has recently shifted its interest from the Commonwealth to Europe. Europe, particularly central and southern Europe, has replaced Britain as the main source of immigrants, posing the problem of digesting the "new Canadians" into the once predominantly British culture.

Economically, the development of Canada has come to depend on the export of new resource products—base metals, newsprint, lumber, iron ore, oil and natural gas—to the vastly expanded American market. The improvement of communications between the two countries has also been steadily breaking down the provinciality and parochialism of Canadian culture in favor of greater cosmopolitanism or, as many Canadians see it, "American cultural domination."

These fundamental changes in the Canadian situation, which are basically reflections on the Canadian scene of world political and economic evolution, underlie the postwar concern in Canada about national identity and independence. With the shift to economic interdependence with the United States and the attenuation of the British connection, traditional Canadian policy has been faced, for the first time, with an apparent conflict between the objectives of economic growth and political independence. Growth points toward closer relations with the United States, and independence points toward greater self-sufficiency at the expense of growth.

Given this conflict, and the historical background of rivalry with and fear of the United States, it is not surprising that Canadian nationalist sentiment should be directed against American economic activities and influence in Canada; nor that in practice it should favor policies of interfering with and regulating rather than seriously resisting those activities. The precise nature of the desired interferences, however, has been conditioned by the postwar evolution of the Canadian economy, and by the ideas of a few key individuals.

The postwar economic history of Canada can be divided into two phases—prosperous growth up to 1957, and subsequent stagnation and severe unemployment—both phases being more extreme in Canada than in the United States.

The phase of Canadian growth involved exploitation of Canadian resources for the expanding American market, and massive investment of American capital in Canadian resource industries and manufacturing for the expanding Canadian market. However, the growing weight of the U.S. economy in Canadian external trade and of U.S. capital in Canadian industry marred Canada's pride in at last achieving the hoped-for growth, and became a subject of nationalist concern. This concern pervaded the Report of the Royal Commission on Canada's Economic Prospects, appointed in 1955. The Chairman of that Commission was Walter Gordon, an independently very wealthy (by Canadian standards) chartered accountant and business consultant in Toronto, now Minister of Finance. The Commission's report bears Gordon's strong personal imprint and contains precise indications of the policies he has since inaugurated. While the report recognized the benefits Canada had enjoyed from American investment and demand, it was concerned with two major objectives: to increase secondary manufacturing in Canada, and to increase Canadian participation in the ownership and management of U.S. direct investments in Canada. For the first purpose the report looked primarily to political pressure on existing businesses to increase the amount of manufacturing done in Canada, and for the second to fiscal incentives to sell equity and give directorships to Canadians—remedies very natural to the thinking of an accountant accustomed to dealing with the top management of Canada's big businesses.

As Finance Minister, Gordon has spoken repeatedly of the first objective, and tried to promote the second in his 1963 budget by changing the nonresident withholding tax and devising investment incentives to discriminate against companies with less than 25 per cent Canadian ownership. As a result of his ineptitude in devising workable principles of taxation, this measure has subsequently been much watered down, while a companion proposal to tax foreign "take-overs" of Canadian enterprises had to be dropped completely. The desire to "Canadianize" U.S. direct investments in Canada also prompted the Canadian objection to the proposed interest equalization tax, which was viewed in Ottawa as a measure to promote direct U.S. investment in Canada.

At the time of the Gordon Report, the two problems mentioned were causes for nationalist worry rather than serious governmental concern, owing to the prevailing prosperity and the absence of any specific tools for applying pressure to increase manufacturing in Canada. But the development of massive unemployment from 1957 on, partly as a result of U.S. developments and partly as a consequence of the inappropriate pursuit of tight money by the Bank of Canada, under Governor James Coyne, provided a strong argument for some form of increased protection to the manufacturing sector as a means of stimulating additional employment.

The speeches of the Governor of the Bank of Canada, which enjoyed wide publicity (and ultimately provoked his dismissal from office), did much to popularize the mistaken notions that unemployment in Canada was due to the country's large current account deficit, that the deficit was due to the inflow of American investment capital, and that the government should attack the deficit by policies promoting manufacturing in Canada, in order both to cure the unemployment and to end the "take-over" of the Canadian economy by American capital. This analysis, which conveniently overlooked the effects of tight money in attracting capital, raising the exchange rate and deflating the economy, not only strengthened the nationalist argument but dovetailed neatly with the views of the two major parties and the Civil Service on the unemployment problem.

According to those views, which have dominated Canadian policy under both the Conservative and the Liberal governments, unemployment is not a general problem to be tackled by expansionary monetary and fiscal policy, but a series of special problems —depressed areas, insufficient training of the labor force, and so on—to be tackled by ad hoc measures. This approach has been reinforced by the conviction, especially strong under Gordon, that the budget must be balanced in order to command domestic and foreign financial confidence.

The Governor's analysis linked the current account deficit, specifically the import surplus in manufactured goods with the United States, with the problems of unemployment and American domination. But the Governor did not suggest any concrete methods for increasing Canadian manufacturing alternative to an increase in tariffs, which was ruled out by popular opposition and the country's international commitments. A solution to this policy impasse, however, was provided by Dean V. W. Bladen, who was appointed in 1960 as a one-man Royal Commission on the automotive industry. Dean Bladen saw correctly that the solution to the industry's problems lay in gaining access to the world market; and he produced a complex plan for industry, the essence of which was to offer the automotive firms remission of duties on imports of vehicles and parts as a subsidy on exports of parts.

The central notion of subsidizing exports by remission of taxes on other transactions of the exporting firms, which ingeniously evades the GATT rules against explicit export subsidization, was seized on by the Conservative government and applied on a limited scale in 1962; it was extended and elaborated by the Liberals in 1963. In its present form, the scheme is directed at subsidizing parts exports by the U.S. subsidiaries in Canada to their parent companies—a rather strange way of asserting Canadian independence. The apparent intention of the government is to extend it to other industries which have an import surplus in their trade with the United States.

A policy of this kind, under current conditions, is a beggar-my-neighbor policy for which there is no reasonable excuse. Given that Canada currently has an overall balance-of-payments surplus and the U.S. an overall deficit, the policy, if successful, will increase Canadian employment at the expense of American unemployment. What forces the Canadian government to such policies is not a real balance of payments problem, but a political mythology about American domination, combined with an erroneous view of how to prevent it, and a fiscal mythology of balanced budgeting that inhibits sensible employment policy.

Whether the Canadian government will travel further down the path of economic nationalism is a politically open question. Gordon's ineptitude in handling his first budget was a serious embarrassment to the Liberals and lost him influence in the government; Mitchell Sharp, the liberal-minded and competent Minister of Trade and Commerce, is reportedly gaining in influence within the government. On the other hand, the Department of Industry, which initiated the new automotive policy, is substantially expanding its top-level staff, with the rumored intention of establishing a system of control over every branch of Canadian manufacturing. Much will depend on the progress of the current Canadian boom; for in Canada, as elsewhere, prosperity is the best guarantee of liberal internationalist policies.

If economic nationalism in Canada continues in its present direction, the U.S. will be faced with an aggravation of its employment and balance of payments problems. However, these adverse consequences of Canadian policy could be averted, to U.S. advantage, if U.S. parent companies could be persuaded to use the Canadian subsidies to increase their Canadian subsidiaries' exports to their European affiliates. The resulting transfer of part of Europe's balance of payments surplus to Canada would ease the U.S. problem, since Canada's need for U.S. capital makes her more willing than Europe to cooperate in supporting the international position of the dollar.

In the longer run it might be advisable to give serious thought to an alternative solution to Canada's manufacturing problems, a solution that Canadian economists increasingly regard as the only rational one and that the new automotive policy is seeking in its own muddled way to pursue—namely, the negotiation of some form of reciprocal free trade between the two countries.

19

United States Foreign Economic Policy and Japan

WARREN HUNSBERGER

Americans can take a great deal of satisfaction in the tremendous economic successes Japan has achieved in the postwar period. The United States has contributed much to these successes and has gained much from them. To a significant degree, the American role was the result of a set of policies based on recognition of the importance to the United States of an economically strong and politically stable Japan. Now that Japan has proved it can make its own way in the world and need no longer be treated as if its economy were sickly, the two countries can look at their relations in a new light. They continue to have important interests in common but each faces some new questions of policy.

The policies that brought Japan and the United States to the early 1960s served both countries well. More benefits can be expected from continuing in the direction set during the past decade. But since the conditions of the 1960s are far different from those of the earlier postwar period, especially for Japan, some new policies may be called for and the emphasis shifted in those that continue. While Japanese-American relations, both political and economic, are at present closer and more harmonious than ever before, the two countries will inevitably be faced with problems that could impair these good relations if handled badly.

Japanese Competition in the American Market

Trade will continue to be the largest problem. The competition of Japanese products in the American market continues to raise

Reprinted in this form by permission from Warren Hunsberger, *Japan and the United States in World Trade* (New York: Harper & Row for the Council on Foreign Relations, 1964), Ch. 12.

more difficult issues than do imports from any other country. Most Japanese goods compete directly and actively with American goods. The United States imports more from Japan than from any other country except Canada, whose products are to a considerable extent not directly competitive with domestic production. The flow of Japanese goods into the American market has been increasing faster than total U.S. imports, faster than U.S. national income, and faster than the growth in world trade. It is evident that some American producers will continue to voice their unhappiness about Japanese competition. Their complaints will pose political problems for the U.S. government and sometimes their situation will present real problems of economic policy as well.

The guiding principle for U.S. policy should be to adhere as closely as is practicable to liberal import policies. Naturally the domestic economy, the balance of payments, and the condition of protesting industries or firms cannot be ignored. To the government official or politician, foreign and domestic considerations will often appear to conflict. As in the past, we can expect a tendency to compromise in the executive branch and in Congress. Also, as in the past, political leaders will tend to favor domestic interests. Here are votes as well as more familiar people, firms, industries, and problems. On the side of foreign relations there are no votes for Americans, the individuals and firms affected are far off and for the most part unknown, and their problems too are more remote. Intellectual arguments about U.S. national interests, especially when they favor the foreign as against the domestic party to a debate, are likely to be regarded suspiciously by politicians and "practical" people. Still, there is need to identify the national interest of the United States and to follow policies calculated to advance it, as against merely balancing the pressures exerted on the U.S. government by interested parties.

The evidence is that U.S. national interests will be served by permitting the rapid increase of imports from Japan and other "low-wage" countries to continue. To serve that interest realistically, that is, to have a policy that works effectively, the United States has to judge, within reasonable limits, how great a flow of imports can be tolerated without undue damage to some part of the domestic economy or the generation of irresistible political pressures for import restriction. It should refrain from restricting imports before this limit has been reached and make sure that, if imports have to be checked, this is done in such a way as to minimize difficulties abroad and interferences to world trade. When this kind of lapse from liberal treatment is politically unavoidable, the restrictive measures should be only temporary. A major task of American policy is to foster the transfer of productive resources from less competitive and profitable activities in the United States to others that are more competitive and therefore more profitable, thus making room for more imports and assisting American industries to compete effectively abroad.

In the Trade Expansion Act of 1962 the United States has a promising instrument for accomplishing these tasks. To ma'e it work effectively will require strong leadership by the administration in Washington in negotiating with foreign governments to expand trade. If it is to resist pressures from domestic producers the administration will also have to work hard to make a success of the act's path-breaking authority to assist American labor, management, and capital to move out of import-competing industries.

The generally excellent records of both the Eisenhower and Kennedy Administrations in limiting the use of the escape clause were marred not so much by the relatively few cases in which tariffs were raised as by the decision to put pressure on Japan to establish export quotas. To maintain a liberal policy during the 1960s, the United States must make it increasingly evident that restrictions of this sort are only exceptions; to do that, it must limit the creation of new exceptions and reduce the number of present ones. While one may hope for the ultimate elimination of such exceptions, that is far less important in the near future than firm adherence to generally liberal policies and convincing demonstrations that exceptions will not grow but rather shrink. Not so much an ideal world as evident progress in the real world is what we should aim for. The Japanese are at least as practical.

An important first step would be to establish standards of due process for determining whether to ask a foreign country to impose export restrictions. There is due process now in the use of the escape clause. The Tariff Commission makes investigations in accordance with law; interested parties have a voice; the Commission makes public its recommendations; the President makes the decision, taking into consideration not only the recommendations but other factors he deems pertinent. No such orderly processes apply when foreign governments are pressed to impose quotas on their exports to the United States. It would be logical, however, and I believe wise, to decide that the U.S. government should not request a foreign country to impose export quotas on goods destined for the American market before the Tariff Commission investigates the facts and recommends action.[1] The same principle could be applied to the long-term cotton textile arrangement. The United States should normally require a Tariff Commission investigation before declaring that market disruption has occurred or threatens. An emergency procedure could be set up for extreme cases, but any restrictions imposed under it should be valid only until the Tariff Commission has had time to make an investigation and recommendation and the President has acted.

The philosophy of the Trade Expansion Act of 1962 is that when domestic producers are suffering from foreign competition the President should examine the possibilities of domestic action to deal with the problem before limiting imports. This would still be the first step under my proposal. Then, if some increase in import restrictions seemed necessary, the Commission should consider all possible methods and in its recommendation should, where feasible, give the President a choice of different measures. Tariff increases should be preferred to quotas. If quantitative restrictions seemed necessary, the use of import quotas imposed by the United States should be compared with the possibility of asking one or more foreign governments to impose export quotas. If either kind of quota was employed, it should normally apply for only a limited period, say a year. At the end of this period every quota should either expire or escalate; those that continued should permit entry of a larger quantity of goods each year. All quotas now in effect should be subject to immediate review by the Tariff Commission, to discover the possibilities of modification or termination or, if necessary, substitution of other measures. Where there were widespread and persistent difficulties, the ex-

---

[1] Perhaps a different procedure would be appropriate for agricultural quotas or those based on considerations of national security which involve quite different kinds of criteria.

ploration of possibilities should include the consideration of a multilateral agreement. The characteristics of some products or the patterns of some kinds of trade would make it difficult to devise workable agreements. In other cases lack of balance in bargaining strength between exporting and importing interests will make it impossible to negotiate an acceptable agreement. Our limited experience of the cotton textile arrangements makes me reserved about the benefits of this approach and suggests that it will rarely prove to be the most desirable alternative.

What is being recommended here is that a heavy burden of proof be put on any proposal to increase restrictions on imports into the United States. The burden should be especially heavy for quotas, American and foreign, existing and proposed, not just initially, but periodically as long as they last. If new restrictions are to be acceptable only after careful scrutiny, and if quotas are to expire after a period, then other measures must also be available to deal with problems arising from the competition of goods from Japan and other countries. Congress and voters will need to be convinced that American producers are not being abandoned to foreign competition. Tariff Commission investigations will have to continue to command respect for objectivity in research and analysis, as well as fairness in conclusions and recommendations. Their speed will have to be sufficient to convince doubters that American firms are not being unduly exposed to "unfair" competition from abroad. Relief and assistance in other forms than import restrictions will have to be prompt and effective enough to carry weight with Congress. And the President will need to remind Congress and the public repeatedly of the advantages to the United States of a trade policy that puts pressure on weak sectors of the American economy in favor of strong sectors.

If such policies as these are followed, Japan should be able to sell in the United States a sufficiently large and expanding volume of exports to meet reasonable needs. The groundwork would be laid for receiving imports of manufactured goods from a growing number of developing countries without repeating the disturbing history of the barring and harassing of Japanese goods in Western markets. Hopefully also, Japanese and others would come to feel they could depend on the receptivity of the American market for imports of competitive products, the limits being those made necessary by the practical prospects of moving American labor, management, and capital out of affected industries and into more profitable activities. If these things happen, measures to provide for "orderly marketing" will have become, not just a new means and excuse for trade barriers, but a positive force for trade expansion as well as order.

The U.S. Balance-of-Payments Deficit

Imports affect not only domestic production but the balance of payments, a matter the United States has had to be concerned about since 1958. This study does not provide the basis for extensive conclusions about a question that affects the whole range of American transactions with the rest of the world but we can put policy toward Japan in a reasonable perspective in relation to the larger problem.

The United States has a favorable trade balance with Japan but, because of aid and military expenditures, the United States paid more dollars to Japan between 1951 and 1962 than came back. Since 1958 special payments have declined (except in 1960) but except in 1961 they more than offset Japan's deficit on current account. Between 1958 and 1962 Japan's gold and foreign exchange reserves rose about $1 billion. Substantial short-term capital movements to Japan have also contributed to the deficit in the U.S. balance of payments. The strengthening of Japan's international financial position has been a significant part of the improvement of its economy. The added responsibility that goes with this improvement was marked by Tokyo's participation in the arrangement worked out in 1962 to provide additional stand-by resources for the International Monetary Fund.

Both the Eisenhower and Kennedy Administrations made a point of abjuring import restriction as a means of rectifying the balance of payments. This is the right approach and an essential one if the United States is to persist in its broad aims of expanding world trade. Of course, if the removal of trade barriers works only one way, resulting in a heavy increase in American imports and no gain in exports, and if other elements in the balance of payments remain unfavorable, the position might prove to be untenable. But if freer importation into the United States is part of a more general removal of trade barriers, including liberalization of imports into Japan, and if adjustments in the American economy move resources to more efficient uses (thus strengthening the country's competitive position), there is no incompatibility between the program advocated here and a proper management of the balance-of-payment problem.

In the series of measures already taken by the United States to help its balance-of-payments position, there are a number which, while falling far short of trade restriction, have had an impact on Japan. Limitations on military expenditures abroad, on the use of American aid funds outside the United States, and on the value of goods tourists can bring back to the United States duty-free have reduced to some extent Japan's opportunities to earn foreign exchange. Whether that result has been justified by the gain to the dollar position of the United States is problematical. Some of the more drastic measures that have been suggested, such as restrictions on foreign investment, would certainly damage Japan and would reduce U.S. exports as well. President Kennedy's proposal of July 1963 for a special tax on foreign securities caused great concern in Japan and brought the Foreign Minister to Washington in a vain effort to get an exemption. While there is no reason for the United States to exempt Japan from measures it is forced to take to meet balance-of-payments needs, it seems likely that the requirements of an effective policy toward Japan do not in themselves greatly worsen the basic American problem, nor do they offer especially significant opportunities for attacking it.

Although the rectification of the balance of payments is ultimately the responsibility of the United States, the problem has given impetus to a significant series of measures of international financial cooperation. Japan should be expected to continue to cooperate in these measures, in accordance with the capabilities and responsibilities that go with its improved international position. This is not only for the benefit of the United States; it is an important step in the process of Japan's becoming fully accepted among the advanced nations of the world.

Employment and Economic Growth in the United States

Like the balance of payments, the slow growth of the U.S. economy in recent years, accompanied by unemployment and the underutilization of productive capacity, may work against a liberal foreign economic policy. For instance, people will ask whether expanding imports from Japan and other countries will not make it more difficult to stimulate rapid economic growth in the United States. Will not imports create more unemployment, perhaps in the very places where it is already highest and most difficult to reduce? Might not a liberal import policy permit excessive human suffering at these points, to gain advantages for export industries that may not particularly need a boost?

Actually, the attack on lagging economic growth is more likely to be helped than hindered by rapidly increasing imports of competitive products. Economic growth results from a vitality, an *élan*, associated with active investing in new productive facilities, with vigorous competition, and with a general feeling among businessmen that change and growth are necessary and desirable. The mood is one of actively looking forward to new opportunities. This is the very opposite of the tone of most protectionist pleas. These reflect generally a backward-looking determination to hold on to existing products, methods, and markets instead of moving forward to better ones. One of the greatest benefits of a liberal trade policy can be to reduce the tendency to hang on to the bitter end, and to encourage—or force—the seeking out of new products, new ideas, and new methods. The effect should be to discourage preservation of investments in high-cost protected industries and to emphasize low-cost competitive activities.

The United States, if it is to be strong and to succeed in its basic policies, must be a leader in the world economy. One of the tasks of the leader is to be first with new and better products and processes. Japan is treading on American heels in some industries, and even the newly developing countries are beginning to do so in a few restricted cases. The proper reaction for American business is to speed the pace of its forward motion, not to contest the rear areas with the foreign producers who are catching up.

Japan's two-way trade with the United States gives an excellent illustration of the American interest. There is ample evidence of Japan's competitive strength and vigor in selling textiles, toys, radios, steel products, and all the lengthening list of other things in the American market. Japan buys American cotton, wheat, coal, turbines, generators, calculators, and other machinery, up to the practical limit of what the nation can afford. Japanese will also in the 1960s buy a greatly expanded volume of American consumer goods—prepared foods, cosmetics, household fixtures, and so forth —if only the foreign exchange is available and the Japanese authorities will permit such things to come in. A liberalizing of this trade will stimulate economic growth in the United States. The export industries that will gain are by no means all concentrated in one sector of the economy or in one region of the country. Moving labor and facilities out of industries that cannot meet Japanese competition will not always require geographical shifts or great losses of skill or investment. What is required is that the workers and businessmen in threatened industries accept the fact that they must choose between competing effectively with imports or shifting to other work. They should not long entertain the possibility of basing their effective competition on substandard wage rates.

Imports will affect some areas and industries, such as parts of the textile industry, which have serious problems of long-term unemployment. These may need special treatment. Tariffs, or even quotas, may be justified for a few years while readjustment is carried out. Readjustment efforts must be stepped up by industries, by localities, by state governments, and by the federal government. One of the most effective ways to stimulate this acceleration is to make it clear that import limitations, especially quotas, are very temporary. Some American cotton textile men evidently do not believe this of present quotas and so are hardly likely to bend their best efforts to getting rid of lines that are not fully competitive, and to move vigorously into activities, perhaps outside textiles, that promise profits in the new, internationally more competitive situation.

In sum, a liberal import policy will in itself do much to stimulate vigorous economic growth in the United States. In addition, specific measures are called for to help those most seriously hurt by imports—to help them move, not stay put. Other measures that effectively stimulate the economy as a whole—such as President Kennedy's tax cut, which was enacted only after his death—will also tend to ease the problem of those adversely affected by imports.

Leading or Pushing Japan?

Both the general tone of Japan's foreign economic policy and many specific measures leave Americans dissatisfied. The reluctance with which the Japanese approach liberalization and the incompleteness of what they have done give rise to complaints. Sometimes American firms receive less favorable treatment than they deem reasonable or the U.S. government thinks justified. Americans think that Japan could do a good deal more for the less developed countries. In dealing with imports from Japan, the United States will continue to face the familiar alternatives of accepting the intensified competition, asking for Japanese export restraints, or, in the end, imposing import restrictions.

On these and other matters the U.S. government has in the past sought to persuade the Japanese of its point of view or to put pressure on them. They have been generally agreeable up to point, but at times they proved themselves extremely tough negotiators, as, of course, the Americans were too. In the 1960s, the status and relations of the two governments are different from what they were in the 1950s, so one of the questions about U.S. policy that needs exploration is the proper approach to Japan.

How much influence can the United States exert on Japan in the future? How can the United States make the most of this influence, considering the political situation in Japan, and particularly the widespread feeling that there is already too much American influence on Japanese policy? One of the strengths of the liberal American import policy I am urging is that it gives a basis for pressing Japan and other countries to do likewise. There are two aspects of this advantage. One is that of example, which may be especially important in relation to Japan. The other is that of bargaining. So long as the United States is prepared to move toward greater liberalization in its own trade policies it can properly ask other countries to reciprocate. The larger the prospective market the United States is prepared to offer, the greater its leverage on other countries. In political and psychological terms reciprocal concessions have the great advantage of enabling each country to show advantages gained for its exports as the counterpart of the import concessions it has granted.

Although the emphasis in American tariff bargaining under the Trade Expansion Act of 1962 may well be on Europe,[2] Japan has a great interest in this matter because the law requires that whatever tariff reductions the United States makes should be extended on a most-favored-nation basis to all but the Communist countries (and those who discriminate against American exports). But the United States will not be willing to have Japan receive such advantages without giving comparable concessions. If American negotiations with Europe should result in substantial tariff reductions for a wide range of products, then Japan will get much and be expected to give much in return. Some of what it has to give will be determined by direct bargaining between the United States and Japan. There will also be more bilateral bargaining between Japan and European countries of the sort that led to a series of significant agreements in late 1962 and early 1963. While the United States may not be directly involved, the most-favored-nation clause will to some extent link all these sets of negotiations.

The immediate purpose of trade negotiations will, of course, be to improve the Japanese market for American goods but one can imagine that considerations of the treatment of capital and other aspects of policy will also be taken into account. Moreover the United States will want to induce the Japanese to play a more liberal part in international economic affairs generally. There is not very much the United States can do to persuade Japan to follow a liberal policy toward the rest of the world, notably Europe, if those countries do not respond in kind. And the United States will almost certainly not have any trade bargaining power

---

[2] This would be particularly the case if the provision of the law could be widely used that empowers the President to eliminate duties on products for which the United States and the European Economic Community account for 80 per cent of free world exports. General de Gaulle's refusal to agree to British entry makes this provision applicable to very few products unless the law is amended to count United Kingdom exports in the 80 per cent, even though Britain remains outside the EEC.

to spare that it can use on Japan's behalf in Europe. Still, it is an important objective of American policy to keep Europe and Japan moving in the same direction.

American influence on Japan's foreign economic policy remains large, and it is proper for the United States to press Japan in ways that benefit both countries as well as world trade. But American influence in Japan has diminished greatly since the Occupation and the United States needs to be careful not to be—or to appear —too overbearing in its approaches. Japan is moving in the right direction, even if too slowly and reluctantly. U.S. interests as well as U.S. hopes for Japan and for the world economy call for Japan to go further and possibly faster. The main feature that is lacking from Japan's trade and payments liberalization so far seems to be a deep Japanese confidence in that kind of policy. U.S. pressure will not generate such confidence. Only as the Japanese develop their own commitment to liberal foreign economic policies can one be sure that each of their specific measures will be sufficiently well rooted to last.

In the circumstances it is not easy to say just how the United States can best approach these matters. Sometimes overt direct pressure will be helpful. Often the Japanese will do better if allowed to decide for themselves without pressure. Sometimes the U.S. example may help to lead Japan in the desired direction. But until Japan has evolved a homemade policy of its own, American approaches must be more circumspect than may be the case once it becomes clear that Japan is no longer susceptible to undue influence from the United States.

An essential requirement of that state of affairs is that the rest of the free world should come to accept Japan on better terms than in the past. As long as they were denied the full benefits of membership in GATT, the Japanese could not be expected to embrace wholeheartedly the principles of liberal trade policy embodied in that agreement. Progress in relations with Europe in 1962 and 1963 coupled with membership in OECD are important steps forward. They reflect an approach to the end of the period of Japanese dependence on American sponsorship. Increasingly Japan can and should rely on its own performance and on the general rules of the free world's economic organizations. Others as well as the United States should have progressively less reason to regard Japan as a special problem.

Closely related is the decline in American ability to influence third countries in Japan's behalf. As Europe has increased its economic strength in the world, the United States has had to mobilize its bargaining power primarily to advance its own interests. What it can do for Japan is a good deal less than before—but Japan can do more for itself. The most promising course for both countries is to cooperate to support principles of international economic relations that hold long-run advantage for all countries. As matters now stand, the liberal principles I have in mind are being given less ardent support than they deserve by either Japan or the United States, and it is no cause for surprise that other countries tend to show more interest in immediate advantages than in principles that yield their benefits mostly over a long period of time.

Japanese Trade with Communist Countries

Japan's trade with Communist countries—and especially China—is a subject of potentially serious disagreement between Japan and the United States. Japanese wishes to expand that trade spring only in part from the normal business interests of a vigorous and eager group of manufacturers and traders. The feeling is widespread that Japan needs new trading opportunities and that China in particular is a natural market of great promise that will be exploited by others if Japan holds back. Underlying these economic considerations are strong feelings that Japan and China should maintain close ties, no matter what the nature of Chinese politics and government. Other Communist countries hold less fascination for the Japanese, but someone in Japan is unhappy whenever an opportunity for any kind of trade slips away.

As Japan's foreign economic policy becomes progressively more independent, it is likely to reflect these feelings, perhaps to an extent that will cause serious concern in the United States. If the Socialists come to power in Tokyo, this development may become politically serious in the American view. Even without this development, the problem is difficult. Most Japanese have far less fear of the Communist menace than Americans have. Many Japanese regard the cold war as a contest between the United States and Russia, or to some extent a contest between the United States and China, in which Japan need not necessarily be involved.

These Japanese may feel that trade with Communist countries is politically desirable as a mark of independence or noninvolvement. For persons with such views, especially those who are eager to demonstrate freedom from American dominance, expanding trade with China, and to a lesser extent with Russia and other Communist countries, takes on a good deal of positive merit.

American concern about Japanese trade with the Communist countries is not based on fear of economic damage through the loss of export markets. Of course, if the trade expanded substantially, some American soybeans, coal, petroleum, and other products may be displaced by products from Russia and China. This is, however, a secondary consideration; the basis of U.S. concern about Japan's trade with the Sino-Soviet bloc is strategic and political. The concern is real but Japan's China trade could expand a good deal without serious danger.

The first condition is continued Japanese adherence to the strategic trade controls agreed on among the free world countries. This will minimize risks, even though some Americans wish the list of prohibited exports were larger. If the Japanese should try to violate or eliminate these controls, one would have to give credence to the view that they would be giving undue support to Communist military preparations.

Even within the strategic controls, Japanese trade with Communist areas still presents problems. For the most part, though, Japanese and American interests are not far apart, even with regard to the touchy matter of credit terms. Japan's refusal to treat the U.S.S.R. and China more favorably than other countries reflects a sound view of Japanese national interest. When it comes to credit, the Export-Import Bank of Japan can be expected to be careful about getting repaid and about the political leverage Moscow or Peking would gain by owing large sums to Japan. While a private businessman might be concerned only about what he could sell, it is difficult to see the normally wary and highly nationalistic Japanese officials permitting themselves to become excessively vulnerable in this fashion.[3] While one could imagine a Socialist government in Tokyo taking a different view of this matter, one

---

[3] Normally conservative, Japanese financial policy has at times turned adventuresome, as in the case of the Nishihara loans which were essentially a political speculation on China during World War I.

should be cautious about assuming that once in power Socialist leaders will let ideology guide them more than nationalism or political astuteness in defending national interests.

Given the conditions of the early 1960s, it appears that any Japanese government looking out for its own national interests in trade with the Communist countries should give the United States little to worry about. Matters would be quite different if Japan were unable to find thriving markets for its exports in the Western world, or if Japan's balance of payments ran into severe deficit, or if there were a serious drop in domestic economic activity. Then pressure to export to any markets might well drive Japan to make dangerous concessions to Communist countries or to disregard the risks of becoming dependent on sales to them. In those circumstances the Communist countries could be expected to make attractive offers for the sake of ultimate political gain.

It is to Japanese and American interest alike to prevent such a situation from arising. To keep Japan from being squeezed in this way the United States and other Western countries should be prepared to provide markets for a volume of Japanese goods rising above the levels of recent years. Beyond this the United States should permit the Japanese to feel they are making their own policy about trade with the Communist areas. Up to now they do not have this feeling—and they are right. Over and above the agreed-on strategic export controls, they have to cope with American pressure on specific matters, as in the case of oil pipe for the Soviet Far East. At some point in Japan's economic resurgence and political evolution, the costs to Japanese-American relations and to Japanese self-esteem of this kind of thing will exceed any advantages the United States gains through such pressure. This point may be reached soon, if indeed it has not already been passed.

PART IV

The Communist World: The Issues

Since the end of World War II, the Communist World has been America's chief ideological and political adversary in a global struggle for power. In 1945 the bloc was clearly a monolith, directed from Moscow and seemingly bent on the destruction of our national way of life. As time moved on, though, the monolith began to crack, and in recent years its internal divisions have become plain for all to behold. On the one hand we see the Soviet Union, still *primus inter pares* but now struggling to maintain a hegemonic grasp on its erstwhile "satellites" in Eastern Europe and Asia. On the other hand we see China, huge and glowering, brusquely challenging Russia's claims to leadership of the world Communist movement. And in between we see the smaller bloc states, some like East Germany and Bulgaria allied closely with the Russians, others like Albania allied with the Chinese, and yet others like Rumania, Cuba, and Yugoslavia attempting to preserve a neutral or independent stance. "Polycentrism" has replaced conformity within the Communist World, and as a result new opportunities have unfolded for the makers of American foreign economic policy.

When the Cold War started, the main objective of American foreign economic policy in relation to the Communist World was the commercial equivalent of our political objective of "containment": to minimize our own and our allies' trade contacts with the bloc in order to deny the Soviet Union and its associates the major benefits of an international division of labor. In the late 1940s, this seemed an eminently logical program, for in those years it was quite obvious that East-West trade was of much greater importance to the Communists than to ourselves. The fuels, industrial raw materials, minerals, and foodstuffs they had to offer we could easily obtain elsewhere. The West, on the other

283

hand, had much to offer that they desperately needed for their post-war recovery and development programs. It followed, therefore, that by cutting off the Communists economically, we could enhance our own national security and the security of our allies at relatively little expense to ourselves. This has remained the basic rationale of our economic policy vis-à-vis the Soviet bloc throughout the postwar period.[1]

Our policy began in 1948 with the initiation of mandatory export licensing controls and was later formalized in the Export Control Act of 1949. This legislation contained two major provisions. First, it withdrew United States most-favored-nation tariff treatment from all Communist states, thereby subjecting imports from the bloc to substantially higher duties than those paid by other trading nations. And second, it automatically denied export licenses for certain "strategic" goods that might contribute to the military potential of the Soviet Union or its associates. In subsequent years additional laws were enacted. One was the Battle Act, which tried to ensure allied cooperation with our policy by threatening to terminate economic assistance, at the discretion of the Executive, to any state exporting strategic commodities to the bloc. Another was the Johnson Act, which prohibited the extension of credit beyond 180 days to any Communist government in default of its obligations to the United States. Czechoslovakia, Hungary, Poland, Rumania, and the Soviet Union came under this category.

Despite the breadth of this legislation, United States policy has been applied with a substantial degree of flexibility. Our policymakers have drawn distinctions among Communist states, and these distinctions have changed from time to time. Thus in the years after Yugoslavia was expelled from the Soviet bloc, most-favored-nation treatment was restored to her exports, and a considerable volume of trade with the United States was fostered. Likewise, after Poland's quasi-revolution in 1956, most-favored-nation treatment was restored, and exceptions were made to the Johnson Act enabling the Export-Import Bank to extend long-term commercial credits. In both cases selective exceptions were made

[1] For a history of our policy during this period, see Nathaniel McKitterick, *East-West Trade: The Background of U.S. Policy* (New York: Twentieth Century Fund, 1966).

to stated policy, our purpose being to encourage the polycentric and nationalistic tendencies of the East Europeans by offering them an opportunity to reduce their economic dependence on the Soviet Union. More recently, we have also begun to offer the same opportunity to the Rumanians, who since the middle 1960s have grown increasingly independent of Russian control.

Conversely, our policy toward the more antagonistic Communist states has been as rigid as possible. Toward China, whose belligerency regarding the United States is well known, as well as toward her neighbors North Korea and North Vietnam and our own neighbor Cuba, a virtual trade embargo has been declared. No alternative policy involving these countries can be validly contemplated as long as the current state of mutual hostility persists. As George Kennan [20] writes, when it comes to trade between Communists and capitalists, "the overriding values here involved are political rather than economic," and politics presently rules out any new trade initiative toward the Communists of Asia and Cuba.

On the other hand, politics does suggest the possibility of a new trade initiative toward the Communists of Europe. In this area of the world, events seem to be moving gradually toward a diplomatic détente and generally improved political relations between East and West. Responding to this development, our general foreign policy has shifted from the objective of containment to an emphasis on peaceful coexistence and "building bridges." And it is clear that among the easiest bridges to build is trade. The question has been raised, therefore, whether the quasi-isolation of the European Communist economies is still in our national interest. The basic rationale of our economic policy vis-à-vis the Soviet Union and Eastern Europe is currently under review. In 1966 President Johnson proposed an "East-West Trade Relations Bill," designed to give the Executive stand-by authority to extend or withdraw most-favored-nation treatment to selected bloc countries and to negotiate commercial agreements for trade in "peaceful" goods. That bill is now before Congress. Our problem here is to consider the merits of expanding East-West trade under present conditions.

Jay Cerf [21] answers his own deliberately ironic query, "Should we or shouldn't we 'trade with the enemy'?," in the positive, and I as well as George Kennan agree with him. Kennan concentrates his attention on the strategic aspects of the issue, emphasizing the potential benefits for the United States. On the one hand, he points out, by liberalizing trade relations we are apt to contribute both to a reduction of East-West political tensions and to the development of polycentrism within the Communist World itself. In addition, there is also the evidence cited by Alec Nove [22] that expanded trade would probably accelerate the tendencies toward economic liberalism and reform visible in several of the bloc countries. On the other hand, Kennan continues, by maintaining our policy of quasi-isolation we are not likely to impede significantly the growth of the Communist economies. It is no longer so obvious as it once was that East-West trade is of much greater importance to the Communists than to ourselves. Circumstances have changed dramatically since the late 1940s, when it was certain that the East could be seriously hurt by American controls. Today, the Soviets and East Europeans are healthy and developing at a rapid pace, and their need for Western imports has diminished.

Moreover, to the extent that needs remain, they can usually be satisfied from sources other than the United States. As Kennan mentions, our allies in Western Europe "often have somewhat different feelings about the whole procedure than we do." For them East-West trade is more essential than it is for us. The East is both a convenient source of relatively low-cost raw materials and foodstuffs and a ready, rapidly growing market for Western finished products. Consequently, Western Europe's policies throughout the postwar period have been considerably more liberal than our own, and their volume of trade many times greater. Indeed, the disparity between their policies and ours has been a source of friction between us, and our efforts to compel Europe to conform to our views have become increasingly costly in terms of offsetting concessions that must be made elsewhere. It is no longer in our power to cut off the Communists economically at little expense to ourselves. But it is still in our power to improve political relations in the West by liberalizing commercial relations with the East. This would be an additional dividend of expanded East-West trade.

Cerf concentrates his attention on the typical arguments heard in opposition to our "doing business with the Communists," which he classifies as either moral, political, or economic. As he demonstrates, not one of these arguments is without its logical or empirical flaws. The fact is that there are no significant risks for the United States in expanding East-West trade. For instance, the commonly cited danger of "dumping," is, as Nove points out, often exaggerated. When dumping has occurred, usually it has been motivated not by a desire to disrupt Western markets, but rather by either a desperate need for foreign currency, or an ambition to gain access to Free World markets, or a lack of familiarity with capitalist pricing practices. And in any event the Communists' ability to dump is severely limited by their comparatively narrow export potential.

The danger that any Western nation or industry would, as a result of expanded East-West trade, become unduly dependent on the Communist bloc for either supplies or sales is often exaggerated, too. There is no single category of exports from the East for which adequate replacements cannot be found in the non-Communist world, and while a loss of an established outlet in the East could be disruptive in the short run, in the longer run any such loss could undoubtedly be made up from the capacity of non-Communist markets. On the other hand, by expanding trade relations we might be able to increase substantially the East's economic dependence on the West, which is the only possible market for many of the bloc's potential exports as well as the only possible source of many of its prospective imports. As Nove concludes, "the Communists stand to lose far more from a disruption of trade relations than does the west. . . ."

Under present conditions it does definitely seem to be in our interest to expand East-West trade, though this is easier said than done. Professor Nove raises the question of whether it is even *possible* for the United States to increase trade with the Communist states and quite rightly emphasizes that it is not simply a matter of our eliminating our existing restrictions. There are at least two other problems to overcome.

One problem, discussed by Nove, stems from the structure of the Communists' own production and trading arrangements. The deficiencies of Communist-style planning are familiar. Foreign and internal markets are kept strictly compartmentalized by a broad division of labor between domestic-production enterprises and foreign-trade enterprises. Consequently, the prices of tradable goods bear no systematic relation to their costs of production, and output is subject to marked variations. Also, because exchange rates are unrealistic, currencies are generally overpriced and inconvertible. All of these factors tend to discourage many Western businessmen from seeking trade contacts in the East, even if restrictions are lifted, for the profits to be made often do not seem worth the uncertainties and administrative delays that must be tolerated. In addition, these factors tend to complicate the task of Western governments seeking to negotiate commercial agreements in the East. What, for example, is the meaning of an agreement for reciprocal tariff reductions so long as Western exporters are barred from competing freely with domestic producers in Communist countries? How can true reciprocity of benefits be ensured? Some of the East Europeans are trying to devise schemes that would ameliorate these kinds of difficulties. But the basic problem will remain as long as the structural differences between East and West persist. And so the volume of East-West trade is likely to remain quite limited, at least until the economic reforms within the Communist World proceed a good deal further than they have.

Yet even then it may not be possible for the United States to increase trade with the Communist states. Still another problem must be overcome: the problem of *what* to trade. It is undoubtedly true that if we were to liberalize our trade restrictions, we would find the East eager to import our industrial products, our technology, and at times our surplus food grains. However, it is less clear that we would be able to absorb Eastern exports, even though, as Cerf notes, the Communists have much more to sell us than merely "caviar and furs." The fact is that the United States is not overly deficient in most of the types of goods that are offered by the East, and in those relatively few cases in which we are deficient, other closer and more convenient sources exist. Cerf is in my opinion overly optimistic when he suggests that the volume of American business with the Communists could grow to sizable proportions.

Nevertheless, I would conclude that the United States should do everything possible to liberalize our trade policy in relation to the Soviet Union and Eastern Europe. As already emphasized, the risks are minimal, the potential benefits numerous. And even if the actual impact on our foreign trade is slight, the impact on our foreign relations could be substantial. In Western Europe we would be eliminating one of the sources of friction between us and our allies, thus enhancing the prospects for our continued political cooperation vis-à-vis the Communist World. At the same time, in Eastern Europe and the Soviet Union we would be demonstrating our good will and our ambitions for truly peaceful coexistence. As George Kennan stresses,

Communist governments . . . have shown a disposition, particularly the Russians, to place a high value on the readiness of others to talk and negotiate, at the governmental level, on governmental measures designed to promote trade. It is evident that they regard such a disposition as having an important symbolic value; and more than once, in the history of Communist diplomacy, trade talks have evidently been regarded, and have served, as an important preliminary approach to more far-reaching political dealings.

In short, by building one "bridge," we could be laying the foundations for a lot more. Here is a clear-cut opportunity to put our foreign economic policy to work in support of the general, global strategy of our over-all foreign policy.

20

East-West Trade

GEORGE F. KENNAN

The problem of what is called East-West trade is scarcely a new
one. For forty-six years our statesmen, and those of other Western
countries, have been facing it in one form or another. So long
and deep is the experience with it that one is taken aback,
sometimes, to see to what extent it is treated in our own public
debates as a new problem, and to what extent the lessons and
precedents of the past are ignored.

Admittedly, these lessons are of limited value. Insofar as they
derive from the prewar period, they relate, of course, only to the
Soviet Union—and only to a Soviet Union in isolation, at that.
Today, we have a wide spectrum of Communist countries to face,
and in almost every case the problem presents certain specific
features. There have, too, been important subjective changes on
our side which have to be taken into account. But there are
certain elements of this early experience of trade with an isolated
Soviet Union which ought perhaps to be borne in mind in any
discussion of the wider problem of today; and it will be well to
mention them at the start.

First, there is the fact that in the period following the consolidation of Communist power in Russia most Western governments, after looking at the problem long and hard, and under the
buffeting of much public debate, settled for policies which drew
a distinction between normal trade, where value was received
for value, on the one hand, and one-sided favors, such as long-
term credits, grants, aid, etc., on the other; and they showed a
disposition, in general, to permit normal trade but to withhold

Reprinted in this form by permission from George F. Kennan, *On Dealing
with the Communist World* (New York: Harper & Row for the Council
on Foreign Relations, 1964), Ch. 2.

the favors. This was the policy of the United States government, as of others, in the period before World War II; and the basic reasons for it are fairly clear. To extend favors to an ideologically hostile country could scarcely be defended, on political grounds; and, except for the insistent Soviet effort to obtain long-term credits, there was little demand or incentive for anything of this nature. "Foreign aid," prior to World War II, was not yet a concept. On the other hand, it was also not feasible, as a rule, to forbid one's own businessmen to take advantage of favorable trading opportunities that came their way, especially where the other side was prepared to give value for value. In addition, there was at no time sufficient solidarity or self-discipline among Western nations to make possible a unified policy in restraint of such trade. If one's own businessmen did not take the trade, somebody else's businessmen did. The result was that normal trade with the U.S.S.R. became a standard feature of the international economic relations of practically every Western country. The statesmen of the 1920s and 1930s would have been amazed to find that the simple principle involved in this practice was being so widely questioned today.

Secondly, trade with Russia never became a very important factor in the economic life of the West. It found its limits in the dimensions of the Soviet capacity to pay. In the absence of any sort of convertibility, this capacity was largely identical with the portion of Soviet production which the Soviet government was able or disposed to make available for export, plus the available gold production of the Soviet Union; and these items were never very great. In the years from 1921 through 1938, Soviet foreign trade averaged only 1.5 per cent of world trade—a small percentage for a country that occupied one-sixth of the world's surface.

The economic significance of what was then called "trade with Russia" was greater in the case of certain other Western countries, notably Germany and England, than in the case of the United States. The turnover of American trade with Soviet Russia ran only in the order of something like $100 million per annum. The Germans, on the other hand, had at times an important volume of machine-tool exports to the Soviet Union, particularly important against the background of the economic crisis of the 1930s;

and British imports from Russia, particularly of timber, were of more than minor dimensions. In general, however, the volume of trade with Soviet Russia was not such as to justify the predictions either of the optimists, who saw it assuming dimensions which would constitute a major boon to Western exporters, or of the pessimists, who had visions of the Western markets being swamped and distorted by vast onslaughts of Soviet dumping.

Thirdly, the technical dangers of permitting private firms in a capitalist country to deal with the foreign trade monopoly of an ideologically hostile government proved not to be very great—certainly not great enough to justify the lively fears entertained in Western circles when the Soviet government first appeared as a trading partner on the world scene. It was clear that such dangers did exist, and had to be guarded against. But Western firms turned out to be pretty well capable of looking after themselves; and where this seemed to be required, as in the case of the German machinery manufacturers or the British timber importers, they found ways of mutual collaboration to guard against their being unduly played off against each other by a stronger trading partner.

These, in the main, were the lessons of the earlier experience of trade with the Soviet Union. They are cited here because all are germane, in some degree, to the problems of the present.

In the recent period, the problems posed for Western statesmanship in this area have been extremely complex, because they are widely differentiated both geographically and functionally. There are a number of different countries or groupings of countries, each of which presents a specific problem from the standpoint of United States policy; and yet there are also certain considerations affecting entire categories of commodities, such as wheat and oil, which have to be taken into account in dealings with the Soviet bloc as a whole. And in addition to this, the problem is different, in many instances, for our allies in the West and East than it is for us; and this raises for us the question of not just what *our* policy should be at any given point, but of what attitude we should take toward the policies of our allies and friends.

Some of these complexities will become evident if one glances at the various geographic entities involved and notes the special situations with which they confront us.

Let us begin with the Soviet Union itself. Here, we have a long tradition of trade; but, as we have just noted, it has always been trade of modest dimensions. Neither for the West nor for the Soviet government has it ever had more than a minor economic significance. Since the recent war it has been even further inhibited by the heightened sensitivity of United States opinion to the idea of shipping to the Soviet Union anything that could conceivably contribute to the growth of Soviet military strength. This has resulted in an elaborate system of American and NATO export controls, reinforced by the provisions of the Battle Act. These measures may have had some effect in slowing down the rate of advance in Soviet military strength. It is doubtful that they could have done much more. There is little, other than the most highly classified sorts of weaponry, and particularly little when it comes to such things as machine tools and other semi-military goods, which the Soviet government cannot acquire either from or through neutral countries or by mastering the necessary techniques and developing the respective production itself, if it sets its mind to it. The significance of these export controls, accordingly, has probably lain more in the subjective satisfaction they have afforded to American opinion than in such objective effect as they may have had. But the states of mind behind them have tended, and still tend, to inhibit any extensive development of United States–Soviet trade; and these states of mind have to be taken into account as an important environmental factor.

Recently, a complication has come into this situation in the form of the sudden readiness of the Soviet government to buy wheat abroad. They, of course, have a great shortage of it—and the United States a great surplus. Both shortage and surplus are the effect of irrational agricultural policies pursued by the two governments for ideological reasons. Neither government is really inclined to depart from these policies merely in order to avoid the shortage or the surplus, as the case might be. In these circumstances, the basis for a deal, or a series of deals, would seem, on the face of it, to be very much present. The United States, by selling its wheat, would make it possible for the Russians to go on giving their farmers inadequate incentive for the production of grain; they, by purchasing it, would make it possible for the United States to go on giving its own farmers too much.

The American statesmen of earlier decades would have been amazed to learn that there could be any hesitation about so obviously advantageous a proposition. In those earlier days, the complaint used to be that the Russians bought only prototypes for industrial equipment, and refused to buy consumer goods; this was cited as evidence that the trade had no proper stability. Now, the Russians have come into the market for consumer goods, and yet numerous echelons of the United States government have had to be occupied for weeks with the decision whether to permit even one such deal to take place. In this, one has an example of the extent to which in the United States the whole question of trade with the Soviet Union has recently become a focal point for political and emotional hesitations.

Turning to the Eastern European satellites, one has a still different set of problems. There is, above all, the general question of whether one wishes to make it easier for these countries to achieve a measure of independence and flexibility in their foreign economic relations, looking not only eastward but also westward for their opportunities; or whether it should be the Western objective to deny them, wherever we can, access to Western markets, both as buyers and sellers, in the hope that this will hamper their economic progress, and embarrass their governments. This last policy, naturally, tends to deprive them of any hope that the West could be of help to them in working out their economic future, and to convey to them that however distasteful the prospect may be (and in some instances it seems very distasteful indeed) they have no choice but to stick closely to the Soviet Union and to look predominantly in that direction for their future economic connections. Both views appear to be represented in Washington; but the second one seems generally to have prevailed when it came to Congressional determinations of one sort or another. This is, of course, a profoundly political question, and one which cuts to the heart of the problem of coexistence, with particular relation to polycentrism. But it is a question to which policy-makers are simply obliged to find answers, because until one answers it, one cannot know whether one should apply to the satellites the same policy concepts one applies to the Soviet Union, or different ones.

A still further problem is presented by Jugoslavia. Here is a country which is not a member of the Soviet bloc and where most of the specific objections raised in the West to the attitudes and conduct of the bloc countries do not apply. Yet there is strong sentiment in the United States Congress for denying to Jugoslavia normal commercial treatment and for doing everything possible, by means of tariff barriers and moral suasion on our own business community, to exclude Jugoslav goods from access to our market. Here, again, the basic question is actually the same one that presents itself in the case of the satellites: whether, namely, one wishes to encourage Communist countries to find independent answers to their economic problems or whether one wishes them to look exclusively to Moscow for these answers. Because the satellites watch the Jugoslav experience very closely, and if one is to penalize normal Jugoslav trade with the West, merely on the grounds that the Jugoslavs continue to call themselves Communists, the satellites can only conclude from this example that even if they were to go a great deal further than any of them have gone or could afford to go in detaching themselves from Moscow's political orbit, this would still not be enough to win them even normal commercial treatment at Western hands.

To all these problems, both with Russia and with the Communist countries of Eastern Europe, a new depth of complexity is added by the fact that the trade of Western Europe with this area is much more important than United States trade. We do about $200 million worth of trade with the entire Soviet bloc per annum. Western Europe does something like $5 billion, or twenty-five times as much. Obviously, restrictive policies on our part are not going to be very effective unless they are also the policies of Western European countries, and unless they are seriously and enthusiastically enforced. This is most unlikely to be the case. Certain important entities—namely, Sweden, Switzerland and Jugoslavia—are, of course, not embraced at all, even formally, in any system of NATO trade controls. But even those Western European countries that are so embraced often have somewhat different feelings about the whole procedure than we do. And commercial discipline throughout this area is not much more adequate today than it was in the 1920s and 1930s for the enforcement of trade restrictions which conflict strongly with the interests of tens of thousands of private traders. These disparities are already sharply reflected in the incongruity of the figures on United States trade with the bloc and that of Western Europe.

Despite this relatively high level of Western European exchanges with the bloc, a shadow falls today over the future of this trade, in the form of the potential internal protectionism of the countries of the European Common Market. These countries are willing enough, as a rule, to export to Eastern Europe; but to what extent they will continue to show themselves receptive to imports from that area, and particularly to imports of agricultural products, is another question. Anxieties on this score exist in several of the Eastern European countries, especially in Jugoslavia and Poland, both of which have an important stake in exports of agricultural commodities to Germany and other Common Market countries. These anxieties are perhaps somewhat exaggerated. But they are probably inevitable, particularly in the light of the fact that it seems to have been impossible for the governments of these countries, to date, to find anyone who would, or could, undertake to discuss responsibly, on behalf of the Common Market, the problems of their future trade with the countries of that area. They are left, in this way, to bat in the dark; and whoever bats in the dark normally has exaggerated fears.

Such anxieties are, of course, not peculiar to the countries of Eastern Europe. They are shared by a considerable number of governments across the globe, not to mention the European neutrals. But there is perhaps a special sensitivity in Eastern Europe by virtue of the political overtones that surround every question of this sort. This has been heightened by the fact that whereas a good deal of public discussion has been devoted in Western Europe to the question of relations between the Common Market and the European neutrals, the similar problem, as it affects the Eastern European countries, has received very little attention, particularly in Germany. In any case, the gravity of this problem for the Eastern European governments, as they face the difficult questions of orientation between East and West, is not appreciably mitigated by the fact that they have company in other parts of the world.

Here again, opinion as to what constitutes the American interest will be divided according to political outlooks. Those who wish to see the satellite countries, and Jugoslavia, deprived of possibilities other than those of a close and exclusive association with the Soviet Union and with each other, will no doubt welcome a Western European protectionism which tends to exclude Eastern European products from the Western markets; and they will continue to regard our own denial of normal tariff treatment to the Eastern European countries as a useful example to the countries of the Common Market. Those, on the other hand, who see value in the achievement by the satellites of a more flexible and independent position, which would permit them to develop trading relations with both East or West as their interests may suggest, will naturally look at it the other way.

So much for the background situation, in so far as the Soviet Union and the Communist countries of Eastern Europe are concerned. China and its satellite régimes in Asia constitute another problem again: one which resembles in many ways that presented by the Soviet régime in its infancy. But since the problems of trade with Russia and Eastern Europe today are probably closely akin to those of trade with China in the future, it may be permissible for purposes of this discussion to stick to the former.

As one attempts, against the background of what has been outlined above, to think out the problems of policy which East-West trade presents for the United States at this juncture, certain broad considerations present themselves.

First, it must be recognized that the overriding values here involved are political rather than economic. Particularly is this true when it comes to United States trade with Russia and the bloc; for here the economic dimensions are entirely of a secondary order. But it is also true when it comes to the question of Western European policies in this field. For while the economic aspects of Western Europe's trade with the East are not negligible, and deserve respect in themselves, its most important aspect is really the effect it will have on the future orientations and policies of the Eastern European countries, and on their relations with one another and with the Soviet Union in particular. The problem of East-West trade is, in short, primarily a political problem, and should be approached as such.

Secondly, I think we should recognize that a policy designed primarily to throttle economic exchanges between the Soviet bloc and the West, as a means of impeding the military-industrial development of the Soviet Union, is simply not apt to be very successful, at least not in the sense of accomplishing anything more than to increase autarkic tendencies within the bloc as a whole and to slow down, to a minor and undecisive extent, the advance of the Soviet economy. It might be questioned whether even a total Western blockade of a region so vast and rich and possessing already so highly developed an industrial base as does the present Soviet bloc could really be effective in accomplishing more than this. In any case, to reduce East-West trade to a level which would have a major and decisive effect along these lines would require, at the least, something like a total Western blockade of the entire Communist orbit. But the effort to establish such a blockade would involve so severe a conflict with natural trading compulsions, and would place so heavy a burden on private as well as national economic interests, that the invitations to evasion would be ubiquitous, and the prospects for success would not be favorable even if the effort was one sponsored by the governments of *all* the major Western trading countries, and not just a portion of them.

In addition, it must be remembered that such an undertaking runs directly counter to the development of a healthy political and economic polycentrism within the bloc. Admittedly, there is as yet no adequate consensus, in the United States at least, as to whether such a polycentrism is what we wish to encourage. But it must be recognized that what is done in the field of trade policy is going to affect this situation one way or another, whether one wishes it to or not. And one should probably expect that the negative attitude toward this question—the view, that is, that polycentrism is *not* to be encouraged and that the West has most to gain by forcing the Communist countries in upon themselves economically—is one that is apt to encounter greater resistance in some European countries than it does in our own.

There is also a fundamental theoretical consideration on which a sharp division must be expected between important segments of American and European opinion. The distinction was mentioned above between normal trade, on the one hand, and such things as long-term credits on abnormally lenient terms or other forms of what is in reality "aid," on the other. Now the question exists as to whether normal trade with a Communist government should be regarded as a favor, extended by us to it, to be requited by concessions to us in the political field, or whether it should not. There are, of course, those who would say that where the law of supply and demand is permitted to operate normally, where value is only exchanged for value, no question of ulterior obligation is involved, and that there is no more reason why we should ask a Communist country to give us some sort of a political reward for permitting such trade to proceed than there is for them to expect the same thing of us. The British, I understand, now go even further, and hold that not even the extension of long-term credit should be regarded as a proper *quid pro quo* for political concessions. It is quite evident, on the other hand, that in the minds of a great many Americans, trade with a Communist country, even on normal commercial terms, represents an act of graciousness on our part for which we should demand political concessions in return. This view is based, as a rule, on the thesis that the scales of values which prevail on the world markets and which normally govern international commercial transactions do not accurately reflect the real extent to which political interests are served on both sides when trade takes place between a Communist country and a non-Communist one. This was the view, for example, of a special mission of the House of Representatives which visited Europe a year ago to study these problems.

We have here a difference as between influential segments of American and European opinion, which, again, will not be easily overcome, particularly because the sacrifices implicit in the American view are ones which would fall much more heavily, economically, on the Europeans than they do on us. To demand political concessions as a *quid pro quo* for normal commercial transactions is, after all, only another way of renouncing trade altogether; for Communist countries will never yield to overt demands of this nature. And obviously, such a renunciation would come harder to some of the Europeans than it would to people in the United States.

But there is another sense in which the suggestion of a connection between trade and politics has greater substance. If Communist governments cannot be expected to give political concessions for specific trading deals, they have shown a disposition, particularly the Russians, to place a high value on the readiness of others to talk and negotiate, at the governmental level, on governmental measures designed to promote trade. It is evident that they regard such a disposition as having an important symbolic value; and more than once, in the history of Communist diplomacy, trade talks have evidently been regarded, and have served, as an important preliminary approach to more far-reaching political dealings. Western governments will do well to bear in mind, therefore, that even if one cannot expect specific commercial deals to be requited with political concessions, there may be times when a readiness on their part to discuss in a constructive manner with Soviet or other Communist representatives the possibilities for a development of commercial relations in general will be appreciated and reciprocated on the other side as important evidence of a desire to improve relations across the board.

With these considerations in mind, it is perhaps now permissible to ask one's self what the outlines of a sensible American policy might be.

When it comes to the trade of the United States with the bloc, it seems to me that the first thing we could usefully do would be to relax and not to make such heavy sledding of it. In economic terms, this trade is still of minor importance. In the case of the Soviet Union, it amounted in 1961 to only one per cent of the total Soviet trade, and something like two-tenths of a per cent of ours. Communist countries are not going to be decisively benefitted if this trade increases somewhat; nor are they going to be importantly injured if we restrict it still further. The Soviet government is not going to fall if we deny it wheat; and the heavens are not going to fall if we permit wheat to be shipped. The amount of agony of decision addressed to this subject in recent months has been out of proportion to what was actually involved.

Secondly, it may as well be recognized that the emotional overtones which this subject carries for much of American opinion, added to the unresolved differences among us over basic questions of political policy toward the bloc, make it idle for us to think that we can approach the problem of our own role in East-West trade on the basis of a cool and detached appraisal of national interest. One does not need to argue about just what the configurations of a policy so calculated would be. Whatever they would be, if they involved any appreciable liberalization of what we have been doing in recent years, they would at once become controversial, particularly in Congressional opinion, to a degree that would militate greatly against their effectiveness. It is, in short, a matter in which we are simply incapable of acting at this time in any purely detached manner. For this, a calmer state of opinion would be necessary, and there would have to be a wider consensus on fundamental questions of policy. For the moment, therefore, anything in the way of a major relaxation of our export controls or extension of our commercial dealings with Russia and the bloc, has to be regarded as simply subjectively unfeasible. The Russians and the satellites will have to understand that if they have favorable chances at all for trade with the West, these chances do not lie in our direction—at least not until there is a marked and prolonged improvement in the political atmosphere.

On the other hand, it should, I think, be recognized that in view of the many variations in the way this problem presents itself to us—the differences, for example, between the considerations affecting trade with the Soviet Union and those affecting trade with the satellites, or between those prevailing in the case of Jugoslavia and those affecting trade with other Communist nations—it is not a problem which lends itself favorably to treatment by sweeping general determinations of policy, and particularly not in the form of legislative strictures. To deal in any way effectively with this problem, we need flexibility of approach—we need the ability to discriminate intelligently. Even a policy which is in essence one of denial or restriction of trade should not be anchored in sweeping legislative injunctions which leave nobody—not even the legislative branch itself—in a position to make intelligent exceptions. It would be better to have a more restrictive and negative policy which rested on a firm understanding between Congressional leaders and the Executive but left somebody free to use his head when it needed to be used, than to try to pursue more liberal policies against the background of a jealous Congressional disposition to prescribe and limit their effects by legislative action.

When it comes to our attitude toward the trading policies of our associates in Western Europe, quite other considerations apply than do in the case of our own trade. Here, again, the best answer would seem to be: relax—but relax in the other direction. If at home the need is for a reduction of tension and controversy by accepting the internal compulsions that make it difficult for us to trade with the bloc, in the case of our European associates it is a question of accepting those external compulsions which make it difficult for them *not* to trade.

This is not to be taken as a suggestion that our European friends should be told that so far as we are concerned anything goes, and that there are no measures of prudence we would consider to be in order. There will still be need, of course, for agreement with them over the definition of what constitutes strategic materials, unsuitable for release to a politically hostile government. There may well be, as in the case of Soviet oil shipments, instances in which it will be necessary for us to take a sympathetic attitude toward, or even associate ourselves with, measures of collective defense, designed to prevent Western markets from being dangerously affected by Soviet trading practices. But whether we should try to bring pressure on the Western Europeans in matters of normal trade with the Communist bloc is another matter. They are not apt to agree entirely, no matter how hard we press, with those outlooks in this country which place such heavy limitations on our own ability to shape policy in this field. Their problems are in many respects their own, not ours. And we, divided and vacillating as we are in our basic judgments as to how to face the problem of international Communism, are not apt to be very helpful guides to others in the shaping of their economic policies in the field of East-West trade.

Continued pressures on our European allies for the restriction of their trade with the Soviet Union and the bloc are unlikely to be very effective in hampering Soviet economic development. But there are two other effects they *are* likely to have. The first, which may be predicted with some confidence on the basis of past experience, is to place further strain on our relations with our European partners and to give us one more thing to disagree and argue about. The second is to throw just enough uncertainty into the minds of the Western Europeans to prevent them from doing anything very effective on their own in the way of giving Eastern Europe the alternative it needs, and to some extent is seeking, to an exclusive economic association with the Soviet bloc. To the extent that the Western Europeans are willing to move in the direction of expanded East–West trade, it would not seem to be our business to attempt to stop them, whatever our own feelings. For the opposite concept, the one which sees Russia's economic advance being importantly impeded by something like a Western blockade, is not going to work anyway beyond a point; and in moving to prevent the first one from being tried, even by our allies, we will simply be assuring that there can be no effective Western policy at all in this field: no effective policy of the denial of trade, because objective conditions do not permit it; no effective policy of its extension, because our pressures will be just sufficient to make it a half-hearted and half-way measure.

These are my reasons for suggesting that, while exercising in regard to our own trade with the East whatever restraint is necessary to retain a reasonably adequate consensus of opinion behind our policy, we reduce the claims we place on the policies of our various allies and associates throughout the world, and leave them greater freedom to decide for themselves what they want to do. This will ease our relationship with them. It will permit us to satisfy our own pangs of conscience about trading with a political antagonist. The loss to be suffered, in terms of the pace of Russia's economic advance, will not be great, even in the eyes of those who see our purposes advanced only by Russia's economic setbacks. And meanwhile, we will at least permit to be conducted, to the extent our Western European friends have the inclination to conduct it, an experiment in which many of us may not greatly believe but which it is unnecessary and perhaps dangerous for us to inhibit: whether, namely, the possibility of better trading opportunities with the West—for Russia, the possibility of a better international division of labor in the interests of her own economic advance; for the satellites, the prospects of a re-inclusion into the community of Europe in at

least one important respect—whether this possibility will not
have a useful effect on the Communist bloc as a whole, and
produce such changes as to cause the entire problem of East–
West trade to assume, eventually, a different and less forbidding
aspect.

21

We Should Do More Business
with the Communists

JAY H. CERF

Should we or shouldn't we "trade with the enemy"? Few questions in American politics are more loaded. And partly because of this, many U.S. leaders would as soon endorse cholera as suggest publicly that a selective increase in East–West trade can promote the U.S. national interest.

In 1934, right after American diplomatic recognition of the Soviet Union and at the bottom of the Great Depression, Will Rogers remarked that the U.S. would probably recognize the devil if it could sell him pitchforks. From the vantage point of 1965, we now know that, though Will knew the devil when he saw him, he was wrong about the pitchforks. In the last 30 years our sales to the Communist bloc have declined to less than 1 per cent of total U.S. exports.

This summer, Congress again renewed its principal law setting forth the terms of U.S. trade with Communist countries. This law (the Export Control Act) requires that almost no U.S. commodity be sold abroad without Government permission. The act further states that no U.S. sale to a Communist country shall be permitted if it "contributes significantly" to Communist military or *economic* potential in a way that would "prove detrimental to the national security and welfare of the United States." It is left to the executive branch to decide what items "contribute significantly" to Communist economic potential. And it is this unique— and often impossible—requirement that lies beneath what has become one of the more ironic elements in modern U.S. foreign policy. (China, Cuba, North Korea, and North Vietnam are not relevant to this discussion. Unlike the U.S.S.R. and Eastern

From the *New York Times Magazine*, December 5, 1965, p. 70. © 1965 by The New York Times Company. Reprinted by permission.

Europe, nearly all trade with these countries is under total U.S. embargo.)

Being equally anti-Communist, our allies join us in refusing to sell to Communist countries items which contribute significantly to Communist military potential. But, going far beyond this agreement with our allies, we have isolated ourselves as the only country in the Free World which legally restricts sales of *nonmilitary* goods to Communist countries. The unsurprising result is that our allies steadily increase exports to Communist countries in many of the very items we prohibit. This homemade strait jacket contributes to the interesting statistic that 94 per cent of the goods the Soviets now purchase from the Free World are purchased from our allies.

How much has the East bloc been deprived during the period since 1949, when our Export Control Act was first enacted? From 1948 to 1963, during which U.S. exports to the East fell by 60 per cent, Free World trade with the same countries tripled. In 1963, the Soviet bloc purchased $2.9 billion worth of goods from the North Atlantic nations; of this the U.S. share was 6 per cent.

The preponderant share of East–West trade developed by our allies as a result not only of their refusal to prohibit sales of nonmilitary goods, but their willingness to open portions of their home markets to Communist-bloc exports. A would-be foreign purchaser, whether Communist or capitalist, cannot spend large numbers of dollars on a continuing basis unless he has a market in which to earn them.

Many consequences of the Export Control Act were obviously not intended by Congress. The natural bureaucratic propensity of administrators to avoid marginal decisions is only one factor which has contributed to the lengthy lists of nonmilitary items whose sales we prohibit. There has also been genuine bureaucratic fear of Congressional and public harassment over individual decisions, a fear which has unfortunately not been without foundation. Moreover, in a field not always characterized by candor or bold political leadership, frenetic oratory in Congress and in public can intimidate the bravest of loyal public servants. Our East–West trade policy, in truth, reflects a national attitude based more on current wishing than on current events.

The ironic result of the policy is that what is intended to impair the enemy has instead impaired us. We have limited our own maneuverability while multiplying trade opportunities for our allies, and have left our adversaries virtually unaffected. In establishing this policy we have argued over problems which do not exist while ignoring problems which do exist. Let us first, then, remind ourselves of what we have been arguing about.

A circular argument underlying many public and Congressional objections to East–West trade is that trading with the enemy must be to our disadvantage because it is trade with the enemy. A recurring variation on this theme is that we now forget the lesson of our sales of scrap iron to the Japanese in the late nineteen thirties. The scrap of the thirties is, of course, strategically comparable to critical atomic isotopes in the sixties. The shipment of such isotopes and other strategic items to Communist states is totally and effectively barred by all Western nations. And even the most venturesome advocates of increased East–West trade urge that these barriers be retained and strengthened where possible.

Other themes frequently advanced to "prove" that East–West trade is advantageous principally to Communists typically fall under moral, political and economic groupings.

The first "moral" argument might be called the theory of the "inherent disadvantage of the moral man." The implication here is that immoral Communist negotiators are by nature somehow more adept at defining their political and commercial interests than are moral Americans, and so, for reasons never quite spelled out, moral parties to trade agreements concede more advantage than they receive. Accordingly, the United States is the loser even when it swaps a portion of its grain surplus for scarce Communist gold—gold which the Russians perforce sell us at $35 an ounce although it is estimated to cost them $65 to produce.

By this theory we lose even if, while sacrificing their scarce gold in the transaction, the Soviets worsen their balance of payments and proportionately benefit ours, or even when we use their gold to build atomic submarines or to finance U.S. economic and military assistance programs, or if the transaction also saves United States taxpayers millions of dollars annually in grain-storage fees. Indeed, it has been said on good authority that the gold sacrificed by the Soviets in the wheat deal is the main reason why in 1963 the U.S.S.R. rejected requests for hard-currency loans from Poland, Czechoslovakia and East Germany.

Of the two "moral" theories, the theory of the inherent stupidity of moral capitalists who sell to Communists is the least unflattering conclusion about the nature of Western businessmen. The second might be called "a plague on all merchants." It is reminiscent of the medieval image of the Demon Merchant and asserts that commerce is commerce and merchants are, *ipso facto*, immoral, regardless of their national allegiance. In the East–West trade dialogue this theory is advanced to explain how United States merchants unhesitatingly, knowingly and willingly place profit above country. To wit: "Dangle a fat dollar before the eyes of an American businessman and, it seems, he will behave like a hungry trout eyeing a fly."

That was written *not* by Lenin but by an irate anti-East–West-trade editorialist in a particularly conservative, well-intentioned United States publication. In fact, Lenin's economic determinism led him to a less harsh conclusion about American businessmen, for Lenin said we would sell the rope to hang ourselves, not wittingly, but only because we are the hapless victims of Marxian inevitability.

The "moral" denunciations of East–West trade are often fortified by three "political" theories: the "Soviet monolith" theory, the "dying gasp" theory, and the "dupes and dopes" theory.

Those who persist in believing that a Soviet monolith still exists in which all East European bloc nations are in effect wholly-owned subsidiaries of the U.S.S.R. deduce that trade with one Communist nation naturally invigorates all Communist nations. Advocates of the monolith theory would be hard-pressed to explain last year's Rumanian-U.S. trade agreement which provoked the ill-concealed anger of the Russians. This new pact was but the latest of a long series of setbacks to the Soviet effort to dictate which satellite may produce what goods and who may sell what to whom.

Nor, apparently, are adherents of the Soviet monolith theory given pause by Poland's agricultural decollectivization, which has been carried out contrary to Soviet will. Nor do they seem fazed by the fact that United States business firms have information offices in Warsaw against the Kremlin's wishes; that Alfred Krupp does business in Warsaw to the displeasure of Moscow; or that many of the "satellites" have supported United Nations peace-keeping forces in blatant opposition to Moscow's efforts to unite the bloc against these policies. Neither do they explain why, in the period during which Yugoslavia's trade with the West became greater than her trade with the East, Yugoslavia also became the most advanced Eastern European country in the adoption of capitalistic techniques. Yugoslavia is now bidding for association with the European Common Market and has already obtained observer status in the non-Communist Organization for Economic Cooperation and Development (O.E.C.D.). Recently, "satellite" Poland has asked for admission to GATT, which is the non-Communist world's principal tariff negotiating body.

The second common "political" argument used to oppose East–West trade might be called the "dying-gasp" or "we've got them where we want them" theory. In its East–West trade version, a Communist trade feeler is seen as a cry of economic desperation; it is a plea for help and a possible sign of imminent collapse; it is a death rattle in the Soviet system.

Since it is free man's inalienable right to choose his own statistics, one can only guess at how the dying-gaspers deal with the fact—if indeed they do—that the deathbed is occupied by the world's largest employer with the world's second largest gross national product, an economy which last year broke its own records in the value of both exports and imports.

I suggest that the dying-gaspers are victims of a miscalculation which is as dangerous as it is benighted. At this late date they still subscribe to the wishful *non sequitur* that if Socialist dictatorships are wasteful, inefficient and despotic, they must also be economically unviable.

A third "political" theme conjures up the old "devil theory" of politics, resurrecting the familiar shibboleth about the "dupes and dopes in the State Department." In effect, one is told that "if only U.S. Government bureaucrats had the skill, the will or the guts to apply the heat to our allies, our sister trading nations would then sell to the Communists only those goods of which we approved." Regrettably, it is true and will probably continue to be true that U.S. diplomats have seldom been able to dictate U.S. trade policy to foreign parliaments or prime ministers.

And, finally, two "economic" theories recur. First is the "Communists-don't-pay-their-debts" theme. The second might be called the "caviar-and-furs" theory. Each begins with truths and ends in confusion.

The notion that "Communists don't pay their debts" starts with undisputed historical truths: The Soviets continue to renounce their World War I Czarist war debts, and they continue to default on their World War II lend-lease loans. These facts are infuriating, but they do not tell the whole story.

U.S. and British banking officials and businessmen alike have been quick to remind us that, in 40 years, the Soviets have not defaulted on a single commercial debt. Western bankers say that nowhere in Latin America or Asia is there a superior record of business debt repayment. Canadian insurance premiums covering credits on Soviet commercial transactions fall in Canada's lowest risk rate category.

But, we are warned, "do not be deceived. Soviet reliability in commercial transactions is but a cunning ruse. Communists would unhesitatingly default in commercial transactions if it wouldn't jeopardize their future credit." How true this is.

However, to call commercial reliability a "cunning ruse" is to call a rose by a dirty name. Loss or jeopardy of credit is always the penalty of default, whether the defaulting party is Communist, capitalist, Fascist, or nudist. The commercial debt repayment record of Communist countries is especially interesting because it underlines their recognition that they, too, are bound by the inescapable discipline of credit jeopardy.

The "caviar-and-furs" theory says that we don't need Communist trade—but that the Communists must have ours. They can offer only unessential frills or superfluous raw materials in exchange for invaluable U.S. hardware and technical know-how. Accordingly, the amount and kinds of potential trade are not worth talking about in the first place.

As with the other theories, the "caviar-and-furs" theory also starts with some valid observations. Obviously, for example, the U.S. not only survives but grows economically without engaging in significant Communist trade. Indeed, this is just as apparent as history's equally clear lesson that Communist countries have survived and grown economically without significant trade with us.

But it does not follow that "caviar and furs" are or shall be the main types of commodities in question. The likelihood is quite the opposite. Communist countries are developing a widening array of articles for export, largely to acquire increased foreign exchange to finance economic growth.

Almost a decade ago, Premier Khrushchev proposed to President Eisenhower a U.S.–U.S.S.R. trade agreement (i.e., a two-country—or bilateral—agreement) in which the U.S.S.R. offered such varied commodities as manganese, chromium, cellulose and paper products, ferrous alloys, platinum, asbestos, potassium salts, modern machinery and equipment, in exchange for U.S. air conditioners, automatic vending machines, city gas pipeline, television sets, medicines and consumer goods.

Following a discouraging response from the U.S., the British took the same list and concluded a Soviet–United Kingdom bilateral trade agreement on terms approximately the same as those rejected by the United States. As has become increasingly the case, our allies made the sale while we gratified ourselves by proclaiming the superior virtue of our position. The Soviets? They were deprived of virtually nothing.

Those who protest the increasing futility of this U.S. trade posture are sometimes reminded that approximately 70 per cent of Soviet foreign trade occurs within the Communist bloc and is therefore not even relevant to the East–West trade discussion. They are told that only 3.5 per cent of world trade flows between Communist and non-Communist countries. But what intrinsic mileage there is in that 3.5 per cent! Though East–West trade at present amounts to a mere $10 billion, few would doubt that greater U.S. participation could have a favorable effect upon our employment and balance-of-payments problems while adding nothing to goods the Communists cannot obtain elsewhere.

Nonetheless, the discussion continues to be dogged by the bizarre notion that trade necessarily rewards enemies more than ourselves. As to "who wins" in commerce, the noted international lawyer Russell Baker recently noted: "Each party to a trade transaction believes that he has gotten the better of the exchange (or he wouldn't have entered into it). And it is in the very nature of trade that in most, if not every, case each is undoubtedly right." Properly put, therefore, the foreign policy question is obviously *not* whether the Communists gain in a transaction, but whether our gain is relatively greater than theirs.

On the rather rare occasions when politicians have contemplated the potential foreign policy advantages in such trade, realism has not always prevailed. A pet proposition, for instance, has been that we should become more involved in trade with Communist countries only after the Russians agree to retreat from key political positions. "We have a historic opportunity," a distinguished U.S. Senator has stated, "in which we would offer grain, equipment and even credits in exchange for such political concessions as removing the Berlin Wall and reunifying Germany on Western terms." However, as the author of the containment policy, George F. Kennan, has noted, it just will not happen that way. To demand major political pullbacks in exchange for normal commercial transactions, Dr. Kennan has observed, "is, after all, only another way of renouncing trade altogether."

The Soviets are not likely to demolish the Berlin Wall or give up East Germany in exchange for conventional commerce, particularly when their domestic economic development is increasing and their external sources of supply are multiplying. Indeed, it could bode ill for us if such a U.S. "strategy" were successful. If Communists were to discover that the U.S. awards commercial concessions in return for political pullbacks, we would in effect be inviting the Soviets to erect new "walls" to obtain U.S. commercial concessions.

Though the walls are not likely to come tumbling down, it is not unrealistic to envisage a calculated U.S. strategy whereby selective trade expansion could achieve specific types of concessions, the aim being to bring Communist countries into a stable international economic order in whose survival they will have a stake.

In future bilateral trade agreements with individual Communist countries, the U.S. can and must insist on arbitration of commercial disputes by third parties, agreed on in advance. Agreements must include airtight safeguards against "dumping" (selling below U.S. market prices to the detriment of U.S. or third-country suppliers), prior acceptance of international covenants on patent and copyright protection, and protection of U.S. property commensurate with rights accorded foreign property in the U.S.

Moreover, U.S. bilateral trade agreements with Eastern countries should include undertakings that U.S. businessmen be accorded carefully defined rights of commercial representation in each treaty country, including authorization for U.S. trade offices and for visits by U.S. trade and cultural missions. To take further advantage of the rapidly growing differences among Communist countries, the President should be authorized to negotiate with selected Communist countries granting tariff concessions comparable to those we grant non-Communist countries ("most-favored-nation" treatment).

In its selective, strategic expansion of trade with the East, the U.S. must remain especially firm in denying long-term credits to Communist countries. Conventional commercial credits are necessary to the normal conduct of commerce. But long-term tie-ups of Western credit money in Communist countries simply permit Communist economies to allocate their limited foreign exchange and gold reserves to their internal economies. As has been correctly stated by Under Secretary of State Ball, a long-term commercial credit policy would be tantamount to granting foreign aid for Communist economic development.

It should surprise no one that businessmen among our allies do not grieve over the virtual U.S. withdrawal from Soviet and East-bloc trade. Many European and Japanese businessmen will admit privately that our active withdrawal from trade with Communist countries is a highly profitable commercial blessing for them. Competitors do not like competition, and we are not likely to shed our self-imposed strait jacket until the U.S. public, and our political representatives, elevate their sights and realistically face these salient facts and figures of trade. When former Secretary of Commerce Hodges spoke of our country's "shameful economic illiteracy," he referred in part to the recent lamentable state of our national conversation on East–West trade.

If one is to judge by the prose one encounters on this subject, we have far to go. For example, leaflets appear which encourage the public not to buy so-and-so beer because it "contains Communist ingredients," and unreconstructed rustics write posters urging that so-and-so department store be boycotted because it sells "Communist merchandise." The authors of this political cant, though undoubtedly loyal and well-meaning, obviously do not have the foggiest notion of the national security question which is *really* involved—namely, what foreign policy concessions has the U.S. received in return for granting a bloc country the right to sell hops to a U.S. brewery or TV stools to a U.S. department store? Such leaflets and posters would strike patriotic Britons, Frenchmen, Germans or Japanese as quaint, to say the least.

With 40 per cent of English jobs, for example, dependent on British acceptance of foreign goods, economically literate Englishmen correctly write off such boycott proposals as a recipe for self-destruction. In the case of Eastern trade, were the United Kingdom to take such extravagances seriously, a source of economic strength would be impaired along with useful leverage to deter disruptive Communist trade practices by linking Communist commercial interests to their own. As a London paper observed not long ago, if Britain traded only with those countries of whose Governments it approved, it would suffer economic collapse in 30 days, and would have done so 300 years ago.

So let us at last challenge neopatriotic rhetoric which labels our retreat from East–West trade a "weapon." Such retreat increasingly impairs our national interest, denies us valuable leverage against Communism and has increasingly become a weapon against ourselves. An aggressive trade policy, embodying intelligent safeguards and pursuing well-defined goals, is probably the one peaceful tactic whereby Communist countries can be maneuvered into adopting civilized international trade practices.

Speaking of our maneuverability, and theirs, I recall the surprise of an audience last year when I responded to an inquiry about whether any trade with the Communists wasn't like going to bed with the devil. I replied that even Will Rogers might have brought his pitchforks to Lucifer's bedchamber if Will had seen a reasonable chance that the pitchforks could be used to limit or even cut off one or more of Lucifer's vital options.

22

Something There Is That Doesn't Love a Trade Wall

ALEC NOVE

This article is a greatly abbreviated and revised version of a research paper prepared within the Program of Research on the International Economics of Disarmament and Arms Control (RIEDAC), under the direction of Professor Emile Benoit of the Columbia Graduate School of Business. The paper in its original form was presented at an international conference in Oslo (August 29–September 1, 1965) held under the auspices of RIEDAC and the Peace Research Institute (Oslo). The right to republish is retained by the author and by RIEDAC.

To start off: a broadly valid generalization—all Soviet bloc countries buy from the west to the limit of their export earnings, plus any available gold. To be sure, the Soviet Union prefers buying from other bloc countries, relying on the capitalist nations only for items that can't be supplied by the communist world. The trouble is so much is unobtainable that, willy nilly, the Russians are keen advocates of expanded east-west commerce.

Their smaller allies are even more unrestrained in their desire to throw open a westward door. For one thing they have higher standards than the Russians and are therefore less willing to be satisfied with second-rate goods. For another they perceive that deals with noncommunist countries provide the means for greater economic and even political independence. A communist official has said: "It is fortunate for Rumania that the new pipeline enables us to be supplied with Soviet oil, because now the Rumanians can sell their own oil in the west and have much more western currency." Rumanian political independence of Russia may well

From *Columbia Journal of World Business*, Winter, 1966, pp. 15–26. Reprinted by permission.

be closely connected with her ability to trade outside the Soviet bloc.

Thus the desire to trade is there. However, the means to trade are often lacking. The balance of payments of all eastern countries is in a state of chronic strain. The list of goods which they wish to buy is always much longer than the means of paying for them. Their secrecy concerning balance of payments statistics, and gold too, is beyond doubt designed to conceal weakness.

It therefore follows that the most important limiting factor in east-west trade is the difficulty of expanding eastern earnings of western currency. The sale of communist goods to western countries is impeded by two principal circumstances: the restrictions imposed by western countries, and failure to make and sell the right goods. Both are important and require some further detailed consideration.

There are a great many restrictions against communist goods applied by nearly all western countries. In some cases the import of a commodity is free from all except communist sources, whereas the communist product is simply banned. More common is the practice of assigning the communist countries a limited quota for a product, while the same import from noncommunist nations is not subject to quantitative restrictions. This quota prevents exports from the east from rising above a given limit, but sometimes impedes trade within these limits too, because it is often not worthwhile to market and service the relatively small quantities of goods (for instance, machinery) permitted by the quota.

Discriminatory quotas stimulate a great deal of bilateral bargaining. Thus France or Britain undertakes to admit a limited quantity of Soviet watches or canned fish, on condition that the USSR allow the entry of British herrings or French hats. A long list of examples of such bargaining about quotas can be collected.

There is also a tendency to insist on bilateral balancing of trade; i.e., confining trade wholly or partly to goods and quantities listed in trade agreements, so arranged that the values in the two directions are more or less equal over the year, or the period of validity of the agreement. For example, Hungary and Czechoslovakia are more or less compelled to spend the whole of their earnings of French francs or German marks on the purchase of goods from

France and West Germany respectively. They are unable to earn convertible currency, and thus while they might prefer to buy a machine from A rather than B, the bilateral agreement in effect ties them to B. This practice, they point out, is inconsistent with our advocacy of freer trade. Nor is the situation improved by the fact that we sometimes read them lectures on the advantages of multilateralism.

Western strategic controls also affect east-west trade, though not so much as was the case when a longer and stricter list was in operation. Obviously, items known to be on the list must be produced in eastern countries, and this affects their investment policies in the direction of greater self-sufficiency. Outside of strictly military items, one wonders if this is in the interests of the west in the long run. Particular harm to east-west trade is caused by uncertainty over changes in the list and by divergent application of the rules by different countries. Thus chemical machinery exported by Britain or by West Germany may contain items covered by U.S. patents, whereupon the United States applies its more restrictive definition and seeks to impede the sale, for reasons which are not too clear to me.

Steel-Pipe Story

The case of the ban on exports of steel pipe is an even worse one. Steel pipe was not on the list, but was banned *ad hoc* because it was an immediate way of causing economic embarrassment. Fear of repetition of such tactics must affect the willingness of eastern planners to rely on western suppliers for important items. It may be that the cancellation of the undertaking to supply steel pipe contributed to the failure to fulfil the plan for gas in 1964, and so led to a fuel shortage. It is a matter of opinion whether this is a desirable objective of western trade policy. It is a matter not of opinion but of obvious certainty that such acts will not encourage east-west trade. The same clearly applies to the cancellation of an American contract to build a tire factory in Rumania, though in this instance it was "unofficial" anticommunism that was responsible.

There are, in addition to the above, the restrictions involved in the Common Market (EEC), which particularly affect those East European countries who traditionally sell much of their produce in the countries of the EEC. However, save in those instances in which the EEC follows a policy of imposing special restrictions on goods of communist origin, the victims of discrimination include *all* outsiders, i.e., Great Britain and the United States as well as Czechoslovakia and the USSR.

Why the West Discriminates

What is the rationale of western restrictions? The Committee for Economic Development report on east-west trade (published in May, 1965)[1] comments, on the whole favorably, on "the unwillingness of the west to extend its own system of freedom unilaterally to the east." The key word here is "unilaterally." The question is: how to define meaningful reciprocity? If a western country grants free access (subject only to the normal tariffs) to a communist country, in other words affords it most-favored-nation (MFN) treatment, what can a state-trading communist country offer in exchange? Tariffs are either nonexistent or unimportant. The Ministry of Foreign Trade could discriminate at any time by an interoffice memorandum urging that preference be given to imports from any particular country. Even if the policy is to buy in the cheapest market, even if the trade corporations are told to behave like "capitalist" traders, there is no means of checking that this is really done. There is no satisfactory way of having any real "access" to the eastern market. No one knows why particular decisions are taken, a by-product of the fact that there are few definable criteria for decision-making in communist economies. The eastern economies recognize this problem, and efforts are being made to alter the situation, as we shall recount below. However, at the present time suspicion of discrimination, as well as the undefinability of reciprocity, stand in the way of granting MFN.

Another restraining influence on western trading policies is fear of "dumping" and "market disruption." Some believe that the USSR and its allies go in for dumping with the avowed object

[1] Committee for Economic Development, *East–West Trade; A Common Policy for the West*, New York, 1965.

of disorganizing the market. Yet all known cases of communist dumping are explicable by one or more of the following circumstances:

a. the necessity to undercut existing prices in order to get into and hold a new market—often in the face of built-in preferences for noncommunist suppliers. This tactic is not unknown to shrewd capitalist traders;

b. ignorance, due to lack of experience on the part of the communist traders, who are sometimes outmaneuvered by slick importers anxious to make a large profit; and

c. pressure to sell very quickly so as to meet extremely urgent bills at a time of severe shortage of foreign currency.

Dumping Is Not the Aim

Under normal circumstances (and on all occasions known to me) communist salesmen were told to maximize foreign currency earnings and sell as dear as possible, provided they did sell the available goods. Because of restrictions imposed in a number of western markets, the effort to make quick sales in the few remaining markets that were open did sometimes have a disorganizing effect, but there is no evidence that disorganization was in itself an objective. Faced with open markets and a surplus to dispose of, eastern traders would surely seek to distribute it so as to maximize foreign currency proceeds. Unless tied by import restrictions and by bilateral agreements, there is no reason why they should seek to "unload" the surplus in any one place.

Though not politically motivated, the occasional communist dumping that does take place is nonetheless damaging to the interests of domestic and foreign suppliers in the west. This damage is all the more unfortunate in its effects since the communist traders often are unable to supply these goods over the longer term, this being the consequence of having to sell such surpluses as may happen to be available, under conditions of variable supply and inflexible domestic prices. (This kind of variation also occurs in agricultural surpluses in many western countries, since prices in this sector are artificial, and this has led many of these countries to impose quantitative restrictions on each other.)

While the policies of the communist salesmen *could* lead to market disruption on occasion, I would add at once that the danger is often exaggerated, because of the limited export potential of the eastern bloc. However, since the danger does exist, it is entirely proper for western countries to maintain reserve powers, which in many instances already exist with respect to imports from any source—namely, the power to impose antidumping duties or quotas.

The Dependency Argument

Finally on the list of justifications for discrimination, there is fear of undue or excessive dependence on communist supplies. This is a point not to be ignored, and indeed operates on both sides. Thus no Soviet planner could fail to have been impressed by the effects on the Soviet pipeline program of the ban on sales of large-diameter pipe which we have already mentioned, and so will avoid such excessive dependence in the future. This whole thought pattern is a quite inevitable by-product of mutual suspicion. One must not be too vulnerable to economic warfare by the other side. This could affect not only import needs, but also export outlets. Thus it is conceivable that either side might make access to its market conditional upon political concessions. Communist China is using such tactics on Japan.

All this is, no doubt, true, but what constitutes "excessive" dependence? Is Italy, who buys a very considerable fraction of its oil from the USSR, or is Britain, who does the same for timber, in this position? One would have thought that if the Soviets attempted to use oil and timber as a means of influencing Italian or British policies, the political and economic harm done to the Soviets themselves would be disproportionate, and in such conditions, alternative supplies would speedily appear. No doubt this constitutes one reason why the Soviet Union does not follow such policies. In any case, the value of the total trade of western countries is far higher than the east's trade, and so the relative importance of east-west trade in the trade of communist countries is much the greater. Therefore, the communists stand to lose far more from a disruption of trade relations than does the west and are not likely to initiate trade warfare.

Eastern countries tend to ask, understandably enough, for elimination of western restrictions. They ask for an end to discrimination, and they claim that, since they buy to the limit of their
resources, the application to them of the principle of MFN is
entirely fair and proper. If pressed, they will admit that their
traders might so disrupt the markets of established suppliers that
reserve powers will be needed to impose antidumping restrictions.
They claim that given due warning that these restrictions are being
contemplated, appropriate action would be taken. They de-
plore various western trade blocs, from which they suffer in common with other outsiders. They suspect also that the effect of the
Common Market will ultimately be to reduce still further the
markets open to them. Thus agricultural deficit countries will tend
to give priority to the imports of surpluses from France rather
than from Poland, and there might well be pressure on Italy to
buy its oil from western companies rather than from the Soviet
Union. Instances have also been known of discriminatory restrictions on eastern goods being imposed by such supranational
western institutions as the Coal and Steel Community.

An Open Market . . .

However, the communist countries are becoming aware that
elimination of western barriers is not enough. It is obvious that
sales to the west suffer from the inadequacies of their own trading
and production arrangements. In this connection one must mention that communist sales have remained poor in the one country,
Canada, which has virtually no restrictions of any kind on imports
from eastern countries—this despite the eastern bloc's very large
deficit with this country. In the case of the Soviet Union this is
partly to be explained by the noncomplementarity of the two
economies, since Canada itself exports many of the raw materials
typically sold by the Soviet Union. But this does not apply to the
other communist countries. The explanation may be neglect of
this difficult market, poor salesmanship, failure to make the right
goods, or all these things at once. Since Canada is so "Ameri-
canized" a market, its experience reinforces the belief that sales
in the United States would also be extremely difficult to make

even if there were no discriminatory restrictions. In general, it supports the view that availability of the right goods at the right price is at least as important as western restrictions in explaining the still modest level of eastern exports. But it also confirms the views of those who discount the need for restrictions. A wide-open hard currency market has *not* led to massive Soviet-bloc dumping or market disruption.

. . . But No Sales Savvy

The Soviet bloc countries organize their foreign trade along lines that obviously impede expanded east-west intercourse. Thus all trade is centered, in nearly all these countries, under the Ministry of Foreign Trade, and is undertaken by specialized trade corporations. This interposes a barrier between the customers abroad and the producers at home. The latter have few if any possibilities to study the foreign market and to make direct contacts with potential customers. Trade corporation executives and commercial representatives abroad often have insufficient technical knowledge and little commercial sense. Of course this is not always so. In some traditional lines, such as Soviet timber or furs, there is much expertise and intimate knowledge of the market. But there are many instances of inefficiency, and such trading countries as Czechoslovakia have suffered from the fact that their experienced traders have been regarded as too politically unreliable to be allowed abroad to trade.

In addition, one need only mention the oft-cited fact that in many eastern countries productive enterprises have no material interest in making any effort to produce for foreign markets, and little or no incentive to improve quality (although this is changing). By contrast there is every incentive to fulfill output plans in quantitative terms. Therefore it is easier to make goods for the less demanding domestic or other communist markets.

The difficulty of making international price and cost comparisons is a further problem. Suppose that it costs 1,000 crowns to produce a given item in Czechoslovakia which could be bought from the USSR for 125 roubles or from West Germany for 750 marks. What should the Czech planners do—import or produce?

The problem seems soluble: one could devise an exchange rate, not necessarily the official one. Cost in domestic currency could then be compared with foreign exchange earnings from sales, less the import content of the exported items. This might help to determine the desirability of importing and the choice of a trading partner. However, there are several reasons why such calculations break down. One is that domestic prices and costs are not particularly meaningful. So far, these prices do not even pretend to reflect relative scarcities, opportunity costs and quality. Since the price of a material does not mirror the fact that it is in very short supply, the assessment of the costs of production of a product which uses this material will not correctly reflect real costs for practical purposes. Lacking reliable measures of real costs, it becomes impossible to determine whether it is wiser to produce or import a given item.

Then there is the complex question which arises because Comecon-country currencies are not convertible into western currencies. Shifting the location of our example, if at a cost of 100 zlotys the Poles could earn either 100 U.S. dollars or 90 roubles, this would represent an identical sum at the official rate of exchange, and indeed might well represent an equal purchasing power at actually existing prices, since this exchange rate was chosen because it is fairly realistic. However, with dollars the Poles could buy almost anything they wanted, anywhere; whereas the roubles would buy only the goods which the Soviet Union was able and willing to supply. In a similar situation in the early postwar years, the British planners used different criteria for earning so-called "soft currencies" and "hard currencies," but since they never devised a workable quantitative measurement of degrees of softness or hardness, it was all very rough and ready.

Finally communist agricultural deficiencies reduce exportable surpluses of farm produce. Failure to invest adequately in agriculture is one example of neglecting export potential in favor of domestic (industrial) development In fact imports of food and fodder, rendered necessary by agricultural shortcomings, are a drain on the balance of payments of several eastern countries.

All of this indicates that deficiencies in the trading arrangements of communist countries are a major factor in limiting east-west trade. However, in a number of eastern nations, experiments are being conducted which could vastly improve these countries' ability to sell in western markets.

Russian Focus Is Domestic

In the case of the smaller communist countries these reforms are directly related to the need for expanded foreign trade. In the Soviet Union, however, the motive of reformers is predominantly to achieve greater efficiency in internal planning. This is hardly surprising, since exports make up only about 3% of the Soviet Union's national income. The need for change has arisen because the old system of administrative instructions and allocation of inputs, with inflexible and economically meaningless prices, has become increasingly unable to cope with the needs of a large and modern industry. Reforms have at least two objectives. First, the planners must be able to choose rightly, in the sense of using resources (especially investment resources) with maximum effect and minimum waste. Secondly, planners must be freed from the futile and time-consuming effort of issuing commands on detailed matters of output, inputs, deliveries, wages, finance, etc. For both these purposes, it is essential to devise appropriate criteria in monetary terms, and on this basis to let subordinate bodies choose much more freely.

Though the focus of Soviet reforms is domestic, the gains in foreign trade planning would be useful by-products. If the measurement of the cost of alternative courses of action helps Moscow to compare the advantage of producing something in Minsk against producing it in Omsk, logically it could facilitate a similar comparison with Prague or even Düsseldorf. If, in order to encourage production and discourage consumption of some scarce material, its domestic price were raised so that it reflected its scarcity, calculations of relative advantage of imports and exports would be facilitated. And, finally, if in order to operate the reformed system, enterprises (or trusts, or combines) are given greater freedom to place orders for their requirements within the USSR, it might bring nearer the day when they can also place orders in another country, subject perhaps to a permit or license, or to import duties. This would be a decisive breach in the present narrow interpretation of the state monopoly of foreign trade. It would place the western importer and exporter in a very different situation and give him new opportunities. It must be emphasized that in the case of the USSR this may not happen for some years after the adoption of reforms because of the strength of the tradition that the Ministry of Foreign Trade and its organs should conduct trade, and also because of shortages of foreign currency and their effects on the minds of the planners. Like British officials in the first years after the war, these planners think in terms of priorities, and will probably regard it as natural that they should be in a position to give preference to "essential" imports by issuing appropriate orders.

Conforming to Capitalist Prices

As noted, in the smaller countries gains in foreign trade are no by-product but the chief object of reform. Thus in Czechoslovakia, Poland and Hungary, there is much talk not only of allowing more enterprises direct access to foreign markets, but also of aligning at least some prices to "world" (i.e., capitalist, or American) prices. The argument is put in the following terms. In the case of goods which are either imported or exported in appreciable quantities, the opportunity cost of the use of the domestic product must be seen as the export earnings foregone, or the import expenditure incurred. Therefore the domestic price should be aligned to the external price. It is interesting to note that such considerations militate against the emergence—often talked about—of a specifically "socialist" market price for use of Comecon countries. To avoid complications, it would be more logical to make Comecon prices conform rather more closely to "capitalist" market prices and to bring domestic prices into line with them. Obviously, this would greatly alter the conditions under which production and trade would be planned, to the considerable advantage (so one would think) of all concerned. However, the logic of such prices must eventually extend to the economy as a whole. For virtually everything is, at least potentially, either exportable or import-saving. This is particularly evident in making choices between alternative investments. Even in the Soviet Union this point has been the subject of published discussion, though not until recently.[2]

An Overview of Reforms

But this is running ahead of decisions actually taken. What has happened so far is important and indicates the shape of things to come, but has not yet had much influence on foreign trade. The reforms thus far are in a number of instances merely experimental, and they differ widely from country to country. This is not the place for a detailed analysis. However, in view of the possible effects on foreign trade, some remarks are called for.

In the Soviet Union, much has been heard of the profit motive as the criterion of managerial decision-making. There have been other proposals too, and the authorities have based their recent experiments on a compromise between a number of different approaches to the problem. Thus the profit motive is by no means the sole criterion, since increased output (sales) must also be achieved. The reforms announced by Kosygin in September, 1965, are not clear about the extent to which the composition of output is still to be regulated by the planners, and how much freedom there will be to purchase inputs. Nor is there yet freedom to alter or fix prices, though there is somewhat greater flexibility, at least with respect to new products or designs. Reforms will probably be introduced gradually and cautiously.

Nonetheless, it does seem that enterprises will be left freer to make their own plans, based on what they think they can sell. They will have a wider range of choice in placing orders for the materials, components, and goods that they want, instead of having to apply for allocations to planning offices. Plans for labor, costs, and profits all become the responsibility of the management. This, if extended further, would represent a major departure from past practices. Great stress would now have to be placed on contracts, on sales and therefore also on salesmanship, a notoriously weak spot in a country where it has been all too easy, for a generation, to sell anything. Obviously, greater attention will have to

[2] The best picture of the problem as seen in Moscow is by G. Shagalov, *Voprosy ekonomiki*, No. 6, 1965.

be paid to the requirements of the user, and therefore to quality. This is, of course, an important part of the motivation of the reform. Production for global output statistics, instead of for the customer, has been (and still is) a major cause of waste and inefficiency.

The reluctance to go all out in this direction is based on a fear that the center would lose command over the macroeconomic magnitudes, resulting in intolerable overstrain, shortages, and even chaos. These fears are far from being groundless. Thus it is hard to see how the center can retain control over major investment decisions without being able to guide the production program of enterprises which make investment goods (e.g., building materials, machinery and the like). Yet many such enterprises (and many such materials and machines) can be used to make consumers' goods, in other words are inputs for those sectors of the economy which would no longer be subject to stringent central control.

Therefore we may find, for several years at least, that in the USSR the "liberalization" is confined to consumers' goods and to materials used to make them (cloth, leather, etc.). Production of, and foreign trade in, most capital goods (for import or export) is likely to remain chiefly centralized. Certain traditional Soviet exports—timber, furs, grain—will also remain under existing arrangements, since these are probably rational and have their counterpart in "capitalist" countries.

In this respect as in many others, reforms will not follow any single pattern. The Soviet type of economy has suffered for too long from a bureaucratic standardization of organizational forms. What is needed is diversity. The west, after all, has all kinds of production and trading organs. Some are nationalized, some are giant corporations, and some are quite small and independent. The units comprising the big corporations have a variable degree of autonomy in making decisions, including decisions involving foreign trade. Sometimes it is considered convenient to negotiate trade deals directly; sometimes it is more sensible to use specialized agencies. Gradually, this need for variety is being understood in eastern countries. Thus some Soviet enterprises are being unified for commercial and planning purposes into a species of trust, now called *firma*, or "firm." These *firmy* are a Soviet reaction to the fact that, for commercial purposes, many Soviet enterprises are too small (and too ill-informed as to needs) to be given autonomy. In some instances the *firma* (or trust) may cover a whole industry. For example, four Soviet phonograph record enterprises are now part of the single *firma*, called *Melodiya*.

This trend toward large trusts is also to be observed in Czecho-slovakia and Poland. In both countries there has been a great deal of discussion about the granting of much wider commercial and planning freedom to productive units, but it is Czechoslovakia that is now (1965) taking a major step in this direction. As in the Soviet Union, production is to be more closely geared to demand by basing the plans on negotiated contracts. Incentives to manage-ment and labor are to be directly related to profits. Indeed, as in Yugoslavia since 1959, the Czech system intends to base the level of wages and of managerial salaries on the total "net revenue" of the production unit, this being defined as total revenue from sales less purchases of materials and fuel, plus depreciation. There is already strong pressure to allow the trusts, into which enterprises are being merged, greater freedom to make deals with foreign countries. They are likely to be allowed greater scope to study foreign markets, to make contacts (if not contracts) with cus-tomers and suppliers abroad, and, last but not least, they will be rewarded for success in exporting.

It is feared by some that the new trusts will be economic min-istries in all but name, and so the essence of the traditional system will remain. However, the intention seems to be genuinely to avoid such a result. The trusts are expected to act commercially and not try to fulfil global output plans laid down by the govern-ment and the central planning offices. If it tells its constituent enterprises to produce for the customer, the trust need be no more "ministerial" than is the head office of a western corporation, which similarly distributes tasks to its factories. The western ex-porter and importer may therefore find himself dealing with a much more responsive trading partner than were the foreign trade corporations, dealing with men with greater technical knowledge, who are closer to production and more interested in the economic consequences to the given sector of the economy of foreign trade decisions. But there would be little or no competition between exporters, insofar as the trust would usually (and in smaller coun-tries perhaps always) cover all the given country's output of the commodity in question. There is less likelihood of this kind of monopoly situation in the case of imports, since many items (for instance, trucks, typewriters, machine tools, metal) can be used in many different parts of the industrial structure.

New Forms of Regulation Needed

Autonomy in buying and selling across frontiers, as and when it comes, must be accompanied by new methods of central regulation of foreign trade. As already mentioned, some system of differential import duties and licensing and a more realistic exchange rate will have to replace the present highly centralized system of operating the foreign trade monopoly.

It is worth mentioning that in Hungary the reform trend is taking a rather different road. Oddly enough—since Hungary has gone far toward liberalization in many respects—the Hungarian reforms have been the least radical, at least on the surface. Economic ministries have been preserved, and some of these continue to control "their" enterprises as tightly as ever. Nonetheless, there is now much greater stress on economic rationality, on commercial advantage and on the customer. A few large enterprises, with a significant role in foreign trade, have for many years been allowed to make direct deals with foreign countries.

In some ministries in Hungary, enterprises are given a greater degree of autonomy. One way of doing this may perhaps be adopted in other communist-ruled countries and may have an effect on foreign trade. This consists of giving an enterprise a plan closely defining part of its activities, and leaving it free to sell and buy with respect to the rest.

It is, in my view, wrong to regard these trends as an evolution toward market capitalism. Profits may become much more important, in the sense of being treated as indicators of efficiency, as criteria for microdecision-making, as the basis on which bonuses are computed, but they still belong for the most part to the state, and the enterprises and trusts will not become in any sense the private property of the management. However, the move toward a more rational price structure and a study of comparative costs will facilitate both the planning of trade (and investments) within the Comecon and the calculations involved in east-west trade. The institutional changes which may accompany the reforms could well have the effect of reducing the objections, voiced by many in the west, to a more liberal and multilateral approach to trade with communist countries.

It appears that the west can contribute to the expansion of east-west trade by adopting more liberal policies, and the east by so altering its system as to facilitate the adjustment of output to consumer demand, abroad and at home. Thus, in conjunction with investments geared to expand output of items which have a promising export potential, better marketing could lead to a major increase in sales. Since the communist countries' imports are only limited by their earnings of western currency (plus gold production, if any) any increase in their sales is bound to lead to a proportionate rise in their purchases. There are many urgent requirements on which they would like to spend the currency they would earn.

What the West Can Do

What specific steps should the west take? In the case of the United States, the immediate measures would seem to be obvious, since her discrimination against imports from most communist countries hits them hard, and the American "strategic" list covers far more purely civilian items than does the list used by her allies. Obviously, if the goal of expanded trade were accepted, the United States would try to eliminate these barriers, which were erected at a time when east-west trade was regarded with distaste.

But the United States is not in itself a promising market for communist goods, even if there were no discriminatory restrictions at all. In the natural course of trade, one would expect the USSR and most of its allies to run a deficit with the U.S., and to cover it with surpluses earned elsewhere. Strict bilateralism, therefore, is not in America's economic interest, nor in the interest of trade expansion generally.

It would obviously be of help if western countries agreed to a *joint* abrogation of discriminatory measures and to abandon any bilateralism, while retaining necessary powers against market disruption. Discriminatory bargaining over quotas is justified because the others do it. It is a form of competition between *western* countries for privileged access to eastern markets. If the French or the Italians were not insisting on a quota for their hats, or cars, or footwear, there would be no reason for the British or the West Germans to do so, and vice versa. This would, of course, require agreement among the major western trading nations, perhaps within the Organization for Economic Cooperation and Development.

What would be the objections to, or the risks involved in, such a step? There is no doubt that it would facilitate "commercial" behavior by the eastern bloc's foreign trade corporations, and also by any enterprises or trusts allowed to buy and sell across frontiers. They would try to buy cheap and sell dear. True, the old bilateral habits may persist, but it is surely for the west to discourage them, not to insist on their retention. Yet there is opposition to such measures.

There is, first, the usual objection to MFN: that the communists will discriminate secretly, or in some other way not grant reciprocity. Yet, if as seems reasonable, we can expect them to spend the western currency they earn, obviously their exports will result in more imports. They would import, in the main, from a western country, or on occasion from a developing country which, like Malaya or Argentina, derives most of its imports from western countries.

Even if the communist country that earns a surplus in francs or sterling expends it in purchases from one of its own allies, this would present no particular problem, since, through procedures already in theory available within the Comecon Bank, the other country would use this western currency to finance its own purchases. True, western currency is at present so scarce that eastern countries are very loath to transfer any to one another. This has led some western analysts to deny the possibility of multilateralism in east-west trade. I must confess myself unable to see the point. Surely the eastern countries could be placed in a position of treating all their resources of western currencies as freely interchangeable. They could then use a surplus in francs to cover deficits in marks, or sterling surpluses to pay Italy, Swedish crowns to pay Britain, and so on.

It is true, of course, that the Czech crown, the Polish zloty, and the Russian rouble are not convertible. That is to say, it is not at present possible for a western country to convert a surplus in one eastern currency. But for multilateral trade to occur it is not necessary that eastern currencies be made convertible. Accounts between eastern and western traders are not settled in eastern currencies. To finance east-west trade, to pay for their imports, the communist countries use western currency. In other words, the multilateral arrangements I have in mind do *not* mean that any country runs up a surplus of inconvertible zlotys or roubles, but that Poland and the USSR can pay in any western currency. And while the net effect of this scheme on any given western country's exports *may* be less favorable than under the system of bilateral balancing, there is no inherent reason why any country should expect this to happen, unless it is pessimistic about the competitiveness of its exports.

To work, such a system might well need an intergovernmental committee to keep an eye on how things are going, to warn the Soviet side if the rules of the game are not being observed, and especially to keep a joint eye on possible market disruption. So far, the more go-ahead countries in east-west trade have regarded suggested western organizations for the conduct of such trade with understandable suspicion. It was thought that they would increase rather than decrease restrictions. However, a joint effort to *increase* trade would be quite another matter.

One common argument for bargaining about quotas is the need to persuade the planners of communist countries to buy what they regard as "nonessentials," i.e., consumers' goods. I am not sure that it is particularly important for us to tell the partners to trade negotiations what they *must* buy. However, if such an attempt is desirable—and it may well be—it could be incorporated in the multilateral arrangements suggested above by introducing some kind of global quota, a sum which the country concerned is free to spend on these so-called nonessentials anywhere in the west (or perhaps even in such a country as India or Japan). Such an arrangement would probably require complex international (multilateral) negotiations, but the possibility exists.

The Question of Credit

What of credits? The eastern countries have been asking in many instances for long-term credits, and the Soviet Union in particular wishes to buy capital goods in this way. Presumably we are referring only to such credits that seem to be in the commercial interest of the country granting them, at the proper commercial rate of interest. No one, so far as I know, is proposing aid—though the United States has in fact granted some aid to Yugoslavia and Poland. No one is proposing artificially favorable terms. Therefore, credits must be considered as an integral part of mutually profitable trade. For example, a Hungarian economist argued for long-term credits to buy fodder to build up a Hungarian export trade in beef. The beef would relieve shortages in the west and would therefore be desirable. These *have* to be long-term credits, because it takes many years to build up beef cattle herds. What is wrong with this? Credits have the effect of relieving immediate shortages of foreign currency on the part of the recipient. If strain and shortage in communist-ruled countries are desirable objectives, then credits should not be granted, but neither should trade be expanded, since we may be sure that communist countries try to obtain by way of trade many items which relieve strain and shortage. The point is that if one accepts the idea of expanded trade one ought concomitantly to raise no barrier to the granting of credits.

But a very real question mark does arise. Suppose the west decides to relax restrictions on trade and on credits. Should it exact a price? By this is meant, of course, a political price. Implied in this formulation is the belief that communist countries derive more benefit from east-west trade than the west does. This view seems to be held, for example, by so balanced and serious a scholar as Gregory Grossman.[3] It would seem to follow that the sale of an item worth, in world markets, $1 million is worth more than that to the USSR, who should therefore be charged more, i.e., a million dollars *plus* political concessions. Certainly a "trade"

[3] U.S. Senate, Committee on Foreign Relations, "East-West Trade," Nov., 1964.

of this kind should not be excluded. Thus the USSR could be given to understand, privately, that some act of theirs would facilitate the conclusion of a highly desirable trading arrangement. There was, it is believed, such an informal agreement between East and West Germany, involving the release of political prisoners by the former. But this would seem an exceptional situation. We cannot, for instance, expect to "trade" MFN for a Soviet troop withdrawal or for a public criticism of Ho Chi Minh. And my own view is that trade is mutually advantageous. I see nothing in the trading methods and practices of the communist countries to suggest that they are capable of extracting more advantage from trade deals than do hard-headed "capitalist" businessmen. In fact statistical evidence, cited by Pryor and by Holzman in their researches, suggests the contrary.

Differentiating Within the Bloc

Should there be differentiation between the countries of the communist bloc—if indeed there is a bloc nowadays? To some extent the United States does differentiate, "rewarding" those who seem likely to take an independent line, while imposing stringent embargos on any trade with China and Cuba. The correctness or otherwise of such policies in the present political situation raises questions which it is unnecessary to pursue here. They concern issues of political-economic warfare. Thus, apart from the rather special cases of China and Cuba, the arguments for discriminating among communist countries are based on the hope or need to weaken the cohesion of the bloc. This may be a perfectly legitimate political objective, which can be effectively pursued by economic maneuvering, among other ways. However, the too-obvious use of economic weapons to drive wedges between the Soviet Union and its allies may backfire, impede the political détente and limit the possibilities of expanding trade.

It would be desirable, however, to devise such rules as will encourage the tendency toward reform and flexibility in communist countries. By this is meant nothing so crude as to make the lifting of trade restrictions conditional upon the adoption of this or that reform of the planning system. This would surely delay change. The point is rather to make the rules for east-west trade such that the trade corporations, trusts and enterprises can make calculations of relative advantage and can base their trading and investment decisions upon such calculations. This will facilitate trade and bring the trading procedures closer to what we in the west would regard as normal. A profit-maximizing "communist" exporter would, no doubt, be a state organization. But it could behave commercially, try to sell at an advantageous price and to buy in the cheapest market. For reasons already stated, this tendency may well be linked, for good internal reasons, with a major reform of the planning system and to greater attention to economic rationality generally. It is a criticism of the present western insistence on what amounts to bilateral barter that it helps to keep the traditional communist institutional structure in being. After all, how can a Czech trust be allowed to buy a given commodity on commercial principles if the foreign currency has been earmarked in laborious trade negotiations for the purchase of this item from, say, France? Obviously, this tends to strengthen the practical arguments for the retention of the Ministry of Foreign Trade and its specialized corporations as the sole authority allowed to deal with foreign countries.

There are a number of other outstanding items on which tough negotiations may be desirable: patent protection and arbitration procedures are two of them. Neither is an insuperable obstacle. Indeed, I have heard of a number of businessmen who like arbitration awards to be decided in a communist capital, because, in their anxiety not to be considered prejudiced, the arbitrators bend over backward to be fair. There are exceptions to this, no doubt, but the problem is not a difficult one.

Patents are a matter of careful inquiry. It must not be assumed that the record of communist countries is so very bad. They are not the only ones to have copied other countries, and they have paid considerable sums for know-how. Their own hope of securing payments for their own discoveries has led the Russians to offer to sign international agreements in this field. More difficult are copyright and royalties on books. Here most communist countries prefer to save scarce currency by disregarding their duty to pay. This is deplorable, and they should be urged to mend their ways. Certainly pressure to achieve this result would form a useful part of east-west trade negotiations. However, the conclusion of such an agreement would not be an unmixed blessing, as it could give the Soviet authorities the right of veto on the kind of Russian books which should be translated in the west. This, clearly, ought to be avoided.

It is not for a moment suggested that the task of facilitating exchanges between different economic systems is an easy one. All kinds of tough obstacles exist in both east and west. The above ideas represent a few possible approaches which could lead to progress. And there are very few areas in which progress is as desired as in this. It would, of course, be absurd to expect that trade would or could by itself eliminate international tensions. Nonetheless, the growth of commercial interdependence and mutual confidence can contribute to the lowering of political barriers, and so help create an atmosphere conducive to a durable political détente.

PART V

The Third World: The Issues

To the south of the Industrial World and the Communist World lies the "Third World": Africa, Asia, and Latin America. Included in the Third World are dozens of nations of every description—large and small, populous and sparsely populated, richly endowed and devoid of resources, united by nationalism and divided by tribalism, democratic and absolutist, brown, black, yellow, and white. Yet, for all this variety, these nations do share from the point of view of American foreign economic policy one vital common denominator: a passionate desire for economic growth and development. This basic theme defines the nature of our economic relations with the less developed countries.

Are there any valid reasons why the United States should need to share the aspirations of the Third World countries for economic development? Is promotion of *their* growth in *our* national interest?[1] If promoting their growth *is* in our interest, then it is expedient for us to sacrifice a certain amount of current income and future wealth in order to accelerate the net flow of real resources to the Third World. Foreign aid is worth our while, and possibly also some change in our commercial and foreign-investment policies as well. However, if promoting their growth is *not* in our interest, then none of these sorts of concessions are imperatives for us. Rather, American economic policies vis-à-vis the Third World can be designed primarily to promote our own growth, perhaps even at the expense of the poor countries.

Now, it is evident that in narrowly economic terms, our national interest is not significantly enhanced by promoting the growth of less developed areas. True, the Third World is an im-

---

[1] For a useful extended discussion of this question, see John Pincus, *Trade, Aid, and Development: The Rich and Poor Nations* (New York: McGraw-Hill, 1967), Ch. 1.

portant source of certain vital raw materials, and we do have a considerable volume of investments built up in many of the poor states. But even so, our economic stake in their development is modest at best. Almost all raw-material imports can be substituted for by domestic synthetics or by imports from within the Industrial World, and although some individual American firms are highly dependent on their investments in the Third World, America as a nation most definitely is not. In general, with only marginal exceptions, economic considerations do not dictate a preoccupation with the growth of the Third World.

Nor, in general, do considerations of military security dictate such a preoccupation. In this respect, too, it is evident that our national interest is not significantly enhanced by promoting the growth of the Third World. The perceived military threat to our independence and way of life comes not from the Third World but rather from the Communist World. Only to a very limited extent are the less developed countries essential to us in the global struggle for power with the Communists. Those that are important are so mainly as bases for weapons and as sources of intelligence and communications facilities, and even here their importance is declining in this era of sea-based missiles and space satellites. Friendly relations with the Third World do not add much to our protection from enemy attack or conquest. On the contrary, even if the entire Third World turned hostile toward us, our prospects for national survival would not be much affected, for our nuclear capacity would be sufficient to keep us safe from military aggression.

The broad considerations of economic and military survival, however, are not the only dimensions of the national interest. Cultural survival, i.e., the survival of certain minimum "core values" such as rank, prestige, material possessions, and special privileges, is also highly prized. It is doubtful whether all of these values could be preserved by a United States threatened by antagonistic states not only in the present Communist World but in much of the Third World as well. At home, the principles of democracy and economic liberalism—the American way of life— would probably be undermined by the gradual development of a kind of garrison-state mentality dominated by a "military-industrial complex"; abroad, valuable foreign investments, commercial concessions, and sources of supply would almost surely be lost or endangered. In the long run, our accustomed way of life can be preserved only by policies conceived and implemented with the object of avoiding the hostility of the Third World, especially those parts of the Third World that are today essential to us for strategic or economic reasons. The policies most likely to achieve this object are those that identify us publicly with the object of greatest concern to the Third World—economic development. In at least one fundamental respect, therefore, the promotion of the growth of poor countries is in our national interest: economic concessions on our part serve as a kind of insurance against belligerency on the part of the less developed countries.

To be sure, the insurance may not always be effective, a point argued by some of the American critics of United States policy cited by Goran Ohlin [23]. The process of economic development, these critics point out, tends to generate political and social disorder. Consequently, by promoting development we may in fact be cultivating the eventual emergence of radical forces even more antagonistic toward us than some of those currently operative. And indeed, in the cases of such countries as Algeria, Cambodia, Egypt, Guinea, and Pakistan, our economic concessions have failed to protect us against acute political hostility. Nonetheless, the practical fact remains that more often than not this kind of insurance has been as effective as we might wish; friendly relations between the United States and strategically or economically important less developed countries have been preserved in enough cases as to justify the continued payment of insurance "premiums." As Goran Ohlin writes:

The American critics here cited contend that the process of modernisation is conductive to instability. . . . This is not denied in any quarter, but the real question, it is answered, is whether by a long-term aid policy "we can marginally influence the course of economic, social, and political modernisation so as to reduce somewhat the risks with which it confronts us."

There is also a second respect in which the promotion of the growth of poor countries is in our national interest. In the global struggle with Communism, ideology is an essential ingredient: the

Communist World sponsors the principles of Marxism-Leninism; we sponsor the principles of democracy and free enterprise. This is not just a matter of preserving the national way of life at home; this is a matter of encouraging others to live the same way. Each side in the Cold War would like to organize the world, in particular the as yet uncommitted Third World, to its own image. Moreover, each side has the capacity to play such a role in shaping the future of the Third World, simply by identifying with its aspirations for development and offering concessions that will guide the development process along lines consistent with its particular ideology. Thus by the very fact of our rivalry with the Communist World, America is committed to efforts to help accelerate the growth of the less developed countries.

Finally, there is a humanitarian consideration. Ultimately, our allegiance as a collectivity to the ideas of political and economic liberalism can be justified only by a fundamental ethical concern for human welfare, both our own and that of others. And certainly economic development is a process that improves human welfare. Furthermore, we are rich, and we can easily afford to ease the misery of economic backwardness in the Third World. Of course, ethics can hardly be described as a central determinant of public policy. But to the extent that ethical factors are weighed at the margin by decision-makers, they constitute a reason why the United States should share the aspirations of the Third World for growth and progress.

Throughout the postwar period the American government has in its statements and actions generally concurred with the arguments outlined above. Indeed, as Harry Johnson [25] observes, "the United States government has repeatedly reaffirmed its commitment to assist the development of less developed countries. This commitment has been expressed in a substantial flow of real resources to these countries." From time to time the public emphasis of government policy has changed, shifting back and forth among strategic, economic, and humanitarian considerations. But always, whatever its current emphasis, our policy has been based on the official assumption that it is broadly in our national interest to promote growth in the Third World. The evolution of the rationale for this assumption is reviewed by Ohlin with sympathy and understanding.

The question now arises of how most effectively to allocate means to ends. The goal of American policy in the Third World is economic development; the problem is to identify the policy instruments best fitted to achieve this goal. In theory, three alternative instruments are available: commercial policy, foreign-investment policy, and foreign-aid policy. In practice, however, the first two of these three have not been much used. Professor Johnson describes how little the United States has offered in the form of trade concessions that might be expected to accelerate the net flow of real resources to the Third World. Likewise, Jack Behrman [26] describes how little we have done officially to facilitate the movement of private investment funds. For the most part, the American government has relied exclusively on foreign aid as a means for promoting economic development; that is why, in reviewing the evolution of the rationale for United States involvement in the Third World's growth, Ohlin is able to speak simply of "*aid* doctrine." Our foreign-aid program in the less developed countries began in the late 1940s with the Truman Doctrine and Point Four and has continued ever since under the aegis of MSA, FOA, DLF, ICA, and, most recently, AID (Agency for International Development).[2]

Presumably the government has preferred foreign aid as an instrument of policy because it is most likely to preserve American influence over the flow of resources to the Third World. Trade concessions yield benefits to the less developed countries that can neither be easily regulated in volume nor controlled in direction from the United States. Similarly, investments by private American corporations give the government relatively little leverage over the policies of host countries; on the contrary, once the investment is consummated, it in fact becomes a "hostage" of the host country, effectively augmenting the latter's leverage over the policies of the United States. Foreign-aid grants and loans, by contrast, are single explicit transactions, each one of which must be separately negotiated and every one of which can therefore be tied up with a variety of "strings." Current income is sacrificed by this country, but not necessarily our power in the Third World.

[2] For a thorough review of United States foreign-aid policy since the late 1940s, see David A. Baldwin, *Foreign Aid and American Foreign Policy* (New York: Frederick A. Praeger, 1966), Ch. 2.

This helps to explain why the American government has resisted pressures to allocate a larger proportion of our foreign-aid funds to multilateral rather than bilateral programs. Robert Asher [24] enumerates a number of strong arguments in favor of placing a greater stress on the former approach to economic development. Multilateral programs can often be more effective than bilateral programs in promoting economic development, mainly because they facilitate coordination of activity and a greater clarity of objectives. Too, they are often more acceptable to aid receivers, for several reasons. First of all, typically fewer strings and conditions are attached. Second, to the extent that conditions remain, they tend to be economic in content rather than political, and hence more tolerable than the conditions often implied by bilateral programs. And finally, as Asher notes, the multilateral approach "is regarded as the wave of the future." Still, the United States has continued to assign the bulk of its aid funds to bilateral programs. Our attitude, it would seem, is that we are interested in identifying publicly with the Third World's aspirations for development, but not in surrendering much of our own international influence in the process.

This attitude has increasingly become a source of tension between us and the Third World. The less developed countries, no less than the West Europeans and the Canadians, resent what often amounts to an American predominance in their economic affairs. Indeed, being by and large even more nationalistic than most industrial countries, they are even more adamantly opposed to any further extension of our foreign economic influence. They want to grow, but not at the expense of their own sovereignty. Thus they would like more economic aid, but from multilateral sources and with fewer strings. They would like more American investments, but not the kind of "neocolonial" control such investments have often implied. And they would like more trade concessions that will enhance their command over foreign resources but not their dependence on us.

In my opinion, the United States ought to compromise with these sentiments. Our aim in identifying with the Third World's aspirations for development is to preserve our political influence. As in Western Europe and Canada, to accomplish this today we will probably have to tolerate a further decline in our net economic influence. This is the reality with which our economic policies in the Third World must deal, no less than our policies in the Industrial World. In the area of foreign aid we should be prepared to attach fewer strings and to rely less on our traditional bilateral approach. And in the areas of trade and foreign investment, too, we should be prepared to make new concessions.

Harry Johnson describes how minor the modifications of United States commercial policy have been in recent years in response to the evolving views and demands of the Third World and how resistant the United States government was to any significant trade concessions at the first meeting of the United Nations Conference on Trade and Development (UNCTAD) in 1964. This negative stance, he argues—I think correctly—cannot be continued: "The United States must regain the political initiative if it is to maintain its influence among the less developed countries." The best way to do this, in my opinion, is to accept the basic principles of the trade proposals being made by the less developed countries themselves, and in particular the proposals concerning preferences. Trade preferences for the poor countries in developed-country markets and preferential arrangements among the poor countries themselves would no doubt produce some negative effects on our economic power position as the world's greatest exporter and importer. But the American economy is not likely to suffer much thereby, and in any event the damage can be contained by careful negotiation of the specifics of the preference proposals. At the same time, by identifying with the basic principles of the proposals themselves, we would probably succeed in preserving our political position in the Third World, which is supposedly the ultimate rationale of our policy.

Likewise, Jack Behrman describes how minor the modifications of United States foreign-investment policy have been in recent years: "It is clear," he says, "that the government's record in this area falls far short of its efforts in other fields." In a sense this weak record is rather surprising, since promotion of private investment as a catalyst for growth would seem to be entirely consistent with our ideological commitment to the idea of free enterprise. But in fact it is not surprising at all, once account is taken of the Third World's firm ideological opposition to the foreign economic control frequently implied by capitalist investments. This opposition usually expresses itself in numerous and complex administrative regulations, in high rates of taxation, and sometimes even in confiscation and nationalization—the prospect of which creates discouraging risks and uncertainties for our businessmen. This is the real problem to be resolved, and so far all efforts on our part have failed. The American government has relied mainly upon a system of investment guarantees, but this program, as Behrman notes, "remains halting and incomplete," and so has never succeeded in overcoming the disincentives that usually confront the United States entrepreneur.

What is needed in this area is a new approach to the concept of foreign investment, an approach that on the one hand protects the legitimate profits of the investor, thereby maintaining his basic incentive to invest, but that on the other hand removes the threat of foreign control, thereby eliminating the cause for ideological opposition on the part of the potential recipients. The best way to do this is to work out arrangements whereby the American entrepreneur is transformed from an owner into something else— a co-owner, a manager, or an agent. This could be accomplished by programs specifying, say, local participation requirements, or management contracts, or perhaps even agreements to turn over control to local partners after a specified time. By taking the initiative in developing such programs, the American government would of course be conceding a probable decline in our net economic influence. Our political relations with the Third World, however, would improve.

Of all the Third World, Latin America is closest to the United States both politically and economically. The Western Hemisphere has always been our special sphere of influence, a buffer against threats to our national security from across the oceans. In addition, it has been our primary source of raw materials and foodstuffs—iron and oil from Venezuela, tin from Bolivia, copper from Chile and Peru, wool from Uruguay, sugar and coffee from Brazil and Colombia, bananas from Central America—as well as a prominent market for our exports. Today, Latin America accounts for about 15 percent of all United States exports and for almost 20 percent of all United States imports. Latin America also accounts for more United States overseas investments than all the rest of the Third World combined.

In view of the intimacy of United States–Latin American relations, it is not surprising that the American government has
taken a particular interest in the problems of economic development south of the border—an interest that was formalized in the
establishment of the Alliance for Progress in 1961. According to
its founder, President Kennedy, the Alliance was conceived as a
broad program for regional cooperation and administration of
economic assistance from the United States. In fact, it has turned
out to be not much more than a dressed-up version of our previous bilateral-aid efforts in Latin America, in principle inspired by
our earlier and successful Marshall Plan in Europe but, as Edward
Mason [27] accurately observes, in practice differing conspicuously
from it. Mason emphasizes the organizational contrasts between
the Marshall Plan and the Alliance, and no doubt these are important. But much more important, I think, are the contrasts of
needs and desires.

At the end of World War II, Europe needed to recover from
six years of military devastation and desired above all else enough
aid to facilitate a rapid rehabilitation. Furthermore, at the time
Europe was relatively unconcerned about American influence in
its affairs, being considerably more preoccupied with the threat of
Communist domination from the East. By contrast, Latin America
today obviously needs to do more than recover; it needs to develop
—certainly a much more prolonged and difficult process. Moreover, Latin America at this time is extremely concerned about
American influence in its affairs. As Mason notes, what the United
States would like to view as common economic interest is felt by
the Latin states as dependence, and they would like to reduce it.
Consequently, they, even more than most Third World nations,
want not just another aid program, but new concessions in the
commercial and foreign-investment policies of the United States.

The kinds of concessions the Latins want are described by
Mason and closely parallel the proposals outlined in the previous
section of this essay. And significantly, the United States has
begun to compromise with the sentiments of the Latin Americans.
At the meeting of Western Hemisphere presidents in April, 1967,
President Johnson pledged complete United States support for a
Latin American Common Market, to be established no later than
1985, and hinted at the possibility of United States tariff pref-

erences for Latin American exports as well. And behind the
scenes the government seems to have begun to encourage the
kinds of foreign-investment programs that would, I have suggested,
help to overcome the ideological hostility that usually confronts
the United States entrepreneur. A continuation of developments
along these lines would seem to be the most appropriate strategy
for American foreign economic policy in Latin America in particular, as in the Third World in general.

23

The Evolution of United States Aid Doctrine

GORAN OHLIN

Two-thirds of all development assistance emanates from the United States, where foreign aid programmes have been prominent ever since the end of the war. In the course of the shift from reconstruction in Europe to development assistance in the underdeveloped regions, the total amounts of foreign aid have declined very considerably, and in relation to GNP or Federal Budget expenditures the drop has been even greater. Thus, in 1949, economic assistance under the Marshall Plan amounted to about two per cent of GNP; at present official economic assistance amounts to one-third of one per cent of GNP. (Military assistance comes to another one-fourth of one per cent.)[1]

In spite of this relatively modest size and declining trend, the foreign assistance programme has never ceased to arouse unease and controversy. One of the manifestations of this has been the steady flow of special committees appointed to review this programme in depth. Since the inception of the Marshall Plan, there have been very few years in which foreign aid has not been the subject of reconsideration by some publicly appointed group of distinguished citizens.

Thanks to their reports and to the continuing dialogue between the Administration and Congress, the picture of United States aid doctrine is a good deal richer than in most other countries. The public debate on foreign aid has also been fuller in the United States than elsewhere. For this reason alone, it would be justified to give much space to the American search for an aid doctrine,

Reprinted in this form by permission from Chapter 2 of Goran Ohlin, *Foreign Aid Policies Reconsidered* (Paris: Organization for Economic Co-operation and Development, 1966), pp. 15–26.
[1] *Proposed Mutual Defense and Development Programs, FY 1965*, p. 4.

as will, in fact, be done in this section. In addition, it might well be argued that the American debate has raised general issues with considerable relevance to other countries.

In the course of over a decade of argument, study, and administrative experimentation and growth, a U.S. aid doctrine has, in fact, evolved with regard to objectives as well as techniques. Yet, it is possible, as sometimes claimed, that public confusion about the premises of United States foreign aid policy is waxing rather than waning. To the public and Congressional unease has recently been added sharp academic criticism and, so far from being closed, the debate about first principles has been revived in the last years.[2]

Technical assistance missions have been undertaken by the United States for more than a hundred years, especially in South and Central America,[3] and the first major programme of economic assistance was, of course, the Marshall Plan. But it was not until 1949 that development assistance as such became national policy. The Point Four programme announced by President Truman in his inaugural address that year, and the subsequent act for International Development of 1950, made it "the policy of the United States to aid the efforts of the peoples of economically underdeveloped areas to develop their resources and improve their living conditions." In his inaugural address, the President described the "bold new program" as a task of "making the benefits of our scientific advances and industrial progress available for the improvement and growth of underdeveloped areas." He said explicitly that "the material resources which we can afford to use for the assistance of other peoples are limited. But our imponderable resources in technical knowledge are constantly growing and are inexhaustible."

This optimism about the catalytic effects of technical assistance also pervaded the presentation of the 1950 Act to Congress, but

---

[2] See, e.g., Edward S. Mason, *Foreign Aid and Foreign Policy* (1964), and the essays collected in Robert A. Goldwin, ed., *Why Foreign Aid?* (1963).

[3] The objectives of such missions are said to have been as mixed as those of modern aid programmes. They "grew out of a compound of economic interests, humanitarian sentiment, and strategic considerations. In most of these cases, the motives were so mixed that American aims were never clearly defined beyond a vague desire to maintain a series of reasonably stable republics." Merle Curti and Kendall Birr, *Prelude to Point Four* (1954), p. 205; cited in Charles Wolf, Jr., *Foreign Aid: Theory and Practice in Southern Asia* (1960), p. 13.

the spokesman for the Administration supplemented the appeal to humanitarianism and the President's call to action against "hunger, misery and despair" by relating development assistance both to the national economic interest of the United States itself and to the broad interests of United States security which had already warranted the massive economic and military assistance operations in Europe and more modest programmes in Asia. It was assumed that economic development could be promoted by U.S. technical assistance, and that it would contribute to political stability and resistance against Soviet penetration.

These objectives—charitable, economic, and strategic—have never been absent in considerations of U.S. aid programmes, and much of the debate about the basic purpose of a programme devoted to economic assistance—rather than military aid which raises fewer problems—has revolved around their interpretation and interrelationship. Whether economic assistance should be divorced, so far as possible, from diplomacy and from other forms of assistance, whether it should be bilateral or multilateral, whether it should be given widely or selectively, on more or less specific political terms—these questions have continued to confound aid policy, although in the end they have found more or less tentative answers.

After the inception of the Point Four programme, the Korean War turned the U.S. foreign aid effort in the direction of military assistance and defence support which claimed no other purpose than that of strengthening U.S. security, and for several years the problems of development assistance received little systematic attention, in spite of the growth of activities in that field. Technical assistance expenditures rose from 30 million dollars to 150 million a year, and a number of ad hoc programmes under the heading "assistance to economic development" found their way into the budget. The PL 480 sales of agricultural surpluses were started. But it was not until 1956–57, after a series of foreign policy setbacks and the appearance of the Soviet Union in the foreign aid field, that the United States foreign aid programme was suddenly subjected to the most intensive study and publicity it had yet received.[4] Reports were prepared by a Presidential Committee of

[4] For a survey of this debate, see the papers by Schelling and Mason in *International Stability and Progress* (Eleventh American Assembly: New York, 1957).

Citizen Advisers, by the International Development Advisory Board appointed under the Point Four programme by the House Committee on Foreign Affairs, and by the Special Committee to Study the Foreign Aid Program set up by the Senate. The Special Committee contracted for eleven studies on different aspects of the foreign aid programme by private research organisations and also dispatched ten individuals to survey foreign aid programmes in different parts of the world. According to the Chairman, Senator Green, the reason for this massive inquiry was the increasing opposition to the foreign aid programmes which seemed "to indicate either that their purposes have not been clearly understood, or that there is a growing belief that they have in some way failed to serve the national interest." The study, which filled over 1,500 pages, was intended to clarify the relationship between foreign aid and the national interest.[5]

What emerged from these studies and reports was a range of positions and a definition of issues rather than a consensus, except possibly on the urgency of a policy vis-à-vis the newly independent states. The most forceful case for a distinctive and enlarged assistance programme, largely divorced from short-run foreign policy, though conceived to serve long-run interests of American security, was made in the report to the Senate Committee on "Objectives of the United States Economic Assistance Programs" by the MIT Center for International Studies, the ideas of which were also reflected in Millikan and Rostow's *A Proposal: Key to an Effective Foreign Policy.* The strategy of a major development aid programme proposed in this study rested on the proposition,

that a comprehensive and sustained program of American economic assistance aimed at helping the free underdeveloped countries to create the conditions for self-sustaining economic growth can, in the short run, materially reduce the danger of conflict triggered by aggressive minor powers, and can, in say 2 to 3 decades, result in an overwhelming preponderance of societies with a successful record of solving their problems without resort to coercion or violence. The establishment of such a preponderance of stable, effective, and democratic societies gives the best promise of a favorable settlement of the cold war and of a peaceful, progressive environment.[6]

[5] U.S. Senate, Special Committee to Study the Foreign Aid Program, *Foreign Aid Program, Compilation of Studies and Surveys*, Washington, D.C., 1957, p. iii.
[6] U.S. Senate, *Compilation*, p. 20.

This proposition in turn rested on the assumptions that assistance could stimulate growth, and that this could promote political maturity, not primarily by a rapid improvement in income, but by focussing nationalist energies, spurring meaningful action and supporting new and modernising elements in underdeveloped countries. Development aid should, it was suggested, be politically neutral:

The United States agency allocating development funds should not have to consider anything beyond the technical criteria which have been established. It should never seek, for example, to influence negotiations on an airbase by granting or denying funds for construction of a hydroelectric station out of economic development appropriations.[7]

Aid should be allocated so as to maximize additional effort, and two indices were suggested to measure such effort: steps to raise the marginal savings rate and capture increases in income for capital formation and the progress made in working out a development programme to enlarge the capacity to absorb additional capital productively. It was also suggested, however, that "capital aid should be offered wherever there is reasonable assurance that it will be effectively used. . . . Absorptive capacity becomes thus the measure of allocation of aid between different countries."[8] Absorptive capacity was thought to be so limited,

that relatively small amounts of capital ($2.5 to $3.5 billion more per year from all sources) would amply suffice even if every underdeveloped country of the free world were to avail itself fully of this opportunity. In practice, it is unlikely that more than 50 to 60 per cent of this amount would be taken up.[9]

These features of the MIT and Millikan-Rostow proposals have been recalled because in many respects U.S. assistance policy has gradually incorporated many of them. Neither in 1957 nor later have they stood unopposed. At the opposite extreme, well-known economists argued that aid programmes "will almost surely retard

[7] *Ibid.*, p. 32.
[8] *Ibid.*, pp. 60–61.
[9] *Ibid.*, p. 61. The study by the Research Center in Economic Development and Cultural Change at the University of Chicago also assumed that $3 billion was the additional need, rising to perhaps $5 billion in 10 or 15 years and then declining. *Ibid.*, p. 236.

economic development"[10] and political scientists that foreign aid programmes could not influence the course of political developments in Asia.[11]

Closer to the mainstream of the argument was the position of those who felt that development assistance inevitably was part of foreign policy, that the actual administration of such a programme neither could nor should be entirely separated from current diplomacy, and that the programme should be selective and generally serve to produce satisfactory political settlements.[12]

In spite of such important differences about the precise relationship between aid policy and diplomacy, there was among those who recognized the need for economic assistance general agreement that the most important motive for such a policy was the concern with present and future political developments in the world. The role and uses of the aid programme were variously interpreted, hopes and assumptions about the relationship between aid, development, political stability, and world peace were rarely spelled out, but it was recognized that, in the end, an aid programme must serve the interests of American national security in a broad sense. Probably nothing has caused greater misunderstanding than this proposition which could be taken to mean anything from the demand that American national policy should serve and not harm United States national interests to the suggestion that the aid programme should be dominated by the strategic exigencies of the cold war, and the furtherance of U.S. influence. Gunnar Myrdal wrote of a "strange suspicion on the part of the American people of their own generous motives" and called it a "slightly perverted element of their Puritan tradition."[13]

The aid-giving relationship was widely recognized as delicate, and the fear of seeming to exact political quid pro quos and instead incurring resentment or even refusals to accept economic aid led to positions such as Millikan and Rostow's, that "a program adopted for the wrong reasons may well be worse than useless."

[10] Milton Friedman, "Foreign Economic Aid: Means and Objectives," *The Yale Review*, Summer, 1958. See also, e.g., the study prepared for the Senate Special Committee by the American Enterprise Association, Inc.
[11] Z. Brzezinski, "The Politics of Underdevelopment," *World Politics*, October, 1956.
[12] See, e.g., Mason, in the paper cited above.
[13] *An International Economy* (New York, 1956), p. 122.

But, whether it was seen as an instrument of short-run influence, or as a bold investment in the future physiognomy of the world scene, the cases for the extension of economic aid took their departure in American interest rather than in that of the receiving countries—although the two were not supposed to be in conflict.

"Economic" cases for the promotion of economic growth in underdeveloped areas were occasionally cited in the 1957 debate. Then, as later, it was not infrequently asserted that the United States cannot indefinitely prosper in a world of poverty, that the development of export markets would be necessary to sustain employment and/or growth in the American economy, or that access to strategic raw material supplies in the underdeveloped regions could be a vital objective of development assistance. Such arguments are difficult to uphold, and few serious students maintained that economic gain in the narrow sense was, could, or should be an objective of economic assistance. Measures taken to stimulate private investment in underdeveloped countries were regarded favourably, especially as a means of transferring technology and skills, but it was never suggested that the promotion of U.S. investment could constitute an objective of assistance policy.[14]

The role of the humanitarian and disinterested desire to assist the poorer countries has aroused heated controversy when held up as an alternative rather than a complement to the security objective. In 1957, as before and after, the generosity and philanthropy of Americans and the moral call to help were mentioned among motives for aid. It is clear that some part of postwar American aid, notably that consisting in private and volunteer action, has had this humanitarian character, it is probable that its importance to the public has been another than to makers of national policy, and it is certainly possible that such motives have attracted individuals to foreign aid work. But it is unlikely that a simple desire to help has been an effective objective of United States aid policy in the

---

[14] A possible exception was the study for the Special Senate Committee on "American private enterprise, foreign economic development, and the aid programs," by the American Enterprise Association, Inc., which made no reference to the political objectives of aid programmes and was profoundly sceptical of the benefits of public aid. But even this report was said to aim at showing "how best to attain our main economic-based security objectives while minimizing the tax burden on Americans." U.S. Senate, *Compilation*, p. 545.

sense that it has affected major decisions. As Charles Wolf, Jr., concluded in his survey of aid policy vis-à-vis South Asia, "in terms of this test, humanitarian objectives are not, nor do they appear likely to be, prominent among the continuing objectives of U.S. foreign aid."[15] In Mason's view, "an aid program of some magnitude would be supported on relatively disinterested grounds," but by and large it would be misleading to assume that any sizable part of United States economic assistance—or that from other countries—has flowed from such motives.[16]

After the stocktaking in 1956 and 1957, the Senate and the House Committees recommended enlarged capital assistance in the form of loans on lenient terms, and with the creation of the Development Loan Fund in 1958 the shift towards development assistance was accelerated. The subsequent reorganisation—the establishment of AID—and the elaboration of U.S. aid philosophy in recent years, may be said to represent a crystallization around some of the positions emerging in 1957.

The foreign aid programme remained a topic of both controversy and consensus. Suspicions of waste and inefficiency were frequently expressed. The growing concern with the U.S. balance of payments made the foreign aid programme vulnerable to attack, and in the 1960's it excited more attention than ever.[17] In President Kennedy's foreign aid message of 1961, it was found necessary to "draw back and ask with candor a fundamental question: Is a foreign aid program really necessary?"

In answer to this question, it was again asserted that "widespread poverty and chaos lead to a collapse of existing political and social structures" which would endanger the nation's security. The need for long-range planning and commitments was stressed, but the objective of development assistance was given special

[15] *Foreign Aid: Theory and Practice in Southern Asia* (1960), p. 284.
[16] Mason, *Foreign Aid and Foreign Policy* (1964), p. 30.
[17] A content analysis of successive State of the Union messages reveals that the percentage devoted to the foreign aid programme was:

Eisenhower:	1955	2 %	Eisenhower: 1958	2 %
	1956	3.5 %	1959	2.2 %
	1957	3.1 %	1960	6 %
			Kennedy: 1962	7.7 %

Cf. Jean Baptiste Duroselle et Jean Meyriat (eds.), *Politiques nationales envers les jeunes états* (Paris, 1964), p. 68.

urgency by the suggestion that many of the less developed nations stood on the threshold of a break-through:

The 1960's can be—and must be—the crucial "decade of development"—the period in which an enlarged community of free, stable, and self-reliant nations can reduce world tensions and insecurity.[8]

In its largest sense, the objective of the foreign aid policy was described as that of creating a partnership between the northern and southern halves of the world, in which other industrialised nations would participate in a common effort. The need for internal reform and self-help in underdeveloped countries was again stated, but with special force in the formulation of a "new working concept" for the aid policy which distinguished between different types of aid and development programmes proper to the recipients' stage of development and indicated that aid would be contingent on efforts to resource mobilisation, self-help, and internal reform.

The latest in the series of public committee reports on U.S. foreign aid is the Clay Report of 1963. The Committee submitting it was appointed by the President and had as its chairman General Lucius D. Clay. Its terms of reference were specific and in themselves express a characteristic of United States aid philosophy: the Committee was to examine U.S. military and economic assistance programmes to determine whether their scope and distribution was effectively contributing to the security of the United States and the economic and political stability in the free world.[19]

It was a brief and terse report. It recognised that the foreign aid programmes served United States interests. Their "basic purpose" was said to be indicated by the high concentration of total foreign assistance to allies and other countries on the Sino-Soviet border which received 72 per cent of total (military and economic) assistance appropriations. The Committee criticised the dispersion of aid to an excessive number of countries. Specifically, it recom-

[18] H. Doc. 117, 87th Cong., 1st Sess. *Foreign Aid*. Message of the President to the Congress.
[19] *The Scope and Distribution of United States Military and Economic Assistance Programs*. Report to the President of the United States from the Committee to Strengthen the Security of the Free World. Department of State, Washington, D.C., 1963.

mended that United States assistance to African countries should be limited to a minimum in view of European responsibilities there; claimed that economic assistance to some non-allied countries in Asia was "beyond that necessary for our interests"; and found the U.S. technical assistance programme too large to be adequately staffed with qualified personnel. The Committee was emphatic on the need for other industrialised countries to increase their aid effort, but believed immediate reductions to be in order in United States programmes, as it was "convinced that the burden of sustaining foreign assistance to the less-developed countries is falling unfairly upon the U.S." (p. 14). It especially urged the improvement of lending terms by other donors; otherwise "international consortia and co-ordinating groups for such countries as India, Pakistan, Turkey and Nigeria will saddle these countries with impossible debt-service requirements and U.S. funds would pay for these short-term and short-sighted debts" (p. 15).

In the long run, the Committee anticipated further reductions of U.S. assistance programmes and expected that repayment of old assistance loans would accelerate and provide an increasing share of the necessary funds.

The Committee favoured a gradual shift towards multilateral administration of aid which would insulate development assistance from political and commercial interests, be less susceptible to charges of infringing upon the sovereignty of recipients, and more co-ordinated than aid by many independent donors. It especially recommended the use of the International Development Association by the U.S. and its partners "as a common channel for aid funds, which would achieve many of our common objectives—a fairer sharing of the burden and the effective and coordinated use of assistance provided on terms both appropriate to the needs of the recipient countries and impartial as among the commercial interests of the contributing nations" (p. 16).

On many traditionally controversial aspects of aid policy, the Committee also took restrictive positions: aid should not be given to establish "government-owned industrial and commercial enterprises which compete with existing private endeavours"; local costs of development projects should not be financed out of external assistance; terms of United States development loans should be harder where debt-servicing capacity was adequate.

The Committee did find the aid programme essential to United States security and noted that the need for development assistance was not merely a function of the cold war. Its tone was one of reluctant approval of a policy basically undesirable and exceptional, a regrettable but transient necessity, and in these respects, it reflected (and in some measure nurtured) the scruples and concerns about U.S. foreign aid policy which made the later Congressional struggle in 1963 one of unprecedented bitterness.

Nevertheless, the Clay report may be described as a brief and qualified endorsement of a policy which over the years has been restated and reviewed repeatedly. In recent years, this policy has been articulated into an AID doctrine which represents a remarkable advance towards the formulation of a systematic aid philosophy. The major objective of U.S. foreign assistance is now tersely described as that of assisting "other countries that seek to maintain their independence and develop into self-supporting nations,[20] as this offers the best long-run prospect of security and peace for the United States.

To use funds available for development aid as effectively as possible, "self-help is . . . the dominant theme" and the first criterion in allocating aid is said to be the effectiveness with which the recipient uses its available resources.

Countries in early stages of development are assumed to have a primary need for technical assistance and institution building, and only limited need for capital assistance, chiefly for infrastructure projects. As the need for capital assistance increases, the need for technical assistance shifts from general to more specific skills. The gradual increase in domestic savings, and a growing capacity to attract private and other conventional foreign capital on nonconcessionary terms will progressively reduce the need for foreign aid. The assumption that the need for aid is temporary and limited is underlined—several recipients in Latin America and elsewhere are expected to attain rapid development in ten to fifteen years, but it is recognised that, in Asia and Africa, the need for aid will remain for a much longer time.

The sharpening definition of the objectives is also expressed in the concentration of funds. In the aid programme for fiscal year

[20] Agency for International Development, *Principles of Foreign Assistance* (Washington, D.C., 1963), p. 1.

1964–65, two per cent of assistance funds were destined to four-teen countries classified as "in transition toward self-support," ten per cent scattered over 37 countries for "limited programs" of different kinds, but 88 per cent concentrated on "major programs" in 25 countries. In this group, funds are further concentrated on seven countries—India, Pakistan, Turkey, Nigeria, Tunisia, Co-lombia and Chile—which are ranked highly in "self-help per-formance" and receive two-thirds of the U.S. development loans. The remaining 18 countries fall into two categories, one in which the "commitment to sound development policies and effective resource use" is found inadequate for programme assistance on a large scale and where aid takes the form of projects and technical assistance, and one in which problems of internal and external stability are overriding and where aid is furnished largely out of funds for "supporting assistance," rather than "development as-sistance."[21]

The official United States aid philosophy has thus reached a high degree of cogency and coherence compared with the early years of the aid programme. This is not to say that it has come to command the universal agreement even of serious students to foreign policy. In recent years, it has come under heavy fire from academic critics, attacking precisely the doctrine and rationale. Professor Hans Morgenthau contended that:

of the seeming and real innovations which the modern age has in-troduced into the practice of foreign policy, none has proven more baffling to both understanding and action than foreign aid.[22]

and claimed that the United States "has yet to develop an intel-ligible theory of foreign aid." In his view, development aid does not differ from the bribes traditionally employed in diplomacy, especially before the nineteenth century.[23] "The pretence and elaborate machinery" of development aid was said to result from a "climate of opinion" in which the obligation to assist under-developed nations and the possibility of promoting their develop-

---

[21] *Proposed Mutual Defense and Development Programs, FY* 1965. Summary Presentation to Congress (Washington, 1964), pp. 22–23.
[22] "A Political Theory of Foreign Aid," *The American Political Science Re-view*, June, 1962, p. 301.
[23] See also George Liska, *The New Statecraft: Foreign Aid in American Foreign Policy* (1960).

ment is accepted. "Economic development has become an ideology by which the transfer of money and services from one government to another in peace time is rationalised and justified" (p. 302). The possibility of promoting economic development in the under-developed countries was sweepingly denied on the grounds that preconditions for modernisation are lacking. Where ruling groups resist economic development, aid will fail in its ostensible purpose, strengthen the status quo, and accentuate social and political problems. Where aid is successful, the social disruption brought about by economic development will lead to political instability internally, and so far from promoting peace and external stability, it will increase the ability of more countries to wage war.

The contrary conclusion derives from the popular, yet totally unfounded, assumption that "poor" nations make war on "rich" nations for economic advantage and that "rich" nations are by definition peaceful because they have what they want (p. 307).

Professor Banfield, like Morgenthau, rejects the hopes placed on aid by reversing the proposition of the Millikan-Rostow chain of argument:

it is unlikely to make much difference to development which, where conditions allow, will come about without it, but in most countries will not;
even if it does, it is unlikely to produce governments that are free, democratic, or even stable;
peace is not promoted by economic development, let alone aid;
even if the new states were to become entirely peaceful, this would not enhance the security of the United States.[24]

As for other benefits sometimes expected to flow from aid, they are described as equally illusory. The effect of aid upon opinion in receiving countries is as likely to be unfavourable as to be favourable, and the possibility of giving aid on a political quid pro quo basis is limited by the sensitivity of underdeveloped countries, but would otherwise be both morally and politically superior to the attempt to manipulate by the creation of diffuse obligations. Aid doctrine is thus said not to

face up to the tragic facts which constitute the problem: that vast areas of the world will probably not achieve a very significant and

[24] Edward C. Banfield, *American Foreign Aid Doctrines* (1963).

widespread improvement in levels of living for at least several generations; that they will probably not learn to govern themselves even
tolerably well; that such development as occurs is as likely to be inspired by hate as by good will or moral respect; that it may, therefore,
prove to be a disaster for the United States and for all mankind.[25]

These sharp challenges of the case for development aid have
been received as salutary antidotes to the clichés of aid discussion
even by writers who find them fallacious and unwarranted.[26] In
part, they rest on pessimistic assertions about social processes
which are no more valid or demonstrable as generalisations than
their opposites. In part, they rest on an appraisal of the realities
of the underdeveloped regions and their importance which, it is
contended, is inadequate. Above all, in their protest against the
extravagant claims sometimes made for aid, they fail to appreciate
the force of what might be termed the minimal case.

As Professor Millikan emphasised in his retort, virtually all recent crises of foreign policy have originated in the underdeveloped
world, and the dangers for world peace and United States security
that arise from political instability in the underdeveloped countries lie less in their potential hostility than in the involvement of
the big powers and the escalation of bloc conflicts. Although indeed there are underdeveloped countries whose prospects of development are poor, there are several in which they are promising,
and there is every reason to pursue a selective and discriminating
policy of allocating aid to countries where it is productively used.
In Professor Mason's view, the basis of a foreign aid programme
can and should be "the demonstrated facts (1) that in at least
a large part of the less developed world foreign aid can make and
has made an effective contribution to economic development; and
(2) that most countries, developed and underdeveloped, desperately want to be independent of external control."[27]

The American critics here cited contend that the process of
modernisation is conducive to instability and that the prospects
of economic growth are in many parts of the world dim and its
consequences unpredictable. This is not denied in any quarter, but

[25] *Why Foreign Aid?* p. 27.
[26] Max F. Millikan, "The Political Case for Economic Development Aid," in
Robert A. Goldwin, ed., *Why Foreign Aid?* Edward S. Mason, *Foreign Aid
and Foreign Policy*, Ch. 2.
[27] *Ibid.*, p. 51.

the real question, it is answered, is whether by a long-term aid policy "we can marginally influence the course of economic, social, and political modernisation so as to reduce somewhat the risks with which it confronts us."[28] The House Committee on Foreign Affairs reached a similar position in 1957 and its terse words sum up a case for aid echoed in many other aid-giving countries. It justified economic assistance on a number of grounds, but concluded:

the most important reason is that nations are determined to develop. Only by participation in that process will we have an opportunity to direct their development along lines that will best serve our interests.

Even though one must take account of the United States' very special position among donor countries, the prolonged debate about U.S. aid is of interest for what it suggests about the intrinsic problems of reconciling foreign aid policy with democratic politics. It reveals a variety of motives for adopting a policy of economic aid to the developing countries, ranging from sheer charity to particular commercial or strategic interests. Much of the controversy has, in fact, concerned the motive rather than the policy, and some of the confusion which has attended the discussion of aid policy on this count has had it roots in simple misconceptions which haunt most aid debates.

In the first place, many arguments about the motives for aid flounder in the shifting sands on the border between conceptions of altruism and enlightened self-interest. The moral or even the political validity of aid is sometimes declared to be nil if there is even the slightest expectation of a benefit, whether in the form of gratitude, prestige, or influence; and scattered voices among Western intellectuals in the former colonial powers have suggested that the colonial era of history has left a burden of guilt requiring some kind of expiation.[29] However, even the saintliest act is easily construed as self-interested, in a broad sense of the word, unless pathological or clearly self-destructive.

Secondly, public policy in a democratic society necessarily finds its support in a variety of motives and purposes. The task of generating effective agreement does not require that all must agree

---

[28] Millikan, op. cit., p. 107.
[29] E.g., Arnold Toynbee, The World and the West (1953).

for the same reason. Foreign aid policies will be approached and interpreted differently, first of all by the various branches of government—departments of foreign affairs, finance, commerce, defence—and secondly by the electorate and its representatives to whom foreign aid policies, even when well understood, will necessarily mean many and different things and be approved or rejected for different reasons. In the United States, as elsewhere, the presentation of the foreign aid programme to the public has put relatively greater stress on the disinterested, humanitarian reasons to extend economic assistance than the deliberations in Congress. Yet, public opinion polls report a substantial majority in favour of foreign aid policies, which is sometimes contrasted with a more hesitant mood in Congress.

Thirdly, the issue of foreign aid tends to bring out sharply whatever doubts exist about the legitimacy or wisdom of pursuing—or appearing to pursue—national interests through diplomacy at all. What George Kennan terms "the legalistic-moralistic approach to international problems" comes to the fore in the uneasy feeling about the aid-relationship. It is strengthened by the internationalist emphasis on moral obligations and by the prickly sensitivity of receiving nations. Here the striving of aid-doctrine, in the United States and all other donor countries, has been to emphasise that, when economic progress is a shared objective, there is a community of interest between donor and recipient, and to separate, wherever possible, development aid from current diplomacy and give it the character of long-run co-operation. Yet there is a persistent preoccupation, not only among recipient nations, with the issue of "strings" in the awarding of foreign aid, and with intervention in domestic affairs in the course of its implementation. Montgomery in his study of U.S. aid policy has even suggested that the doctrine of nonintervention has served to obscure the degree of involvement of the United States in other countries and weakened the diplomacy of foreign aid. "Repeated assertions of the non-political character of foreign aid have deceived Americans more than they have the leaders of the underdeveloped countries." What in his view is lacking is "a rationale for the legitimate and inevitable involvement that occurs in foreign aid relationships, and an understanding of both the opportunities and the limitations of such involvement."

24

Multilateral Versus Bilateral Aid:
An Old Controversy Revisited

ROBERT E. ASHER

At the beginning of the 1960s an unsophisticated observer—meaning, of course, someone other than the reader—might have concluded that, in the United States at least, the long-standing controversy over multilateral versus bilateral aid had been laid to rest. The funeral oration had been pronounced by no less a personage than President Eisenhower when he addressed the General Assembly of the United Nations in September 1960. He went right down the line for multilateral assistance via U.N. channels.

He recommended increasing the United Nations Technical Assistance Program and the United Nations Special Fund, then operating at a level of approximately $75 million per year, to a combined total of $100 million per annum by 1961. He endorsed a United Nations Fund of another $100 million for the Congo. He urged an "all-out United Nations effort to help African countries launch . . . educational activities." He said the United States would cooperate in devising a scheme to provide surplus foods through the United Nations system. He made proposals to expand the Operational and Executive Personnel Program of the United Nations (OPEX), and the work of the International Bank, the International Monetary Fund, and the Food and Agriculture Organization.

A few months earlier—before his nomination as the Republican Party's candidate for Vice President in 1960—Ambassador Henry Cabot Lodge, in a well-publicized speech, had ticked off nine "clear" advantages of the multilateral way of providing econom c

Reprinted in this form with permission from *International Organization*, Autumn, 1962. Address of March 7, 1960, before Tenth Annual Conference of National Organizations called by the American Association for the United Nations, Washington, D.C. (USUN Press Release 3367; Department of State *Bulletin*, April 4, 1960 [Vol. 42, No. 1084], p. 525).

aid. In the process, he more or less equated multilateral with U.N.

If these were the views of the dominant wing of the Republicans—notoriously more suspicious of the United Nations than the Democrats—what boundless support might one expect from the more internationally-minded Kennedy Administration, especially after that eloquent Inaugural Address in which the vigorous young President said:

To that world assembly of sovereign states, the United Nations, our last best hope in an age where the instruments of war have far outpaced the instruments of peace, we renew our pledge of support—to prevent it from becoming merely a forum for invective—to strengthen its shield of the new and the weak—and to enlarge the area in which its writ may run.

But less than 60 days later, when President Kennedy sent to Congress his message on the Alliance for Progress, the writ of the United Nations was not noticeably enlarged. Of the $500 million requested, $394 million was to go to a new Western Hemisphere institution, the Inter-American Development Bank (IDB), $100 million to a domestic agency, the International Cooperation Administration, and $6 million "to help strengthen the Organization of American States [OAS]." The OAS, President Kennedy said, "is also working out cooperative arrangements with the United Nations Economic Commission for Latin America and the IDB. These three regional agencies will work together in making regional studies, and in sponsoring conferences. . . ."

A few days later, another major message informed the Congress of the "basic concepts and procedures" that would govern the over-all foreign aid efforts of the Kennedy Administration. Except for a bow to the potentialities of the new Organization for Economic Cooperation and Development (OECD) and a passing reference to the World Bank, the message was devoid of any reference to international machinery.

It would be unfair to conclude from the foregoing that the present Administration is less dedicated to the United Nations as a promoter of development than its predecessor was. There were no important executive orders, congressional messages, or policy directives issued after President Eisenhower's return from the

General Assembly, to give practical effect to his words. The balance of the fifteenth session of the General Assembly—Khrushchev's pounding of the table with his shoe, the Soviet proposal for a three-headed directorate of the U.N., and the increased strength of the underdeveloped bloc in the U.N.—might have given even greater pause to the Eisenhower Administration than it did to the Kennedy Administration.

A fair conclusion is that the controversy is not dead and one cannot blithely assume a steady increase in the proportion of development assistance coming through multilateral channels in the 1960's. The debate will have to come to grips with many new factors and be conducted at a higher level of sophistication than heretofore.

The thesis of this article is that the case for multilateral aid through U.N. agencies is as strong as it ever was. Powerful reasons for utilizing multilateral machinery outside the U.N. framework have also arisen. Paradoxically, the case for bilateral aid, too, remains strong. We shall therefore continue to employ a variety of channels during the foreseeable future. However, we need a more rational basis for a division of labor than has yet been presented. Some guidelines for a better *modus vivendi* are accordingly suggested—more in the hope of stirring up thought than of promptly influencing policy.

But first a bit of general background.

A Bit of Background

Much of the early debate was naïve. It tended, by and large, to be conducted in terms of generalities. Multilateral meant "U.N."; bilateral meant "U.S." Little practical experience with either type of program had been accumulated. As time went on, changes in the economic, military, and political picture attached qualifications to the generalities, but by then the generalities were already in orbit, living a life of their own and reluctant to return to earth.

The first major-postwar foreign aid program was administered by a short-lived multilateral agency, the United Nations Relief and Rehabilitation Administration (UNRRA). During the early

month of UNRRA's existence, there was very little controversy
about multilateral versus bilateral aid. The mood from 1943 to
1945 was predominantly internationalist.

UNRRA was a pioneering, precedent-setting effort. Though it
bore the U.N. label, it was never formally a part of the U.N. system. It proved disillusioning in several important respects. The
United States furnished more than 70 percent of the aid, but had
only one vote in the Council. Many Americans felt that those who
paid the piper should have a stronger voice in calling the tune.
Much of the UNRRA aid, moreover, went to Byelorussia, the
Ukrainian Soviet Socialist Republic, Poland, and other eastern
European areas that were being sealed off from the West by an
iron curtain. In some cases, the aid itself was alleged to be
strengthening the Soviet hold on the area, indirectly making it
more hostile to the United States. At the same time, the economic
situation in western Europe was deteriorating rapidly, with obvious implications for the United Kingdom, the second largest
contributor to UNRRA, and for other non-United States sources
of funds.

In the circumstances, the swing to bilateralism is understandable. One of the lessons of the UNRRA experience is the difficulty
of operating a sizable multilateral program on the basis of one
vote per member government, when the bulk of the funds comes
from a single source and the prospects for any wider sharing of the
burden are fading. Furthermore, although the major recipients do
not have to love or marry the major donor, complications will arise
if they become implacably hostile.

The World Bank, which opened its doors for business at about
the time UNRRA was closing shop, escaped several of these
dangers. Although in fact it operated almost exclusively on United
States resources in its early years, this was obscured by a capital
structure in which the U.S. subscription represented less than 40
percent of the capital stock. Voting, moreover, was weighted
roughly in accordance with subscriptions to the capital stock.
Every member government has a quota and is a contributor as well
as, in theory at least, a potential borrower. The Soviet Union, although an active participant in the Bretton Woods Conference,
has consistently remained aloof. Poland and Czechoslovakia suffered brief, unhappy memberships. Cuba was a founding member,

but withdrew in late 1960. The Bank's three presidents have all been Americans, and strong, capable management has been a feature of most of its history.

Though the Bank has had its share of critics, its prestige has increased steadily, and it has acquired a major and a minor satellite —the International Development Association (IDA) and the International Finance Corporation (IFC). The International Monetary Fund has become less doctrinaire and more flexible in its approach to the problems of the developing countries. The United Nations Children's Fund (UNICEF) has always been popular. The U.N. Technical Assistance Program, off to a shaky start, has survived several crises though it remains far from a model of efficiency. The World Health Organization, the International Civil Aviation Organization, and the U.N. Special Fund continue to be highly regarded.

Despite the successes of various international agencies, bilateral aid programs have dwarfed the multilateral programs since the dismantling of UNRRA. It could hardly have been otherwise so long as the United States was the sole important source of funds. During most of the 1950's, moreover, military aid was far more acceptable to the United States Congress than economic aid, and "defense" was therefore made the umbrella for as much American assistance as possible. Now economic aid is out from under the shade of that umbrella and again respectable in its own right— though with diminished public faith in the miracles it can perform. For the first time since the end of the Marshall Plan, the economic aid expenditures of the United States in the fiscal year 1961 exceeded expenditures for military assistance.

Some multilateral economic programs have fared well financially, and there may even be a correlation between how well they have fared and how well they are run. (There is an obvious inverse correlation between their prosperity and the extent of participation by members of the Soviet bloc.) The enlargement of the resources of the World Bank in 1950 was readily accepted, as were the initial subscriptions to the capital resources of the Bank's affiliates, IFC and IDA. The U.N. Special Fund has grown more rapidly than the U.N. Technical Assistance Program. Regional agencies not related to the United Nations, including the Inter-American Development Bank and the Development Fund of the European

Economic Community (EEC), have acquired resources and been assigned significant roles.

The total flow of public capital from the more developed to the less developed nations of the world has increased steadily during the past decade. Within this larger flow, the share of international agencies has increased somewhat, rising from about 10 percent of the total in the fiscal years 1954–56 to about 12 percent in 1958–59. It has risen further since then, but probably does not exceed 15 percent today.[1] At this rate, the international agencies in 1970—and "international" includes the Development Fund of the EEC and the Inter-American Development Bank as well as the U.N. agencies, whereas "national" excludes Sino-Soviet aid programs—will still account for less than one-quarter of the total flow.

The Arguments Pro and Con

The case for bilateral aid may be good, but is it as overwhelming as the statistics imply? Let me review the arguments for and against multilateral aid, particularly aid through U.N. channels, commenting as I go along and revealing my biases in the process.

1. *Coordination.* Uncoordinated efforts to promote development will not deliver aid of the right types, in the right amounts, to the right places, at the right times. With few exceptions, the developing countries are unable to do the coordinating job, though it has to be done initially on a country-by-country basis. Neither the United States nor any other major donor can possibly assume the coordinating function. It must therefore be undertaken multilaterally.

[1] United Nations Department of Economic and Social Affairs, *International Economic Assistance to the Less Developed Countries* (New York, 1961), p. 48 (for 1954–1956 and 1958–1959 figures). See also Document E/3556, *International Economic Assistance to the Under-Developed Countries: Statistics of Official Contributions in* 1960 (October 4, 1961); Organization for European Economic Cooperation, *The Flow of Financial Resources to Countries in Course of Economic Development,* 1956–1959, and Organization for Economic Cooperation and Development, *The Flow of Financial Resources to Countries in Course of Economic Development,* 1960. The figures are subject to a number of qualifications set forth in the aforementioned reports.

This argument for a multilateral approach has assumed importance only since the list of donor countries has lengthened and since country programming has become the order of the day. So long as the United States was virtually the sole source of assistance and aid was provided on a project basis, the proponents of the bilateral approach—or an uncoordinated series of bilateral approaches—had a pretty good case.

By the latter part of the 1950's, the United States no longer was, or needed to be, the only source of funds. The economies of western Europe and Japan had recovered from the disruption of World War II and were moving toward ever-higher levels of prosperity while the United States was encountering serious balance-of-payments deficits. The beneficiaries of earlier American aid programs recognized a responsibility for the progress of the emerging countries and became contributors to numerous bilateral and multilateral programs. The opportunities for irritation, confusion, duplication of effort, and pockets of neglect are obviously greater when twenty donor nations operate more or less independently of each other than when two or three do.

As demonstrated, however, by the Indus and Mekong River Projects, the consortia for India and Pakistan, and other efforts, a substantial measure of coordination is possible without a pooling of funds if there is a mechanism for reaching agreement about who will do what.

2. *Acceptability to aid-receivers.* It is often argued that we must use U.N. machinery because aid provided in this manner is more acceptable to the receiving nations. If acceptability were the major objective, we ought to consider dropping convertible currency from high-flying planes. Acceptability is less important than effectiveness, though the two are clearly connected.

Reasons for the great acceptability of U.N. aid to a majority of the developing countries will become clearer before the end of this discussion. We should note at the outset, however, that not all aid recipients prefer U.N. channels. The leading Indians, it is reported,

do not want to be thrown into the same statistical bin with two or three dozen other countries in a lower stage of development readiness; they fear the inappropriate egalitarianism that international politics injects into the parceling out of funds under multilateral operations.

The Indian Government, moreover, wants to keep its foreign aid bargaining dispersed. . . . Not only may the present arrangement occasionally allow India to play off one benefactor against another; it maximizes the autonomy of Indian developmental planning. And the latter is something that a government of the independence and stature of the Indian is no readier to surrender to the World Bank or the United Nations than it is to the United States or the Soviet Union.[2]

What is true of India may be true also of Pakistan and, though not necessarily for the same reasons, of South Korea, Vietnam, Indonesia, Turkey, and a number of other countries.

Receivers, having learned that they do not automatically enslave themselves by entering into a bilateral relationship, have become more interested in the size of their aid checks than in the signatures upon them. Assuming the same total of aid funds, those whose receipts would be reduced by the criteria they anticipate under the U.N. are not particularly eager to have more of the fund flow diverted to the multilateral channel. By the same token, those who are not especially favored by any present bilateral relationships have an added reason for preferring the multilateral channel.

3. *Strings on aid.* The acceptability and effectiveness of assistance are also functions of the conditions under which it is made available—the strings attached to it. Fears of strings on aid have subsided markedly as the number of nations and agencies in the aid-dispensing business has increased. Receiving governments that think they are chafing under Western or Eastern restrictions can buy leeway by threatening to switch their patronage. Moreover, by drawing on both sources, they can protect themselves from opposition charges of being pro-Western or pro-Eastern.

The discussion of strings was always a bit confused because appearances in this respect tend to be as important as realities. Thus, it has been said that aid should come without either strings or the appearance of strings, and that the U.N. is therefore a better channel than the U.S. Others have argued that aid should come with strings, provided they are of the right kind, and that the U.N. is better able than the U.S. to attach such strings.

It does seem that the U.N. family is, on the whole, less capri-

[2] John P. Lewis, *Quiet Crisis in India: Economic Development and American Policy* (Washington, D.C.: The Brookings Institution, 1962).

cious than the United States or any other major power and less vulnerable to blackmail. Consequently, if the only strings in which the United States is interested are those that will promote economic progress, it can afford to untie some of its more irrelevant strings.

The notion of "aid without strings," whatever that means, is a most fitting slogan for a Soviet policy concerned primarily with the political climate that it can create and with the unfavorable contrasts with Western imperialism that it can draw. Its appeal largely depends on its remaining aloof from the recipient's internal problems and on its ability to reduce its visible "strings" to a minimum. For us, however, "strings," in the sense of conditions concerning economic policies to be adopted by the recipient government, are indispensable to the success of the objectives we seek to obtain. The real imperatives for us are to exercise appropriate restraint, to impose only such conditions as are relevant to the technical objectives of our aid, to simplify as much as possible our complex controls and safeguards that are such a constant source of annoyance in the recipient countries, and to avoid using our power to enforce compliance with our own ideological preferences. But to try to adopt an ostentatious pose of "no strings" would be transparently out of character and counterproductive for us.[3]

4. *Nonpolitical character of multilateral aid.* Some claim that multilateral aid is preferable to bilateral aid because the multilateral agencies are "nonpolitical." The claim deserves examination from several points of view. What do we mean by nonpolitical? Are there pressures forcing bilateral programs to be almost as nonpolitical as multilateral programs? Do we want aid to be nonpolitical?

Some multilateral economic agencies are obviously less political than others. The free world's OECD is less political than the communist world's Council for Economic Mutual Assistance (COMECON), but the adjective "nonpolitical" is nevertheless usually reserved for U.N. agencies. Though the United Nations can conceivably be used as the instrument of a political bloc, it was not created to promote the foreign policy interests of particular members or groups of members. U.N. agencies are consequently less suspect than the United States, the United Kingdom,

[3] Hans Heymann, Jr., "Soviet Foreign Aid as a Problem for U.S. Policy," *World Politics*, July, 1960 (Vol. 12, No. 4), p. 532.

the Soviet Union, or Communist China acting alone. Receivers as well as donors of aid have a voice in shaping their policies and an opportunity to place in their secretariats fellow-nationals in whom they have confidence. As a result, actions taken by the U.N. agencies reflect a far broader consensus and are generally more acceptable than those of a single foreign office. They are not always acceptable to aid-receivers, however, and international agencies have from time to time been accused of attaching unreasonable conditions or interfering unwarrantedly in the internal affairs of aid-receiving governments. The World Bank has had its troubles with Turkey, the International Monetary Fund (IMF) with Brazil, and the International Atomic Energy Agency with India.

To the extent that Americans approve of the political neutrality of the U.N. family, it is largely because they expect the agencies to be neutral in favor of the free world. Their charters and constitutions, drafted when American prestige was at its highest, were heavily influenced by Anglo-American concepts, and we rightly expect those charters and constitutions to be upheld.

Our occasional insistence that it is both desirable and possible for the United Nations to function as an impartial agent, serving the real interests of both sides by filling a vacuum neutrally and thereby reducing the tendency of Cold War blocs to move into it competitively, has been confused and made less credible by our more general tendency to regard the organization as an instrument to be used by the West in the struggle against the East. The ambiguity cuts deep into our own thinking; we should like the organization to be able to alternate between serving Western interests and presiding with what everyone must regard as majestic impartiality over the interests of the contending blocs.[4]

There may be some confusion here between neutrality, which implies a kind of indifference to the battles of others, and objectivity, which implies absence of bias or prejudice in reaching decisions. An American expectation that the U.N. will apply objectively the principles of the Charter is by no means incon-

[4] Inis L. Claude, "The Containment and Resolution of Disputes," *The United States and the United Nations,* edited by Francis O. Wilcox and H. Field Haviland (Baltimore: Johns Hopkins Press, 1961), p. 122.

sistent with a view that the U.N. is a useful arena in which, and a useful instrument through which, to pursue the aims of American policy.

Nevertheless, the provision of economic aid through the United Nations—through what Henry Cabot Lodge referred to as programs "obviously insulated against political manipulation"—implies a considerable loss of flexibility for donor nations. The U.N. can decide not to provide aid for certain purposes or unless certain eligibility requirements are met. But once it decides the terms on which aid should be available for the build-up of industry or agriculture, the establishment of development banks, or the improvement of civil aviation facilities, it cannot afford to discriminate arbitrarily among qualified applicants. India and Pakistan, Egypt and Israel, Mexico and Cuba, Albania and Libya ought to be judged according to the same standards.

Many who regard foreign aid as an instrument of national policy consequently consider it imperative that we retain the right to use that instrument in accordance with our own interpretation of our best interests. The United States is not interested solely in rapid economic progress in underdeveloped countries, but also in a host of short-term and long term objectives whose attainment may be made easier by the ability to withhold foreign aid, or to put in additional aid, or to direct it to particular projects within the underdeveloped country. Sometimes this serves very broad interests, as in the recent withholding of American aid from Laos to facilitate the formation of a coalition government, or from Peru to protest the military deposition of a democratically constituted government. The flow of American aid can be stepped up as well as suspended in order to promote the United States or the general interest; there is nothing reprehensible in wanting freedom to be more generous to a decent, friendly government than to an indecent, unfriendly one.

Whatever theoretical advantages bilateral programs may confer in terms of freedom of action, the longer such programs remain in existence, the less freedom they allow. There are built-in pressures to extend the program on identical terms to more and more nations. Bilateral programs initiated to help friends in particular regions (western Europe in the case of the United States, and eastern Europe in the case of the USSR) soon spread out globally. Discrimination between friends, enemies, and neutrals becomes increasingly difficult over time.

The same pressures that lengthen the list of countries receiving aid make for broader programs within recipient countries. Each major donor views its program in a political as well as in a humanitarian and technical context. Eager to maximize the political impact, it tends to offer the complete cafeteria of types of assistance, often on terms that undermine the standards the same donor is trying to uphold in the World Bank, the International Atomic Energy Agency, or some other multilateral body.

Once a donor has invested in a receiving country, further investment tends to be regarded as the surest way to preserve the initial investment. After the program has been continued for five years or so, it becomes both a right in itself and a right in relation to aid extended to third countries. Thailand is almost as concerned about the level of United States aid to Cambodia as about the level to Thailand itself. The same is true for Pakistan and India, Peru and Ecuador, Greece and Turkey, and other pairs of countries. When the Congress, in an understandable fit of pique, tries to punish some receiving country (that may also in a fit of pique have boxed itself into an impossible position), the executive branch has to exert itself strenuously to undo the damage. In the process it argues, in effect, that although flexibility is needed, it must be vested in the President rather than the Congress.

Conflict between the executive and legislative branches of government is not a feature of life behind the Iron Curtain, but there must be large numbers of people in the Soviet Union and Communist China who, if they dared speak out, would ask variations of the same questions that are asked in the United States. "Why," they might ask, "are we communists squandering scarce resources in Egypt, Iraq, Yemen, and India? Egypt locks up its communists and vies with Yugoslavia for leadership of the neutral bloc; Iraq has *not* gone communist; Yemen is hopelessly reactionary; India, that ungrateful nation, played a key role in rescuing the United Nations Congo operation at the time Russia most wanted to torpedo it. Why, moreover, is Russia offering India planes that might be used against China? Why are stadia being built with communist help in Indonesia and roads in Afghanistan, when housing is so desperately needed in Moscow and Peking? What does Guinea mean by accepting our aid and then kicking out our ambassador? Why don't Russia and China co-operate and share the aid burden sensibly instead of competing with each other in a number of countries?"

Despite these difficulties, the communists can no more turn the aid spigot on and off capriciously than can the United States. They, too, live in an interdependent world and, in their curious way, must bear a decent respect for the opinions of mankind.

5. *Neutrality of U.N. secretariats.* In theory, the policies of international agencies are established by member governments and administered by secretariats. In practice, the secretariats breathe operational meaning into the broad generalities agreed upon at the intergovernmental level. The confidence of member governments therefore depends to some extent upon having respected nationals of their own, or of friendly governments, in responsible secretariat positions.

The maintenance of a comparatively neutral, objective secretariat, in which all members can have equal confidence, and the initiatives of which can be expected to be in the collective interest, has become more difficult for the world-wide agencies in at least two respects. The newer African and Asian members are even more eager than the dominant founding group for agencies that, if neutral, will be neutral in their favor. In addition, the communist governments have stepped up the pressure for secretariat jobs for their nationals.

In the secretariats, economists, scientists, technicians, and administrators—communist as well as non-communist, underdeveloped as well as overdeveloped—should behave as representatives of the total membership and accept the value premises implicit in the U.N. Charter and the constitutions of the specialized agencies. There is evidence that this presents no insuperable obstacles for non-communists. The growing proportion of staff from the developing countries may temporarily reduce the efficiency of the Organization, but will not alter disastrously the course of its work.

On the other hand, there is a widespread conviction in the West that the obstacles are almost insuperable for communist nationals.

Mr. Khrushchev's belligerent assertion that there are no neutral men,[5] his proposals for reorganizing the secretariat, and the long lists of secretariat posts that he wishes promptly to fill, cannot help but give pause to those who would put more of our eggs in the U.N. basket.

6. *Efficiency.* In the multilateral-bilateral controversy, efficiency of the organization is relevant but not really a primary consideration. The bilateral programs of Canada, Israel, and Australia are, to the best of my knowledge, impressively efficient. A dedicated employee of the United Nations, who has done a first-class job of running a major project involving bilateral and multilateral participation, told me that it is easier to deal directly with every one of the eleven governments he has to consult than with any one of the ten multilateral organizations involved. Nevertheless, certain of the multilateral programs enjoy enviable reputations for efficiency.

At the opposite end of the spectrum, the competition is equally keen. Outstandingly inefficient, as well as outstandingly efficient, organizations have been created by means of intergovernmental cooperation. The American government, relying only on its own resources, ingenuity, and know-how, has also erected monuments to inefficiency. Just as one starts wringing one's hands about the U.N. technical assistance program, one remembers, with equal sadness, our own Agency for International Development.

Efficiency in a public agency, I conclude, depends not on its multilateral or bilateral aspects, but on the clarity of its objectives, the wisdom and professionalism of key people at headquarters and in the field, the ability of those people to obtain intelligent, dedicated subordinates, and the environment and administrative tradition in which they operate.

7. *Relative costs.* Debate about relative costs has been as fuzzy and inconclusive as debate about efficiency. Americans have sometimes argued that multilateral programs are unnecessarily costly. More often they have argued—without the support of any very convincing statistics—that the United States has been bearing an excessive, if not an intolerable, share of the aid burden. The

[5] See Walter Lippmann, "Today and Tomorrow," *Washington Post*, April 17, 1961.

desire to shift part of that burden to western Europe and Japan accounts for much of the early U.S. enthusiasm for the Organization for Economic Cooperation and Development. The fact that other industrialized nations have stepped up their aid to less industrialized nations is, however, no reason for cutting down our assistance unless requirements are shrinking. They are not shrinking.

Administrative costs constitute an insignificant proportion of program costs. Nevertheless, in the capitals of the countries in which the United States has its own aid programs, the United States operations mission tends to be embarrassingly large and prominent. This is due primarily to the number and variety of specialists we try to supply, the standard of living they try to maintain, and the red tape in which they are enmeshed. This embarrassment to the United States could be reduced by a different delineation of multilateral and bilateral responsibilities in the field of technical cooperation.

Irrespective of the effect on the size of local United States missions, it is periodically asserted that U.N. programs are preferable because the United Nations can select its experts from anywhere in the world, thus obtaining better personnel while at the same time paying them less than the United States government would pay. But the business of hiring experts from all over the world (including some whose expertise is dubious), evaluating their qualifications, welding them into teams, and operating in several languages, has its uneconomic and awkward features, too. Even if the U.N. Technical Assistance Program is cheaper, man for man, than the U.S. bilateral program, it is probably more expensive, man for man, than the programs of Israel, Japan, and a number of other countries now supplying experts pursuant to bilateral agreements.

8. *Balance-of-payments effects.* Technical assistance, which is a low-cost form of aid, has negligible effects on the balance of payments of the supplying country. The effects of capital assistance are more worrisome. The loans made by the World Bank and the Inter-American Development Bank are not tied to supply sources in particular member countries, but grants and loans made available bilaterally are, for the most part, used only for purchases in the donor country.

So long as the aid-giving nations adhere to the practice of tying their bilateral aid, each is deprived of the opportunity to earn funds from the expenditures of others, to the detriment of its most efficient producers. Thus, the tying process tends either to raise the total cost of aid programs over what they would be if purchases were made in the cheapest market, or to procure less aid for the same amount of money. In the receiving countries, tied aid increases costs by complicating the job of matching requirements with availabilities.

Under a policy of tied aid, however, the donor countries can be reasonably sure that their foreign aid programs will not reduce their reserves or affect adversely their balances of payments. This, plus pressures to help their least efficient rather than their most efficient producers, makes donor countries slow to take advantage of the alleged economies of multilateral operations.

9. *Availability of funds.* If exclusive reliance on multilateral agencies resulted in substantial economies but even greater reductions in the total availability of aid for developmental purposes, the receiving countries would be worse off economically because of the shift. For the foreseeable future, I think, this would be the case insofar as funds from the United States are concerned.

Congresses and parliaments—always reluctant to appropriate funds—remain on the whole considerably more reluctant to vote them to international than to national agencies. The continuance of bilateral programs results in a competition that is not entirely deplorable and swells the total level of aid to needy countries.

10. *Gratitude, friendship, and credit for services rendered.* Reliance on the multilateral channel, it is said, prevents us from reaping the political credit we deserve for the aid we give. The usual rebuttal is that gratitude is not the objective of our foreign aid programs. Our objective is not a group of grateful satellites, allied to us militarily, voting with us in the United Nations, sharing fully our views on private enterprise, and publicly thanking every visiting official who comes their way. Our basic objective is the creation of self-respecting, increasingly prosperous nations, willing and eager to live in peace and freedom with other nations.

If the objective were gratitude, it could not be purchased by foreign aid. This has been learned by the United States and is being learned by the Soviet Union. India, which should understand the point of view of an aid-receiving nation better than the United States or the Soviet Union, is also learning the hard way. Prime Minister Nehru, deploring what he recently called "an astonishingly virulent" newspaper campaign against India in neighboring Nepal, is reported to have said, "That is what we are getting in exchange for all the friendship and help we have given in the last ten years or so."[6]

Not only is the good will obtainable through direct donor-recipient relationships persistently overestimated, but the good will obtainable from responsible participation in a multilateral undertaking is often underestimated. The prestige of the Scandinavian countries and of a number of others has been significantly enhanced because of the role they have played in U.N. activities. And the Soviet Union, in joining the U.N. Technical Assistance Program after attacking it for years, was undoubtedly aware of the favorable public relations impact of its abrupt reversal.

Though gratitude is not a primary objective of foreign aid programs, it is a highly prized by-product, and ingratitude is always distressing.[7] Multilateral programs are less affected by day-to-day variations in the fever chart of international relations than bilateral programs but, as I indicated in recalling the UNRRA experience, they are not immune.

11. *Satisfactions of the multilateral approach.* Throughout the world millions of people silently share President Kennedy's previously quoted assessment of the United Nations as "our last best hope." The way to strengthen it is to use it. To use it for economic and social purposes helps nurture the nascent sense of international community, helps build the consensus that is a prerequisite for greater achievements in the political and security sphere, and helps broaden the foundation for international law.

6 *The New York Times,* January 7, 1961.
7 Intangibles like good will are, of course, hard to measure and, after aid has become a factor, one cannot know what the state of international relations would be in the absence of such aid. Some may share the view of a prewar American investor recalled in a letter to *The New York Times* on August 10, 1962: "It cost us $100,000,000 to lose the friendship of Peru, when we could have lost it for nothing."

If all member governments have a sufficient voice in establishing the policies of a multilateral agency, they will feel that those policies are about as equitable as can be expected. The confidence enjoyed by the agency may then permit it to be tougher in its appraisals than any single member country could be. The International Bank may be more probing in its review of India's Third Five-Year Plan, or the World Health Organization in its consideration of a project from Guinea, than any member or group of members acting alone.

Although thoroughly frustrating at times, the multilateral approach is often profoundly satisfying. It is regarded as the wave of the future. Everyone who has participated in a hard international bargaining session that winds up with some kind of agreement is aware of the deep and lasting feeling of accomplishment that has been called the satisfaction of shared experience. The confrontation of differing viewpoints modifies the participants' assessments of their own national interests. The voice of the international community may seem weak in competition with the powerful voices of domestic interests, but it is nevertheless peculiarly penetrating.

Every nation must come to terms with the fact that, though the force of collective interest is so great that national policy must be based upon it; yet also the sensitive conscience recognizes that the moral obligation of the individual transcends his particular community.[8]

One of the lessons of the 1950's, however, is that this broader sense of obligation may be less than global in scope. There are many rest houses en route and multilateral is no longer synonymous with U.N. The OECD, the Alliance for Progress, the *ad hoc* agreement of a group of interested countries to help some other country surmount its economic troubles—these, too, are multilateral. One can lament the United States failure to invest as much time and talent in making certain U.N. organs function as it has invested in, say, the OAS and the OECD, but the grand design of the Kennedy Administration—creating an Atlantic

[8] Reinhold Niebuhr, *The Irony of American History* (New York: Scribner, 1952), pp. 36–37.

Community before building a world community—is indubitably worthy of a great nation.

The Upshot of the Arguments

The arguments, I think, add up to a case for considerably more multilateral assistance than the present division of funds would indicate. But until the relationships between economic, social, and political change in low-income countries are better understood, until the development process becomes less of a mystery and the role of foreign aid in influencing the process is clarified, debate about the auspices under which the aid is made available cannot be conclusive. As Hans Morgenthau has said in a provocative and gloomy article:

The popular mind has established correlations between the infusion of capital and technology into a primitive society and its economic development, between economic development and social stability, between social stability and democratic institutions, between democratic institutions and a peaceful foreign policy. However attractive and reassuring these correlations may sound to American ears, they are borne out neither by the experiences we have had with our policies of foreign aid nor by general historic experience.[9]

A fundamental need, therefore, is the accumulation of studies in depth from which more valid generalizations about economic, social, and political development can be made. Whatever such studies prove, they will not invalidate a major underlying reason for foreign aid. The human conscience no longer tolerates affluence for the few while the many are deprived of necessities. The kind of inequality that exists among nations is no longer permitted within the progressive nations, and the world has become too small for fellow-feeling between men to stop at political frontiers.[10]

Insofar as the multilateral-bilateral controversy is concerned,

[9] "A Political Theory of Foreign Aid," *The American Political Science Review*, June, 1962 (Vol. 56, No. 2), pp. 304–305.
[10] See "The Vienna Declaration on Cooperation for Development," adopted by the Conference for Economic Cooperation and Partnership, July 1–7, 1962 (Vienna: Theodor Körner Foundation, mimeographed), paragraph 2.

arguments about cost, gratitude, and acceptability are in reality peripheral. More central are questions concerning focus and coordination—how to transfer the right amounts and kinds of assistance to the right places at the right time; which of the alternative organizations is best equipped to attach relevant and meaningful conditions; how even-handed the organization can and should be; and how willing the legislatures are to entrust it with funds.

Receivers and donors are both pathologically insistent on maintaining maximum freedom of action. All are consequently hesitant to put too many eggs into a single basket. Yet, the freedom of action so highly prized by every nation is increasingly illusory in the aid business. A variety of forces makes it ever more difficult for donor nations to discriminate among aid recipients and advantageous for them to protect themselves against the temptation to do so. Distributing more of the available aid multilaterally is a way of obtaining the necessary protection. Non-discriminatory treatment may have long-run advantages that far outweigh its short-run disadvantages. In a world of competing power blocs, strength lies with the weak. The ultimate sanction—discontinuance of aid while "need" still exists—seldom proves to be a realistic alternative for either bilateral or multilateral programs.

Nevertheless, the Soviet Union will, I predict, continue to rely almost exclusively on bilateral agreements.[11] The Chinese and other members of the bloc will take the same line. The free world will be more open-minded.

For the foreseeable future, the United States will prefer to channel any multilateral aid involving substantial amounts of capital through the International Bank-IMF complex or the Inter-

11 According to Joseph P. Lash, "While the Russians were delighted to use the U.N. as a lever with which to evict Western interests from the Congo, they were also probing for ways by which they could move in. . . . Alone of all the powers contributing food in response to the U.N. appeal, the Soviet Union furnished it directly to the Congolese Government rather than through the U.N. And one of the first Soviet planes flying in food also brought in André Fomin, a top Soviet political expert on Africa, to direct Moscow's on-the-spot operations. Fomin went around Leopoldville openly telling the Congolese they were foolish to expect technical help from the U.N.; they would be much better off to follow the pattern of Guinea and make a direct deal with the Soviet bloc." Joseph P. Lash, *Dag Hammar-skjöld: Custodian of the Brushfire Peace* (New York: Doubleday and Co., 1961), pp. 241–242.

American Development Bank rather than through the United Nations itself or any new organization which includes Soviet bloc members. This preference will be less marked for activities that require smaller expenditures—technical assistance operations and pre-investment surveys by the U.N. Special Fund. The United States will be influenced primarily by political considerations but also by the fact that additional World Bank financing through bond sales on the American market does not show up in the U.S. budget whereas government subscriptions to U.N. bonds do.

Despite a large reservoir of American support for the United Nations, the tortuous course of the U.N. bond issue through the Congress reveals considerable uneasiness about the future of the global organization. Will Soviet intransigence paralyze it? Will the growing strength of the underdeveloped countries distort it? Will the Secretariat live up to the role set for it by Dag Hammarskjöld?

The United Kingdom, a loyal supporter of the World Bank, will at best be lukewarm toward the U.N. proper. France will not promptly become an enthusiastic supporter. The Federal Republic of Germany favors bilateral aid administration and now stands second to the United States in the number of countries which it aids bilaterally. It is not a member of the United Nations, though it belongs to all the specialized agencies. Israel, rich in technicians and know-how and compelled to leapfrog the Arab boycott if it is to survive, has strong political reasons for continuing a sizable program of bilateral aid. The receivers of aid, as I have indicated, are no more eager to become wards of the U.N. than satellites of the United States or the Soviet Union.

25

U.S. Trade Policies
Toward Less Developed Countries

HARRY G. JOHNSON

Though some elements of its rationale for development assistance are debatable, and there has been increasingly serious questioning of the effectiveness of and necessity for the foreign aid program in recent years, the United States government has repeatedly reaffirmed its commitment to assist the development of the less developed countries. This commitment has been expressed in a substantial flow of real resources to these countries through the foreign aid, military assistance, surplus commodity, and other programs. In absolute terms, the United States is by far the largest donor of development assistance in the world. However, its predominance is largely a consequence of its size and wealth. If development aid is measured as a proportion of national income, and especially if loans are reckoned at the value of the real resources they transfer instead of their nominal value, the U.S. contribution is only about half as large as that of France, though over double that of any other leading noncommunist aid donor.[1] If aid contributions are compared with what would be assessed on the basis of an income tax on individual citizens as progressive as the average national tax system, the United States does not

From Chapter 1 of Harry G. Johnson, *Economic Policies Toward the Less Developed Countries* (Washington, D.C.: The Brookings Institution, 1966). Reprinted in this form by permission.

[1] See John A. Pincus, "The Cost of Foreign Aid," *Review of Economics and Statistics*, Vol. 45 (November 1963), pp. 360–67, especially p. 364. Pincus estimates French aid commitments in 1962 at 1.32 percent of gross national product, U.S. at 0.66 or 0.55 percent (depending on whether P.L. 480 aid is valued at official prices or at world market prices), and German, Dutch, and U.K. commitments at 0.27, with Japan, Portugal, Canada, and Italy being committed for successively smaller proportions of their gross national products.

appear to be bearing a disproportionately large share of the aid burden.[2]

Foreign Aid

Foreign aid in the form of grants, loans, and sales of surplus agricultural commodities for local currencies, together with technical assistance, has been the prime means through which the United States has contributed to the economic development of the poor countries of the world. The general technique, developed to meet the postwar reconstruction needs of the European countries during the period of dollar shortage, was transferred to the new problem of promoting economic development as the demands for such assistance became more pressing and Europe's problems were overcome. The fact that the two problems were essentially different was scarcely appreciated at the time, and failure to recognize the fundamental difference in their amenability to quick solution by foreign aid is largely responsible for the growing disenchantment with development aid. Europe possessed industrial skills, modern technology and entrepreneurial ability and could be revitalized by marginal contributions of real resources and foreign exchange supplied over a limited period. The less developed countries must modernize their economies by accumulating stocks of "human" capital as well as material capital, starting from a low level of virtually every asset.[3] Limited contributions of aid can scarcely have a catalytic effect on these economies, for the process of getting economic development started is bound to be prolonged, expensive, and grossly inefficient by the standards of investment productivity normally applied in developed countries.

Despite the burden that the transfer of resources through foreign aid places on the U.S. taxpayer and the U.S. economy—a sub-

[2] See I. B. Kravis and M. W. S. Davenport, "The Political Arithmetic of International Burden-Sharing," *Journal of Political Economy*, Vol. 71 (August 1963), pp. 309–330.
[3] For discussions of economic development as a generalized process of capital accumulation, see Harry G. Johnson, *The Canadian Quandary* (Toronto: McGraw-Hill, 1963), Chap. 14, and T. W. Schultz, *Transforming Traditional Agriculture* (Yale University Press, 1964).

stantially lighter burden than is indicated by the money amounts involved in surplus disposal under Public Law 480 or total aid during periods of abnormally high unemployment—primary reliance on foreign aid in policy toward the less developed countries represents a "soft option" for both parties, not merely the recipient country.[4] For the beneficiary of aid, the real resources and foreign exchange provided reduce the pressure to develop industries that can compete efficiently with those of the developed countries in the domestic and foreign markets. Aid in the form of surplus agricultural products reduces the incentives to increase productivity in agriculture (which tends anyway to be starved of investment resources by planners interested in industrialization) even though it is typically the largest, and an obviously backward, sector in the less developed countries. For the donors the giving of aid excuses the maintenance or adoption of commercial and domestic economic policies that restrict the opportunities for less developed countries to develop on the basis of exporting to their rich and growing markets. Aid in the form of agricultural surpluses enables a domestic problem to be shifted to the world market under the guise of charity. In short, the giving and receipt of aid permits both parties to avoid harder choices involving conflicts between the requirements of economic efficiency and other objectives of economic policy.

An incidental but significant consequence is that some part of the potential contribution of aid to development is nullified by the greater inefficiency that aid permits both sides to tolerate. In addition—a matter of importance in view of the value attached by the United States to the free enterprise system—the process of aid giving inevitably obliges the donor to insist that the recipient practice some sort of central economic planning, since this appears to provide a relatively simple basis for testing aid-worthiness. Moreover, the administration of aid given directly by one country to another places officials of the donor country in the recipient country in a rich-man/poor-man relationship that is scarcely conducive to mutual respect and political amity.

In the early stages of promotion of development through assistance—broadly speaking, the 1950s—the U.S. policy of con-

[4] P. T. Bauer and J. B. Wood, "Foreign Aid: The Soft Option," *Banca Nazionale del Lavoro*, No. 59 (December 1961), pp. 403–18.

centrating on the provision of loans and grants meshed reasonably closely with the demands of the less developed countries and with the requirements indicated by the prevailing theory of the development problem. Nationalistic development policies, modeling themselves on the examples of the United States and especially the Soviet Union, aimed at the creation of a self-contained modern industrial economy. Such an economy was to be created by transferring labor from the traditional export industries and the subsistence sector to an industrial sector, which was to be developed by investing resources obtained through foreign aid and the taxation of traditional exports in "economic infrastructure" and in domestic production of industrial goods formerly imported—the policy of development through import substitution. The prevailing theory of development, derived from the Keynesian theory of unemployment in advanced economies and the extension of it into a growth model by Harrod and others, stressed the necessity of material investment to draw supposedly surplus labor from the subsistence sector into productive industrial employment, and of foreign aid to fill the gap between the available domestic savings and the investment required for a satisfactory rate of economic growth. Since both policy and theory emphasized development of production for the domestic market, on the simplistic assumption that the shortage of capital and the absence of economic planning were the root causes of underdevelopment, it appeared that all the developed countries could usefully contribute was foreign aid coupled with technical assistance in planning and executing its investment.

Demands for New Trade Policies

With the accumulation of experience of the development problem, the growth in the number of countries claiming assistance, and the steady increase in the rate of economic growth to which those countries aspire, however, it has become clear that foreign aid is no longer a sufficient means of promoting economic growth. The less developed countries and their sympathizers have thus begun to press for other forms of assistance. In the first place, the prospective requirements of the less developed countries for external resources to implement their target rates of development are substantially greater than the amount of aid the developed countries are likely to provide. This has led on the one hand to growing pressure both for increases in the amount of aid provided and for changes in the form and terms of aid designed to increase its real value. On the other hand, and of more fundamental significance, it has generated a new interest in the possibilities of obtaining external resources through trade rather than aid. The variety of demands on the developed countries for changes in their policies that directly or indirectly affect their foreign trade ranges from demands for higher prices for the primary products on whose export the less developed countries depend for most of their foreign exchange earnings (to be achieved by international commodity agreements) to modification of policies associated with agricultural protectionism that restrict the market for such exports. In the second place, those less developed countries that have achieved sufficient progress to be capable of exporting industrial products and are anxious to expand such exports as a means of earning external resources have become aware that the developed countries place serious obstacles, both tariff and nontariff barriers, in the way of such export expansion. They, and other less developed countries expecting or hoping to arrive at a comparable stage of development, have been voicing demands for reduction of these barriers and beyond that for preferential treatment of their exports of manufactured and semimanufactured goods.

These criticisms of the approach of the developed countries to assistance for the less developed countries, and recommendations of changes in trade policy to benefit the latter, have been mounting in volume and seriousness through the 1960s. They have increasingly occupied the attention of GATT (the General Agreement on Tariffs and Trade, the international body concerned with the rules of commercial policy and the conduct of trade negotiations) where they have been the subject of sharp divisions both between the less developed and the developed nations and among the latter. They culminated in the convening of the United Nations Conference on Trade and Development (UNCTAD), held in Geneva from March to June 1964, which served as a forum for the expression of the views and demands of the less developed countries (they were all somewhat euphemistically rechristened "developing countries" before the occasion) and which has since been made a permanent organ of the United Nations.

Modifications of U.S. Policy

The United States has modified its policy in certain respects in recent years in response to the evolving views and demands of the less developed countries and also as a result of its special commitment to the economic development of Latin America. Its previously rigid opposition to international commodity agreements intended to raise and control prices has been modified, as evidenced by U.S. participation in the international coffee agreement. Within GATT, the United States has affirmed its general sympathy with the evolving program for unilateral action by the developed countries to assist the export endeavors of the less developed countries. This sympathy was reflected concretely in certain provisions of the Trade Expansion Act of 1962, notably the authority to eliminate tariffs of 5 percent or less, the authority to eliminate duties on tropical agricultural products and hardwoods if the European Economic Community would do the same, and the authority to bargain about nontariff barriers to trade. On the other hand, in the past few years the United States (like some other developed members of GATT) has continued to take policy actions particularly harmful to the export interests of less developed countries, such as the imposition of more restrictive sugar quotas, restriction of imports of cotton textiles, and the imposition of quotas on meat imports and petroleum.

The modifications of U.S. policy have been extremely minor by comparison both with the changes sought by the less developed countries and with those the other developed countries have shown themselves prepared to contemplate. Increasingly the United States has appeared to be isolated from the general trend of thinking and discussion about problems of the less developed countries, a lone voice of negation confronting a chorus of hopeful positive suggestions. This was certainly the impression registered on the other participants and the observers and commentators at UNCTAD. The United States appeared as the most forceful (and often the only) opponent of the less developed countries' proposals for new arrangements to increase their export earnings. In particular, it flatly rejected any proposal for preferences for their exports—the most novel and appealing proposal that had emerged both from the discussions of GATT and from the preparatory work for UNCTAD.[5]

After the experience of UNCTAD, it is virtually an international political impossibility for the United States to maintain its traditional economic policies toward the less developed countries. In the first place, its political objectives cannot be promoted by an adamantly negative attitude toward policy changes whose desirability has been endorsed by the less developed nations acting as a cohesive political group in the United Nations setting— especially when its stance has not been supported by the other developed countries of the West with which the United States must ultimately work in concert and which have offered positive alternatives for consideration. The United States must, if it is to serve those political objectives, evaluate and propound solutions for the problems of the less developed countries as those countries, and not the United States alone, understand them. Secondly, though the solutions proposed at UNCTAD and elsewhere for those problems are in many cases highly questionable from an economic point of view or politically and administratively not feasible, the problems themselves are genuine and deserve serious consideration, analysis, and remedial action. The position of leadership of the United States imposes a responsibility to formulate constructive policies to deal with them. Thirdly, the United States cannot evade the demand for action in the trade field by offering substantial increases in foreign aid, which appears to have been its strategy at UNCTAD and is clearly unacceptable to the less developed countries. That course, even if it were possible, appears to be precluded, at least for the present, by

[5] "The United States Delegation appeared to lack both an understanding of the basic needs of the less developed countries and any desire to gain one. An American observer remarked of the chief delegate of his country: 'He had nothing to offer and so he offered nothing.' The U.S. became clearly identified as the least willing of the industrial countries to even consider a 'new' international division of labour which would permit the developing countries to industrialize." J. C. Mills, "Canada at UNCTAD," *The International Journal*, Vol. 20 (Spring 1965), p. 214.

domestic political opposition to further enlargement of the aid program and by the mounting cost of the war in Vietnam.

U.S. Policy Problems After UNCTAD

In the face of the demands of the less developed countries for drastic changes in the organization and conduct of international trade, the United States appeared at UNCTAD as the arch-defender of a system of international trade they believe to be strongly biased against their trade and development interests and the chief opponent of changes they believe essential to the foundation of a more equitable international trading order. The United States had reasons for the stance it adopted, reasons rooted in the historical evolution of its economic and political relations with the other developed nations and with the less developed nations, in the lessons of past experience with some of the proposals refurbished by the less developed nations at Geneva, and in the logic of the basic principle of U.S. commercial policy and of GATT, the principle of nondiscrimination. To an important extent, also, the United States served as scapegoat for other developed countries, especially the European Common Market countries, carrying the burden of resistance to the demands of the less developed countries while the other countries avoided commitment through abstention from voting.

After the confrontation in Geneva, however, the United States cannot persist in maintaining this predominantly negative stance. In purely political terms it has suffered a serious defeat from the less developed countries group, and has moreover been revealed to be partially isolated from the other developed countries and less sympathetic than they to new movements of opinion among the less developed countries. The United States must regain the political initiative if it is to maintain its influence among the less developed countries. As a result of UNCTAD, too, the opportunity to do so exists, for the preparatory work and proceedings of UNCTAD have demonstrated conclusively to the less developed countries the inability of the communist bloc to offer them trade opportunities comparable in magnitude and substance to those of the developed Western countries. UNCTAD also generated increasing skepticism about the usefulness and feasibility of the Common Market proposal for a comprehensive system of organized markets.

The United States has the opportunity to develop a positive program of constructive proposals for mitigating or resolving the real problems underlying the discontents that prompted and were vented vociferously at UNCTAD, while minimizing or avoiding the new difficulties that would be created by implementation of at least some of the solutions there proposed. A positive program would serve not only the political but the humanitarian interest of the United States in the economic progress of the less developed countries, if only because of the moral superiority of development through trade over development through aid. It would also serve the enlightened self-interest of the United States. In the first place, if the demand for assistance of the less developed countries has shifted from grants, loans and technical assistance to expanded opportunities for export earnings, it is to the U.S. economic interest to respond by shifting its emphasis from aid to trade, so as to maximize whatever returns it obtains from such assistance per unit of cost, or minimize the cost per unit of return. If the less developed countries want patronage rather than philanthropy, it is inefficient of the United States to insist on confining itself to the role of philanthropist. In addition, by adapting its trade and domestic policies to match the needs of the less developed countries as they see them, the United States may be able to exercise more influence in pressing the less developed countries to modify those of their domestic and trade policies that the United States believes are restraining their economic development.

The United Nations Conference on Trade and Development raises three major issues for U.S. policy toward less developed countries. The first concerns the "mix" of trade and aid; the other two concern the new proposals for the organization of international trade endorsed by the less developed countries in UNCTAD: broader market access and international commodity arrangements for primary commodities, and preferential arrangements for manufactures both between developed and less developed countries and among the less developed countries.

Consideration of a possible shift in emphasis from aid to trade requires an analysis of the comparative contributions of these two policy approaches to development; for though they have generally been considered as substitutes, in reality they are not so, from the point of view of either the assistance-giving or the assistance-receiving country. Concrete evaluation of the trade alternative raises some difficult economic problems, since what is in question is the offer of improved market opportunities whose real value depends on a variety of factors and is not readily comparable with aid. Further, assistance through trade encounters political-institutional problems of two sorts. The first arises from the possibility of conflict with domestic policy objectives, such as the desire to support farm incomes or to protect established producers from violent market disturbances, a conflict whose resolution requires the development of new methods of implementing these objectives. The other, and in some ways more difficult, arises from the network of institutions, principles, and practices governing commercial policy among the developed nations, and particularly from the principle of effecting tariff reductions by bargaining on a basis of reciprocity.

In order to assist the less developed countries by expanding their export opportunities, the United States may well have to choose between the principles of reciprocity and of nondiscrimination. Specifically, while the United States and other GATT members have waived the requirement of reciprocal concessions for the less developed countries in the negotiation of tariff reductions of special interest to those countries in the Kennedy Round, the result has been to establish a new principle of reciprocity—equality of tariff concessions to the less developed countries. This new principle, like the old, makes successful tariff reduction depend on the willingness of more than one major trading country to negotiate, and so may block progress along this line within the framework of GATT—as indeed it has already been doing. In this case, if the United States still wished to open trade opportunities for the less developed countries, it would have to choose between according unilateral tariff reductions to both developed and less developed countries to preserve the principle of nondiscrimination, sacrificing reciprocity from both groups, and according preferential tariff reductions only to the less developed countries, preserving the principle of reciprocity with respect to advanced countries at the sacrifice of the principle of nondiscrimination. These alternatives, however, pertain to the technical problem of enlarging trade opportunities for less developed countries within the GATT framework; the best form of trade assistance to the less developed countries is a question of a different order.

The specific question of broader market access for primary products raises the same problems of conflict with domestic policy objectives as does trade assistance in general and necessitates the consideration of similar alternative methods of resolving the conflict. The more far-reaching proposal of measures to raise and stabilize primary product prices and earnings raises questions of probable effectiveness and necessitates consideration of the choice between the broad alternatives of buffer stock and compensatory financing schemes, as well as of problems of administration and of equitable distribution of burdens and benefits.

The two related issues of trade preferences for less developed countries in developed country markets and preferential arrangements among less developed countries raise a variety of thorny issues in the theory and empirical analysis of preferences. For the first type of preference, a great variety of alternatives has been propounded, the main axes of differentiation being between temporary as against permanent preferences, preferences for unlimited quantities as compared with preferences subject to quotas, preferences for all or most products as contrasted with a selected list of products, equal preferences for all less developed countries as contrasted with differentiation among less developed countries, and preferences granted multilaterally by all developed countries as contrasted with preferences granted individually by each developed country. An important consideration in examining the differing effects of these alternatives on economic efficiency and in the promotion of development is the magnitude and elasticity of the supply potential from the less developed countries. The second type of preference, regional or other arrangements among the less developed countries, has been accepted in U.S. policy without critical examination, perhaps as a consequence of earlier acceptance of discrimination against the United States by the European countries, and of the comfortable assumption that the less developed countries are too unimportant to U.S. trade for such arrangements to cause concern. There are, nevertheless, some issues connected with trade preferences among less developed countries that should be explored.

Examination of the issues raised by the new proposals for trade assistance to the less developed countries will require some questioning and critical reexamination of the established principles and presumptions of U.S. international trade policy and domestic economic policy, which some will find discomforting and even sacrilegious. The choice is not between a perfect or easily perfectible world economy attainable by traditional policies and a world economy eternally condemned by the adoption of new economic heresies; in an imperfect world, imperfect policies intelligently applied may produce more desirable results than theoretically perfect policies only in fragmentary fashion. Though many of the new policies demanded at UNCTAD appear to be in sharp conflict with the traditional principles of U.S. foreign economic policy, there are precedents for the application of more of them than might appear at first thought. In addition, the United States has in the past given the equivalent of temporary preferences for less developed countries to its former dependencies; in the new automotive agreement with Canada it has accorded preferential entry for a single product group to a country that considers itself "developing" rather than "developed"; and in its sugar policy is has established the equivalent of a managed market providing prices above the world level to a favored group of less developed countries. These are of course minor exceptions to the austerely nondiscriminatory grand design of U.S. trade policy; but they concede the principle of discrimination that the less developed countries have been advocating for more general application.

26

The Case of the Cautious Matchmaker

JACK N. BEHRMAN

For the past twenty years the U.S. government has been acting the part of a self-conscious and somewhat ambivalent marriage broker. On paper committed to consummating the union of the U.S. investor and the less-developed country (LDC), it has in practice been guilty of a great deal of indecisive foot dragging, with the result that many an opportunity for bringing the shy and tentative (one might say almost reluctant) lovers into contact has been ingloriously muffed.

In consequence, though the parties have gotten together on occasion—with moderately pleasant results—the connection has proved neither extensive nor habit forming. The overall volume of U.S. private investment in the LDC's has remained relatively small. For example in Latin America—a favored area for U.S. investment—the hoped-for flow of $300 million annually during the 1960's has not yet materialized in a single year; rather, in 1962 the net total U.S. outflow to this area was negative, although net manufacturing investment topped $100 million. In the same year U.S. manufacturing investment in Africa, South Asia, and the Far East was a bare $24 million, nor did it climb appreciably in 1963 and 1964, totaling $31 and $48 million respectively.

In truth, the attractiveness of the investor-LDC relationship is at times suspect; and, in particular, the pulling power of manufacturing, though not extractive, investment in the developing world is something less than sensational. These are three possible explanations for this state of affairs: (1) some companies are categorically opposed to investment in developing countries; (2) investment is made highly unpleasant or risky by the attitude of

From *Columbia Journal of World Business*, Spring, 1966, pp. 31–40. Reprinted by permission.

host governments; or (3) the techniques of persuading investors to embark on such ventures are inadequate to the task.

The aversion to investing in the LDC's is quite strong in many U.S. firms, often so strong as to be proof against any reasonable efforts at persuasion. This attitude may arise from two circumstances: (1) domestic demand may be too great and the total company operation too small for foreign involvement; or (2) the company may wish to move abroad, but seeks a more secure association first—such as in Canada, Europe, Australia, or Japan—before essaying a more tenuous relationship in the LDC's.

There may be little that can be done to change a policy based on the first set of problems. As to the second set, much can be done, and here our marriage broker—the U.S. government—has played a curious role, for in discouraging investment in the advanced countries, ostensibly for balance-of-payments reasons, she has helped undermine the flow to the nonindustrialized world.[1] This has been demonstrated by the drop in inquiries in late 1965 from U.S. industry on the programs of the Agency for International Development in support of private foreign investment in the LDC's, after a banner increase in fiscal 1965. It is obvious that private companies will not become persuaded of the benefits of investment in the LDC's unless they maintain contact with potential hosts through this agency.

Aggravating the difficulties is the behavior of some of the developing countries themselves. Many of these favor foreign investment on economic grounds but maintain a hostile climate for political reasons. Still others have welcomed foreign investment but have done nothing to build a foundation of domestic enterprise within which foreign enterprise could flourish.

Recognizing the manifold difficulties, several developing nations have made strong efforts—some successful—to improve the climate for foreign investment through passage of foreign investment laws (e.g., Turkey, Pakistan, India, Thailand, etc.). But the administration of these laws has at times left something to be desired, and the existence of a law is in itself not a sufficient attraction to foreign investors. Pakistan, despite a "model" law on foreign investment and an investment treaty with the U.S., found

[1] See my article, "Foreign Investment Muddle: The Perils of Ad Hoccery," *Columbia Journal of World Business*, Volume I, Inaugural Issue, p. 51.

that little additional capital was flowing in—to its great disappointment.

Much of the work of the U.S. government has been designed to develop programs mitigating some of the unfavorable investment conditions in the developing world, e.g., the threat of currency inconvertibility, the danger of expropriation, and the lack of "national treatment" for U.S. corporations. Some of this work has been done; but by no means all. Moreover, there is considerable doubt that the government has approached its task with the singleness of purpose and clarity of direction necessary to overcome the major obstacles to a sustained outflow.

Long on Advice, Short on Achievement

If the government has been derelict, it certainly has not been for want of advice. There has been no end of talk about the requirements of a balanced program that will effectively promote the attractiveness of foreign investment in the LDC's. Indeed, little is ever done in Washington without a report or study of the need for "considering the desirability of establishing a program" (read: doing something). Often, however, little is done even *with* the vaunted reports, and such is the case in this area. Government accomplishments have unquestionably failed to keep pace with the copious outpourings of the dozen or so task forces, official and unofficial, that have been impaneled over the past decade and a half. The most prominent suggestions (some enacted, others tabled, and still others consigned to oblivion) made by these various bodies—starting with the Gray Report in 1950 and concluding with the most recent effort, that of the Advisory Committee on Private Enterprise in Foreign Aid (the Watson Committee) in July 1965—are summarized below:

1. Government guarantees against certain risks of investment: currency inconvertibility, expropriation, and war—and more ambitiously, guarantees against devaluation, insurrection and "creeping expropriation" (i.e., legislation that is damaging to private enterprise but which stops short of expropriation).

2. Tax relief:

a. Adoption of the principle that foreign income from businesses overseas should be taxed "only in the country where the income

is earned and should therefore be wholly free of U.S. income tax."
Alternatively, reduction of foreign tax by 14 percentage points (as
under the Western Hemisphere Trade Corp. Act);

b. U.S. incorporation of a foreign-base company which would be
exempt from taxes on income it received from a foreign affiliate
so long as the income was not remitted to the U.S. parent;

c. A tax credit—a 30% credit on investment in LDC's is currently the most popular request; older proposals have included the
use of a tax certificate permitting a minimum return on capital of
5% after taxes to be used by U.S. companies in selected enterprises as a credit against their U.S. income tax liability when such
minimum return is not achieved;

d. Insistence upon tax sparing, whereby the U.S. government
agrees not to raise the tax on the foreign income of enterprises
whose taxes have been reduced by their host countries;

e. A tax deduction against current taxable income for losses due
to devaluation; and

f. Allowance as a deduction for ordinary income of losses on
liquidation of stocks or securities of companies operating in LDC's
in the Western Hemisphere.

3. Negotiation of bilateral commercial treaties and adoption of
a multilateral investment code.

4. Appointment of a deputy director in the AID agency charged
solely with encouraging private enterprise.

5. Creation of a new affiliate of the World Bank to assist private
enterprise.

6. Liberalization of antitrust treatment.

7. Government-financed or -aided investment feasibility studies.

8. Assistance in meeting the problem of currency devaluation by
the creation of a substantial pool of local currency funds for loans
to the private sector, to be available to both U.S. and locally owned
enterprises.

9. Greater support by embassy officials of U.S. overseas interests.

Protection Not Promotion

How do the programs of the government match those proposed
and what has been missing? At first glance one of the most obvious
things missing has been a sense of urgency. It took fifteen years to

get an investment guarantee program that operated on a reasonably simple contract; it required five years to appoint at an appropriate level an officer in the AID agency responsible for private enterprise; and it took ten years to obtain a program of feasibility studies. Another missing element has been the failure to adequately appreciate the importance of investment promotion. Until very recently the government has sought more to protect than to promote overseas ventures. Let us first glance at the record in its area of primary concern before considering its somewhat belated "selling" endeavors.

The record of the government's fifteen-year-old investment guarantee program covering inconvertibility, expropriation, and war is not auspicious. The volume of investments covered by the three types of guarantees from 1950 to mid-1965 was $2.5 billion, or about $1 billion of separate projects if duplications of coverage are removed; this equaled less than 10% of the investments made in the LDC's over the past fifteen years.

The major problem has been that not all countries where risks are involved are covered under the program and that, until 1965, there has been a backlog of applications amounting to several times the annual outflow of dollars to the LDC's—at one time, in 1964, well over $1 billion worth of projects. As noted, it took AID and its predecessors fifteen years to work out a contract that could be processed quickly enough for business to make investment decisions. It may now be that with the backlog worked off, processing will move along nicely. (Indeed, 623 guaranties worth $803 million were issued in fiscal 1965 compared to 302 worth $596 million in fiscal 1964; the same investment is, of course, covered under two or three separate guaranties.) But there are still important countries not covered, since they have refused to sign the bilateral undertakings.

Congress thought that it had solved the problem of the "nonsigners" when it approved AID's request for authority to extend the guarantee to investments in countries that refused to sign, *if* this was in the U.S. national interest. AID has not used this authority because it would undercut its efforts to induce reluctant countries to sign the bilaterals. The major problem in obtaining signatures is that the agreements usually have to be ratified by parliaments or legislatures, and the implication in the bilaterals is that the government must guarantee to another government that it will not do what it has already said it would not do *or* what it may want to do in the future. Legislatures frequently view this as interference by a foreign government, and the political risks of proposing such a measure have been too great for some foreign heads of state. For these and other reasons, in Latin America, Mexico and Brazil are not covered on any risks; while investors in Peru have no guarantee against expropriation or war, and those in Costa Rica, El Salvador, Haiti, Honduras, Guatemala, Paraguay, and Uruguay have no war insurance. In other areas, Burma, Ceylon, Lebanon, Libya, Iraq, etc., remain uncovered and many others exclude war risk.

A means of removing the objections of many countries would be the establishment of a multilateral guarantee system, under which all member countries would agree to help repay any losses. It has frequently been argued that a multilateral system would discourage expropriations and the like, since the less-developed countries, being themselves partially liable for the losses, would pressure the offending party to reconsider. This type of system has been given passing consideration by the government for the past four years, but it has not been thought important enough for all-out support. A study by the staff of the World Bank did not find the question of a multilateral code impossible of solution, but the Bank itself apparently has given the matter a relatively low priority.

Two Gaps in the System

Thus, the guarantee system remains halting and incomplete. And, in the view of some users, guarantee insurance is more costly than it should be, because of separate charges for each of the three risks covered and the high premium rates. Finally, sufficient coverage has not been worked out to stimulate institutional investment or for the protection of working capital against devaluation. The former would expand the sources of funds significantly, and the latter would open up a new flow of funds in a critically tight area.

Although many have been interested in opening the institutional source, the guarantee limitation—no more than 75% of the investment—has left a parent company with too much risk, and little has been accomplished. As to a guarantee against devaluation to protect working capital, there are still some in the Administration who do not think that loss of capital through inflation is a real problem; they see it in terms of a book loss offset by a book gain on the revaluation of assets and sales—unrealized until there is liquidation of the business; prior to that time, the extent of "loss" or "gain" is undeterminable. While this is true to some extent, it is also true that subsidiaries require varying volumes of working capital and at times simply cannot expand without an inflow of capital for this purpose—especially when local borrowing is too expensive or just not available. Furthermore, such inflows are frequently repaid once the need has passed or when the volume of local repayment rises so that normal turnover can finance working capital.

Following some months of efforts by both business and government officials to establish a dialogue on these two guarantee questions, the most recent task force—the Watson Committee—picked up the subject in its report. But there has been no agreement as to how to establish adequate guarantees or whether it might be done multilaterally. Neither problem is impossible to solve; it will merely take the kind of continued pressure that was generated within and outside the government for the special housing guarantee program, of which AID is now so proud.

Offsetting the guarantee program has been a stance taken by government officials that little could be done directly to prevent property of U.S. citizens from being expropriated by foreign governments. And business has considered most official representations ineffectual. A notable exception was the settlement of the International Telephone and Telegraph expropriation in Brazil, gained as a result of the continued interest of the U.S. government. But business's concern over the stance of the U.S. government on expropriation has been so great that it obtained, through the good offices of Senator Burke Hickenlooper (Republican-Iowa), an amendment to the AID legislation requiring the termination of aid to a country which expropriated without prompt, just, and adequate compensation. This amendment was used against Ceylon and resulted in a standoff that did not help U.S. policy objectives.

To help guide it in the application of the provision—which it had not wanted—the State Department established a Committee on International Business Problems. A special assistant was appointed to the Undersecretary to develop an agenda for the committee, which was headed by Clarence B. Randall. The committee, composed of businessmen and lawyers, heard cases in which the supplicant wished to have the Hickenlooper amendment imposed or which required government representation to prevent the situation from reaching such an extreme.

No One Was Listening

Had there been adequate communication between business and government, leading to a closer working understanding, there would have been no Hickenlooper amendment. And had the representation of embassy officials been either more adequate or effective *or* more effectively explained to the businessmen concerned, there should have been no need for the Randall Committee. Both are evidence of the absence of an effective rapport between business and government on this issue.

Another protection program has included the negotiation of "investment treaties," i.e., treaties of friendship, commerce, and navigation. While these have been signed with a number of the less-developed countries and purportedly guarantee to U.S. investors national treatment, they have not always been effective, and, as has been indicated, their administration by host countries has been fraught with problems. Since administrative practices are obviously far more important to the U.S. investor than the formal treaty, the signing of a treaty has, in many cases, failed to materially improve the investment flow. Moreover, some countries will not even sign a treaty to provide equal treatment—again on the grounds that it is not necessary and infringes on their sovereignty.

AID Efforts Abort

Turning now to promotional rather than protective efforts, it is clear that the government's record in this area falls far short of its efforts in other fields—e.g., the Export Drive. While both AID and the Department of Commerce have assumed responsibility for this activity, the program has little shape or urgency. After repeated prodding by Congress, AID appointed an assistant administrator responsible solely for the development of private enterprise abroad and private financing. He was given line responsibility for the investment guarantee program and a staff function in relation to each of the regional assistant administrators. He thereby had no power over the assistance programs for any region, and the tendency in each of these has generally been to discount the contribution of the private sector. Thus, although there are "industry officers" attached to the AID missions overseas, many do not know the local business community well and are not charged with discovering investment opportunities abroad. An attempt was made by AID to set up a deputy assistant administrator in the Latin American area, responsible for private enterprise, but after a few weeks on the job, the only incumbent resigned with a feeling that inadequate support would be given to that part of the total program. Thus, despite valiant efforts by a few, AID has not significantly expanded the role of private enterprise in its assistance programs.

AID also offers a program of support of investment feasibility studies undertaken by private companies. If the company approaches AID beforehand and obtains its approval, it can sell the resulting study to the agency for half of the cost in the event that the results prove unfavorable to investment. While this arrangement may induce companies to look into situations they might not otherwise pursue, it does nothing to arouse interest in an investment in the first instance. Yet it is in taking the first steps that U.S. business is weakest. It was for this reason that COMAP (Commerce Committee on the Alliance for Progress) was formed: to underwrite expenses of businessmen for the discovery of projects which in turn would be made known to private industry. The idea foundered on the problem of conflict of interest and the necessity of obtaining financial support for the projects uncovered. The former probably requires congressional action, and the latter needs more concentration by AID on the problems of financing projects that are marginal to private business. Action on the Watson Committee recommendation that local currencies owned by

AID be made available to U.S. businessmen and that the transfer of technical and managerial know-how be subsidized would be a significant step in the right direction.

Shortage of Staff

The COMAP goal of improving procedures for the location of overseas projects has been supported by a number of AID efforts, such as the collation of surveys that have been made over the past decade or so and the establishment of a mechanism for rapid recovery of information in them on specific projects. The reports are not all current, however, and still more could be done to uncover investment projects—just as export opportunities are uncovered by embassy personnel. The Department of Commerce has joined AID in an effort to maximize the exposure of its collated surveys, and some follow-through promotion is done by its Office of International Investment; but the manpower devoted by both agencies in Washington, abroad and in the field, is grossly inadequate.

Encouragement Begins at Home

When attacked for not having provided a larger role for the private sector, despite the strictures of Congress, AID officials fall back on the proposition that *all* of their programs will be useful in promoting private-sector investment, in that they are strengthening foreign economies and improving their growth rates. While this is undoubtedly true, two significant actions have not been taken. One is the granting of a higher priority to assistance projects which have a more direct impact on the private sector—either through support of some new enterprises or the financing of projects that permit a continuing participation of U.S. investors. The second is paying more attention to the means used (or not used) by the recipient government to make certain that the private sector does in fact grow. In some countries, not even the *area* of private-sector operations is well defined, leaving uncertainty as to where investment is permissible or safe. In others, there is no thought in the overall economic programming of how the private sector fits in or how the AID-financed projects can more directly benefit growth in the private sector. Although there was a committee established within the Inter-American Economic and Social Council on private-sector financing and industrial development, the deliberations showed that much more attention will have to be paid by AID itself to growth in the private sector before recipient governments feel that they must take the matter seriously.

On its part, AID feels that the private sector must demonstrate a more active and responsible role than previously, else it is not worth the effort to try to involve it more extensively in ongoing programs. And there the matter rests—or almost!

The private sector did come forth in the late 1950's with a suggestion that technical and managerial assistance should be given directly from industry in the advanced countries to companies in the LDC's, by-passing governments in both countries. The proposal was followed up in 1963 and pushed to completion under President Johnson, who in 1964 officially welcomed the establishment by a group of dedicated businessmen of an International Executive Service Corps.

Patent Protection Lags

But while the government was encouraging this effort at buttressing the private sector, it was passing up another key opportunity by its failure to adequately protect industrial property rights in host countries. Industrial property rights (patents on products, processes, and designs; trademarks; know-how; and copyrights) provide the basic guarantee that creative efforts, inventions, and innovations will not be pirated. Without such protection, the danger of "borrowings" makes new endeavors too risky. Although the U.S. government provides a strong system of protection at home, it has not been very active in encouraging the spread of such a system into the developing countries which it is aiding.

Although some concrete steps have been taken by the fourteen African states in the African and Malagasy Accord, providing for a single central office and a common system for filing and maintaining industrial property rights, no such common action has been achieved in the Latin American countries, which might have much to gain by such a move. In fact, only four of the nineteen Latin American republics are members of the Paris Convention on the Protection of Industrial Property. More active support of this Convention and the objectives thereof might well have avoided some of the problems on patent rights which have been raised to the diplomatic level. This is not to say that all friction on patent rights will be avoided by such membership, for Ceylon is a member while India is not, and yet difficulties have been raised in both for foreign companies holding patents on drugs and related products.

Accompanying the low priority on promoting patent and trademark systems is a reluctance by the Administration to "interfere" in *ad hoc* cases involving patent rights abroad. An example of this was the unwillingness of some officials to press strongly for appropriate regulations or remedies when patents on pharmaceutical items were attacked in India during 1963–1965.[2] Some U.S. companies failed to recognize the danger to their own position, arguing that "pharmaceuticals are different; they won't touch us." These firms were later convinced that such an argument does not hold. The official U.S. representation that was forthcoming was made difficult by lack of full support from the American community in the countries concerned, and by the fact that pharmaceuticals had been under strong congressional fire at home. Apparently no concerted effort had been made by embassy staffs to explain to foreign governments the difference between the questioning of company actions under an accepted system of protection and attacking the system of protection itself.

A final deficiency in the promotion area is the feeling of business that its interests or potential contribution to growth in the developing countries have not been fully appreciated by our embassies. There has not been a close working relationship between

[2] A bill was introduced by the government to force the licensing of drug patents under terms which the companies considered amounted to abolishing patent protection. Although the U.S. ambassador was concerned and made some representations, it required considerable pressure within and outside the government to cause the State Department to back up the ambassador strongly and order further representations at top levels.

AID industry officers and U.S. businessmen, nor have U.S. ambassadors in general gone far in supporting private sector contributions in AID programming.

It is fair to say that both in word and deed the present government program of encouragement of private investment in the LDC's leaves much to be desired. However, before any programs of inducement can be effective, the government must clarify its position on foreign investment—for the long term as well as the short. No sizable investment will flow into the LDC's if business considers either that the supports are likely to be withdrawn or, worse, that constraints will be imposed for "overriding" or "emergency" considerations. While some temporary reversals can be sustained, it is the persistent "doubting posture" on the part of the government that hampers an expansion of U.S. business in the LDC's. This doubt takes the form of questioning not only the possibility of a contribution by the private sector to overall U.S. economic and political objectives but also the appropriateness of such a contribution in economies that are tending toward socialist institutions.

This dilemma of posture was *apparently* resolved, at the highest levels at least, in favor of increasing the contribution of the private investor, as evidenced by the executive branch's oral support in 1963, 1964, and 1965 of the 30% tax credit for investment in the LDC's. However, the fact that the proposals did not come to a hearing reflects some continuing indecision in the Executive, as well as a tight congressional calendar, the complexity of the bill itself, and a mixed response on the part of business.

Just to get approval of the proposal within the Executive Branch required continuous bargaining and pressure from those interested. Passage will require a higher priority next year and more concerted efforts on the part of business than have been forthcoming. To date, indications are that many companies have not yet formed "a corporate policy" on the question. Those responsible for tax matters want a removal of all taxes on foreign income (once again!) or better yet a repeal of some of the worst provisions of the Revenue Act of 1962 (which are really not relevant to the issue of incentives). Most of those responsible for international operations would like to see such a credit enacted, but many do not want to be placed in the position of having to testify in support of a "subsidy for overseas business"—especially at a time when the outflow of capital is under question.

These problems were foreseen by those participating in the White House Conference in 1963 in the panel on Foreign Investment and Exports. It was clear to them that the business community had not been able to make its point on the total impact of foreign investment, including its long-run balance-of-payments effects, and that any further testimony before Congress should include very clear statements on these questions. Thus, if the 30% credits is to be supported, companies must be able to demonstrate the *need* for it and show that it will, in all probability, do the job of accelerating economic growth in the LDC's by increasing private investment. They do not have to *request* such a credit; the Administration has done that on grounds of overall foreign objectives. But they will probably be required to demonstrate that, in the longer run, foreign investment is a big plus in the U.S. balance of payments.

Tax Credit in Jeopardy

However, at this writing, it is not apparent that the business community will get the chance to support the proposals. It will have to be acted on by Congress during the current session, in an election year, and the likelihood of this happening is further reduced by the Treasury's action in negotiating a 7% investment credit in its tax treaty with Thailand. The motive behind this move—to put the foreign investor on an equal tax footing with his domestic counterpart—is laudable, but the mere granting of a 7% credit to investors in one country does not do the trick. In fact, the 7% credit would have to be extended in a blanket fashion if tax equity were the objective. Instead, the credit is being used as a negotiating device. But if negotiating strength were desired, a 30% credit would have been even more useful.

It would seem doubtful that the Congress will approve country-by-country investment credits before approving the principle for LDC's. On the other hand, the fact that the treaty is before the Senate for ratification will be a convenient excuse not to take up the 30% credit. Further, the fact that such treaties are being negotiated with other countries increases the likelihood that consideration of the 30% credit will be deferred.

In such a confused situation, the business community will have to determine its interests fairly early and press for them both in the Congress and within the Executive Branch. But it is doubtful that the business community sees this case as the test that it is. It took considerable pulling and hauling within the Administration to get the bill into submittable form and to the Congress. There are some officials who are unwilling to use up their congressional credit on such a bill and others who do not think it would lead to much further investment in any case. The stakes are high. The AID Administrator has given the bill his full support as a means of opening further the door for private enterprise and has asserted that, if it works, he will be willing to move even more strongly in the direction of private-sector development. It is, therefore, a harbinger of further steps—but only if business can show government that it can work in harness for a common objective.

Since the comprehensive report to AID and the Congress by the Watson Committee, business has had two choices in advancing its cooperative efforts with government: it can attempt to obtain the full range of recommendations made by the committee, or it can select some that it can agree are most important and press first for these.

The first course is not impossible, but will undoubtedly require the "laying on of hands" by the President himself. The initiative taken by business must, therefore, be high-powered itself and start from the top in government (both in the Executive and in Congress). Nothing less, in my opinion, could succeed. The potential results are well worth the effort. But, given the nature of business disagreements in the past, it will be hard to get an across-the-board support for the committee's recommendations. Also, it is in the nature of things in Washington that compromises are frequently required, and if the package is to be torn apart, business should be clear as to which parts it feels it should insist upon. Finally, such a substantial shift in emphasis may require time to implement, and it may be necessary to take the recommendations piecemeal; again a selection is necessary.

If it becomes apparent that a selection is the best strategy, business should emphasize those proposals that can achieve the most significant results. In the area of encouraging the outflow of capital and techniques, three seem most important: (1) passage of the 30% credit, covering both direct and portfolio investment; (2) assistance in spreading technical collaborations, including a subsidy to licensors; and (3) assistance in the preparation and presentation of investment opportunities.

In the area of encouragement to local private enterprise (so as to create a more receptive climate) the three most promising steps are: (1) assistance in the formation of local capital markets; (2) assistance in establishment of management and technical training institutes; and (3) emphasis on private participation in economic planning procedures so as to guarantee that the country's full resources will be tapped. In connection with the last point, industry officers in AID missions abroad should be instructed to help uncover and promote private opportunities for both local and U.S. investors as well as make certain that governmental programming does not neglect the private sector. Both local and U.S. businessmen can also be helpful in filling program gaps and pointing to projects which would aid private-sector growth. For the longer run, U.S. companies in a given industry should be induced to make studies of the potential of various areas (e.g., Central American Common Market or Latin American Free Trade Association) in their industrial category so as to provide guidelines for resource use.

A Question of Priority

These specific actions are less important than that business and government agree on what the next steps should be and then *take* them! There are a variety to choose from—and have been over the past fifteen years! But, as stressed by the Watson Committee, the first agreement must be to change priorities under the aid programs, in order to involve the private sector much more deeply. This objective has been stated and pressed by Congress in various legislative acts, but performance has been far shy of the mark. This lack of action is probably a key factor in the committee's suggestions that administrative changes may be required—especially institutionalizing the contacts between business and government.

The desire of Congress to alter the priorities and give greater emphasis to the private sector has been echoed within past Administrations. Consideration was given during the Eisenhower Administration to developing a separate program for private assistance; it was proposed that Congress enact separate legislation for such a program, to be centered in the Department of Commerce. In order to assure coordination of this new program with overall foreign economic policies and the aid program itself, the program was to be under the direct supervision of the Vice President, who was to assume Administration leadership in foreign economic matters.

Some officials in the Kennedy Administration were also never quite satisfied with the contributions of private enterprise and with the government's program. They considered seriously the establishment of a Private Enterprise Development Corporation, with responsibility for all efforts at encouraging such activities overseas. The corporation was to be an independent agency for the simple reason that it seemed impossible to obtain a sufficient priority within AID, nor was it feasible or economic to compartmentalize the program within existing government bureaus.

The bill for a "Peace by Investment Corporation" (S. 2785), introduced in 1964 by Senator Morse with the endorsements of Senators Javits, Beall, Hartke and Humphrey, follows up on this initiative. The corporation envisioned in this bill would have power to make equity investments in participation with private enterprise, function as an investment trust, and issue broadened insurance to private investors, thus assuming and widening authorities now discharged by AID.

While such a separate agency is a possibility, it is hoped that the priorities can be changed under the present setup so as to harmonize the purposes of government and those of private enterprise. The Watson group has laid out the guidelines and charted the way. It is now up to both business and government to move quickly and in unison.

27

The Alliance for Progress

EDWARD S. MASON

The preceding chapters have not attempted to emphasize the regional differences among countries in the underdeveloped world, though these obviously have an important bearing on the process of economic and political development and on the character of foreign aid as an instrument of U.S. foreign policy. Latin America, however, has a special set of economic and political relations with the United States that has recently been recognized by the establishment of the Alliance for Progress. The Alliance is the first attempt since the Marshall Plan to introduce regional organization into the administration of foreign aid, and the differences and similarities between the Marshall Plan and the Alliance will concern us later in this [article].

The U.S. trade and investment relationships with Latin America are, of course, closer and more significant than with any other less developed area. Approximately 50 per cent of Latin American exports flow to the United States, and approximately 50 per cent of Latin American imports come from the United States. For Mexico, Colombia, and Guatemala the figures are closer to 75 per cent. It is only in Argentina and Uruguay that trade is more closely tied to Western Europe. For Latin America as a whole, roughly 95 per cent of exports take the form of agricultural products, minerals, and fuels. The percentages vary from 99 per cent in Colombia and Bolivia, to 92 per cent in Brazil. Since the prices of many of these exports are highly volatile and since, after 1952, the terms of trade have tended to run rather strongly against Latin American exports, an interest of long standing in the instru-

Reprinted in this form by permission from Edward S. Mason, *Foreign Aid and Foreign Policy* (New York: Harper & Row for the Council on Foreign Relations, 1964), Ch. 4.

mentalities for stabilizing and raising the price of raw material exports has been reinforced. Any consideration of aid for Latin America tends to become involved with trade policies. And since the United States is by far the largest market for Latin American exports, it is American trade policies that are of primary concern.

By 1962 U.S. private investment in Latin America was in excess of $12 billion, which is a multiple of the total of U.S. private investment in the remainder of the less developed world. Traditionally, this investment has flowed into minerals and fuels and, until recently, into public utilities, but since World War II there has been a substantial investment in manufacturing, particularly in Brazil and Mexico. Recently, however, the flow of U.S. private direct investment on a net basis into Latin America has all but ceased. From $618 million in 1956, and $1,163 million in 1957, net direct U.S. private investment declined to $141 million in 1961 and a negative $32 million in 1962.[1] These figures are, of course, misleading as indicators of the current contribution of foreign private investment to Latin American productivity and development. They do not take into account either the very large reinvestment by American firms in Latin America of earnings and depreciation allowances or the attendant flows of new techniques and managerial competence. Nevertheless, both the size of the U.S. investment stake in Latin America and the recent lessening of external additions to this stake, suggest aspects of Latin American development, and of the U.S. interest in this development, that are intimately related to foreign aid policy. The question of the appropriate role of private investment in the foreign aid program is particularly significant and relevant for Latin America.

The special political interests of the United States in Latin America have been manifest since the announcement of the Monroe Doctrine in 1823. This was a unilateral declaration, un-

---

[1] These figures are heavily influenced by variations in petroleum investment. In 1962, the net outflow of capital to Latin America by various categories was as follows:

Mining and smelting	— $3 million
Petroleum	—115
Manufacturing	114
Other	— 28
Total	—$32 million

Survey of Current Business, August, 1963, p. 18.

enforceable during the nineteenth century except for the benign assistance of the British navy. Nevertheless, though unilateral, it was welcomed by the newly independent Latin American republics and enshrined more than a century later as an inter-American doctrine in the Act of Chapultepec in 1945 and the Reciprocal Assistance Treaty of 1947. In the interval, more active rather than purely defensive, interests of the United States in Latin America had been made evident by the acquisition of territory from Mexico, the promotion of the Panamanian revolt against Colombia, the several armed interventions in Central America and the Caribbean during the administration of the first Roosevelt, and in Mexico during the early years of the Wilson administration. After World War I, under the astute ministrations of Ambassador Dwight Morrow, the United States made its peace with Mexico and this effort, well begun, blossomed in the 1930s into the Good Neighbor Policy. The policy carried the strong implication of nonintervention, at least unilaterally, in Latin America; and despite the action in Guatemala in 1954 and the abortive Cuban incident in 1961, it would appear to be established policy that the United States is no longer likely to intervene in Latin American affairs except in concert with its fellow members of the Organization of American States. The Organization is the outgrowth of a long series of inter-American conferences beginning in 1890, and, though relatively weak, is one of the indications of the special regional characteristics of U.S. relations with Latin America.

This long but chequered, hot-cold relationship between the United States and Latin America must be borne in mind in considering the problems now faced by the Alliance for Progress. There *is* a strong consciousness of common security interests among the American States, but the history of U.S. intervention—some of it fairly recent—suggests to Latin America that the United States is perhaps too prone to substitute its own interpretation of these interests for the common judgment. Latin America *is* more closely tied by trade relationships to the United States than to any other part of the world, but this is apt to be felt as dependence rather than common economic interest. The overwhelming predominance of the United States as a military and economic power is not conducive to an easy relationship among members of the Organization of American States. Nor has the history of our foreign aid activities prior to the formation of the Alliance for Progress given much comfort to Latin America.

Until recently it has been assumed in the United States that trade and foreign private investment were the appropriate sources of foreign exchange for Latin American economic development. Apart from relatively small technical assistance programs, public financial assistance has been pretty much limited to loans from the Export-Import Bank and International Bank at close to commercial terms. This has, of course, contrasted strongly with the treatment by U.S. foreign aid agencies of other parts of the world. Immediately after the war, the United States furnished some $14 billion in economic assistance to Western Europe on a purely grant basis. After the Marshall Plan, Asia and the Middle East became the favored areas, later to be followed by Africa, with grants and soft loans the preferred media of assistance. Finally, it would have to be said that not since Sumner Welles occupied the position of Under Secretary of State has there been an American government official in a top policy-making position whose primary interests have been in Latin America.

Beginning in 1958, a series of steps have brought about profound changes in U.S. policy toward economic relations with Latin America. In that year President Kubitschek of Brazil published his proposal for Operation Pan America concerned with the collective responsibility for economic development in Latin America, and the United States agreed to the establishment of an Inter-American Development Bank. In 1960 President Eisenhower promised financial assistance for social development programs in Latin America, and the Act of Bogotá was signed committing the Latin American countries to a series of institutional reforms and the United States to financial assistance. This was followed in the early months of the Kennedy administration by the launching of the Alliance for Progress. All this represents an almost revolutionary change, but Latin Americans may, perhaps, be forgiven for thinking it a somewhat belated response accelerated by the security shocks connected with the treatment of Vice President Nixon in Peru and Venezuela in 1958 and by the Cuban revolution in 1959. The deductions drawn therefrom concerning appropriate ways of inducing American foreign aid generosity have plagued the first two years of the Alliance for Progress and still represent a problem to be managed.

Although increased access to foreign exchange is not a sufficient condition for sustained growth in most Latin American countries, it is a highly important condition. In the public sector the capital requirements for necessary expansion of social overhead facilities —railways, roads, communications, electric power, port facilities, and the like—are high and the import content per dollar of investment tends to be large. In the private sector the rather rapid expansion of manufacturing capacity that has occurred in a number of countries has tended to concentrate on consumer goods and assembly operations; and although this has meant extensive import replacement and foreign exchange savings for these items, it has also meant increased demand for machinery, spare parts, raw materials, and fuel, which had, in large part, to be imported. At the stage of development at which most Latin American countries find themselves, growth is difficult without an expansion of imports, and these countries are no exception.

Trade within Latin America is negligible. Not over ten per cent of Latin American exports go to other Latin American countries, and, although efforts are being made to encourage intra-American trade through the Central American Economic Integration Treaty, the Latin America Free Trade Association, and in other ways, the development of intraregional exchange is very slow. Latin American exports are mainly competitive rather than complementary, and the lack of currency convertibility makes it difficult to take advantage of whatever opportunities for trade triangulation may exist. There is no reason to expect that this situation will continue indefinitely. After all, the exports of the several States following the American Revolution were as noncomplementary as are Latin American exports now, and trade among the states was a small fraction of shipments overseas. But the development of intraregional trade in Latin America has a very long way to go, and, in the meantime, these countries will have to depend on imports from the United States and Western Europe.

By far the most important source of foreign exchange to pay for imports are export earnings, and, as we have seen, the United States is by far the largest importer of Latin American products.

The U.S. share of both exports from and imports into Latin America has declined substantially since the mid-1950s as Western European markets and export capacity have increased rapidly. But the United States will undoubtedly continue in its predominant position, a position that has led one observer to say of Latin American countries, "Whenever difficulties arise with respect to prices received for their exports, the tendency is to put the entire onus upon the United States rather than upon the world market."[2] Certainly the United States is expected to do what it can in the area of commercial policy to stabilize and increase Latin American export earnings, and, consequently, trade policy becomes a potentially important element within the Alliance for Progress in promoting Latin American development.

The areas of trade policy that appear to be of greatest concern to the Latin American countries are the following: discriminations against Latin American exports imposed particularly by the preferential systems of the British Commonwealth and the European Common Market; barriers to traditional Latin American exports imposed not only at the frontier but in the form of high internal taxes on the consumption of tropical products; the lack of preferential treatment for the manufactured exports of less developed countries as against similar exports from the developed countries; and, most importantly, international arrangements for stabilizing and increasing the price of various export commodities. To the extent that Latin American export earnings could be increased by action in any or all of these areas it would, of course, relieve the pressure for increased foreign aid.

All of these areas of trade interest are emphasized in the Charter of Punta del Este and its appended resolutions. The discussions under the auspices of the General Agreement on Tariffs and Trade (GATT) of the so-called "Kennedy Round" have on the agenda the question of preferential treatment (nonreciprocal tariff reductions) for exports from less developed countries. And the United Nations Conference on Trade Policy scheduled for 1964, in the preparations for which Latin American participants have been very active, is expected to examine all feasible ways of increasing the export earnings of the underdeveloped world. Recent

---

[2] Reynold E. Carlson, "The Economic Picture," in The American Assembly, *The United States and Latin America* (New York, 1959), p. 123.

calculations indicate that if the underdeveloped world as a whole had paid 1958 prices for their 1962 imports, they would have benefited to the extent of $200 million; and that if they had received 1958 prices for their 1962 exports, they would have benefited to the extent of $1,400 million. Trade and trade policy as an instrument of development is much to the fore, and perhaps the central issue, as the Latin Americans see it, is how can the international division of labor be restructured in the interests of the less developed countries of the world.

It is impossible, within the scope of this chapter, to do justice to this range of issues. Our primary concern is the relation of trade to aid in the context of the Alliance for Progress. What can and should the United States do in the area of trade policy to promote economic development in Latin America, and how is this likely to affect the requirements for economic assistance? We have a common interest with Latin American countries in reducing the discrimination involved in the preferential system of the British Commonwealth and the European Common Market. Our primary concern is the discrimination against U.S. manufactured products. The Latin American concern is primarily with the discrimination against their raw material exports to Britain and Western Europe. But we also would benefit from increased Latin American exports to Western Europe since a high percentage of their foreign exchange earnings are spent in the United States. There is every reason to make common cause with Latin America in seeking a reduction of these discriminations. It does not follow, however, that we can do much about these arrangements of long standing which, moreover, enjoy the blessing of GATT. It might be possible to use the leverage of our large foreign aid programs in India and Pakistan to dislodge these countries from Commonwealth preference. But it is far from clear that to do so would be in our long-run interest, or of any benefit to Latin America.

With respect to nonpreferential barriers to traditional Latin American exports, the United States does not appear in a particularly favorable light. We drastically limit oil imports, including oil from Latin America. We have, on occasion, imposed quantitative limitations to imports of lead, zinc, and copper. We have, sometimes for health reasons, imposed barriers to the importation of Argentine beef. If Argentina and Brazil should exploit to the full their comparative advantage in the production of beef cattle, it is doubtful whether they would find an open market in the United States. We have traditionally imposed a high tariff on wool, which particularly affects Uruguay and Argentina. All these barriers need to be re-examined in the light of our participation in the Alliance for Progress. It would, however, take a bold prognosticator to foresee rapid progress here.

Internal taxes limiting the consumption of tropical products are heaviest in Western Europe. Recent trends have been toward a lowering of these taxes, and there is some reason to believe that this trend will continue. Coffee, sugar and cocoa would probably be the chief beneficiaries among Latin American exports, but here, of course, these exports meet competition from within preferential trading areas.

The underdeveloped world, including Latin America, has been pressing strongly for nonreciprocal reductions by developed countries of tariffs on manufactured products. It is plausibly argued that without preferential entry, at least for a period of time, such exports are unlikely to be able to meet the competition of established manufacturing enterprises in the developed world. Such an unreciprocated reduction is unlikely to come about except by concerted action. But such a proposal has been put forward for discussion in the "Kennedy round" and it should, and presumably will, receive the full support of the United States. Latin American countries have evinced little interest in this proposal presumably because it is to be discussed under the aegis of GATT, which is regarded as an outworn instrument of the industrial countries interested in maintaining the existing pattern of world trade in which the underdeveloped world exports raw materials and the developed world exports manufactured products. They prefer to put their faith in the United Nations Conference scheduled for 1964, which they hope will find a way to restructure world trade on the basis of a "dynamic" future look at comparative advantages rather than an existing "static" examination.

Although a diversification of exports from the underdeveloped world in the direction of manufactured products must come about if this world is to attain satisfactory growth, it would have to be said that Latin America has lagged behind in this development. Not more than ten per cent of total exports from the under-

developed world now consists of manufactured products, and no
Latin American country is to be found among the principal exporters, despite the fact that Brazil, Argentina and Mexico, at
least, are among the most highly industrialized countries in the
underdeveloped world. This may indicate that industrialization
in Latin America has too heavily concentrated on indiscriminate
import replacement behind excessive tariff barriers rather than
on a selective cultivation of industries offering, at some stage,
export possibilities. In any case, it suggests that developing an
export market for manufacturers is not entirely a matter of removing import barriers in the developed countries.

This brings us to the subject of commodity arrangements,
which has for decades been high on the list of Latin American
trade preferences. If the purpose of commodity arrangements is
to raise the level of commodity prices rather than merely to
stabilize fluctuations around a trend, they should properly be
regarded as a form of aid. The aid is financed by higher prices to
consumers rather than by higher taxes for taxpayers. The United
States has a certain "burden sharing" interest in this form of aid
to the extent that U.S. consumption of the commodity "stabilized"
is less than our share of aid rendered in some other way. On the
other hand, this type of aid would go only to countries producing
the commodity under agreement in proportion to their share of
total exports. It would appear excessively difficult to negotiate
commodity agreements in such a way as to provide anything like
the present relative shares of aid to aid-receiving countries. Furthermore, such aid would presumably be rendered without bargaining
for a *quid pro quo* in the shape of self-help measures to assist
economic development. This might or might not be a disadvantage.

The Latin American countries are clearly now more interested
in the level of prices than in their stability. In the case of certain
recent sharp declines in export earnings brought about, for instance, by a fall in the prices of Chilean copper or Brazilian coffee,
the Export-Import Bank has shown a willingness to step in with
sizable loans. The International Monetary Fund, also, sees such
occasions as providing justification for the exercise of drawing
rights. This method of handling the situation leaves the Latin
American countries with a debt burden; but, if price declines are

in fact variations below the long-term trend, they will presumably be followed by variations above the trend which, at least, present the possibility of liquidating debt burdens. Whether or not this is a satisfactory method of dealing with fluctuations in exchange earnings, Latin American interest, stimulated by recent declines in the terms of trade, is much more in the level than in the stability of commodity prices.

As one looks at Latin American commodity exports, however, it becomes doubtful whether the United States can do much more than it is now doing or contemplating. Half of those exports, by value, consist of oil and minerals. Production is mainly in the hands of firms at least as interested in higher prices as the producing countries and frequently capable of doing something about it. Here, the problem of Latin American governments is one of securing an adequate share of the proceeds. In the cases of oil and of copper, where the Chilean tax amounts to some 80 per cent of the net income of copper producers, they seem to have succeeded; perhaps, in fact, too well. Other exports, such as wheat, wool, or beef, run into the problem of competition from domestic sources in the importing country or from alternative sources not likely to be covered by agreements. A recent examination of the possibilities for international commodity agreements pretty much narrows the range, so far as Latin American exports are concerned, to coffee, cocoa, sugar, and possibly bananas. We have already distributed the former import quotas of Cuban sugar to the advantage of a number of Latin American countries. We are now members of an international coffee agreement and are considering participation in a cocoa agreement.[3]

This represents a substantial change in U.S. policy which, until recently, except for wheat and sugar, has been opposed to supporting the international price of raw materials. This change, it is fair to say, has been undertaken with considerable misgivings concerning the practicability of such arrangements. No such arrangements, to the best of my knowledge, has ever met successfully the problem of reducing output and exports from high-cost sources in favor of increasing output and exports from low-cost sources, particularly new ones. Under these circumstances the

[3] The cocoa negotiations broke down in October 1963 over a difference of opinion between producing and consuming countries on the question of price. Whether and when negotiations will be resumed is not yet clear.

arrangement becomes a support for the *status quo* until such time as it is overwhelmed by pressures from low-cost sources inside or outside the agreement or from synthetic substitutes, and from consuming countries anxious to take advantage of these opportunities. Although there does not seem to be much long-term future for such agreements, it may well be that, for a time, coffee and cocoa agreements could bring Latin American exporters a somewhat higher price than they otherwise could expect.

As one surveys the prospect for changes in trade policy favorable to Latin American export earnings, one must conclude that no revolutionary improvement is in the offing. Recent changes in U.S. policy concerning commodity arrangements may offer some short-run advantage. There is also a real possibility that within the next few years concerted action on the part of the industrialized countries will provide preferential entry to manufactured exports from less developed countries. To take advantage of these opportunities, however, will require more realistic exchange rates in Latin America, and a greater concentration in industries with export possibilities than has hitherto been evident. The United States has a strong obligation, under the Alliance for Progress, as well as a strong interest, in supporting changes in trade policy favorable to Latin American export earnings. But it is improbable that improvements in this area will, over the next few years, sharply diminish the need for public capital flows.

Foreign private investment is another potentially important source of financing for Latin American economic development, and a few words need to be said concerning its probable role within the framework of the Alliance for Progress. As I have already pointed out, the stake of United States investors in Latin America is large, particularly in comparison with their interests in the rest of the underdeveloped world. At the end of 1962, U.S. private investment in Latin America was valued at $12,190 million, of which $8,472 million was direct investment. But, as I also pointed out, net U.S. capital flows to Latin America have been declining rapidly and reached a negative figure of $32 million in 1962. It should be noted, however, that the reinvestment of earnings of American firms in Latin America totaled $287 million in 1962.[4] The decline of net capital flow in recent years,

4 These figures are taken from the *Survey of Current Business*, August, 1963.

and current prospects for private investment in Latin America, raise serious doubts as to whether the $300 million a year counted on from U.S. private investors in making up the $2 billion of capital inflow deemed necessary to finance the Alliance program can be realized.

It would have to be said that the Charter of Punta del Este does not place a heavy emphasis on the role of foreign private investment. It is said in Chapter IV of that document, on External Assistance in Support of National Development Programs, that, "The economic and social development of Latin America will require a large amount of additional public and private financial assistance on the part of capital-exporting countries. . . ." But this is the only mention in the Charter of foreign private investment. It is declared to be an Alliance objective, "To stimulate private enterprise in order to encourage the development of Latin American countries at a rate which will help them to provide jobs for their growing population. . . ." But nothing is said about foreign private enterprise. There are numerous resolutions concerned with education, public health, taxation, programming, and the like, but none devoted to the conditions propitious to the flow of foreign private funds.

Nor, during the first year of the Alliance, was any particular stress put upon foreign private investment. The emphasis in Latin American statements was on the expected flow of public funds from the United States. The emphasis in American statements was on the need for development planning and for self-help measures and social reforms designed to increase local resources available for development and to improve the well-being of the masses.

It required the impetus provided by the rather drastic decline in foreign investment mentioned above, and substantial evidence of a sizable flight of domestic capital from Latin America, to turn the attention of the Alliance to this problem. Accurate information on the volume of capital flight is lacking, but reliable observers think it may have reached an annual level of from $500 million to $800 million. If this is so, the adverse effect on the Latin American balance of payments of the decline in new foreign investment, plus the export of domestic capital, may have exceeded the beneficial effect of the flow of U.S. public funds during the first year of the Alliance.

Secretary Dillon forcibly brought this matter to the fore in his statement at the first annual review of the Alliance in Mexico City, October 1962:

There is one area in which during the past year we have not only made no progress but where we have suffered a serious setback. Private investment, both domestic and foreign, has suffered damaging blows and has lost confidence. Not only has foreign private investment in Latin America declined, but private domestic capital has been seeking safe havens outside Latin America. This capital flight has in some cases reached serious proportions.

The plain fact of the matter is that private enterprise has not always been made to feel that it is truly a part of the Alliance.[5]

Whatever the influence of this admonition in Latin America, there is no doubt that in the United States it has received attention. Earlier in 1962 the Secretary of Commerce had established a Commerce Committee on the Alliance for Progress, composed of leading businessmen with interests in Latin America. The Report of the Clay Committee laid heavy emphasis on the role of private enterprise in economic development. The President, in recommending to Congress the Foreign Aid Bill for 1963, said that "the primary new initiative in this year's program relates to our increased efforts to encourage the investment of private capital in the underdeveloped countries. . . ."[6] And, within AID, under the vigorous Assistant Administrator for Development Finance and Private Enterprise, increased attention is being given to the promotion of U.S. private investment in Latin America. It remains to be seen, however, in the absence of effective cooperation of the Latin American partners in the Alliance for Progress, how much can be accomplished in this area.

Apart from tax incentives and loans from the Export-Import Bank, most of the devices for promoting U.S. private investment abroad are now administered by AID. These include participation with U.S. firms in the financing of investment surveys, dollar loans to private investors ineligible for Export-Import Bank

[5] *Report of the First Annual Review of the Alliance for Progress*. Pamphlet for the use of the Committee on Foreign Affairs, House of Representatives, p. 5.
[6] On business reactions to the Alliance for Progress and the role of private enterprise in economic development, Emilo G. Collado, "Economic Development Through Private Enterprise," *Foreign Affairs*, July, 1963, p. 715.

borrowing, loans from P.L. 480 local currency, and a broad range
of investment guarantees. It is impossible to estimate the net
effect of these aids on net investment, but it would seem that
the government has gone about as far as it can go to promote
U.S. private foreign investment in Latin America without outright
subsidization.

The action of American firms in adapting themselves to the
changing situation has probably been of greater importance in
sustaining foreign private investment in Latin America than anything the government could do for them. They have trained and
promoted local officials to high positions; they have taken the lead
in the provision of housing and social services to their employees;
they have actively sought out local suppliers; and they have increasingly invited the participation of local capital, although in the
area of joint ventures they have lagged behind the goals favored
by the U.S. government. One of the most interesting and successful private attempts to encourage both domestic and foreign private investment has been the activities of the Creole Investment
Corporation in undertaking minority equity investment in Vene-
zuelan enterprises. Another promising venture is the Atlantic
Community Development Group for Latin America, initiated by
Senator Javits and European colleagues, which is expected to
channel equity capital from Western Europe and the United
States into the private sector in Latin America. Altogether, we
have come a long way from the era of Banana Republics.

And yet, foreign private investment lags. To understand why
this is so, the scene has to be shifted to Latin America. It would
be fruitless at this point to undertake a rehearsal of the arguments
for and against the proper role of foreign private investment in
economic development. In my own view, it could make a large
contribution, particularly in Latin America. But the questions that
primarily concern us here are how large a contribution will it be
allowed to make in view of Latin American attitudes and policies
and what, if anything, can be done to improve the prospects for
foreign private investment within the Alliance for Progress.

Traditionally, the two areas in which foreign investment in
Latin America has been large have been public utilities and the
extractive industries. Since the war, there has been a substantial
flow of U.S. private funds into manufactures, particularly to

Mexico and Brazil. This flow continues despite the drying up of investment in other areas. In 1962, when U.S. foreign investment as a whole in Latin America reached a negative figure, there was still a net investment of $114 million in manufactures.

During the nineteenth and early twentieth centuries, the flow of private investment funds into Latin American utilities, both from Europe and the United States, was large. Given the whole history of this investment, marked by numerous repudiations and expropriations, it is doubtful whether it yielded a positive return.[7] It should be clear, by now, that public utility investment within the context of the typical Latin American inflationary process is a losing game. Although the capital requirements for overhead facilities continue to be large and the foreign exchange content high, such foreign funds as are available are exclusively from public lending agencies and from this source only if the debt becomes an obligation of the borrowing government. Certainly, as an area of foreign private investment, public utilities can be removed from further consideration.

The largest area of U.S. private investment in Latin America is, of course, in the extractive industries. Here the prospects for increased investment are problematical. On the one hand, the Latin American governments have made it clear that they want to hold this investment to a minimum. On the other hand, the foreign demand for oil and most minerals is rising rapidly, the capital requirements are large, and it is difficult to dispose of outputs in the absence of distributing organizations in the raw material consuming countries. Latin American opinion and government action have left no doubt that this type of foreign investment is viewed with disfavor. The Mexican government now grants a 50 per cent tax rebate to mining companies with 51 per cent, or more, Mexican ownership. Brazil has long forbidden exploration by foreign oil companies, and has recently eased out an American iron ore mining operation. The reversal of policy in Argentina which permitted private oil exploration has met with widespread political opposition and, in fact, the reversal has recently been declared unconstitutional. How far abrogations of contracts made under the Frondizi government will be carried

[7] The British experience has been recently reviewed by J. Fred Rippy, *British Investments in Latin America, 1882–1949* (Minneapolis, 1959).

and what compensation, if any, will be offered is unclear as this is written. Chile has taxed the U.S. copper companies up to 81 per cent of net income, and whether the tax situation will be adjusted to permit new investment is still under consideration. Attractive opportunities for investment exist in Bolivia or, rather, would exist given similar treatment to foreigners as Bolivia gives to its own nationals. Of the extractive industries as a whole, it would have to be said that while the investment opportunities could be large, it is doubtful whether they will generate any sizable new flows of foreign private funds.

While the prospects are more favorable in manufacture, the total U.S. investment in this field in Latin America is still small as compared with the investment in extractive industries. At the end of 1962 it amounted to $1,900 million. This investment is there mainly to produce for the local market. Its orientation is very similar to that of domestic manufacturing investment, i.e., in the direction of import replacement. If U.S. manufacturers are flexible in their adjustment to the local scene, willing to accept local partners, developing products not yet locally produced, responsive to the attitude of local competitors where they exist, and willing to blend into the environment, then there is no reason to think that investment opportunities will not continue to be good. As Latin American incomes rise, the market for goods that American producers are accustomed to produce will rise proportionately. Nevertheless, it cannot be denied that there is a growing hostility to foreign investment, even in the manufacturing area, not only from left-wing intellectuals, but also from the business community. This will probably increase as local businessmen emerge as competitors to foreign entrepreneurs. Vernon has remarked on this attitude in Mexico, but it exists elsewhere in Latin America, also.[8] It is a mistake to think that a Latin American blessing of private enterprise, where this is forthcoming, also necessarily embraces foreign private enterprise.

It would be foolhardy in this uncertain situation to forecast the flow of net U.S. private investment to Latin America. Yet I confess I would be surprised to see it touch, within the next few years, the $300 million a year envisaged by the Alliance for

[8] See Raymond Vernon, *The Dilemma of Mexico's Development* (Cambridge, Mass., 1963).

Progress. To evaluate the contribution of private investment to Latin American development only in te.ms of the net flow of funds from outside is, of course, highly misleading. Reinvestment of earnings of U.S. firms approximates $300 million per annum and this, plus investment of depreciation allowances, brings with it new equipment, new techniques, and a valuable complement of technical assistance. But despite this, it seems unlikely that foreign private investment will fill the role the United States would like to see it play in the Alliance for Progress.

Can anything be done about this, either by the United States or by the Latin American governments, within the context of the Alliance? The United States Congress has already intervened in a negative sort of way to protect U.S. private investments by enacting the Hickenlooper amendment. As one might expect, this amendment has not been greeted with favor in Latin America or elsewhere in the underdeveloped world. The Brazilian ambassador to the United States, Roberto de Oliveira Campos, one of the most respected of Latin American officials, put the case against the Hickenlooper amendment as follows:

Such a provision, unless wisely administered, may become a source of interminable friction in United States relations with the Latin American countries, which are likely to question (a) the implied assumption that compensation in convertible foreign exchange is required under international law when legal tradition supports only the requirement that compensation be made in a "useful" form of payment; (b) the premature internationalization of disputes, in view of the fact that, unless and until denial of justice by local courts is demonstrated, litigation between individual companies and sovereign states remains a matter of internal and not international law; and (c) the possibility that foreign assistance programs may be transformed into a dangerous leverage by private interests in support of exaggerated claims on foreign governments.[9]

This is a good legal argument, and it is more than a mere legal argument in the sense that without wise administration the Hickenlooper amendment could create interminable friction and could be used to support exaggerated private claims. The argu-

[9] "Relations Between the United States and Latin America," in Mildred Adams (ed.), *Latin America: Evolution or Explosion* (New York, 1963), pp. 49, 50.

ment on the other side is that American taxpayers can hardly be asked to shoulder the burden of financing a flow of public funds made appreciably heavier by the unwillingness of Latin American governments to tolerate foreign private investments and that, in particular, they should not be asked to finance the expropriation of American firms. The issues that have arisen in Latin America have concerned Dr. Campos' country and, on the whole, the amendment seems to have been wisely administered. Its existence will probably serve as a strong deterrent to incautious action, and, without such a deterrent, it is doubtful how far U.S. opinion would continue to support a large outflow of public funds.

Can and should the foreign aid program be further used to promote U.S. private investment in Latin America? It is taken for granted that the foreign office of any country supports the legitimate claims of citizens abroad to the best of its ability. And, despite the frequent complaints of U.S. businessmen concerning the lukewarmness or incompetence of State Department support, there is no evidence that it is less forthcoming than the support by other governments of their citizens abroad. The possible uses of foreign aid as an instrument go further than this. Should foreign aid be withheld or conditioned on particular treatment for U.S. investors? To do so, except in egregious cases of inequity, would seem to me to tread on dangerous grounds. We are concerned in the Alliance for Progress, and in our aid program in general, with a much broader and deeper range of interests. These could easily be sacrificed by a narrow concern for U.S. private investment, even though we are convinced that private investment makes an important contribution to economic development.[10]

10 Many of the issues involved in the use of aid as an instrument to protect and promote U.S. private investment are illustrated by the situation of the American copper companies in Chile. Two companies, Anaconda and Kennecott, account for over 90 per cent of Chilean copper production, and copper exports account for nearly 70 per cent of Chilean foreign exchange earnings. In 1955, the companies jointly negotiated a tax agreement with the Chilean government that provided for a basic tax of 50 per cent of net income and a supplementary tax of 25 per cent which was reducible in proportion to expansion of output. By 1960, Anaconda's total tax liability had been reduced to 60 per cent of net income though Kennecott's was somewhat higher. In 1961, the agreement of 1955 was abrogated by the imposition of two new taxes at 8 per cent and 5 per cent of net income. This raised Kennecott's tax obligation to 81 per cent and Anaconda's to a somewhat lower figure. The companies maintain that at this level investment is unprofitable but that

In sum, the United States would like to envisage a large role for foreign private investment as an instrument of Latin American development within the framework of the Alliance for Progress. To this end, the government has devised and administers an impressive array of incentives to induce private investment. American business, furthermore, exhibits an increased willingness to adapt itself to local conditions. Nevertheless, investment lags primarily because foreign private investors do not find the current climate in Latin America particularly congenial. There is probably not very much the United States can do by itself to improve this climate, even with the leverage of a large foreign assistance program. If foreign private investment is to play the part envisioned for it in the Alliance for Progress, the principal responsibility for action would appear to be lodged in Latin America.

It has been emphasized that an essential condition of economic development in Latin America is increased access to imports. For various reasons discussed above, it appears unlikely that the necessary increase will be provided, at least within the next few years, either by higher export receipts or by an increased flow of

---

they stand willing to make large investments at a more reasonable level of taxation guaranteed over a sufficient period of time.

The companies' case has been argued vigorously and at length by the U.S. government in Santiago and in Washington. The question that concerns us is whether the leverage of aid can and should be brought into use. Specifically, should fair and equitable tax treatment of the copper companies be made a condition of aid along with the conditions agreed to in connection with a stabilization program? On the one hand, it can be argued that an increase in foreign exchange earnings is necessary to Chilean development; that the only large and readily available source of increased earnings is an expansion of copper exports; that such an expansion of exports requires a large increase in investment; and that a failure to make such an increase possible simply shifts the burden to U.S. taxpayers who are asked to finance public loans and grants to Chile. On the other hand, that two foreign companies account for 70 per cent of Chile's foreign exchange earnings and that the tax returns from these companies amount to perhaps 15 per cent of Chilean government revenues gives these companies high political visibility. Attacking the copper companies is an established route to political power in Chile, and this route is by no means travelled exclusively by left-wing partisans. The additional taxes in 1961 were imposed by the conservative party then and now in power. And in general, the conservative element in Chile, while extremely resistant to anything in the nature of domestic reform, is quite willing to join in any attempt to lay Chile's burden on the foreigners. Under these circumstances, it seems highly dubious whether equitable tax treatment of the copper companies could or should be considered as a condition of aid.

private investment. But it has also been emphasized that increased capacity to import is not enough. Self-sustaining growth in Latin America is unlikely to be attained without increased investment and a better use of domestic resources. This may require changes in fiscal, monetary, and exchange policies and in budgetary practice, and it may also require far-reaching institutional reforms.

The Alliance for Progress recognizes the double-sided nature of the problem and proposes an ambitious cooperative method for dealing with it. The primary initiative for the Alliance came from Latin America, and the Charter of Punta del Este represents only the most recent in a long series of steps to achieve concerted action in Latin America in dealing with questions of economic development and political and social reform. It is a series to which the Economic Commission for Latin America, the various existing and proposed free trade areas, President Kubitschek's Operation Pan America, and the Committee of Twenty One, whose final product was the Act of Bogotá, have all made contributions. United States policy had also been moving slowly but perceptibly away from unilateral action and exclusively bilateral dealings toward the goal of more serious regional cooperation.

The Alliance is, in many ways, a remarkable conception. As Alberto Lleras Camargo, former President of Colombia, emphasizes,

Neither the Charter of Punta del Este nor the Declaration to the Peoples of America, which preceded it, nor any of the annexed resolutions, has the formal character of ordinary international agreements, covenants and treaties. . . . The governments bind themselves, not so much to the other signatory nations as to their own peoples, to carry out a policy which will, in effect, be the product of the closest international collaboration. Any of the 20 states may, without previous notice, withdraw from the Alliance simply by communicating the fact. Any state, moreover, may renounce the economic, political and social principles agreed upon in the various documents. The Punta del Este agreements, then, are no mere diplomatic instruments, but the final adoption of a great conjoint policy which is itself the result of a deep collective conviction.[11]

The Alliance does not rely on treaty obligations or formal commitments. Nor is the organizational and administrative machinery,

[11] Alberto Lleras Camargo, "The Alliance for Progress: Aims, Distortions, Obstacles," *Foreign Affairs*, October, 1963, p. 26.

designed to achieve a common course of action and to execute it, very extensive or, to date, very impressive. A Committee of Nine was established as a group of impartial experts (seven Latin Americans, one from the United States, and one from Europe) to appraise the proposed economic and social development programs of Latin American countries and to act as arbitrators between the sources and the recipients of funds. Beyond this, the Alliance relies on an annual meeting of the Inter-American Economic and Social Council to review its progress and propose new courses of action. The Council is a subordinate body of the Organization of American States, and it would have to be said that the O.A.S. does not enjoy high prestige in the United States and even less in Latin America. The Administrator of the Alliance for Progress in Washington does not have a Latin American counterpart, nor does he have a chief representative in Latin America. The Inter-American Development Bank is located in Washington as, of course, is the Export-Import Bank, the World Bank, the I.M.F., and other sources of funds. Such administrative machinery as the Alliance possesses is markedly oriented toward the United States.

In the absence of formal commitments and any very extensive machinery, the Alliance must perforce depend heavily on a recognition of common goals and of shared purpose. In the words of Roberto Campos, the Alliance "is a work of social engineering, requiring from the people a passionate involvement. In this sense it has to act as counter-myth to the Communist ideology which, despite its wanton brutality, has been rather successful in conveying to neglected masses a feeling of participating in the construction of new societies."[12] And Governor Muñoz Marín of Puerto Rico has said, "The ideals of the Alliance must be fused with the national ideals of each country." In the words of Lincoln Gordon, our Ambassador to Brazil, "A political mystique is indispensable to the success of the Alliance for Progress and . . . leadership in the creation of this political mystique must come from Latin America."[13]

It is to be doubted, however, whether mystique is enough, or rather, whether the proper mystique can be developed without a closer involvement in common decision-making than the Alli-

[12] *Op. cit.*, p. 55.
[13] Lincoln Gordon, *A New Deal for Latin America: The Alliance for Progress* (Cambridge, 1963), p. 111.

ance has been able to achieve thus far. In this connection it may be useful to refer to the experience of the Marshall Plan, our only previous venture in regional administration of aid. There is no doubt that the Marshall Plan developed a mystique, but this emerged through a set of arrangements and practices very different from those now visible in the Alliance for Progress. I believe that the Alliance must work toward something like the Marshall Plan arrangements both in Washington and in Latin America, though this is likely to be a rather slow process.

It is frequently pointed out that the problems of the Alliance are very much more difficult than those of the Marshall Plan in the sense that (a) the need in Europe was for a flow of imports for a period of time long enough to restore the export earning capacities of economies capable in all other respects of sustained growth, while in Latin America many other conditions for sustained growth need to be fulfilled; and (b) Western Europe had a well-developed managerial class both in the public and private sectors, while this exists in Latin America to a markedly smaller degree. Both of these differences are real and important, but they are not in themselves insuperable barriers to the development over time of an effective regional organization.

The organization differences between the Marshall Plan and the Alliance for Progress are very great both in Washington and in the field. Marshall Plan assistance was administered through an independent operating agency, the Economic Cooperation Administration, which looked to the State Department only for the most general policy guidance. There was no P.L. 480 program or Peace Corps lying outside its jurisdiction, and the Export-Import Bank was not lending in Europe. The independent status of the agency and the novelty and importance of the task made it possible to attract some of the ablest Americans to senior positions, and the quality of its staff has rarely been equalled by government agencies. Trade and monetary policy were an integral part of the assistance operation and although E.C.A. met with opposition from the State Department and the Treasury, it was strong enough to carry through a thoroughly regional program for Western Europe. Of course, the building up of a European trade and payments union discriminating heavily against American exports would have been impossible—nor would it have been attempted—in the absence of our overwhelming balance-of-payments surplus.

In contrast, the organization for the Alliance for Progress in Washington is a loose attempt to coordinate the activities of a large number of independent agencies each with its own point of view and special interests. The position of the Administrator is one of much responsibility and little power. The initiative for trade policy is with the State Department, and although we have modified our attitude toward commodity agreements with Latin American interests very much in mind, there is no disposition, as in the days of the Marshall Plan, to depart very far from traditional trade practices in favor of regional interests. The authority for P.L. 480 disposals lies with the Secretary of Agriculture, and the Peace Corps is an independent agency. The Export-Import Bank, which is a large lender in Latin America, may be influenced but is certainly not controlled by the Administrator of the Alliance for Progress. Actions in Washington affecting the Alliance are the product of a large number of interagency committees on which the Administrator is represented along with the spokesmen for many other interests. Under these circumstances, Washington finds it difficult to speak with one voice in affairs concerning the Alliance.

But it is in the organizational arrangements outside of Washington that the Marshall Plan contrasts most strongly with the Alliance. The European centerpiece of the Marshall Plan was the Organization for European Economic Cooperation which not only provided a frequent meeting place for responsible ministers of state, but possessed a large and highly qualified staff of civil servants working continuously on problems of European recovery. The United States participated *de jure* in O.E.E.C. activities only as an observer; but, *de facto*, Ambassador Harriman, the first chief E.C.A. representative in Europe, and his large staff in Paris participated fully in the formulation of recovery policies. In the course of time, the staff of O.E.E.C. and their American counterparts came to regard themselves more as international civil servants than as representatives of particular countries, and the mystique of the Marshall Plan grew out of this intimate collaboration.

The United States came to depend on O.E.E.C. for the annual estimate of country requirements. This estimate was, of course, not binding, but it was accepted in Washington with relatively few modifications. It was hammered out in a process of give-and-take in which U.S. representatives participated, and it inevitably involved a large measure of intervention in what are normally regarded as the domestic affairs of the member countries. Marshall Plan aid was quite definitely not "aid without strings." The conditions in the form of sensible economic policies and practices in the receiving countries involved extensive intervention, but it was mainly intervention via the deliberations of a European organization with American participation rather than via bilateral negotiations.

One of the major reasons why an organization like O.E.E.C. was possible in Europe and is not, at least at this juncture, in Latin America is that in an economic sense Western Europe is much more of an integrated region than is Latin America. Before the war, the volume of intra-European trade was a large fraction of the total foreign trade of the area. These trade connections had been broken in the 1930s and during the war, and one of the most difficult problems facing O.E.E.C. was the establishment of multilateral clearing arrangements and the removal of commercial policy restrictions to intraregional trade. This was possible at all only because of a common recognition on the part of the participating countries that unimpeded intraregional trade was a *sine qua non* of recovery. The task was also facilitated by our rather extraordinary complaisance toward a set of policies discriminating against the United States.

Nothing remotely resembling the O.E.E.C. has yet been established within the framework of the Alliance for Progress. The task of the Committee of Nine is a very different one, namely to facilitate bilateral negotiations between the United States as a source of funds and individual Latin American countries which present programs of economic and social development and give evidence of adequate attempts to help themselves. There is a growing recognition within the Alliance for Progress of the need for a Latin American organization performing at least some of the functions of O.E.E.C. and a realization that the Organization of American States and its subordinate bodies will not serve this purpose.[14] It can hardly be expected, at this juncture at least, that

14 At a meeting in Mexico City of the Inter-American Economic and Social Council to review the first year of the Alliance for Progress, it was agreed "to entrust to two outstanding citizens the study of the current structure of the

such an organization could undertake the delicate task of formu-
lating the financial requirements for development country by
country. There is, however, increased awareness of the fact that
the presentation of large claims for balance-of-payments support
on the part of one country may well mean less in the form of
development assistance for others. And it is quite possible that
in the course of time Latin American pressure against the domestic policies that generate such claims can be more effective than
tough bilateral bargaining.

As I have pointed out, the intraregional trade in Latin America
is less than ten per cent of the total exports of the area. The close
economic interdependence that gave meaning to much of the
activity of O.E.E.C. is at present lacking. But this trade can
develop with time, and it should be one of the interests of a
Latin American arm of the Alliance to encourage it. Furthermore,
there are strong regional ties deriving from language, culture, the
rather similar course of political development, and a significant
set of common organizations. Certainly, there are reasons for
treating Latin America for development purposes as a region
that do not apply to southern or eastern Asia or to Africa. But if
the Alliance is to be conceived as a regional development organization, it is high time that Washington install machinery capable
of producing a consistent set of policies relevant to Latin America
and that the Latin American partners create an organization
capable of understanding some of the repercussions on regional

---

inter-American system as it relates to the Alliance for Progress. . . ." This task
was given to former President Kubitschek of Brazil and former President Lleras
of Colombia and in June, 1963, these representatives submitted their separate
reports to the Council of the Organization of American States. Both of these
reports recommended the formation of an Inter-American Development Committee representing all the members of the O.A.S. but with a smaller executive
body devoting full time to the affairs of the Alliance. Both recommended
Washington as at least the initial seat of the Committee, but it is suggested
in the Kubitschek report that in time the Committee, the Inter-American Development Bank and the Committee of Nine should be based in some Latin
American capital. There are certain differences in the recommended composition of the Committee and in the definition of its functions which were
left for the consideration of the Inter-American Economic and Social Council
at its meeting to review the second year of the Alliance for Progress. It seems
probable that some serious moves toward "Latinizing" the Alliance and
strengthening its capacity to act as a regional agency are in process.

development of the action of individual countries and doing something about it.

Doing something about it means intervention in the traditionally domestic concerns of countries. And intervention is an ugly word. There will be intervention in any case in the sense of conditions, more or less onerous, attached to aid. The only question is whether this intervention takes the form of persuasion and pressure generated within an organization of which all are members and in which all have a voice, or whether it is brought to bear in bilateral negotiations. If Latin America really is, or can be made, a region in a significant sense for development purposes, it seems probable that external influences on domestic policies can be both more effective and more acceptable if mediated by a regional organization.

The alternative for the United States and for the Latin American countries is periodic confrontation in which the Monetary Fund, the World Bank and possibly the D.A.C. may participate but in which the United States, as the principal creditor, essentially calls the tune. During the first year-and-a-half of the Alliance, this has in fact been the standard procedure. The Committee of Nine has exercised some influence as a mediator and has imparted a slight regional flavor, but, in the main, the Alliance has operated through tough bilateral negotiations. The results to date have not been very encouraging. The conditions for assistance to Brazil from the United States and other sources were a set of promised actions looking toward monetary stabilization. But the price level promises to rise in the neighborhood of 70 per cent in 1963. The conditions not having been fulfilled, most of the assistance is not forthcoming, and Brazil's financial position is highly precarious. Colombia, for reasons not entirely within its own control, is finding it impossible to meet the conditions on which large assistance commitments were made in 1962. Indeed, despite notable successes in particular areas and special programs, there are very few countries that have made substantive economic progress over-all during the first two years of the Alliance.

The fact is that the Alliance for Progress to date has not developed the capacity to act, in the words of Ambassador Campos, as a creditable "counter-myth to the Communist ideology." As one observes the military take-overs in Argentina, Peru, Ecuador,

Guatemala, Honduras, and the Dominican Republic since the initiation of the Alliance, a rather different type of alternative to Communism appears to be emerging. It seems highly improbable that this kind of regime is a real alternative or that it can stand for long, though it is equally improbable that we have seen the last of such take-overs. Internal struggles for power arising from the sharp class cleavages and irreconcilable ideological differences characteristic of Latin America seem inevitable in a number of countries.

It does not follow, however, that because military dictatorship is usually not an effective alternative to Communism, there are no effective alternatives. The forces behind the Alliance in Latin America standing for a moderate, evolutionary and democratic approach to change are real and potent forces, and it is highly probable that the future belongs to them. The military regimes in Argentina and Peru have already surrendered power to democratically elected governments, and this is likely to happen elsewhere. It is strongly in our interest to support the forces behind the Alliance and it is very much in their interest to have the support of the United States. The economic difficulties confronting Latin American development can hardly be overcome without a substantial flow of public funds, principally from the United States. And the changes in domestic policy and, over time, the changes in domestic institutions in Latin America will certainly be easier if the external pressures come from a regional organization in which the Latin countries have an effective voice. Although the time schedule of the Alliance for Progress has been drawn too optimistically, the Alliance continues to represent the only approach to Latin American development that holds much promise for the future.

Suggested Further Reading

I. General

Balassa, Bela (ed.). *Changing Patterns in Foreign Trade and Payments.* New York: W. W. Norton, 1964.

Douglas, Paul. *America in the Market Place: Trade, Tariffs, and the Balance of Payments.* New York: Holt, Rinehart and Winston, 1966.

Dowd, Douglas F. (ed.). *America's Role in the World Economy: The Challenge to Orthodoxy.* Boston: D. C. Heath, 1966.

Kenen, Peter B. *Giant Among Nations: Problems in United States Foreign Economic Policy.* Rev. ed. Chicago: Rand McNally, 1963.

Reuss, Henry S. *The Critical Decade: An Economic Policy for America and the Free World.* New York: McGraw-Hill, 1964.

Zupnick, Elliot. *Primer of U.S. Foreign Economic Policy.* "Headline Series," No. 169. New York: The Foreign Policy Association, 1965.

II. The Financial Framework

Aliber, Robert Z. *The Future of the Dollar as an International Currency.* New York: Frederick A. Praeger, 1966.

Aliber, Robert Z. *The Management of the Dollar in International Finance.* ("Studies in International Finance," No. 13.) Princeton: International Finance Section, 1964.

Aubrey, Henry G. *The Dollar in World Affairs: An Eassay in International Financial Policy.* New York: Frederick A. Praeger, 1964.

Committee for Economic Development. *The Dollar and the World Monetary System: A Statement on National Policy.* New York: 1966.

Committee for Economic Development. *Gold, the Dollar, and the World Monetary System.* New York: 1965.

Cooper, Richard N. *The Economics of Interdependence: Economic Policy in the Atlantic Community.* New York: McGraw-Hill for the Council on Foreign Relations, 1968

Gray, H. Peter (ed.). *The Dollar Deficit: Causes and Cures.* Boston: D. C. Health, 1967.

Hansen, Alvin H. *The Dollar and the International Monetary System.* New York: McGraw-Hill, 1965.

Kindleberger, Charles P. *The Politics of International Money and World Language.* ("Essays in International Finance," No. 61.) Princeton: International Finance Section, 1967.

Rolfe, Sidney E. *Gold and World Power: The Dollar, the Pound, and the Plans for Reform.* New York: Harper & Row, 1966.

Roosa, Robert V. *The Dollar and World Liquidity.* New York: Random House, 1967.

Roosa, Robert V. *Monetary Reform for the World Economy.* New York: Harper & Row for the Council on Foreign Relations, 1965.

Ruff, Gunther. *A Dollar Reserve System as a Transitional Solution.* ("Essays in International Finance," No. 57.) Princeton: International Finance Section, 1966.

Shannon, Ian. *Gold and the American Balance of Payments.* Chicago: Henry Regnery, 1966.

Triffin, Robert. *The World Money Maze: National Currencies in International Payments.* New Haven: Yale University Press, 1966.

Young, John Parke. *United States Gold Policy: The Case for Change.* ("Essays in International Finance," No. 56.) Princeton: International Finance Section, 1966.

III. The Industrial World

American Assembly. *The United States and Japan,* Herbert Passin. Englewood Cliffs: Prentice-Hall, 1966.

American Enterprise Institute. *U.S. Foreign Trade Policy After the "Kennedy Round."* Special Analysis No. 3. Washington, D.C.: April 27, 1967.

Aubrey, Henry G. *Atlantic Economic Cooperation: The Case of the OECD.* New York: Frederick A. Praeger for the Council on Foreign Relations, 1967.

Balassa, Bela. *Trade Liberalization Among Industrial Countries: Objectives and Alternatives.* New York: McGraw-Hill for the Council on Foreign Relations, 1967.

Committee for Economic Development. *Japan in the Free World Economy: A Statement on National Policy.* New York: 1963.

Committee for Economic Development. *Trade Negotiations for a Better Free World Economy: A Statement on National Policy.* New York: 1964.

Evans, John W. *U.S. Trade Policy: New Legislation for the Next Round.* New York: Harper & Row for the Council on Foreign Relations, 1967.

Galbraith, Virginia L. *World Trade in Transition.* Washington, D.C.: Public Affairs Press, 1965.

Hinshaw, Randall. *The European Community and American Trade: A Study in Atlantic Economics and Policy.* New York: Frederick A. Praeger for the Council on Foreign Relations, 1964.

Humphrey, Don D. *The United States and the Common Market: A Background Study,* Rev. ed. New York: Frederick A. Praeger, 1964.

Jensen, Finn B., and Walter, Ingo. *The Common Market: Economic Integration in Europe.* Philadelphia: J. B. Lippincott, 1965.

Johnson, Harry G. *The Canadian Quandry: Economic Problems and Policies.* Toronto: McGraw-Hill, 1963.

Johnstone, Allan W. *United States Direct Investment in France: An Investigation of the French Charges.* Cambridge: M.I.T. Press, 1965.

Krause, Lawrence B. (ed.). *The Common Market: Progress and Controversy.* Englewood Cliffs: Prentice-Hall, 1964.

Layton, Christopher. *Trans-Atlantic Investment.* Bologne-sur-Seine, France: The Atlantic Institute, 1966.

Strackbein, O. R. *American Enterprise and Foreign Trade.* Washington, D.C.: Public Affairs Press, 1965.

IV. *The Communist World*

American Management Association. *East-West Trade: An Analysis of Trade Between Western Nations and the Soviet Bloc.* New York: 1964.

Committee for Economic Development. *East-West Trade: A Common Policy for the West: A Statement on National Policy.* New York: 1965.

McKitterick, Nathaniel. *East-West Trade: The Background of U.S. Policy.* New York: Twentieth Century Fund, 1966.

Uren, Philip E. (ed.). *East-West Trade: A Symposium.* Toronto: Canadian Institute of International Affairs, 1966.

V. *The Third World*

Baldwin, David A. *Economic Development and American Foreign Policy, 1943–62.* Chicago: University of Chicago Press, 1966.

Baldwin, David A. *Foreign Aid and American Foreign Policy: A Documentary Analysis.* New York: Frederick A. Praeger, 1966.

Banfield, Edward C. *American Foreign Aid Doctrines.* Washington, D.C.: American Enterprise Institute for Public Policy Research, 1963.

Committee for Economic Development. *Trade Policy Toward Low-Income Countries: A Statement on National Policy.* New York: 1967.

Dreier, John C. (ed.). *The Alliance for Progress: Problems and Perspectives.* Baltimore: Johns Hopkins Press, 1962.

Eisenhower, Milton S. *The Wine is Bitter: The United States and Latin America.* New York: Doubleday, 1963.

Feis, Herbert. *Foreign Aid and Foreign Policy.* New York: St. Martin's, 1964.

Goldwin, Robert A. (ed.). *Why Foreign Aid?* Chicago: Rand-McNally, 1962.

Gordon, Lincoln. *A New Deal for Latin America: The Alliance for Progress.* Cambridge: Harvard University Press, 1963.

Johnson, Harry G. *Economic Policies Toward Less Developed Countries.* Washington, D.C.: Brookings Institution, 1966.

Mason, Edward S. *Foreign Aid and Foreign Policy.* New York: Harper & Row for the Council on Foreign Relations, 1964.

Montgomery, John D. *The Politics of Foreign Aid: American Experience in Southeast Asia.* New York: Frederick A. Praeger for the Council on Foreign Relations, 1962.

Nystrom, J. Warren, and Haverstock, Nathan A. *The Alliance for Progress: Key to Latin America's Development.* Princeton: Van Nostrand, 1966.

Pincus, John. *Trade, Aid, and Development: The Rich and the Poor Nations.* New York: McGraw-Hill for the Council on Foreign Relations, 1967.

Ranis, Gustav (ed.). *The United States and the Developing Economies.* New York: W. W. Norton, 1964.

Westwood, Andrew F. *Foreign Aid in a Foreign Policy Framework.* Washington, D.C.: Brookings Institution, 1966.

DATE DUE

7-15 DEC 12 1900			

68 69 70 71   7 6 5 4 3 2 1

AMERICAN FOREIGN ECONOMIC POLICY

ESSAYS AND COMMENTS

ESSAYS

AND

COMMENTS

UNDER THE ADVISORY EDITORSHIP OF *William G. Bowen*